Praise for CANTONA

'*Cantona – The Rebel Who Would Be King* is the most rounded portrait of the United legend yet published . . . Fans will miss Cantona even more once they have dived into Auclair's excellent biography. Drawn to his countryman but never blinded by love for his subject, the London-based author seeks to flesh out the catalogue of extreme acts, ranging from the genius on the ball to the explosions of temper, which made Cantona so controversial and compelling. The book is a search for Cantona's soul and Auclair gets to grips as well as anyone has with what made the Frenchman tick . . . But where the book breaks new ground is in tracing the career-long battle between Cantona the sportsman and the frustrated, perfection-seeking artist' **Matt Dickinson, *The Times***

'Here at last is a definitive account of Cantona's extraordinary life which couldn't be more timely . . . Auclair's portrait of Cantona's relatively comfortable early life in Marseilles is definitive, moving and disproves many myths . . . Auclair writes with an elegance most native sportswriters might envy . . . A truly great book . . . with this book Auclair announces himself as an outstandingly gifted biographer' *GQ*

'At once elegant and exhaustive, this book by Philippe Auclair, though sympathetic to Eric Cantona, doesn't attempt to hide the arrogance and violence which, as much as his enormous skills, have characterized the man . . . This is a book about an outstanding gifted footballer by an outstandingly accomplished journalist. A tour de force' **Brian Glanville**

'*Cantona* is as impressive a book as the best of its subject's goals. Auclair modestly declares himself "neither Joseph Conrad nor Valdimir Nabokov", but succeeds in crafting prose in his adopted language which is never less than incisive, fluent and elegant . . . As a biography of an icon for the near fourteen years of his football career, Auclair's book is poignant, admirable and without equal' *TLS*

'For years, football biography has been the lowest form of literature. Philippe Auclair's biography of Eric Cantona may just change that. It is, in the main, simply a superior example of what has gone before (although saying that is like saying that a Ferrari is a superior example of a handcart) . . . But there is also a more unusual side to the book, a series of passages dotted through the text. In them, Auclair muses on a series of quasi-philosophical themes: what is it, for instance, that makes a great goal? Or exactly what is the interaction between fan and game? . . . The result is a fascinating and unusual book, one that might just usher in a new age of football biography. Football literature has been growing up at a rapid rate, and this is a further sign of its growing maturity' **Jonathan Wilson, *FourFourTwo***

'Cantona was hailed as a devil, a martyr, a saviour, a genius, a psychopath, a divine inspiration and a diabolical advocate of violence . . . But Philippe Auclair knows that football is always about more than a football . . . This, indeed, is the soul of Auclair's remarkable book . . . This dichotomy and its brilliant dissection by Auclair grabs the reader by the lapels, or in an affectionate embrace, as one's sympathies alternately swing towards the player and then violently away from him . . . But Auclair saves his best, gentlest, most insightful whispers for his examination of Cantona the man. It is what makes this the best of biographes' **Hugh MacDonald, *Herald***

'Many of us watching [Cantona's] wonderful and bizarre career here felt that the key to his character was that he was, well, French (arrogant, entrancing, etc), but it's fascinating to discover from a new biography by Philippe Auclair that the French found him enigmatic as well . . . The author . . . establishes this book as the likeliest text on which future historians of the game may base their judgment of this extraordinary man' ***Telegraph***

'Here are some words and phrases you don't expect to read in your average biography of a football player: leitmotiv, Velázquez, post-structuralist historians, *L'Instinct de mort*, Jacques Derrida and the "absolute nothingness that lies beyond the pitch", political nihilism. I don't think any of that stuff cropped up in Wayne Rooney's scintillating autobiography, unless I missed them . . . A fascinating portrait of an exquisitely talented and intelligent but also petulant and arrogant monkey who illuminated and perhaps changed for ever the British game: Eric Cantona' **Rod Liddle, *Sunday Times***

'Auclair offers fascinating insights to the player's personality, with the aid of early interviews and anecdotes from his youth . . . A difficult man to understand, perhaps, but Auclair's absorbing book goes a great deal of the way towards unraveling Cantona's story. And he is, we learn, but a man' ***Irish Times***

CANTONA

Philippe Auclair has been a correspondent with *France Football* for over a decade, and is a prolific freelance journalist on both sides of the Channel. He is also Radio Monte Carlo's main match commentator and English football analyst, and a bestselling author in his native France. He lives in London.

PHILIPPE AUCLAIR

CANTONA

THE REBEL WHO WOULD BE KING

PAN BOOKS

First published 2009 by Macmillan

This edition published 2010 by Pan Books
an imprint of Pan Macmillan, a division of Macmillan Publishers Limited
Pan Macmillan, 20 New Wharf Road, London N1 9RR
Basingstoke and Oxford
Associated companies throughout the world
www.panmacmillan.com

ISBN 978-0-330-51185-8

9 8 7 6 5 4 3 2

A CIP catalogue record for this book is available from
the British Library.

Typeset by Ellipsis Books Limited, Glasgow
Printed in the UK by CPI Mackays, Chatham ME5 8TD

To Jean-Marié and Marion Lanoé

Contents

Foreword

Les Caillols – the village square.
The sign reads: 'No Ball Games'.

I'd originally thought of giving this book a different title: *The Life and Death of a Footballer*. This was not to satisfy a desire for gratuitous provocation. Éric Cantona, the footballer, really died on 11 May 1997, when he swapped his Manchester United jersey with an opponent for the last time.

Throughout the three years that this book took to research and write, the idea that this 'death' – a word Cantona himself used liberally when speaking of his retirement – was also a suicide became a conviction of mine. In January 1996, when he was at the height of his powers, he turned down the chance to rejoin the France team. He chose not to be part of an adventure that would lead to a World Cup title in 1998. Why and how you shall see for yourselves. At this stage, it should be enough to say that this apparently incomprehensible decision fitted in with the strange logic of his progress so far, an eccentric parabola the like of which French and English football had never seen before, and are unlikely to see again.

There have been many accounts of Cantona's life, perceived failings, failures and achievements over the years; too many of them published in the immediate wake of his prodigious success with Manchester United to stand the test of time. Some have focused on his 'troubled personality', and sought clues to his 'instability' and tendency to explode into violence. Others were mere picture books or collections of match reports which could only satisfy the hungriest and most easily sated of fans. Some (particularly in France) were attempts to make a martyr of him, a victim of the establishment or of xenophobia. Others deplored the self-destructive undercurrent in his character, which had prevented him from becoming one of the game's all-time greats.

One thing united these attempts at making sense of the man who transformed English football to a greater extent than any other player of the modern age: as I soon discovered, even the most thoughtful and penetrating of them were reluctant to question the mythical dimension of Cantona. To question – not to deny, as so many of his deeds instantly became, literally, the stuff of legend.

Éric himself helped build this legend. His sponsors exploited it with glee. It provided writers with tremendous copy. A strange balance was thus found: it was in nobody's interest to look beyond the accepted image of a prodigiously gifted maverick, a gipsy philosopher, a footballing artist who could be exalted or ridiculed according to one's inclination or agenda. Cantona attracted clichés even more readily than red cards.

I'll not claim to have unearthed a truth that had proved elusive to others; my ambition was to write this work as if its subject had been a sportsman (or a poet, or a politician) who'd left us a long time ago. Which, in Cantona's case, is and isn't true. It is true because he scored his last goal in competition twelve years ago and because the Éric who still exerts such fascination, the Éric one wants to write and read about, ceased to exist when he last walked off the Old Trafford pitch. What followed – his efforts to turn beach soccer into an established sport, which were remarkably successful, and his attempts to be accepted as a bona fide actor, which were largely ignored outside of France – are part of another life, a life after death if you will, which I will only refer to when it has a relevance to what preceded it. It isn't true because his aura has not dimmed since he stopped kicking a football. Manchester United fans voted him their player of the century several years after he'd retired, ahead of the fabled Best-Law-Charlton triumvirate. More recently, in 2008, a poll conducted in 185 countries by the Premiership's sponsor Barclays found him to be this competition's all-time favourite player. That same year, *Sport* magazine chose the infamous Crystal Palace 'kung-fu kick' as one of the 100 most important moments in the history of sport. Ken Loach has made him a central figure in his latest film, *Looking for Eric*. The ghost of Éric Cantona will haunt us for some time to come.

True, legends have a habit of growing as actual memories are eroded by time. But I didn't want to 'debunk' this legend: those looking for scandalous titbits and innuendo will be disappointed, I'm afraid. But I wished to interrogate the myth and chart Éric's steps from promise to damnation, then redemption and idolatry, with the exactness of a mapmaker. What I can promise is that there will be a few surprises along the way.

The first decision I took was an easy one for me, even though it intrigued several of my friends, and will puzzle a number of readers. I informed Éric Cantona that I was writing a book about him, first by fax through a mutual acquaintance, doing it twice for good measure, then in person, on the occasion of one of his regular visits to England. I was told that he was aware of my project and that I could consider this an unspoken assent. I had confirmation of this when he thanked me for my undertaking during one of his visits to England, and that was that.

He had, after all, already put his name to an autobiography published shortly after he'd won his first title with Manchester United in 1993, *Un Rêve étrange et fou*, which was so haphazard in its overall conception, and so inaccurate in its detail, that it clearly showed that the idea of going over the past made little sense for him. I was also wary that his entourage might try to exert a control over the finished work that I wouldn't be willing to accept. Éric's previous chroniclers have all encountered the same problem: their subject has been demonized to such an extent that those who love him feel a natural urge to protect him with a fervour bordering on fanaticism. To achieve what I'd set out to do, I had to refuse to choose a camp, something which would have been impossible had Cantona himself been looking over my shoulder. In fact, he'd have been holding my pen.

I must conclude this short foreword with a word of apology and a recommendation. I know that it is not customary for a biographer to appear as transparently in his narrative as I do in these pages, but I strongly felt, *mutatis mutandi*, that my own experience of England, where I settled five years before Éric, could inform what is also a reflection on exile in Britain. Following Erik Bielderman's advice, I also took the liberty to extract from my original draft a number of digressions – some of them of an anecdotal nature, others more akin to essays – which, whilst giving a sense of context to Éric's story, would also have interrupted the narrative flow: the first of these is both a coda to this foreword and a prelude to what follows. The reader should feel free to skip these asides and peruse them at leisure should he or she feel so inclined, which is very much my hope. But I must now leave the stage to the man who really matters: Éric Cantona, and start where it all started, a rocky spur above Marseilles, a city unlike any other, where a footballer unlike any other was born.

Marseilles often appears not to be part of France at all. A Parisian friend had told me: 'Marseilles is the only city in France where you don't feel you're in province'. I, coming from Rouen (Flaubert's home town), know all about the province – the cafes which empty at 9pm, the picturesque town centres with their gothic churches, markets, maisons de bourgeois and opulent civic buildings. Beyond the city walls, space has been found to house those who have less money, the immigrants in particular. For them, concrete tower blocks and, should they be more affluent, bungalows and pavilions have been built, dotted on land which was cultivated not that long ago, with not a shop in sight. A drive away, hypermarkets and vast branded warehouses are selling anything from sportswear to cheap leather sofas. This drab, mind-numbing template is repeated from Lille to Strasbourg, from Nice to Bordeaux. Marseilles, however, seems out of place on this map of prettiness, pettiness, anonymity and boredom. My friend was right: to the first-time visitor, Marseilles does not look, smell or feel remotely like it belongs to La République. Tourists hardly ever visit Cantona's hometown. Holiday-makers, wary of its reputation for excess and violence, troubled by the extraordinary number of 'foreigners' who walk its streets, might stop briefly in one of the dozens of restaurants which serve approximations of the traditional bouillabaisse around the magnificent old harbour. They then move on to the more reassuring surroundings of the Riviera resorts, unaware that they're leaving behind the most beautiful and vibrant of cities.

There's a whiff of danger about the Massalia of the Greeks, their first settlement in the western Mediterranean, which has been inhabited far longer than almost any other region in France. When Marseilles makes the national news, you can pretty much bet that the news is not good. Torched cars. Corruption scandals in the local administration. Drug traffickers and mafiosi. Local rap artists preaching insurrection (or something similar, but oddly incomprehensible, because of the 'funny', unsettling nature of their speech). Supporters of Olympique de Marseille throwing flares on the pitch, beating up visiting fans, reprising their thirty-odd years' war against Paris-Saint-Germain. Éric Cantona.

So Marseilles and its 1,600,000 inhabitants are pretty much left alone, which suits them fine. Cantona is truly one of a breed: Marseillais care little for their reputation. Their sense of dignity, the conviction that they are, somehow, not just different from, but superior to the rest of France, feeds on the unease they sense in those who come from the outside. Half a century ago, their image, shaped by the novels, plays and films of Marcel Pagnol, was more benign. Pagnol's Marseillais played cards, drank pastis, told tall tales with an endearing, song-like accent. The sardine that blocked the harbour of Marseilles was one such story, which I heard many times around respectable tables in my youth. 'Ah, those Marseillais . . .' – only there was a note of affection for the Southerners. Their amusing pomposity somehow redeemed their tendency to listen to the hot blood rushing in their veins rather than to the cool voice of reason. How things have changed since then. All because of the immigrants, of course, whom non-Marseillais are quick to call 'foreigners', missing the point that Marseilles' cosmopolitanism is of a unique kind. Whoever comes to the old Phocea takes root in its fluid, amazingly fertile soil, and that includes the hundreds of thousands of 'pieds-noirs' and 'harkis' (the predominantly Muslim soldiers who remained faithful to the Republic throughout the war of decolonization) who fled Algeria in 1962 and disembarked at the Vieux-Port. Most of them had left with nothing; but public opinion did not see victims in the refugees who carried their belongings in cardboard suitcases. They were the cause of all their own problems, and of those they had inflicted on the métropole – the terrorist attacks, first by the independence fighters, then by the OAS loyalists. This first wave was soon followed by the mass immigration of Arabs from the Maghreb, who had been invited by the French government to lend their arms to the manufacturing and construction boom of the 1960s and early 1970s. Quite naturally, like the banished colons*, the formerly colonized settled in vast numbers in the Marseilles region,* *mostly in the huge housing estates that sprang out in the eastern and northern parts of the city. Zinédine Zidane would be born in one of those ugly, featureless ghettos.*

Such was the hostility towards the new arrivals ('they've kicked us out of Algeria, now they come to eat our bread') that the perception of Marseilles changed markedly over less than a decade, and not for the better. It shouldn't have, or certainly not to that extent. Every Marseillais' ancestor had, once, been an exile himself, and the Cantonas were no exception.

A matter of history, perhaps. From the day the city was founded – some six hundred years before the birth of Christ – Massalia's doors have always been open to the populations of the Mediterranean. Some came there in search of trade; others sought a refuge from poverty or persecution. At some point in the eighteenth century (no one knows exactly when), Catalonian fisher-men had established a small colony on one of the hills surrounding the harbour, not far from the Pharo and the Fort St Nicolas: it bears their name to this day ('Les Catalans'). Closer to us, tens of thousands of Italians, mostly from the impoverished South, had made a beeline for Marseilles. Reminders of this constant flow of population are everywhere to be seen, including in the village where the Cantona clan built a home, Les Caillols, which is where I found myself in search of Éric in the autumn of 2007.

London, April 2009

1

Eric's studio at home in Auxerre.

I AM THE KING!
I AM THE KING!

'As soon as I walked, I played football. My parents have told me: as soon as I saw a ball, I played with it. This is something I have in me . . . Maybe, on the day I caressed a ball for the first time, the sun was shining, people were happy, and it made me feel like playing football. All my life, I'll try to capture that moment again.'

To find the house in which Éric Cantona was born, you board a gleaming, air-conditioned tram that takes you uphill from the heart of Marseilles' Old Town. Just before La Palette, ten minutes at the most from the quayside of the Vieux Port where fishmongers sell live sea bream on a multitude of small slabs, you find yourself suddenly in Provence. The trees growing alongside the boulevard will bear olives in the autumn; the road's gradient becomes steeper; and the pine-covered hills of the Garlaban, the backdrop to Marcel Pagnol's *Jean de Florette* and *Manon des Sources*, draw nearer. A few modern housing estates are peppered between tile-roofed villas enclosed in small walled gardens.

Once in the village of Les Caillols, the names on the mail boxes tell their own story. Hardly any of them sounds 'French'. Italian, yes; Spanish, too. Every Marseillais has an ancestor who was once an exile, and the Cantonas were no exception. No French city is more truly cosmopolitan; the social division of the city does not prevent an easily carried elegance in the rapport between the communities. Only in London have I seen so many friends and lovers cutting across racial and ethnic distinctions. Marseillais we are first, French second – maybe. In a video he shot in 1995, shortly after the end of the eight-month ban which nearly precipitated his second and final retirement from the game, Éric Cantona chose to address the camera clad in a T-shirt on which can be read: '*Fier d'être Marseillais*' – Proud to be a Marseillais. Alone among the conurbations that have doubled or trebled their size in the last fifty years because of the influx of North and Western African immigrants, Marseilles exudes the sense of vitality and youthful exuberance one would associate with cities where new lives can be made.

As I walk along the dusty alleyways that arrow from the Grand-Rue, each of them leading to a modest house set in a clump of small trees, a lady – Madame Ferrero – calls from her doorstep. She's seen me jotting a few words in my notebook, and I realize that I must look out of place. In Les Caillols, no one wears a suit when summer lingers so warmly in October. There is curiosity in her voice, but no abruptness. Am I looking for something? she asks. When I tell her I have come to see the place where Éric Cantona grew up, she points out to a hill in the distance. 'You see that white house, there?' It's hard not to. It is already halfway up the mountain, pink and white against the green of the pines; gigantic compared to the modest dwellings in the village. 'That is where they lived.'

In fact the house is still theirs, even if they have now acquired another home in the Basses-Alpes, and Éric's brother Joël has moved towards Notre-Dame de la Garde. The postcode tells us we haven't quite left the great city; everything else, the plane trees, the monument to the dead of the Great War, the unpretentious church, the ground cleared to play boules or *pétanque*, all this speaks and smells of Provence. Marseilles is a peculiar city: its dozens of villages have been swallowed by the metropolis over time, but, once there, the air you breathe still carries the fragrances of the countryside. The Marseilles Éric Cantona grew up in had little if anything in common with the concrete jungle that gave some shade to Zinédine Zidane and his friends when they hit a football in the Castellane *quartier*. It is a 'poisoned city', where unemployment tops 50 per cent and firemen hesitate to answer a call, as they fear being stoned by feral youths. But if La Castellane speaks of a fractured city within a fractured country, Les Caillols sings with a Provençal accent. The breeze that freshens its few streets carries the scent of tomatoes gently simmering with garlic at lunchtime. What

Zidane kept of his tough upbringing is a volatile, sometimes violent temperament. But Cantona's rebelliousness flowed from a different source – certainly not from his own environment, which was loving and, in many ways, idyllic.

According to Éric's father, Albert, 'this land didn't cost much, because no one thought it would be possible to build a house on such rocky terrain'. After a long search, in 1954 or 1955 (depending on which member of the family is speaking) Albert's mother Lucienne had found this site located on the border between the 11th and 12th *arrondissements* of Marseilles, all stones and weeds. This, she decided, is where the future home of the Cantonas would be built. Come the weekend, picnicking families would unfold their tablecloths on the slope to enjoy the magnificent view, as yet uncluttered by tower blocks – from there you could see the Garlaban mountains and the rugged outposts of Cassis, rising as if they were close enough to touch; on clear days, the first houses of Aubagne, St Marcel and La Vierge de la Garde could be glimpsed on the horizon. Later, when the young Éric walked onto the terrace, he could watch players kicking the ball some 500 yards away on the pitch of the Arsène-Minelli stadium, the home ground of his first club, Sports Olympiques ('SO') Caillolais.

But view and price aside, this piece of land had little to commend itself. Local tradition had it that the German army used this promontory as a look-out in the last months of the Second World War; but if they had, no trace of their presence is left. All that Lucienne's husband, Joseph (a stonemason by trade), could find as shelter when he embarked on the huge task of building a house on the face of the hill was a small cave, covering a bare nine square metres, which the couple protected from the elements with a curtain in winter. Contrary to legend, Éric himself never lived the life of a troglodyte, but his teenage father most certainly did. Nicknamed '*la chambrette*', the cave survived the erection of the family home, a memento of the hardship Joseph and Lucienne had to overcome.

It's true that hardship had long been a companion of the Cantonas. Joseph's roots were in Sardinia, whose odd language, with its ghostly remnants of Phoenician and Etruscan, was still spoken at home when he grew up on the Boulevard Oddo, the first port of call for transalpine immigrants. To his own parents, Marseilles had been what the New World represented for the Italians who could save enough to pay for their passage overseas. Money was hard to come by; when winter came, with no electricity, proper heating or running water, Lucienne had to cook pasta in melted snow; but her husband's energy and the fierceness of her determination overcame shortcomings like these and, slowly, a house rose from the dust. This was followed by a second one, built on top of the original to accommodate Albert's young family.

Albert was nicknamed '*Le Blond*' ('the Fair One'), not because of the colour of his hair, but because of his eye for the ladies. He had fallen in love with Eléonore ('Léonor') Raurich, the handsome daughter of Catalan refugees named Pedro and Paquita. Poverty and exile looked over her side of the family too, with a measure of tragedy. In 1938, Pedro, a republican partisan, had suffered a serious injury to his liver while fighting the Franquist forces in Catalunya. He sought medical help across the Pyrenees, only to be caught by the Vichy police two years later and sent to a detention camp set up for the 'undesirables' of the collaborationist regime. Upon his release, after a forced stay in the town of St Priest in the Ardèche, the passionate anti-fascist finally settled in Marseilles – accompanied by the much younger Paquita. Pedro would never see his parents again. With such a background, which combined fidelity to one's own and almost constant displacement to an inextricable degree, is it surprising that Éric understood the attraction of nomadism better than most?

In 1966, with already her four-year-old son Jean-Marie to care for, Eléonore (a seamstress by trade), was about to have a second child. Their house was nowhere near ready to be lived in but, contrary to the legend that would have Albert taking the family to Paris (where he had found a job as a psychiatric nurse), it was in Marseilles that she gave birth to Éric Daniel Pierre Cantona on 24 May. A third son, Joël, would follow in October 1967, completing the family. Work had now sufficiently progressed for all of them to occupy the home that Joseph built, though it was by no means finished. The three boys would jump over heaps of concrete bricks and bags of cement until they became teenagers. Their house, as if carried on the shoulders of the grandparents' home, cut a striking silhouette on the hill. Like the family who lived in it, the house was different, which enhanced the status of the boys and their parents in the small community of Les Caillols.

A singular presence on the rocks, surrounded by dark trees, the seat of the clan spoke for the values it shared: hard work, stubbornness, pride, and reliance on each other. The Cantonas were by no means outcasts; their diverse origins held nothing exotic for the neighbours for whom, as we've seen, settling in Marseilles was still part of living memory. Nevertheless, it took time for 'outsiders' to gain their confidence and be invited to the huge table where three generations of Cantonas sat, always eating together, laughing at the ceaseless jokes cracked by Albert. As Éric's brother Joël recalled to one journalist, 'These Sardinian and Catalan roots, adapted to Marseilles, [had] created an unusual mix. Our parents had a strong personality, which everyone respected, as my father was a natural leader. So, yes, there was [a sense of] honour, but also the typical warmth of Mediterranean families.' Despite Albert's strong sense of discipline, there was also mayhem, more often than not involving Éric. The little boy 'loved playing, but loved to win above everything else', Jean-Marie told *L'Équipe Magazine* in 2007, thinking of one incident when, having been beaten twice in a row at table tennis (which the brothers somehow managed to play in the attic which doubled up as a painting studio for Albert), the younger Cantona, beside himself with fury, managed to jump on the table with such force that it broke in two. And 'ping-pong' mattered little to Éric compared to football, of course.

Éric's father, Albert, had been a decent goalkeeper himself, not quite good enough to cut it in one of the better clubs of the area, but sufficient to become the coach of his three sons. The situation of the house made playing with a proper ball quite a tricky exercise; the patio offered a bit of space, but a misdirected kick easily sent the ball rolling all the way down the hill, where it would be fetched and brought back by a grumbling neighbour. The brothers were so caught up in their game that they'd crumple old newspapers into the semblance of a sphere to carry on playing, rather than run down the slope themselves. Other matches were played at night, in their bedrooms. The legs of a wardrobe became goalposts, and rolled-up socks were close enough in shape to the real thing to kick and argue about.

'We could hear them talk all the time,' Albert recalled. '"Did the ball cross the line? No, it didn't!" We sometimes had to pick one of them up by the scruff of their neck to make the others stop.' Stop – but not for long.

The passion for football that ran through the three sons ran through the father as well. He could have punished the unruly children by preventing them from attending Olympique de Marseille (OM) games at the Stade-Vélodrome; in fact, he took them there himself, to watch Josip Skoblar ('the Yugoslavian goal-machine') and the Swedish winger Roger Magnusson, who produced some of the most ravishing football seen in Europe in the early seventies. On one of these early visits to Marseilles' stadium, on 20 October 1972, Éric, perched on Albert's shoulders, was one of 48,000 spectators who saw Ajax, the European champions, beat Marseille by two goals to one. The beauty of this Dutch exhibition struck the six-year-old boy to such an extent that, to this day, no other team (not even the Brazilians, 'who pass the ball as if it were a gift') has taken the place of Johann Cruyff's in Cantona's pantheon. Cruyff, 'a real artist, a visionary', inspired such a devotion to the *Oranje* in the young boy that when, in the autumn of 1981, France met the Netherlands for a crucial World Cup qualifier, he prayed for the defeat of his countrymen. France won 2–0. Marseillais first, footballer second, Frenchman a distant third.

Around the time he conceived this violent passion for Ajax's 'total football', at the age of six, Éric was old enough to sign his first registration form. Just as the elder Jean-Marie had done, and like Joël would do, he joined SO Caillolais, where he was asked to go in goal. This was a logical choice for Albert's son, but did not hold much appeal for him, and was a waste of his prodigious gift. How prodigious that gift was soon became apparent. In any case, he'd had the good fortune to grow up almost next door to the very best football school Marseilles could provide.

Sports Olympiques Caillolais was already an institution by the time Éric joined in 1972. Founded in 1939, a few months before France declared war on Germany, it had established itself as a feeder club nonpareil to the best teams in the Provence-Côte d'Azur region, including the 'giants' Olympique de Marseille and OGC Nice. Its youth teams regularly made mincemeat of what opposition other *quartiers* dared to enter in local competitions: the mass of cups and medals that greet the visitor to the club today bears witness to this enduring success. Its most famous product, until Cantona became 'Canto', had been Roger Jouve, a midfielder who was capped by France seven times in the seventies and won the national title with RC Strasbourg, having been the heartbeat of OGC Nice for thirteen seasons. The great Jean Tigana joined the club the same year as Éric, though he was his elder by more than ten years; and to this day, no fewer than eleven Caillolais have progressed through the club's ranks to become professionals, an astonishing number considering the not-for-profit association's lack of resources, and its complete reliance on the generosity of unpaid coaching and administrative staff. Cantona could not have wished for a better footballing education.

One of his teammates at the time, who also sat with him at the desks of the local *école communale*, was Christophe Galtier, no mean player himself.* Cantona did not take long to make an impression. Galtier recalled how his friend, having played just one game between the posts, insisted on joining the forward line. As was their habit, the cocky Caillolais had scored some fifteen goals without reply, and their new 'keeper hadn't had as much as a touch of the ball. Football was not supposed to be that boring, something Éric articulated in loftier terms once he had retired from the game: 'Even as a footballer, I was always being creative. I could never have played a defensive role because I would have been forced to destroy the other players' creativity.'

A few weeks after the massacre to which he had been a frustrated witness, the reluctant goalie got his way and was deployed upfield at a prestigious under-twelve tournament held in Cannes. Les Caillols won (naturally), Cantona earning the distinction of being voted the

* Galtier played for a number of professional teams from 1985 to 1999, including Lille, Nîmes and, twice, Marseille, and finished his career holding together the defence of Liaoning Yuandong, in China. He then became the most trusted assistant of manager Alain Perrin, following him from club to club – among others Portsmouth FC, Olympique Lyonnais and, at the time of writing, St Étienne. Galtier was also a key member of the French under-21 side that gave Cantona his only international honour, the European Championships of 1988.

competition's best player. The young Éric still put the gloves on from time to time, however, when his team was practising penalties on the rugged pitch, or when the three brothers (joined by Galtier) hit the ball in one of the club's two car parks, a battered bus shelter having become the goal. Like Maradona and Platini, Cantona learnt the game 'dribbling with tin cans in the street'; he would always feel that these impromptu kickabouts not only helped him refine his skill, and taught him how to exploit the most exiguous of spaces, but also represented a more noble, more authentic form of the game he loved. As he told a French journalist in 1993: 'My luck is that I have kept the spirit of street football. In the street, when I was a *minot* ['a lad', in the patois of Marseilles], if a player had a red shirt, and I had it too, we played together, in the same team. There was no strategy, no tactics. Only improvisation. And pleasure. What I have kept from this time is pleasure, the uncertainty of the result, and spontaneity. Whatever else is said, in today's football, despite everything, a player remains more spontaneous than artists who claim to be spontaneous themselves.' Not everyone shared these convictions, as he was to discover later.

Albert didn't mind Éric deserting the net. He knew enough of the game to realize what a special talent the second of his sons possessed. 'It wasn't necessary for my father to tell me I was good, I could see it in his eyes. It's better if it's not said but shown in other ways.' Of the 200-plus matches Éric played wearing the blue and yellow of SO Caillolais, only a handful were lost. Nobody knows quite how many goals he scored. But, without giving in to the Marseillais penchant for embellishment, it must have been hundreds, and this when the bob-haired youth often played against much older opponents ('at nine, he was already playing like a fifteen-year-old' is a comment that I have often come across). The quality of his first touch, his assurance in front of the goal and, above all, the confidence he had in his mastery of the ball set him aside from what, even by Les Caillols' high standards, was the best generation of footballers the club had ever seen. Yves Cicculo, a man whose life has been enmeshed with SOC for six decades, from playing in the youth team to assuming the presidency, has often commented on the 'pride', 'the natural class and charisma' of the little boy he first saw shortly after his sixth birthday: 'That attitude is not for show – that is the real Cantona. He was one of those rare players you knew would become a pro. He made us dream even when he was a small boy. He didn't need to be taught football; football was innate in him.'

His family did nothing to discourage Éric from feeling 'special'; far from it. Albert provided extra coaching; words of advice too, as when he told his son after a rare defeat: 'There is nothing more stupid than a footballer who pretends to be more indispensable to the game than the ball. Rather than run with the ball, make the ball do the work, give it and look quickly. Look before you receive the ball and then give it, and always remember that the ball goes quicker than you can carry it' – words that Cantona claimed to remember verbatim when, in 1993, he dictated his somewhat eccentric (and factually unreliable) autobiography, *Un Rêve modeste et fou** ('A Humble and Crazy Dream'). But Albert was not the only Cantona to position himself on the touchline when Sunday came; in fact, the whole family gathered behind the railings. Éric's paternal grandmother, Lucienne, was never seen without an umbrella; the story goes that she didn't use it just to protect herself from the light of the sun, but also to accompany her diatribes against whoever had had the cheek to rough up her grandson.

Whether because of jealousy, or out of genuine concern for the child's well-being, not everyone took kindly to the Cantonas' behaviour. In 1995, immediately after Cantona's infamous assault on a thuggish fan at Crystal Palace, the *Mail on Sunday* dispatched a reporter to Marseilles with a clear brief: to find out whether there was a cloud of darkness over Cantona's childhood, which might explain his life-long conflicts with authority and outbursts of violence. The journalist didn't come home empty-handed. Jules Bartoli, who had been Éric's coach in the under-11s team of Les Caillols, painted a picture of a child who

* This title, *Un Rêve modeste et fou*, is taken from Louis Aragon's collection of poems 'Les Poètes', and was set to music by the French communist/romantic troubadour Jean Ferrat. An approximate translation of that stanza could read, with apologies to Aragon, 'To have – maybe – been useful/This a humble and crazy dream/It would've been better to silence it/You'll lay me in the earth with it/Like a star at the bottom of a hole'.

was far too easily indulged by his parents, Albert in particular: 'In French we say '*chouchouter*' ['pamper'] – he had special treatment and was obviously his father's favourite. There were three sons, but the father seemed interested only in watching Éric. He was very systematic about it. Maybe Éric received too much attention from his parents.' More interestingly, Bartoli is quoted as saying: 'Éric did not know how to lose because his team simply never lost. In one season, he scored forty-two goals and the team didn't suffer a single defeat. If he had learned how to lose, maybe he wouldn't do so many stupid things now.' It is tempting to add – 'and he may not have scored so many goals either'. Yves Cicculo, usually so full of praise for his most famous player, concurred, up to a point: 'If Éric had enjoyed a more normal adolescence, he might have had more serenity. But he started with our club at six and had left home by fifteen. Parents don't think of the sacrifices their children must make. Some children crack straight away. Éric didn't, but the experience may have destroyed his youth. It certainly changed his character.' Perhaps there is an element of truth in these opinions, provided Cicculo's 'may' is understood not as a figure of speech, but as a mark of genuine uncertainty. Whenever Cantona himself has spoken of his childhood, which he has often done, it has always been in nostalgic terms, as if the higgledy-piggledy house on the hill had been built in some Arcadia. This idealized vision was not exclusively his; the few who were allowed to enter the inner circle of the clan, like Christophe Galtier, have spoken of its 'love, warmth and lack of hypocrisy' with fondness and a deep sense of gratitude for having been accepted within it.

Even if one concedes that Bartoli 'may' have had a point, Les Caillols was not the kind of nightmarish place inhabited by many other gifted athletes in their youth. Éric did not become a performing monkey dancing to his father's tune. He *did* suffer from bullying, however, not at the hands of those closest to him, but when he was singled out by the son of his very first schoolteacher, 'someone you knew was very unhappy' – Éric's words – when he was only five years old. The teacher's son, a leather-clad biker, visited his mother from time to time in the classroom, and used Éric as a target for his own anger. The form this bullying took can only be guessed at; but the little boy never once complained, and only betrayed his disarray when he was asked by the bully's mother to stand up and read a poem or a story in class. Éric must have complied, but with such unease that one of the lasting effects of his trauma was a phobia of speaking or reading in public. He only confessed to this three decades later, when he had already embarked on an acting career. Trust him not to do things by halves, even when it comes to catharsis.

Exceptional as Éric's talent was, and keen as his parents were on pushing him to the fore, his childhood was not just a long game of football played in the bosom of a proud and protective family. Marseilles might have been the country's third largest city; but the boy's and the teenager's desires were more attuned to what the scrubby woodland of the nearby Garlaban had to offer – the walks, the daydreaming, the shooting parties in the company of his father. Rising at dawn, the two of them would look for 'larks, thrushes and woodcocks', Éric simultaneously pacified by the hush of the forest and inebriated by the scents of the undergrowth. From a very early age, silence and solitude held a strong appeal for him, an inclination which, coupled with his boisterousness and frequent explosions of temper, made him something of an enigma to his schoolmates. Christophe Galtier has described him as 'a bit of a *poète*' in the classroom. Éric's mind easily drifted into a world of his own creation, with little regard for the consequences this might have on his work or on his teachers' judgement of this unusual child. He could be charming one minute, appallingly rude the next; he wouldn't harm anyone out of sheer viciousness, but could cause serious hurt nevertheless. One of his first football coaches is said to have been so shocked by a public attack on his tactics and team selection that he resigned his position there and then.

Yet there was always the other Éric, the playful, mischievous, exuberant Éric, who was never more in evidence than when the family uprooted from Les Caillols for the Christmas and summer holidays. The Cantonas had two favourite destinations, the Provençal Alps and the Côte Bleue, a stretch of coastline between L'Estaque and Martigues where Éric's paternal grandparents owned a *cabanon* – a wooden hut – right on the shore of the Mediterranean. The whole family, Joseph and Lucienne included, seven people in all, crammed into a Lancia which had seen better days. The drive was mercifully short, and as soon as they had arrived the three brothers set up camp on the beach. The first object out of the boot was, more often than not, a football. Jean-Marie remembered blissful days spent diving from rocks, swimming and fishing for whatever Lucienne needed for the evening soup, then sitting round a bonfire, listening to the Gipsy guitarists who had been invited by his grandfather Joseph. Éric relished these regular escapades, which also gave him a chance to indulge his passion for scuba-diving, though not of the usual kind. Buying the requisite equipment was out of the question; but using one's imagination cost nothing and could be just as rewarding. So Éric collected empty water bottles, and tied them together with a piece of string. Once he had thrown this apparatus on his bare shoulders, it was easy enough for him to pretend the bottles were filled with oxygen, and that he had joined the crew of Jacques Cousteau's ship, the famous *Calypso*.

Then there was art or, more precisely, painting. Albert, again, would be a perfect guide for his son through the mastery of his craft, his culture and, above all, his sensitivity. 'He was passionate about many things,' Cantona told *L'Équipe Magazine* in 2007. 'He explained something to you and then he would start to cry. He gave us this passion and love for life. That's very important: when your education is built around that, it is solid. And you can cry, even when you are a strong man. You can find something beautiful and cry simply because it is so beautiful. You can find emotion in the beauty of things and, to me, that's love.' Albert had obviously been a convincing teacher. Éric would sit by his side when he mixed his colours and painted brightly coloured landscapes in the style of the *école marseillaise*, with post-Impressionist Pierre Ambrogiani a favourite of both. Albert could see a bit of himself in Ambrogiani, a self-taught Provençal of working-class extraction who had worked as a postman for many years, before the patronage of Marcel Pagnol had launched a career spent exclusively in Marseilles. Albert, who also introduced Éric to Van Gogh's work, was by all accounts 'an accomplished amateur', someone who had mastered his craft to a far greater degree than most Sunday brush-pushers. Éric watched, and learnt.

Judging from an early photograph, taken in his first two years at the *communale* of Les Caillols, the cherubic little boy possessed a strong sense of colour, using vivid blues and yellows eerily evocative of Joan Miró, a painter he would idolize later on. Though he never lost his admiration for the Ambrogianis of this world (his father included), his taste soon moved away from the figurative. Éric's need for 'expression', and his somewhat naïve belief that 'expression' represented the be-all and end-all of the creative act, pushed him towards darker universes, such as the 'spontaneous' creations of the short-lived CoBrA school and the astonishing still-lifes of Nicolas de Staël – an inclination that should be proof enough that there was nothing pseudish about his visceral response to art. Cantona never felt much affinity with painting as production of imagery (think of Magritte); he instinctively responded far more to colour, rhythm, abruptness of manner as well as harmony of composition – in short, what is most 'painterly' about painting. Yes, Éric Cantona was an unusual child. So what could be done with him?

The answer lay a few miles away, at La Grande Bastide college, in the Mazargues quarter. If Éric was serious about becoming a professional soccer player, this had to be the place to put his dedication to the test. La Grande Bastide housed a *sports-études* section, which was open to talented local athletes, provided they passed a stiff admission examination (three-quarters of all applicants failed). The college's purpose was to ensure that the natural sporting ability of its pupils could be nurtured by dedicated staff, while the children, aged twelve to fifteen, followed the national curriculum as any other student would have done in a normal secondary school. Institutions like these were dotted all over France in the 1970s and had already proved extremely successful in producing elite sportsmen, tennis players in particular. La Grande Bastide provided a superb environment for an aspiring footballer to make the transition from youth club to apprenticeship in a professional context; should he fail to make the grade, he could rely upon a solid preparation for vocational training; reintegrating into mainstream French state education was another possibility. The scholars' routine must have seemed like paradise for Éric, who had no trouble securing a place at the college. After a couple of early lessons, mornings were set aside for training, from 11:30 to 13:00, and afternoons for study, with the odd coaching session thrown in whenever possible, which left long evenings for kickabouts in the schoolyard and weekends to terrorize whichever opposition was thrown in the path of Les Caillols. What's more, Cantona had not just found a school ideally suited to his needs and aspirations. Luck also gave him one of the best teachers he could have been blessed with, a man who had the experience, the nous and the warmth of heart to deal with as ill-disciplined a boy as the 12-year-old prodigy was at the time.

The name of Célestin Oliver appears in few French football encyclopaedias, which says more about how little France cares about its sporting past than about what Cantona's first real mentor had been worth both as a player and a coach. Oliver was forty-eight when Éric enrolled at La Grande Bastide and had retained much of the athleticism that had made him one of the main artisans of Sedan's rise to the elite of French football in the late fifties. He won the French Cup with them in 1956, just one year after *Les Sangliers* ('The Wild Boars') had achieved promotion. A lean, muscular midfielder who could look after himself on the pitch (his black belt in judo might have given him a measure of protection), he had travelled with the French national squad to the 1958 World Cup in Sweden, together with far more celebrated players like Just Fontaine, Raymond Kopa and Roger Piantoni. There, the first 'golden generation' French football had ever known gave a perennially under-achieving sporting nation its first taste of international success. This group of players finished in an unhoped-for third place in the tournament, and everyone was of the opinion that they alone had provided a genuine threat to Brazil, the future world champions. Oliver himself hadn't played. His talent was not in doubt (he had featured in two of the qualifiers), but squad rotation and substitutions weren't part of the game in those days. Once back in France, after three disappointing seasons with Marseille, and a further three years spent with Angers and Toulon, he turned his hand to coaching, and had just left second-division Toulon for La Grande Bastide when 'the player who gave [him] the most pleasure in [his] life, an absolute joy to coach' stormed into his school. And 'storm' is no hyperbole.

When I met the dapper, elderly gentleman his friends call 'Tico' and everyone else 'Monsieur Oliver', age and illness hadn't dampened the impression the youngster made on him when they were first introduced to each other. We were sitting a stone's throw away from his 'home from home', the Stade Vélodrome, at one of the *buvettes* where OM supporters gather on match days. Madame Oliver, who had accompanied her husband to many dinners at the Cantonas' house on the hill, was there too, perhaps apprehensive that 'Tico', who was ill at the time, would struggle to find the right words to describe how much he had loved, and still loved, this impossible boy. She needn't have worried.

New to his job, Oliver had not heard of Cantona's talent – or reputation – before the boy's arrival, which must have made the discovery of such an exceptional footballer even more exciting for the new coach of Mazargues' *sports-études*. 'He had huge qualities already,' he remembered. 'He was already top class at the age of thirteen. He might have been a little less powerful – physically speaking – than the others at the very beginning. But he could do exceptional things without thinking about them, as if they were normal.' Soon, however, a spurt of growth changed the spindly teenager into a superb athlete. 'Aged fourteen, he could control the ball on his chest; none of the others could do it. He really stood apart.' And this, when the group of twenty-odd young footballers Oliver took care of was, by his own reckoning, the strongest he would ever see in his career. There were still flaws in the teenager Oliver considered to be 'not a football player – but a footballer'. He could dribble past defenders with such ease that he sometimes took the ball too far, carried away by his own ability. But 'he had two feet, he could head the ball, control it, pass it, he could do everything!'

So the former international gave Éric far more freedom than he granted others. Some rules were inflexible ('I first taught my youngsters to behave on the field. If someone insulted the referee, or showed a lack of respect to his teammates or his opponents, I'd take him off'), but Oliver, drawn by Éric's smile, and astonished by his ability, was willing to bend others to enable the teenager to blossom. He let him practise on his own. He forgave him minor infringements against the school's regulations, certain as he was that he would be repaid tenfold for his forgiveness. Encouraged by his own delight in Cantona's gift, Oliver chose not to ignore what his heart was telling him. Éric was tricky and overreacted when he was needled by his schoolmates, but the only way to have access to what was best in him, the human being as well as the player, was to trust him. Is it any coincidence that the managers who got the most out of Cantona in his career – Guy Roux, Marc Bourrier, Gérard Houllier, Michel Platini and Alex Ferguson – all made the decision, driven by their affection as much as by their judgement, to do precisely the same, and trust him, even when his behaviour must have sometimes felt like a betrayal?

Célestin Oliver didn't wish to wander round the darker alleys of Cantona's character; his sense of shared loyalty prevented him from fishing out an anecdote or two which might have clouded his judgement of 'a charming, adorable boy'. I felt this very keenly, but opted not to find out how tautly the string could be pulled. This is something I noticed very early on when talking to people who had fallen in friendship, or in love, with Cantona at any stage in his and their lives. It is as if they had signed a pact in which, it must be said, Cantona hated to relinquish the upper hand. Célestin Oliver himself admitted as much when he said that, should he miss one of the beach-soccer tournaments the Cantona brothers regularly organize in the area, '*ooh-la-la . . .*' – and he wasn't referring to the song they would sing in Leeds or Manchester.

An extreme example of this is given by Bernard Morlino, the author of *Manchester Memories* – a loose yet riveting collection of Cantonesque reminiscences as yet untranslated in English, which is a pity. Morlino, a disciple of Surrealist poet Philippe Soupault (whose path we'll cross again), justified his forgiveness of what others judged unforgiveable (the Crystal Palace kung-fu kick, for example) by quoting the novelist Roger Nimier. 'If a friend of yours commits a murder, you do not ask "Why did you do that?" but "Where is the body?"' Admirable, foolish, foolishly admirable, or admirably foolish, others can be the judges of that.

Oliver made his decision early. His reward was to gain the confidence of a man who didn't pick his friends lightly, even if he sometimes withdrew this confidence for the flimsiest of reasons later in life. 'For me, he was a pure centre-forward,' Oliver recalled, 'but he could also be deployed in many other positions, which he did with good grace. "We'll give it a go, Monsieur Oliver!" and, oh, he certainly did.' From the outset Cantona, this most individualistic of players, was keenly aware of the collective nature of his sport. The personal urge for self-expression which alone could justify considering football an art form, in the romanticist sense of 'art', remained a worthless impulse if it was not inextricably, almost incomprehensibly, wedded to the victory of a team. Maradona had to be the greatest of all footballers not because he danced past scores of English and Belgian defenders in the 1986 World Cup, but because his virtuosity made Argentina world champions. Cruyff's only blemish was that the Dutch team of 1974, *his* team, didn't win the trophy. Just as revealingly, the 'emotive' adolescent (which is how Cantona was described in a school report his parents received during his first year at La Grande Bastide – not just sensitive, but unafraid of showing how his sensitivity had been hurt) could take justified punishment with equanimity. And what greater punishment could there be than to be cast aside from the first XI?

'Once,' Monsieur Oliver told me, 'after he hadn't done, well, what he should have done during the week, I didn't put him in the team that was to play Nice – the biggest game for us. I put him on the bench. With ten minutes to go, the score was nil-nil, and I sent him on. Of course, he scored the winner with a tremendous header. He asked me after the game: "Monsieur Oliver, why didn't I play from the beginning tonight?" I just looked him in the eye and replied: "You know as well as I do, Éric." "I understand," he said. And that was the end of it.'

Not everyone could untie the knot of Cantona's conflicting impulses as adeptly as his coach. He grew up in one of the largest cities in France, yet felt himself drawn to the countryside. He loved the parties his grandparents improvised on the beach, revelled in their gregariousness, sang with the Gipsies, and then dived into the ocean, alone with his fantasies. Most adolescents experience this duality of character, halfway between the secret garden of home and the jungle that lies outside, but few have as great a talent as Éric, and the confidence that flows from it. Only within the cocoon of his family could he truly be himself. Even then, his shyness would sometimes get the better of him. He would retreat to his room, just as he did at La Grande Bastide, without warning or explanation. Christophe Galtier, who was as close to him as an outsider could be at the time, remembered Éric leaving the communal table in the middle of supper to listen to music (The Doors were a favourite of his then and still are, as was Mozart, who had 'been a great friend for many years'; 'In Mozart,' he said, 'there's art) or he'd go to the cinema on his own. 'He had to be by himself', Galtier said. 'He never said why, and we didn't ask.' This need to withdraw from the company of others, this capacity to isolate himself when surrounded by a crowd, would remain with him all through his life. My friend Jean-Marie Lanoé, who had been assigned the task of following Cantona for our magazine *France Football*, at Auxerre, Marseille, Montpellier and the under-21 national team (at a time when 'following', for a journalist, meant sharing rather more than five minutes in the car park of a stadium), has never forgotten how, on the evening of a 2–2 draw against England at Highbury in 1988, the two of them ended in a deserted London nightclub. With no one but a journalist to talk to, Cantona got up and walked to the dance floor and 'started to move alone, rapt, unaware or uncaring, for what seemed like hours. The oddest thing is that others would have seemed ridiculous in this situation, whereas Cantona was simply Cantona.' Célestin Oliver insisted on the 'maturity' of the teenager he looked after so sympathetically. Whether the teenager matured much further is not that clear. His models, after all, had been part of his life from the very beginning.

Joseph, his Sardinian grandfather, embodied loyalty – even more than Albert, in Oliver's perception. Pedro, the free-spirited Catalan who had as little time for the surplice as for the army uniform, personified something different from rebelliousness for its own sake. Defying authority was a matter of honour, as experience had written in his flesh what instinct had whispered to him before: authority's main purpose was to crush the individual, to extinguish the dream within ourselves. If Pedro had stood up to Franco, Éric might as well tell anyone else what he really thought of them. In one of the most telling passages of his autobiography (one of the few paragraphs in which I feel that his voice rings true),* he remembers how, in the summer of 1978 – immediately before becoming a boarder at Mazargues – Les Caillols, having already won the Coupe de Provence, were on the verge of completing the double; all they had to do was beat Vivaux-Marronniers in the final of that competition. The match didn't go according to plan, however. With five minutes to go, Vivaux-Marronniers went 1–0 up, and deservedly so. 'We're playing added time,' Cantona recounted in a tone that reminds me of the mythical Finn MacCool's superhuman exploits, as told by Flann O'Brien. 'It is the moment I choose to spring from the back and run towards goal, having dribbled past a good half-dozen opponents, as in a dream. I am alone, a few metres from goal, and if I score, maybe we'll be champions tonight.'

But Les Caillols would not add the 1978 championship of Provence to the list of their trophies. The referee blows his whistle. Éric's bootlaces have come undone, and the regulations are clear: a footballer's laces *must be tied*. 'The game is over. Tears flow in the dressing-room.' That day, Cantona had 'discovered stupidity or injustice, whatever you wish to call it'. The tale's most revealing trait must be that neither the child nor the grown man could tell the difference between the two. There was, of course, nothing 'unjust' about the referee's decision. Call him a bigot, a cretin, any name under the sun, but 'unjust'? No. 'Unfair', yes, as when a child complains of something 'unfair' when he's not given what he thinks he deserves. Had the goal been

* That book, published in France by Robert Laffont in 1993, written with the help of ghostwriter Pierre-Louis Basse, was hastily translated into English a year later under the title *Cantona: My Story*. Éric himself seems to have shown little interest in its preparation, and, as the deadline loomed, two members of his entourage were drafted in to fill in gaps in the text. In the first two pages, the reader was informed that Time [sic] Square was in London and that Gérard Philipe (died 1959) was France's main screen idol at the time of Cantona's birth (1966). Other factual inaccuracies include the date of Cantona's signing his first professional contract with Auxerre.

scored, and validated, the victim of the 'injustice' would have been Vivaux-Marronniers, not Les Caillols. But I doubt that anyone could persuade Cantona that his perception of right and wrong in what is, after all, one of the most regulated areas of human activity – team sports – was and remains deeply flawed. To him, when the official signalled a foul, it was as if he had killed a butterfly for no other reason than it was a butterfly, regardless of its beauty and harmlessness. To him it was a crime. Justice is an instinct, not a rulebook. No rules should circumvent invention. Those who have the ability to imagine beyond the rules have a right, maybe a duty, to break them, and damn the consequences.

For those who were satellites around the family sun, it was more a matter of 'managing the unmanageable, sometimes in impossible circumstances', as one of them told me, of finding accommodation with a fascinating, endearing and 'emotive' young man who could charm and exasperate those who cherished him most within a matter of seconds. His English teacher at La Grande Bastide, Evelyne Lyon, adored Éric, yet felt compelled to warn him that he 'had better watch out, because talent was not enough, and if he didn't change his character, he would have problems later on'. He was 'someone you always had to keep an eye on', she said. But this she did with as much gentleness as she could muster, even when her pupil ran riot outside her own classroom. Oliver chuckles at the recollection of Cantona dashing through the corridors after a training session, 'shouting in English, "*I am the king! I am the king!*"' Célestin Oliver could see the surprise on my face. Others would call him that later, wouldn't they? 'I think it had to do with Muhammed Ali,' he says, with another smile. How he loved his boy.

Cantona was thriving at La Grande Bastide, but word of his achievements on the field hadn't spread – yet – beyond Marseilles and Provence. OM had had a look at him, but, according to Oliver, their management had decided that Cantona was 'too slow' and passed on the chance to add the fourteen-year-old centre-forward's name to their books. Jean-Marie and Joël, who also entertained dreams of becoming professionals,* were similarly unsuccessful. Such a rejection cast a threatening shadow over Éric's future career; if a child of Les Caillols couldn't make it in his home-town club, who could he turn to? Thankfully, and not for the last time, luck lent a helping hand.

The French FA had divided the country into districts whose borders mirrored the country's *départements* and regions. These constituted the foundations of a pyramid, at the top of which sat national teams for each age group; a system of filters, if you will, a distillery of talent, one which would prove remarkably efficient at identifying and supporting emerging players. The chronic lack of success of *Les Bleus* in major tournaments, their inability to build on the exploits of the 1958 national squad, had prompted inspired administrators like George Boulogne and Fernand Sastre to undertake a complete reorganization of the detection system. Judging by the paucity of their results in European competitions, clubs couldn't be trusted to identify and develop promising footballers – the Federation would have to take care of that. To that end, regular tournaments or 'test-matches' were held at every level, in Provence as elsewhere.

Cantona may have failed to attract the attention of OM, but at fourteen-and-a-half was still good enough to be considered for selection in this context. The then technical adviser for the Marseilles region, Henri Émile, had been in touch with Célestin Oliver, who had warmly recommended Cantona for inclusion in a 'Mediterranean squad', a group of thirty-five players who were then separated into two teams, the 'possibles' and the 'probables'. To his amusement, Émile, who would become one of the most pivotal figures in Cantona's career, can't remember which of these two teams the boy was assigned to. 'Éric himself has a very vivid memory of the occasion, which we often talk about when we're travelling together,' Émile told me at the French FA's Clairefontaine

---

* Jean-Marie, the least gifted of the three brothers, became a businessman and later rejoined the footballing world, but as an agent. He still looks after a number of French professionals, the World Cup-winning goalkeeper Fabien Barthez among others. Joël managed to carve a peripatetic career with Olympique Marseille, Stade Rennais, FC Antwerp, SCO Angers, Ujpest and . . . Stockport County, a point at which his story and Éric's become entangled for good, as you will see.

headquarters, 'but was he a "possible", or a "probable"? He doesn't know. He had no idea what these terms meant!' It hardly mattered, as Cantona produced a magnificent display that afternoon in the spring of 1981. What mattered was that the match had been watched by a couple of scouts from Auxerre, an up-and-coming club from northern Burgundy which had risen quickly through the divisions under the tutelage of the wiliest of managers, Guy Roux. They had made the trip to the ground in order to monitor another player, whose identity has been forgotten by everyone. But they had seen Éric, and that was enough.

No one was keener than Roux to poach the best young talent available; his club had only acquired full professional status a couple of years earlier and its ground, the Stade de l'Abbé-Deschamps (named after the Catholic priest who had founded the Association de la jeunesse auxerroise, or AJ Auxerre or AJA), was minuscule by first-division standards. Roux had to scrape for every penny, which, it should be said, agreed with the parsimonious nature he had inherited from his peasant roots. Twenty-seven years later, as we sat down to a distinctly non-frugal lunch in one of Chablis's restaurants (after a lengthy visit to one of the area's most renowned cellars), Roux recalled how his chief scout's report – his name was Jean-Pierre Duport – had been glowing enough to convince him that Cantona's trail should be followed by the club's second-in-command, assistant manager Daniel Rolland, in whom Roux had total confidence.

So it was that Rolland repeatedly drove down the *autoroute du soleil* to judge for himself. 'Everybody could see he was "above" the others,' says Roux – but no one as clearly as the astute coach from Burgundy, who, feigning innocence, called Oliver to ask him what he really thought of 'this lad . . . Éric Cantona, yes?' There was some risk attached to uprooting an adolescent from sunny Marseilles to one of the sleepiest towns in the sleepiest of regions. As Henri Émile says, 'You never know how far a player can go at this age. You can feel a potential. But there are things you cannot control. Psychological things – as when a player thinks he's "made it", too soon. They can stall. You can see a great player's potential but you don't have certainties. Competition alone reveals whether the player masters all the criteria of the highest level.' But – and it is a crucial but – the way that the OM reject had seized his one opportunity to shine showed that there was steel in his character as well as skill in his boots. The importance of the occasion had not fazed him. Still, Émile cannot help thinking of a 'what if': 'Éric's told me on several occasions that, if he hadn't been picked in this team to start with, he might not have had the same career. Maybe he could have slipped through the net . . . which just goes to show!'

Roux still had some work to do to land his catch. Cantona's performance for the Provençal scratch team had not escaped OGC Nice – a club with a reputation and a collection of honours that Auxerre could only look up to. This was the club for which Roger Jouve, another product of Les Caillols, was still playing three seasons earlier, and whose colours had been worn by another of Cantona's early heroes, the Bosnian striker Jean Katalinski. Oliver himself kept telling his pupil that he should 'go for it' and rush down the coast to join Nice for good. By contrast, Auxerre was neither the most obvious nor the easiest choice for a stripling footballer who had not yet reached his fifteenth birthday. The medieval town, built like a low ribbon of stone along the slow waters of the Yonne, had a discreet charm, but few attractions for a teenager who had grown up in the warmth of the Mediterranean. There, in the north-eastern corner of Burgundy, autumns turned sharply to harsh Continental winters, almost as soon as the vineyards had been unburdened of their last bunch of grapes. Fog was common, snow too, often at unseasonal times. Going back to Marseilles would entail long hours on the train or in the family car – the high-speed TGV link between Paris and Marseilles was only completed in 2001. Nice, with ten times the population of Auxerre, had a casino, fine restaurants, nightclubs, beaches, palm trees and girls in monokinis by the seaside. Auxerre, on the other hand, had a few choice *charcuteries*, splendid white wines and a clutch of cafes which closed early when they deigned to open at all (Sundays are a very quiet affair in this town).

When it came to football, Nice, again, had dwarfed Auxerre for almost its entire history. Both clubs had been born roughly at the same time – AJA in 1905, OGC Nice three years later – but there the similarities ended. Whereas Nice's *Les Aiglons* had won four French championships, two French Cups, and twice reached the quarter-finals of the European Cup, Auxerre owed its small measure of fame to its dramatic rise from the amateur ranks to the final of the 1979 French Cup, thanks to the genius of one man – Guy Roux. Glamorous Nice should have held all the cards in the duel for the acquisition of the exciting but yet unproven Cantona; but it played its hand badly. Perhaps the *Niçois*, who must have been aware of Auxerre's manoeuvring, believed that the prestige attached to their red-and-black jersey, coupled with the interest they showed in the teenager, would suffice to overwhelm him. AJA was small fry after all. But Nice totally misjudged the young man's temperament and hardly bothered to find out what could possibly prevent him from becoming one of their dozens of apprentices. Cantona finally made the trip to Nice as planned, but came back to his family laden with disappointment. He had decided to turn his back on OGCN for what seemed like the flimsiest of reasons – which he daren't confess to his father at the time. He had asked if he could be given a jersey and pennant of *Les Aiglons*; quite ridiculously, the club insisted he should pay for them. He paid, but didn't forget how little his prospective employers appeared to care for him.

However, when Cantona accepted Roux's invitation to Auxerre a few weeks later, nothing had been decided yet. The Auxerre manager had behaved with typical subtlety in his dealings with Célestin Oliver. 'One day,' Tico says, 'Guy Roux called me, and said: "Have you got a decent player in your class?" I told him – Cantona. "Send him to me."' Guy Roux is a very, very clever man . . .' Éric was just to take part in a small, seemingly informal clinic. The date was 1 May 1981.

The memory of these first few days spent together brings a smile to Roux's face. 'We'd just finished our first year as a professional club. I was there, of course. There were quite a few of these youngsters: Galtier, Darras, Mazzolini, all these kids . . . and Éric Cantona.' The atmosphere was more reminiscent of a holiday camp than of a test which could and did decide the future of these carefree teenagers. 'They were larking about like toddlers, because we had a pool . . . well, a bath for the players, about the quarter of the size of this place,' Roux says, gesturing towards the dining room of Au Petit Chablis, which would not have accommodated the larger kind of Bourguignon wedding reception. 'But there were very few pools of that kind at the time. They were having such fun . . . I chatted with the lad, and, after a few minutes, he tells me: "I'd like a shirt"; at that time, a shirt was something . . .' When Roux, cunning as ever, slipped a few jerseys in Cantona's bags when time had come to bid him farewell, builders were still at work finishing the academy's main hall. Its next recruit, filled with delight by the generosity of his future manager, still had to convince his family that the choice he had made in his heart would feel right for them too. This time, though, he was prepared to be his own man. The first decision he had taken on his own would prove to be one of the best in his whole life.

Now is as good a moment as any to interrupt the chronological thread in Cantona's story, to address once and for all the comments his love of painting, alluded to in this first chapter, attracted later in his life, when everything he said or did became a target for the cheapest kind of mockery. A footballer who paints – how comical, how ludicrous is that? In the macho world of football, and particularly English football, an artistic inclination, especially as genuine an inclination as Cantona's, only ranks below homosexuality if ostracism is what you're looking for. To his enemies, Cantona's attachment to art brought another proof of his insufferable arrogance. 'I paint' meant 'I am better than you'. This is a profound misunderstanding (one among many others) of the man's personality. Vanity had nothing to do with the need he felt to look into himself in this way. Later in life, he always resisted the temptation – I would go as far as to say that he never felt it – to use his fame as a sportsman to stage public exhibitions of his work. Painting was a private pursuit, a means to relax, too, when he would take his paintbox and head for the garrigue – the wild coastal scrubland near his home – on his own, with no other company than his two dogs. He was also aware that if he possessed a real gift, his technical ability didn't quite match Albert's, and that it would be cheating to pretend that he was as much a genius with a brush in his hand as with a ball at his feet. Insecurity combined with his instinct for self-protection to keep painting an interest that could only be shared with people he trusted. He was not coquettish or ashamed of what he was doing, no; he might organize a private show of some works for the benefit of close friends and members of his family, but not more than that. The few who had access to this much-spoken-about, unfairly ridiculed and hidden part of his world, and have spoken to me about what they saw, invariably stressed the dark, even 'tortured' nature of most of his work. They also insisted on its quality – Gérard Houllier in particular was struck by the originality of what he was shown. Photographer Didier Fèvre, who was among Cantona's closest friends in the late eighties and early nineties, saw him experiment with supports other than canvas, cutting up photographs which he then half-covered with brushstrokes. It is clear that, moving into adulthood, Cantona was retreating in more ways than one from the Provençal idyll his father had tried to capture. He was also developing an increasing sense of his own mortality, as a hypersensitive footballer-artist could not fail to do; once he had reached the age of thirty, physical decline would precipitate his rapid 'death' as an athlete, a subject which became a recurrent theme in the interviews he gave late in his career, an awareness that contributed to precipitate the announcement of his retirement in 1997.

The language he uses when speaking of the artists he admires today is revealing. Of Zoran Mušič, a Slovenian painter who left haunting etchings and engravings of the Holocaust he survived: 'It's powerful, you feel a power . . . You feel that if he hadn't painted, he'd have died [the French crevé, *or* burst, *almost carries the stench of death, but has no equivalent in English].' Of the Catalan Antoni Tàpies: 'He gives another life to objects which are fated to die.' His Picasso puppet featured on* Les Guignols de l'info *– the French equivalent of* Spitting Image *– was nothing but a gross caricature of the man's sincerity and talent. It is to Cantona's credit that he bore these cheap shots at his 'difference' with good grace. He genuinely enjoyed seeing his latex alter ego make a fool of himself on television with incomprehensible pronouncements (which, more often than not, concluded with his throwing his shirt away in disgust). And why not? He had long been aware of the absurdty of his public persona. The superb copy he threw away to journalists in his early twenties was littered with self-deprecating quips about his supposed 'intellectualism'. Some got it, most didn't. Caught between the urge to be recognized and the desire to be left alone, he laid shoals of red herrings on the slab, finding amusement, and a kind of security, in the willingness of others to gobble up his catch. Talking of which, sardines were not spared in a splendid advertising mini-feature – two-and-a-half minutes long – purportedly shot for the benefit of an electronics* *manufacturer shortly after the denouement of the Crystal Palace affair, in the spring of 1995. In that film, arms aloft on the top of a cliff, seagulls screeching over his earnest baritone, his whole body shaking in the presence of the Muses, Cantona laughed at Cantona. This was probably the finest acting performance of his career. He might not agree with this judgement. But he would probably smile at it.*

2

Cantona and his 'band of merry men'.

AUXERRE: THE APPRENTICE

Éric's parents didn't share his enthusiasm for moving 600 kilometres north of Marseilles – to put it mildly. He had just celebrated his fifteenth birthday; it was one thing to board a few nights a week at Mazargues, quite another to find himself among people he knew nothing of, with only the telephone to link him to the clan. 'Why not Nice?' they asked him. 'We could come and see you every weekend.' Jean-Marie, the most even-tempered and 'reasonable' of the three brothers, also advised him not to pack his suitcase for Burgundy. But Éric stood his ground. Some of the arguments he used when the family discussed his future showed him to be rather more than a stubborn, hot-headed teenager who could be bought for a few shirts. He wouldn't be the first child of Les Caillols to seek success a long way away from the Provençal sun, he said. Five years previously, René Marsiglia had left SOC for Boulogne-sur-Mer when only thirteen years old, and was now an established professional with Lille Olympique Sporting Club. It was well-known that southern clubs had a perverse tendency not to look after their own, and that local fans easily turned against footballers who had grown up in the same streets as them – as Marseille fans would when Éric joined their club in 1988.

Éric had a profound respect for Monsieur Roux. He felt at ease in the unprepossessing atmosphere of Auxerre, where he had had such fun splashing about and training with what he knew instantly was an exceptional group of youngsters. Crucially, AJA trusted their young players to represent the club in the third division championship, where the reserves played, whereas he would be likely – no, certain

– to be ignored by the management of haughty Nice for such games. And how could he improve if he didn't play? Thanks to Henri Émile's recommendation, he had recently been called up by the French under-seventeen national squad. This meant two things: his qualities were now recognized within the game, but he would also need to fight even harder to survive in the football world. Auxerre would provide him with a chance to measure himself against tougher opponents in a competitive environment. Little by little, Éric won over his family. Albert took his son's decision with good grace in the end. Auxerre wasn't the end of the world after all.

So Joseph and Lucienne drove Éric to Burgundy, where they enjoyed lunch with Guy Roux on the banks of the River Yonne. 'When we were served dessert, I told them, "But you just have to come back to see him!" His Italian grandfather replied, "Oh, Auxerre is far, I'm old, I don't know . . ." "Listen to me," I said. "When he plays for France the first time, you'll have to come and see me." Well, he was nineteen when he played against [West] Germany – and the grandfather hadn't forgotten.'

Within a matter of weeks, the recruit had become a full-time apprentice, the youngest in his age category, and was training with the reserve team. The summers spent in the shade of Joseph's and Lucienne's *cabanon* belonged to the childhood he had left behind; should he return to the Côte Bleue, it would be like opening, briefly, a window on his own past. But Éric felt sure he could live with the brutality of this break with his former life. He wasn't cowed by his new surroundings, quite the contrary, in fact. Was it because Albert and Eléonore were not there to keep him in check any longer? The 'difficult' teenager turned into a genuine hellraiser. Célestin Oliver had seen in him a 'born leader'; but maybe not of the kind of gang that soon congregated around the imposing youth. Their misdemeanours were confined to the club – for the most part. Basile Boli has recounted how this 'gang', which Roux called 'Canto and his band of merry men' (on that occasion, Cantona, Prunier, Vahirua, Basile and his brother Roger), would buy clapped-out cars and organize 'rodeos' – lifesize dodgems – in the local rubbish tip. Roux never knew about this, thankfully; had he done so, the punishment would have been severe. A strict disciplinarian, he thought nothing of fining trainees who earned barely anything. Once, several of the youngsters, who'd taken part in a remarkable victory over the reserves of St Étienne, were spotted in a nightclub after the game. Roux was told by one of his many spies, and dug into the culprits' pockets to buy a billiards table for the academy, which was referred to as the 'Boli-Cantona' table for years afterwards.

On the whole, however, the merry men kept themselves to themselves. They did not vandalize phone booths or terrify the good burghers of Auxerre. But they played pranks, wreaked havoc in the dormitory, and generally brought the coaching staff close to a communal nervous breakdown. 'These kids were very close to each other,' Roux told me. A brief pause, then: 'They were also up to no good most of the time. Daniel Rolland, a lovely man who adored them, and who was probably the best educator in French football at the time, just couldn't cope with them.' 'And what did you do?' I asked. 'Me? I was the court of appeal. Éric came to my office when Daniel Rolland just couldn't bear it any more. Éric was very violent, in his language too. But also charming when he could keep his temper in check. Generous, and hard-working, with a really good heart behind all the excesses. Tell me – between a nicey-nicey lazybones with no talent and a super-worker with an awful temper on him, what would be your choice? Mine was quickly made.'

Something had struck me: to qualify Cantona's 'awful temper', Roux had used the adjective *caractériel*. It is a very strong word indeed, one you wouldn't use to describe a naughty child – a disturbed one, rather, who might need medical attention. Was it really the word he had meant to use? Roux looked me in the eye and said: 'Yes.'

Thankfully, most of Éric's horseplay was 'naughty' rather than '*caractériel*', and Roux noticed a marked improvement once the wrench of being parted from brothers, parents and grandparents was gradually blunted by the comradeship he developed with his new teammates. In that respect, Auxerre had been a wise choice, as no other elite club in France had a better claim to call itself 'a family'. A husband-and-wife duo took care of the youth team at the time (Roux gave me their names, but omitting them might spare a few blushes, even now), a couple of ex-factory workers who looked after their meals, their kits and, sometimes, their sorrows. Once a week, Mrs X— left home after dinner to attend a late gym class in town. Mr X— did not waste much time in switching on the television and slipping an adult film into the video player. Word got round the academy of what was going on at the X—s' home, and it became one of the week's highlights to clamber over the dormitory walls and watch both Mr X— and watch what he was watching. What could Guy Roux do but smile?

Smiles, however, were scarcer on the training ground. Roux loved skilled players, and stuck to the enterprising 4-3-3 formation which had taken his team to the top division in the country and to a French Cup final two years earlier, in 1979. But he could also be implacable with players who did not show the drive he never lacked himself. There are numerous stories of his 'breaking' young footballers who did not possess enough steel in their characters to withstand the toughness of Auxerre's upbringing. Éric's teammate Basile Boli, Guy Roux's other 'son', could write in his remarkable autobiography *Black Boli*: 'Auxerre [was] a real factory. I've seen many kids whose dreams exploded like a football that's been inflated too much. Formation is a gamble. When you win, you have a career. When you lose . . . you lose everything, really.' Roux, who had been convinced of Éric's talent ever since he had laid eyes on him, still waited for proof that the fifteen-year-old had the mental qualities required to put himself in contention for a place in the first-team squad. Both player and manager agree that this proof was shown late in the spring of 1982, shortly before the end of the season. Roux enjoyed pitting his reserves against the first team's pros; nothing but pride was at stake, but it was proud men he was looking for, and a stupendous second half by the young Marseillais proved to him – and to everyone else – that, barely a year after he had left Provence, the prodigy of Les Caillols was ready to step up a level.

There was no holding back Éric Cantona, in more ways than one. On that sunny afternoon, the victim of his cheek was Lucien Denis, an experienced defender who, according to Roux, 'went mad'. Incensed by the youngster's dribbling, he fouled him crudely on several occasions. But if Denis was not amused, he was in a minority of one. 'I could see he was already at the level of the pros – and he hadn't celebrated his sixteenth birthday yet!' Roux's delight was shared by his apprentice. 'Life was beautiful,' Éric recalled in his 1993 autobiography, all the more so as his first season at Auxerre was to end with a magnificent opportunity to demonstrate his talent to a far larger audience than his club's management team on a training pitch.

An international friendly was to be played in Lyon between the France of Tigana, Giresse and Platini and Bulgaria on 15 May 1982, providing the national manager Michel Hidalgo with a last chance to deploy *Les Bleus* before the World Cup. As was the tradition at the time, the game would be preceded by a curtain-raiser, between the under-17s of France and Switzerland on this occasion. Éric played out of his skin. Everyone now knew that Guy Roux and his scouts had unearthed a gem, who signed off his first appearance for his country with the winning goal. The *cadets* of Auxerre also won the Coupe Gambardella – the French Youth Cup – that year, putting six goals past Nancy. 'The kids we then had at the academy were of exceptional quality,' says Roux. 'Usually, out of a group of fifteen, if a third of them make it, you'll be delighted. Well, out of this lot, twelve became pros, and four were capped by France at senior level: Basile Boli, Pascal Vahirua, William Prunier* – and Cantona.' Life was beautiful indeed.

Still, nutmegging Lucien Denis in a seven-a-side game back at l'Abbé-Deschamps hadn't given Éric a licence to queue-jump his way into the first team. He first had to further his education in the dour and unforgiving environment of the French third division, where upstarts of his kind are choice targets for the dirty tricks of so-called 'hard men' – and for the jealousy of teammates not quite good enough to be called from the reserves. Éric survived both tests with some ease, thanks to his irrepressible enthusiasm, his talent and his astonishing self-confidence, creating mayhem on the field of play as well as off it.

---

* Prunier would be Cantona's teammate at Manchester United in the 1995–96 season; see page 414.

The lightly built teenager of Marseilles was also turning into a stupendous athlete, and revelling in his physical transformation. The Ivorian-born defender Basile Boli, who had been turned away from Paris Saint-Germain, had arrived at Auxerre at the start of the 1982–83 season and, though seven months younger than Éric (according to his passport), had immediately joined him in the third division team. Both had the bodies of men several years their elder, and constantly looked for occasions to find out who was the quickest, the strongest, the most resilient. To Roux's amazement, they were way ahead of everyone else in the reserves, and in every single department. A sprinter, held back by his weight and his muscular mass, would normally hit the wall when asked to complete more than a single lap of the track; not Basile, not Éric, who were both built like boxers rather than footballers of that day and age. A dancer needs powerful arms, shoulders and thighs (not to mention a torso like a lumberjack's) as well as exceptional balance and coordination to perform his art; Cantona's own brand of ballet should remind us of that truth: he was gifted the ideal body to become himself.

The speed with which he had adapted to life in the reserves meant it was only a question of 'when' rather than 'if' Guy Roux would give him his debut with the first team. Quite astonishingly, or perhaps characteristically, when asked by his amanuensis Pierre-Louis Basse to relive the occasion, Cantona would remember the date as 21 October 1984, against Nancy. He had got the opponents right – and the day wrong, by almost a year. In fact, it was on 5 November 1983 that he was at last given a chance to play alongside established internationals such as goalkeeper Joël Bats and striker Andrzej Szarmach, one of the heroes of Poland's magnificent 1974 World Cup, where they were a whisker away from qualifying for the final (Éric had cried when Beckenbauer's and Müller's West Germany made Cruyff's Netherlands pay for the arrogance of their play). Auxerre waltzed past Nancy that day – and Cantona was 'on a cloud'. 'I knew little of Szarmach,' he remembered, 'but I was reassured by his simplicity, his kindness and his humility. I discovered what it meant to be a footballer of great talent, but also a man who had class.' The Pole had done everything in his considerable power to offer a goal to the teenager, without success. Cantona's own generosity to younger teammates, which was to have such an impact at Manchester United, was perhaps kindled on that day.

Reports published at the time didn't dwell on his contribution, however. He had done well, well enough to last over an hour; but he was not quite ready yet, nor was he when Roux called on him again for the visit of Lens six weeks later. Lens capitulated 4–0 at l'Abbé-Deschamps, just like Nancy had done, but he would have to wait until March 1985 to join the first-teamers again. Cantona had talent in spades, no question; but it was proving rather hard to bend this precious ore the way the manager would have wished. Cantona's temper could short-circuit without warning, never more spectacularly than on one evening of this 1983–84 season. Here is how Roux retold the incident, with the same mixture of pride and concern he must have felt all those years ago.

'We were playing against Cournon-Le Cendre on a Saturday night. These guys were tough. They came from a mining town of the Auvergne. One of their central defenders hacks him down, nastily. Éric gets up. The referee says nothing. Cantona is hacked again, and this time reacts. The other guy didn't finish the game. His teammates were not happy. My assistant Daniel Rolland had already gathered our kit and left the ground, but I was still there, and so was Cantona, who hadn't left the dressing-room. All the Cournon players are around me, next to the door. I asked them: "What are you waiting for?" "We're waiting for Cantona." "Well, listen, in any case, the evening will finish badly for you. If you give him a hiding, I'll call the police and you'll end up in a cell; but he might also give you a right thrashing, and you won't be able to complain." "There's ten of us!" "You'll see!" Then Canto gets out – he sees them – he doesn't wait. He swings his bag around, and catches one of the guys on the head – out for the count – he punches a couple of others, throws the bag, and starts kicking them – yes, already! I can see a disaster about to happen. And what can I do? I wasn't much at the time; but, instinctively, I scream "*Halte!*" at the top of my voice. Everybody stops. "Right," I say, "enough. If there are any injuries, we go home and treat them." We all troop back to the dressing-room. I get the first-aid kit . . . Éric had hurt his hands. But he sat with them as if nothing had happened! He was afraid of nothing.'

Cantona was also mightily strong, as was proved when Roux took advantage of the long winter break to take his team to the cross-country ski resort of Prémanon. Éric had by then achieved his transition to the senior level, at least in terms of sporting achievement; boarding with much older pros presented other challenges that he still wasn't quite ready to confront. 'But, once on the snow,' adds Roux, 'he was half an hour quicker than anyone else.' The last day of their stay coincided with the French Youth Cross-Country Championships. The Auxerre staff asked the organizers to keep the tracks open and to put their medical facilities at their disposal. Roux then asked his players to take part in 'our own little race, ten kilometres long, chocolate bars for the winner'. No prizes for guessing who pocketed the chocolate bars. Cantona ran out a clear winner, 'by a mile', ahead of Polish international Waldemar Matysik, whom his coach describes as 'a very tough guy'. In fact, had Cantona taken part in the French Championships, his time would have placed him among the five quickest finishers. This is remarkable for a child of Provence who had never been on skis before.

Week in, week out, Cantona had to measure himself against the mix of promising youths, convalescent first-teamers and professional journeymen who made up the vast majority of third division teams, many of which doubled up as reserve sides for the elite clubs. Auxerre was the exception; Auxerre was about youth – all-conquering youth. Cantona and his friends took the title with some panache, his future brother-in-law Bernard Ferrer only being outscored by Éric himself, who finished the season with twenty goals to his credit, the last one ensuring AJA's victory in the championship final. There were only 100 spectators in the Valence stadium to see what the correspondent of *L'Yonne Républicaine* described as a 'stroke of genius' from Cantona. The local paper was the only publication to report Auxerre's 1–0 victory over the club that Éric might have joined had he not been asked to pay for one of their red-and-black striped shirts: OGC Nice. Cantona lost his marker, started a solitary raid from the halfway line, and scored. He also got a yellow card.

In almost any other club of Auxerre's standing – short on resources, long on ambition, but lacking too much of the former to fulfil the latter – Éric would have undoubtedly become a focal point of the team's attack before the 1986–87 season, when Roux finally unleashed him for good. But the *Icaunais* suffered from a surfeit of high-class forwards at the time. At nearly thirty-five years of age, Andrzej Szarmach was not quite the force he had been, but was still strong enough to warrant an automatic place in the starting line-up. Patrice Garande, Éric's elder by six years, was enjoying the most prolific form of his career – which included a gold medal with the French team at the 1984 Olympic Games, a couple of months after having been awarded the 'Golden Boot' for his 21 goals in the French first division championship, one more than the Polish striker had scored. For Roux, who never cared much for reputation, Cantona came third in the pecking order, and then only just, ahead of Philippe Fargeon – who would become a French 'A' international – and Michel Pineda, a close friend of Éric's who would soon enjoy some success with Espanyol in the Spanish Primera Liga. It seemed as if all the seeds Guy Roux had sown were flowering at the same time. The under-17s were crowned champions for the second year running. Daniel Rolland led the reserves of the reserves (!) to the fourth division title. Auxerre thrashed Laurent Blanc's Montpellier-La Paillade 3–0 in the final of the 1985 Coupe Gambardella. Éric scored all three of his team's goals that day. But even a hat-trick wasn't quite good enough to enable him to break into a playing unit that delighted the whole of the country with its fast, intricate, inventive, counter-attacking brand of football. Roux still harboured doubts about Cantona's ability to rein in his self-destructive impulses; hardly surprising given that Éric regularly gave him sound reasons for having such doubts.

In January 1984 the French *juniors* were invited to take part in a six-team indoor tournament in Leningrad. Éric had been made welcome in this set-up. His head coach, the late Gaby Robert, enjoyed a very close relationship with him, for Robert was a Marseillais too, a jovial, kind-hearted man who knew when to shrug his shoulders or look the other way, and when to have a heart-to-heart with the 'unmanageable' youngster he treated like a son. Robert, however, found himself at the centre of another potential Cold War crisis when Éric, incensed by a refereeing decision, spat in the face of the Soviet official. The official in question was a colonel in the Red Army, who sent him off on the spot in front of an aghast French delegation. Diplomats did what they had to do. Nothing came of it, somehow, and Éric flew home with his teammates; but word of his exploits had already been passed on to the Auxerre manager. Roux quietly dropped him from the first team (with whom he had played two games already, as we've seen), and started to work on his next move.

Éric turned eighteen in May of 1984. For all Frenchmen of his generation, reaching that age meant a call-up to the army. Then again, 'call-up' signified many things. For most, twelve months of tedium, loneliness and ritual humiliation in a remote provincial town or, if you were particularly unlucky, in Germany. A few weeks of drill, then the mind-numbing routine of life in the barracks – dodging ill-tempered and foul-mouthed adjutants during the day, downing Kronenbourg beer and playing table football, pinball or billiards in the evening. Students, who benefited from a suspended sentence (conscription could be postponed until they had completed their degree, up to the age of twenty-two), hoped for a posting abroad. One of my friends ended up promoting French cinema on behalf of French consular services in Ottawa, which should tell you everything about *piston*, France's answer to the Anglo-Saxon old-boy network. Elite sportsmen dreamed of joining the *Bataillon de Joinville*, an army in shorts and tracksuits that never saw a gun, and was expected to carry the flag in international competitions instead.

The *Bataillon* had, shall we say, something of a reputation. Joinville was conveniently close to Paris, and one-night desertions were tolerated by the military. Roux, an expert in the *piston* system, usually preferred to have his young players assigned to the local *gendarmerie*. Conscript footballers were allowed to return to their club for the weekend's games as a rule; should they become *gendarmes* in Auxerre or Chablis, they would also be able to attend a number of training sessions – and Roux could keep an eye on them, of course. But is a *gendarme* a soldier? Not quite. Perhaps misguidedly, the Auxerre manager thought that his rebellious Marseillais would encounter sterner discipline in the *Bataillon*, and phoned his friend Joseph

Mercier – who happened to be the man in charge of this unit's footballing squad. Mercier, who is now well into his eighties, chuckled when I asked him why Roux had made an exception to his rule in Éric's case. 'Oh, Guy always hid his boys at the *gendarmerie*! But Cantona posed a few problems to Auxerre, because of his well-defined personality.' (Mercier is a master of the understatement.) 'He told me, "I'm sending you a top lad" . . . that made me laugh. I knew exactly why he was doing this. To have the lad knocked into shape.'

When I put this version of events to Roux, I was hit by a barrage of not entirely convincing incredulity. 'I had no choice,' he blustered. 'Éric was already an international footballer with the under-21s [*not quite: with the under-19s, but you get Roux's point*]. He had to go to Joinville!' I could imagine Mercier's chuckle in the background. Whatever the truth may be, the experience was only a qualified success. The little control Cantona may have had over the wilder side of his character was lustily relinquished. 'We burned what was left of our adolescence,' Éric told Pierre-Louis Basse. This 'we' refers to Éric and Bernard 'Nino' Ferrer, who, though he was two-and-a-half years older, had been conscripted at the same time: Roux obviously thought that Éric needed company. 'We prepared ourselves to spend a year sleeping during the day, and having fun at night' – which is precisely what they did.

Their behaviour would have shocked a hussar of Napoleon's army. Mercier, a prudent man, had asked to be relieved of his duties shortly after Éric's arrival at the *Bataillon*, and only supervised a handful of international games, including one against West Germany, before passing on the baton to Jacky Braun. Braun declined to be interviewed for this book, as he would 'only have unpleasant things to say' about Cantona. A pity. He might have shed some light on an eventful tour of Gabon which saw Éric 'flirt with death', that is: experience a very nasty trip after smoking the local dope with strangers in the capital Libreville. 'Fear quickly took the place of curiosity,' he wrote in his autobiography. 'The fear of dying. [. . .] I had been looking for artificial paradises, but it is anguish that was waiting for me at the end of such a journey. One does not resist the attraction of the forbidden fruit . . .' Tellingly, a rite of passage had become a brush with the Grim Reaper. Éric never did things by halves.

Cantona's understanding of the logic that led to his being assigned to Joinville differed from Mercier's and Roux's. To him, his mentor had connived with an accomplice to give him a chance to sow his wild oats before he settled down with a fiancée or a bride – like most professional footballers do at a very young age – to a life of 'sleeping, eating, playing, travelling without having the time to comprehend the countries [they] go through'. It's hard to see in this anything but an attempt to justify the recklessness of his behaviour at the time, which was exacerbated by his visceral rejection of any kind of institutional authority. He knew that Joinville conscripts enjoyed a privileged status. They could do pretty much as they pleased, and get away with acts of indiscipline that would have earned ordinary squaddies a few nights in jail. He exploited this leniency to the full. Roux, who paid weekly visits to the barracks, was appalled by what the colonel in charge of the *Bataillon* told him. A general had announced his intention to meet the flower of France's youth; but Cantona had developed an aversion to shaving at the time, and looked like an extra from *Papillon.* Unfortunately, this particular soldier had very personal views on what constituted an order. His adjutant tried to cajole him into getting rid of his coal-dark stubble, but to no avail. The colonel didn't fare any better. 'I do not shave,' was Cantona's answer, each syllable of '*Je-ne-me-ra-se-pas*' enunciated in a low, forbidding baritone. The officers relented. They put Éric in a lorry and sent him on an impromptu trip to Orléans, a hundred and fifty miles away, to collect bags of potatoes.

This chore must have felt like a victory, another white flag hoisted by the men in uniform. It is no wonder that Éric, unlike 99 per cent of his contemporaries, had fond memories of his time at the service of the nation. Five years later, he crossed Mercier's path again, when Montpellier played a game in Châteauroux, to where the coach had retired. Coming out of the dressing-room, he recognized his benevolent manager, gave him a mock military salute and exclamed: 'Ah, Monsieur Mercier, yes, sir!' – in English. 'The first thing I told my players,' Mercier explained, 'was – do not discuss a referee's decisions more than a US Marine would discuss an officer's order.' Roux's plan to have 'the lad knocked into shape' hadn't quite worked as planned.

It hardly mattered, though. Right at the end of the season, as Auxerre were striving for a place in the UEFA Cup for the second time in their history,* the uncontrollable Éric gave two magnificent demonstrations of what Roux does not hesitate to call his 'genius'. The first of these was on 14 May 1985, in the antiquated décor of the Stade Robert-Diochon, in Rouen, nine days before Cantona's nineteenth birthday, when he scored the first of his 23 league goals (in 81 appearances) for the Burgundy club. 'It was a rotten game,' says Roux. 'My three 'keepers were unfit. In the end, [Joël] Bats played – but couldn't kick the ball. It was pissing down. This is Rouen, the chamber-pot of France. Water everywhere. Over an hour had been played. Canto started from the middle of the pitch and ate everything: the puddles, the defenders, he left everything behind, he munched the lot, and scored with a piledriver.' Auxerre won 2–1, thanks to a complete unknown. Two weeks later, more drama, more Cantona.

Strasbourg this time, at the Stade de la Meinau. AJA need a single point to guarantee a place in Europe, and things aren't going too well. 'My son was studying there at the time,' Roux says. 'He's listening to the game on the radio. We're losing 1–0 at half-time. We've got to do something, I tell them, we're not going to miss out on Europe like this! We were dead. I didn't have a go at them, as I knew they couldn't do more. Cantona said something like: "I'll take care of it." And he did. He took the ball in midfield. He pushed it once, and whacked the ball from the centre circle. Goal. 1–1, Auxerre is in the UEFA Cup.' Cantona himself relived his equalizing goal with the clarity of a dream. No, he wasn't in the centre circle – a little over 25 yards from his target. But as soon as he had received the ball in his own half (that much is true), he had known that something special, preordained ('I've always felt I was watched over by something greater than me') was about to happen. That was the day, 28 May 1985, on which an exceptional footballer emerged from the chrysalis. To think that, the day before the game – something that Guy Roux's spies had failed to report – Éric, accompanied by his friend Nino (a nickname

* AJA had finished third in the league in 1983–84, and, having drawn Sporting Lisbon, exited the UEFA Cup at the first hurdle.

Bernard Ferrer owed to sharing a surname with one of France's most popular sixties pop singers), had drifted from bar to bar, nightclub to nightclub, girl to girl, until four in the morning. To think that within a few weeks, the teenager would meet the woman who would anchor him at last. Cantona's apprenticeship was over.

3

Cantona at Auxerre, May 1985.

AUXERRE: THE PROFESSIONAL

For 'Nino' Ferrer, the time to settle down to the life of 'sleeping, eating, playing, travelling without having the time to comprehend the countries [footballers] go through' came that summer, when he got married, at the age of twenty-one. Éric was one of the first names on his list of guests, naturally. At the wedding reception, his eyes fell on Nino's sister Isabelle, whom he had already met, albeit fleetingly, when she had visited her brother in Chablis, where she could revise for her exams in peace.

Three years Éric's elder, Isabelle could not have been further from the archetypal WAG, be it in looks or personality. When I met her more than twenty years later in Marseilles – she and Éric had been living apart for five years by then – she retained the charm and allure which had convinced Éric he had met the woman he wanted to grow old with. She came from a humble background not dissimilar to his, and spoke with the delightful southern lilt of the Provençal working class. She had been studying literature at the University of Aix-en-Provence and had done very well there, supporting herself by working as senior clerk in a supermarket. She was graced – *le mot juste* – with beautiful dark eyes and a sunny, yet slightly melancholy smile. She was no bimbo, but a very attractive young woman who was not afraid to let her heart rule her reason, as she showed when, after spending two weeks in Éric's Auxerre flat, she jumped from the train taking her back to Provence to spend another couple of days with the man she loved. Thus was born the apocryphal tale of a near-mad Cantona forcing that same train to stop by jumping on the track in front of the locomotive. The truth was simpler, sweeter, and more fitting. She would be the discreet and faithful companion of Éric throughout the turmoil and the triumphs of his whole career; to borrow from Cantona's favourite poet Arthur Rimbaud, she was the rock to which Éric could always moor his drunken boat. Isabelle, whom I've always heard being talked about with affection, respect and even admiration, cannot remain a silent silhouette cut out from the backdrop of Éric's melodrama. Her selfless love for her husband ennobled him, and I don't believe you can tell a man's story if you do not speak, even that briefly, about the woman he loved more than any other.

But settling down like his teammate Nino had done was not on Éric's mind just yet, despite the passionate nature of his first real relationship. A footballer's summer lasts but a few weeks: Éric had to go back to the training ground, Isabelle to her books, hundreds of miles away. Already disoriented by the violence of his feelings, and by the frustration of being so far from the one human being he wanted to be with, he also saw the beginning of his 1985–86 season ruined by a viral infection that kept him out of the first team from mid-August to early October – precisely at the time when Andrzej Szarmach's departure meant that he could claim a place in the Auxerre forward line. Roux had promised to give him a string of games to establish himself, and was true to his word, but Éric, his mind elsewhere – in Provence – failed to capitalize on the chance he had been given. He didn't score a single goal in the six games (one victory, two draws, three defeats) he could take part in before the virus struck him down; and when he had recovered his fitness, it was to find that another striker had claimed his spot in Roux's first eleven: Roger Boli, brother of man-mountain Basile, a quick, clever centre-forward, whose goals had kick-started Auxerre's stuttering season.

AJA won at Nice thanks to him, then recorded the most brilliant victory in their history by beating mighty AC Milan 3–1 in the first leg of the UEFA Cup's first round. Boli had scored again, and Cantona found it hard to share fully in the joy of his teammates. What's more, when he rejoined the team, on the occasion of the second leg, it was to be on the receiving end of a 3–0 drubbing. Any player would have suffered a blow to his pride in such circumstances; and Cantona's pride was as strong a current in his character as insecurity, strong enough to flood him when so much in his life was already in a state of flux. Roux, who loved him and understood him better than any manager other than Alex Ferguson (some of Éric's teammates openly teased him about his relationship with 'Papa Roux'), was at pains to comprehend why the player who had lit up the end of the previous campaign had retreated into his shell. That is, until he was told by one of his many spies that Éric's Renault 5 had been spotted on the motorway, heading towards Aix-en-Provence. 'All my guys were stationed at toll-gates between Auxerre and Paris,' he explained to me. 'But it so happened that one of them had taken the place of someone who worked between Auxerre and Lyon, on one of these nights when Éric was driving south! I'd never have known about it otherwise.' Roux asked for an explanation; Éric gave it to him. 'I want to see her,' he said. 'It's her I love.'

What to do? According to Roux, he picked up his phone and called the coach of FC Martigues, Yves Herbet, whose club had sunk into the relegation zone – and that was relegation to the third division. Herbet remembers things differently: he desperately needed a quality striker, and it was he who called the Auxerre manager. In any case, both men clearly saw a splendid opportunity to address their own ongoing problem, and seized it. But if Éric was easily sold to Martigues, who could do with all the help they were given, how could Martigues be sold to Éric? The 'Venice of Provence' – it is criss-crossed by canals and waterways – was the same size as Auxerre; its club was not. But the sun shone on its picturesque city centre. More importantly, Éric and Isabelle could live together, as Aix was less than an hour's drive away, and Auxerre's canny manager had made sure to talk to the young woman first, before informing her lover of his suggestion. Martigues would provide the young couple with a small flat, from which Isabelle could commute to work every day. Her response had been enthusiastic, and so was Éric's. Roux's plan, cleverly designed, subtly executed, must rank among the most inspired decisions he ever took in over forty years of management. He had judged Cantona perfectly, as a man, and as a player of immense promise. To make sure of the man's gratitude and of the fulfilment of his promise, he was willing to deprive his team of one of its greatest talents. Let him live on love and play in front of crowds of a few hundred people, if that's what it takes to calm him down; if that's what it takes to save Éric Cantona.

Another thought had crossed Roux's mind: 'Éric's going to kill himself on the road.' It's only as Jean-Marie Lanoé and myself were on our way back to Paris that I remembered a slip of the manager's tongue which I would have thought nothing of, had my friend not reminded me of Michel N'Gom's tragic story. You'll remember that Roux had mentioned Cantona's battered Renault 5. But Cantona, who had passed his driving test in August, drove a (battered) Peugeot 104. He'd have loved to own one, preferably an 'apple-green 5TS, with black spoilers', the car he much later said he dreamt about when he was a child. It was *N'Gom* who owned a Renault 5. He was a brilliant young player of Senegalese origin who, like Cantona, had been educated at La Mazargue, before joining Marseille, Toulon, Marseille again, and PSG, with whom he won two French Cups. Roux had recruited him for the 1984–85 season. He played ten games for Auxerre, all of them pre-season friendlies, before he was killed in a car crash on 12 August 1984, aged twenty-six. N'Gom was a bon vivant who, during his three seasons in Paris, had spent a great deal of his spare time in the nightclubs of the capital. Once at Auxerre, he travelled incessantly in his car to catch up with the friends he had left behind in Paris. It was on his way back from one of these escapades that, surprised by the presence of a tractor in the middle of the road, he crashed a few hundred yards from his home, where his parents were expecting him for Sunday lunch.

And this is why Éric Cantona, French under-19 international, was loaned out for seven months to a club that had won nothing in sixty seasons, bar a brace of Coupes de Provence.

Two weeks after Auxerre had been knocked out by Milan, Éric packed all his belongings in his 104, including a large black-and-white television set which he strapped in the front passenger seat, and made his way down the *autoroute du soleil*. His move to Martigues attracted very little attention in the media, though his six months there didn't entirely pass without incident. Éric did his job, and did it rather better than is suggested in his autobiography, where this half-year-long episode is only alluded to. A return of four goals in fifteen appearances might seem modest at such a level, until you know that this made him Martigues' leading goalscorer for that period. 'He was a pivotal player for us,' Herbet told me. 'He was the main reason we stayed up.' His new coach had been a fine footballer himself, a member of the French team that hadn't disgraced itself when losing 2–0 to England in the 1966 World Cup. Built like a flyweight, he had relied on skill, speed of thought and imagination to build a professional career, and was naturally receptive to Éric's artistry.

'This boy could do everything in front of goal,' he recalls. 'Left foot, right foot, first touch, headers, volleys – he had it all.' Cantona being Cantona, Herbet needed to show patience and understanding too. 'Yes, he had a real temper on him. He lacked maturity. But I quickly saw that you needed to build him up to get the best out of him. When you brutalize Cantona, he hits the wall. So I trusted him. We spoke about painting – not something I've got much knowledge of, but he enjoyed talking about it. And, in the end, it all went well. I'd been told that he'd had problems relating to some of his Auxerre teammates; but with us? No. Deep down, he is a good man.' A good man who could, of course, 'blow a gasket' on occasion, especially if, as he said later, with some exaggeration, that he had 'almost forgotten football' at the time, being too busy building a life with Isabelle.

The young couple – he was still nineteen, she twenty-two – spent their evenings poring over maps of Provence, choosing destinations for their Sunday escapades in the countryside. The holy site of Saintes-Maries-de-la-Mer, sacred to Gipsy pilgrims, the wilderness of the Camargue, where white horses roam the marshes and flamingos dot the lagoons, the pink, ochre and purple rocky desolation of Les Baux. This was a time for romance, not football. Back at home, Albert wondered why his son barely sent him news. Éric himself had all but forgotten about Guy Roux. His on-field discipline suffered. He had never been sent off in a competitive game when at Auxerre, but at Martigues was shown the red card on two occasions. The first incident occurred, quite perversely, in the easiest game of the *Martégaux*'s campaign, a 5–0 slaughter of Grasse in the French Cup, on 15 December

1985. This fracas was eerily similar to what happened at Selhurst Park in January 1995. As Herbet recalls it, a spectator seated near the touchline had showered abuse on Éric, who reacted, ran to the perimeter fence and gave as good as he had got, far too much for the referee's taste, who sent him off there and then. That was quite a day for the Cantonas: Éric's normally reserved elder brother Jean-Marie apparently injured his hand jumping over the fence, trying to put right the same spectator. But unlike the hurricane that blew up in the media when Éric flew, feet first, into the crowd at Crystal Palace, Éric's temporary loss of self-control only warranted a couple of lines in the local press match reports, as did his second sending-off – for reasons no one I've spoken to can remember – against Cannes, in the penultimate game of the season.

Encouraged by the reports on Éric's progress at Martigues, Roux decided the time had come to tie him to Auxerre on a long-term contract, which *L'Équipe* reported to be for eight seasons. On 1 February 1986, the AJA manager travelled to the Stade Gerland, where Lyon were hosting the *Martégaux*. The Lyonnais, who had promotion in their sights, could not break down Herbet's defence, and had to satisfy themselves with a 0–0 draw. Shortly after the final whistle, somewhere in the cavernous underbelly of the stadium, Roux came across Éric's father, and told him all his son had to do to fulfil his ambition of becoming a professional footballer was to sign the papers he had brought with him. Auxerre being Auxerre (and Guy Roux being Guy Roux), Cantona wouldn't earn a great deal of money, not much more than a mid-ranking executive of a mid-ranking company would expect to find on the bottom line of his wage slip. To Éric and Isabelle, who had survived on a pittance in Aix-en-Provence, this was a fortune. What's more, back in Burgundy, Cantona would be 'free', by which he meant 'free to put cartridges in my shotgun, and go and shoot thrushes or pigeons as soon as training was over', as he had been doing in the hills of the Garlaban. 'Free to undergo psychoanalysis without people saying I was mad', as he did 'out of curiosity', because it was 'enjoyable to make visible things which are invisible', in order 'to better understand others by better understanding myself' – quite a remarkable statement in the mouth of a twenty-year-old, especially when this twenty-year-old kicked a football for a living. 'Free, yes, to paint and to live 20 kilometres away from Auxerre, with my girlfriend and my [two] dogs,' Brenda and Balrine. And as ever, Roux would be there to watch over the young man he would come to care about as if he were a son.

'Isabelle and Éric were the first people to live in a house I'd built in Poilly,' he told me. 'They didn't have a home. My village had put aside a whole plot of land for development; but bang in the middle of it was a stretch of acacia woodland, which belonged to my grandfather, who refused to sell it, because it came from his own grandfather. I told him: I'll buy the land from you, and I'll build a house on it. It won't leave the family. He agreed. And when the house was built, Cantona was the first person to live there. They were just by the trees . . . He was a perfect lodger. Then they bought a house in Poilly-sur-Tholon, a village with a beautiful church, where they got married.'

The wedding took place in February 1987, a ceremony that the manager – father figure and now landlord – did not attend, as he had to supervise a youth team game that afternoon. Indeed, according to legend, Éric and Isabelle nearly missed the ceremony themselves. I cannot resist retelling this legend myself: somehow, in the middle of winter, they came across a basket of cherries, and gathered handfuls of *bigarreaux* to festoon their nuptial clothes; time flew by; as they were still dressing each other with fruit, the guests looked at their watches, as did the mayor – another few minutes, and the next couple would be ushered in. Happily, just in time, the couple walked in, looking like an Arcimboldo fantasy, and exchanged their vows in front of a nonplussed but relieved congregation. It is pure invention, of course, but somehow fitting of a most unlikely couple: the footballer and the graduate. What is true is that no invitations had been sent in the post, as Bernard Ferrer remembered twenty years later: 'In our country, you normally send out notices when you get married, but Éric did it the other way round. He sent out the wedding announcements afterwards. This is typical of him.'

It is tempting to view Éric's footballing life as a non-stop rush towards fame, success and self-destruction in almost equal measures; and over the three years this book took to research and to write, I became more convinced by the day that, all along, there had been a quasi-suicidal streak in the would-be footballing artist, a temptation to equate triumph with death, be it real – Jim Morrison overdosing in Paris – or symbolical – Arthur Rimbaud cutting short his life as a poet to become a slave merchant in Abyssinia. For every trophy won, there appears to have been an outburst of violence, an outrageous public statement, or yet another controversy to fill the back pages (and in his case, the front pages too) of newspapers. He revelled in thinking of himself as a victim, as it brought him proof that he too, like the 'geniuses' he admired, was doomed to be misunderstood and vilified. But there have also been moments in his career when, helped by Isabelle's presence, and guided by an understanding manager, he was able to appease his feverish impulses, and almost forgot to behave the way he believed or felt Canto should. The 1986–87 season was one of these plateaux of – relative – serenity, as the campaigns of 1993–94 and 1995–96 would be at Manchester United.

Back in Auxerre, with Szarmach retired, the newlywed was given the keys to Auxerre's attack by Guy Roux, and repaid his manager's skilful handling by stringing together magnificent performances for the club. It took him a while to find the target, finally scoring in his ninth game of the campaign, a 3–0 victory over St Étienne on 13 September; but as soon as he did, AJA, who had endured another pitiful start to to the campaign (not a single victory until Éric broke his duck), took off quite spectacularly, and steadily climbed up the league table to finish in fourth spot. Éric's superb vision and assurance in front of goal (seventeen successful strikes in all competitions that season, six of which transformed draws into victories, plus four with the French under-21s) were the difference between uneasy survival in the soft belly of the *Première Division* and qualification for Europe. Even a two-month lay-off due to injury, the longest he had had to suffer in his career so far – from the 20 December to the end of February – failed to hold him back; and when he returned to the first team, he was the catalyst for a superb series of results: Auxerre would remain undefeated in the league until mid-May.

As French journalists are prone to say, Cantona 'exploded' that year – on the field, in the best possible way, and in his countrymen's consciousness, not just because of his prowess with a ball at his feet, but also because, one evening in early September 1986, he paid a visit to a hairdresser in Brittany and came out of the salon looking like a convict, his head as smooth as a snooker ball. Remember: there was a lot of hair on show when teams assembled for their annual official photograph in those days. Éric's whim might have been not much more than a schoolboyish prank, but it certainly made him cut him a bizarre figure in the ultra-conservative village of eighties football.

Guy Roux's amusement is not feigned when he tells the story: 'We went to Roscoff three or four days before facing Brest, a strong team at the time, with players like Bernard Lama, Julio Cesar, Paul Le Guen, Martins, and quite a few others. As Roscoff is twinned with Auxerre, we were treated to a civic reception at the town hall. Speeches, canapés, nothing was missing . . . except my youngsters, all of them. No one knew where they'd gone. Dinner was served at seven. No sign of Canto and his band of merry men . . . Dutuel, Prunier, Mazzolini, Tarras . . . I could see the street outside from my seat. Fifteen, twenty minutes later, I catch a glimpse of him, straight-backed as usual. He walks in, sits down without a word. He's waiting for me to scream at him. But I don't. Nobody dares say anything. You'd have thought they were serving supper in a Trappist monastery. Finally, when dessert is brought in, I make an announcement: "I'll give my verdict tomorrow at 22:00."' After the final whistle, of course.

Roux beams. 'We were 3–0 after 15 minutes' play.' (*Which, by the way, is not true. Auxerre drew 0–0 that day, 3 September 1986; but Guy Roux is not the kind of raconteur to spoil a good story by something as trivial as a scoreless draw.*)

He went on: 'Cantona had had his head shaved! And all his friends had gone to the barber's with him! That evening – what fun! – I had the room opposite his. I go out of my bedroom, and here he was, talking to Isabelle on the phone: "Yes, Isa! I am completely bald . . . no, not a hair left . . . and I'm so cold!"'

Cantona had acted on impulse, as usual, to fulfil a sudden desire to 'feel the freshness of water, the power of the wind' on his bare skull; maybe. But there must also have been the mischievous itch to test his boss's patience, to find out how far the staunch traditionalist would allow his twenty-year-old striker to bend the rules his rebellious way.

Roux himself didn't take the bait. But the sight of a bald teenager on the pitches of the *championnat* was unusual enough to catch the attention of a number of French publications. It hardly mattered that Cantona had scored the grand total of six goals in thirty-nine games for Auxerre so far – and would have to wait until 13 September to open his account for the 1986–87 season.

Interviewers made a beeline for the Stade de l'Abbé-Deschamps and Éric's home in the forest, where he supplied them with enough quirky quotes and references to poets, painters, philosophers and the like to try and convince their readers that a rather different, previously unsuspected species of footballer had been discovered in northern Burgundy. *Paris-Match*, the magazine one could find in every French dentist's waiting-room at the time, allowed space for Éric's stream-of-consciousness effusions beside its regular instalments of comings and goings at the princely court of Monaco, marriages of uncrowned Ruritanian royals and the odd half-serious report about some war taking place somewhere else. Over the next nine months, Cantona became the first *celebrity* footballer in his country's history, when others – Platini, Kopa – had merely gained fame for their on-field achievements. Éric would later revile the 'media circus' that would follow his every move and misdemeanour, perhaps forgetting how willing a subject he had been at the time, and how much it would help him to appear – at least for a couple of seasons – to be the answer to the question 'What now?', which followed France's defeat by Germany in the semi-finals of the 1986 World Cup.

That summer, the 'golden generation' led by Michel Platini had fired its last bullets in Mexico, winning an unforgettable game against Brazil before surrendering to the Germans. Their tournament, which also included a 2–0 victory over world champions Italy, ended with a sadly predictable whimper, predictable inasmuch as the team which had emerged eight years before in Argentina had reached the end of its life cycle. One by one, the heroes of Seville 1982, *Les Bleus*' most mythical game (they were denied a place in the World Cup final by the Germans on penalties, having led 3–1 in the first period of extra time), announced their retirement from the international game, within weeks of an epoch-closing defeat. Some were too old. Others were spending more time in the physiotherapist's treatment room than on the training ground. The rest suffered from burn-out. Of the superb squad gathered by national coach Michel Hidalgo, who also took his bow and passed on the baton to the former Nantes midfielder Henri Michel, only a couple survived: left-back Manuel Amoros and defensive midfielder Luis Fernandez. France was in mourning. The search was on for a new Giresse, a new Trésor – one dared not say a new Platini.

Éric's timing was as crisp as a Brian Lara on-drive. Out of nowhere, it seemed, had appeared – Kojak-headed, his chest puffed out like one of Napoleon's field marshals – a pro who talked like no other pro dared to talk, and could play a bit too, as he proved by scoring on his debut for France's under-21s, a 4–1 'friendly' thrashing of Hungary, which took place nine days after he had startled the great and good of Roscoff. On 10 October his two goals gave a far more significant 2–1 victory over USSR in Le Havre – the game that sparked a magnificent adventure for *Les Bleuets* of Marc Bourrier, another of these southern managers who had an instinctive appreciation of and affection for the maverick of Marseilles. His team would be crowned European champions in June 1988, with Cantona suspended, as we'll see. And the closer one looks at the legendary misfit, the more one is struck by how snugly he fitted in the tangle of aspirations, doubts and fantasies of French football as it saw its most successful troopers and generals head for *Les Invalides*.

Cantona's star wouldn't have risen as spectacularly, and rapidly, if these fantasies hadn't had a new medium to feed on: subscription TV channel Canal+, then a byword for modernity and trendiness. Just as Sky television would use coverage of football in all its guises as a battering ram into British homes, Canal+ exploited the epic progress of France's best young footballers in Europe for something more than what it was worth. Until then, this competition – of which France had never even reached the final – had been pretty much ignored by media and public alike. But the up-and-coming TV channel needed to differentiate itself from and compete with the established, government-controlled terrestrial networks, which held exclusive rights over the senior team's games. Canal+ was about the new, the untried, and sold itself as an outsider, a trend-bucker on its way to becoming a trend-setter. X-rated films on Saturday nights. Marc Bourrier's *Espoirs* (literally, 'The Hopes') on match days. What Canal+ heralded, of course, was not an age of quasi-anarchistic freedom and hedonism, but of consumerism and instant gratification, in which it would come to represent a different kind of Establishment. Few saw it that way at the time.

The contrast between the exuberance of Marc Bourrier's hopefuls and the drabness of a declining national team couldn't have been starker. Cantona and Co. took risks, scored outrageous goals – and won. Henri Michel's eleven stuttered, looked for and couldn't find an identity – and would miss out on the European Championships and World Cup qualification. The horse that Canal+ had picked was rushing home, when it could have cantered to the line. The next year-and-a-half was the making of Cantona as a footballing icon in France.

If everyone soon knew how different Éric was, very little had filtered through of his more erratic behaviour at Auxerre. Roux, who employed spies not just on motorways, but also in every nightclub in Burgundy, was known to hop on his moped in the small hours of the morning to drag home a player who had been spotted on the dance floor of some rural disco. He was equally good at keeping his extended family's linen washed in-house. No one was aware then of one particular hair-raising incident which had taken place a few months previously, during a pre-season visit to Poland. According to Roux, it could have led to a diplomatic incident. 'Auxerre took part in a tournament in Mielec, in the south-east of Poland. Cantona treats the public to a scissor-kick, then to a magnificent goal . . . but they don't like it, oh no. As we're walking off, a guy throws an egg, which explodes on his thigh. He loses it completely, I try and hold him by his coat-tails, but no way, it was as if I were water-skiing behind a speed-boat!' One is rarely bored in Guy Roux's company. One sip of Irancy, then: 'Éric climbs in the stand – looks for the guy – and I'm thinking: "Let's hope that guy is hiding somewhere," and I'm saying, "Éric, if you hit him, we're in communist Poland, you'll get ten years, and we won't be able to get you out!" Bernard Ferrer was yelling, "Think of Isabelle!" But here we are amongst these Polish miners, those guys who go down 2,000 metres every day – but he couldn't find the egg-thrower, and we were saved.'

Roux, however, loved Éric more than he had ever loved any other of his young players, and, more often than not, reached for the carrot, not the stick. He took no action when, on 21 February 1987, word got out that Auxerre's goalkeeper Bruno Martini had been on the receiving end of Cantona's anger; word – and pictures. Martini sported a magnificent shiner. The door he had walked into was Éric's head. ('Make sure people know Éric didn't throw a punch!' Roux exhorted me, 'and tell them it was all Daniel Rolland's fault!') It's fair to say that Martini, a superb 'keeper who had already been selected by France, and would become a long-term member of *Les Bleus*' technical staff, did not court popularity with his teammates, and that the rough justice meted out by Éric would have found an acquiescent jury in the Auxerre dressing-room. Like Cantona, Martini affected to find the life of a footballer tedious in the extreme, but unlike Éric, he made no efforts to balance his world-weariness with the kind of horseplay familiar to young footballers the world over. Martini preferred the company of authors like Goethe, Montherlant and Céline to that of fellow players, and listened to Handel oratorios at home. That morning, he made the mistake of demonstrating his contempt by refusing to help the first-teamers and the academy players who were trying to clear the pitch for the final of the Coupe des Alpes, which would pit Auxerre against the Swiss champions Neuchâtel-Xamax. The broadcasting rights of that half-serious, half-friendly encounter had been acquired by Canal+ for half-a-million francs – manna from heaven for a small club like AJA.

Unfortunately, heaven had also sent down a copious amount of snow – three inches of it – during the night, and the surface of l'Abbé-Deschamps was unplayable. Armed with advertising boards, the whole squad helped to push the slush over the touchline; all the squad – bar Martini. Roux picks up the story: 'Rolland, who'd been there since the break of dawn, noticed it and told the 'keeper: "Hey, Bruno, maybe you could . . .", and Canto said, "Absolutely!" Martini made a dismissive gesture with his hand. He shouldn't have. Canto went up to him, and bang! That evening, I had to explain to the Canal+ presenter that we'd been practising headers, and that Martini had taken a knock . . .' Amusingly, Éric, who was still recovering from the injury he had sustained in December, took no part in Auxerre's 3–1 victory in that game. But Martini did.

I should add that the veracity of Roux's account was vouched for by several witnesses of the incident, who accompanied their assent by a knowing smile. Later, when it became a national English pastime to demonize Éric, the Martini 'punch' always featured high in the list of his greatest hits. Hardly anyone – no one, in fact – bothered to check what had really happened. The British public was told that 'Auxerre had punished Cantona with a suspension' for his assault on Martini. False. He played in the very next game, a 2–0 win at Laval. But who cared about the truth by then? It was enough that another dark spot could be found in his character, and there were so many of those that the picture emerging was black, black, black. The man was a maniac. He had knocked a teammate out cold on the training pitch. Roux knew otherwise. Éric repaid his manager's clemency by giving his all when it mattered; and all through this magnificent season, it seemed to matter each and every weekend. It was no longer a question of if, but when Éric would make the transition from the under-21s to the national team, and Roux's prediction to Cantona's mother and grandmother would be fulfilled.

That season came to a close very late for Éric, as late as 16 June, when the *Bleuets* fought out a 2–1 victory in Norway in which he had, again, been decisive, and which gave Bourrier's players a place in the quarter-finals of the European Championships. Two weeks later, after the briefest of holidays, he was back in training with his club, and taking part in another staging of the Coupe des Alpes, won 3–1 by Auxerre over Grasshoppers Zurich, Éric adding another goal to his collection. Then the *championnat* took over, the footballer's bread and butter, in which AJA dipped a tentative toe, as usual, with a solitary success in their first four games. But Éric's form remained stupendous throughout, and nobody was surprised to find his name in the squad that Henri Michel announced on 4 August, eight days before France was to play West Germany in Berlin.

It is customary for players who celebrate their first cap to serve up heartfelt platitudes such as 'a dream come true', or 'the proudest day in my life' to journalists who're not too demanding about what ends up on their plates. Not unexpectedly, Éric switched off the autopilot, and the comments he came up with after he had walked off the pitch, having scored the goal that brought the home team back to 1–2, left quite a few taken aback.

'I didn't feel any pressure on me,' he said with the straightest face he could conjure up for disbelieving hacks. 'I am not an emotional person,' (*Really?*) 'and I took this game as if it were a banal league game.' (*Excuse me?*) 'Why should I have made a huge thing of playing against West Germany? The questions I asked myself were purely tactical. I thought about my game. I concentrated. That's all.' (*But you scored – a clinical finish from ten yards – surely this means something special to you?*) 'It meant nothing to me. Maybe if it had been the equalizer. But then, nothing. I told myself we had fifty minutes or so to re-establish parity.' (*But . . .*) 'Giving up is not a habit of mine. I've got my own mental attitude; every one's got his. But mine suits me perfectly. If I were a coach, I'd transmit it to my players. Because I think I am in the right. In France, we have a tendency to tell a player he's the most beautiful, the strongest. That's awful. Nobody will manage to destabilize me or to make me lose my head. I'm quite happy for people to compliment me, but I take it with enough detachment to take it or leave it. In fact, I prefer criticism. My wife told me I hadn't been good. She knows nothing about football. But I'll try to please her next time round.' (*Thank you.*)

Was this arrogance, stupidity, or playfulness? Or simply the urge to provide the press with the kind of copy they had been expecting from him for the last nine months, and which flattered him far more deeply than he cared to show? Cantona kept a close eye on what was said and written about him. So did the clan, back in Marseilles. As Gérard Houllier told me forcefully on several occasions, the more talented a footballer is, the more insecure he feels about his ability – and Éric didn't lack in talent. To illustrate his point, Houllier told me of Juninho Pernambucano, Lyon's superb midfielder, being physically sick before a number of 'crunch' games – in which he almost always performed superbly. Éric might have been his own man, but in this he was no different from most of the players he conversed with on the pitch. What set him apart was his strategy, how he coped with the demands he and others put on himself. He managed his own persona as it pleased him, and with such efficiency that even genuine slips into automatic, quasi-primal speech became indiscernible from calculated statements. He would provoke, attempt to wrong-foot his questioners, with an audacity that verged on the suicidal (that word, again). British reporters seldom came across this side of his character later on. The linguistic barrier might have contributed to this – but only in part, as it became another weapon in Éric's armoury; his English was good enough, as we'll see, despite the enduring legend of a sombre, lapidary and barely comprehensible Frenchman at odds with his adopted country's language.

Late in September of that year, 1987, a *France Football* reporter paid a visit to Cantona at the Stade de l'Abbé-Deschamps and came back with an astonishing interview which was published on the 29th of that month. This was twelve days after Éric had missed a number of chances in Auxerre's 2–0 defeat at Panathinaikos, which seemed to condemn Guy Roux's team to a first-round exit from the UEFA Cup. As Éric made himself increasingly scarce with the media over the years, papers desperate for Cantona-isms cannibalized this remarkable outpouring of juvenile angst and anger as if it provided the alpha and omega of his personality. Despite Éric's ingenuous admission that he 'talked a lot of bullshit', it became an unreferenced and frequently butchered *Urtext* in the Cantona canon, which is why I have added it as a postscript to this account of Cantona's Auxerre years, exactly as *France Football* readers discovered it in the autumn of 1987. It has never been reprinted since, and I have only excised those parts which dealt with circumstances which would lose all relevance as soon as Panathinaikos did, indeed, usher Auxerre out of the UEFA Cup. (Cantona, who had promised he would win the return leg 'on his own' after his poor display in the first match, was almost as good as his word: on 30 September he scored one of Auxerre's three goals. But the Greek side hit back with two of their own, and that was that.)

This extended question-and-answer session gave a fascinating glimpse into the naïve, contradictory, but also profoundly sincere and sometimes strikingly expressed convictions of a very young man. It also shocked and divided that part of public opinion which paid attention to football enough to cut the country into two camps, whose garrisons would entrench themselves deeper and deeper as years went by. To some, he was not so much a breath of fresh air as a tornado that swept away the hypocrisy of the *bien-pensants,* a non-conformist who could literally do no wrong, victimized by cowards and careerists. To others (the majority, to begin with), a mildly deranged, self-justifying, self-aggrandizing *voyou* who talked nonsense and could get away with it as long as he put footballs into a net. At the first sign of weakness, Cantona would be shot down by his critics. Tellingly, it was his own actions that provided them with the ammunition.

'If I have a piece of advice to give to the young, it is to count on nobody but themselves to succeed. It gives me pleasure that ten-year-olds have my poster on their bedroom wall. But I ask those who, one day, will be contacted by professional clubs, to tear that poster up'.

'That poster' could have been a blown-up photograph taken by a man who met Éric on the very day he gave that infamous interview. Didier Fèvre – who snapped *France Football*'s cover shot – had started pointing his camera at sportspeople only six months previously. His pedigree was unusual in many respects – his father had been the favourite printer of Robert Doisneau and Henri Cartier-Bresson – and Didier himself was accustomed to rubbing shoulders with film actors and directors rather than footballers. Despite, or because of this background, he became close to a number of players whose interests extended beyond the playing field or the after-match visit to a nightclub – Dominique Rocheteau, Gerald Passi, Éric's great friend Stéphane Paille, to name a few. But it is with Cantona that he established the most passionate of these friendships – almost a love affair in its intensity, whose sudden and unpredictable breakdown Didier has not quite got over, seventeen years later.

'Our relationship was one of exchange, an enrichment for the both of us,' he told me. 'Éric was so keen to discover new things, to open himself to new experiences,' like sitting down in Fèvre's Parisian sitting room to watch Max Ophüls's films – *Le Plaisir* was a favourite – and talk for hours about the great creators the photographer had met in his youth. Didier saw a side of Éric's character that was off limits to his football acquaintances: a shy aspiring artist experimenting with mixed media, applying layers of colour to cut-outs of photographs, modest about his own talent, eager to discuss his work, and genuinely open to criticism and suggestions. The pair would spend their family holidays together, often joined by Paille and his wife. As he was drawn ever closer to the epicentre of the Cantona circle, Fèvre became party to information his workmates at *L'Équipe* would have killed for, and which he had to keep secret, putting himself in ever more delicate situations. But Éric had put his trust in him, fully, without afterthought or calculation. He valued loyalty above all other virtues, and, demanding as he was, also showed himself to be the most generous of friends – that is, until he felt, often without justification, or for reasons only he could fathom, that this trust had been abused or betrayed, two words which could pass for synonyms in his vocabulary.

As often with Cantona, a friendship would be born when he found himself confronted by someone who had the courage to question him, or willing to stand his ground when challenged by authority. That afternoon in Auxerre, in Fèvre's case, authority took the shape of Guy Roux. 'I didn't know much about Cantona,' Fèvre recalls, 'but I'd been struck by the way he celebrated his goals, with a movement of his arm, his fist clenched, very imperious, chest upright, like a Roman Caesar. I was quite shy – I wasn't really part of the world of football yet. Roux agreed to give me fifteen minutes with his player. I asked Canto if he wouldn't mind doing this gesture for me. He – an actor to the core – complied and started gesticulating on his own. Guy Roux noticed it, and told me: "You're not here to make my kids behave like clowns." I heard myself replying: "Mr Roux, when it comes to football, I am in no position to give you any advice; but leave the photography to me." Canto was astonished! Guy Roux too, I suppose. He wasn't used to people talking to him like this, and he just said: "All right, all right, do your thing." And I guess this is how Éric first noticed me, the first step he took in building up our friendship.'

A few of Didier's pictures appear in this book, which show a man very different from the 'Roman Caesar' who was, again, the fulcrum of Auxerre's side in the 1987–88 season, a year of consolidation, confirmation and eventually turmoil for the newly capped international.

*

Éric needed to be at his best for the *Icaunais*, who had lost a key player – his brother-in-law Bernard Ferrer – as early as 19 August. Ferrer had suffered a fractured thighbone in a home game against Laval, in which Cantona took part. Such injuries are extremely rare in football, and no one could be sure that Ferrer would ever play again. Éric and Isabelle spent half the night by Nino's bedside. 'Bernard brought me great confidence,' Cantona explained to journalists who wondered why Roux's team was making such a hash of things when it had been expected to challenge for a European place again. 'Whether we dominated play or not, I knew that, at some stage, I'd receive a pass I could score from.' Not any longer. With Nino out for a year, Éric had to shoulder yet more responsibility. He did so with a huge heart, played some magnificent football, showing that for all his flicks and tricks, he was no Flash Harry, but an extravagantly gifted footballer who was born with a rare sense of the collective nature of the game. Roux is still visibly moved by the memory of one of these games when the supposed egotist sacrificed himself to the team cause – a desperately needed 2–1 victory at Le Havre, on 6 October 1987.

'What an awful day it was,' he told me. 'A hurricane was blowing from the sea, the rain was lashing down. In the first half, we are playing with the help of the wind, and we score [*through Éric, as it happened*]. In the second half, Cantona positions himself on the penalty spot – our penalty spot! He clears every corner kick. Each ball he gets, he gets past five players, he manages to bring us 50 metres further upfield, he gives us time to breathe . . . He did that for the whole game. I can still see him. He was so proud of himself! This game was a present from him to us.' There was steel in the twenty-one-year-old. At a time when Auxerre, short of players and short on form, needed fighters on the pitch – five 0–0 draws in six league games from 24 October to 27 November – he was the most committed of them all. From mid-October to the New Year, every time he scored – three times – Auxerre won, and on no other occasion.

France too had its problems, and these Éric couldn't solve on his own: the France of Henri Michel, that is, not the France of Marc Bourrier. Cantona found himself in a unique position. Still young enough to play for the *Espoirs* until the end of their two-year European campaign – should it take them to the final – he had also gained by right a place in the starting eleven of the senior squad, and featured in four of the five matches it played until February 1988 (he only missed a 1–1 draw in the Soviet Union because of a slight injury). The contrast between the elation he felt when joining the under-21s and the soul-searching that accompanied every outing of the full international side couldn't have been starker. Michel's players huffed and puffed from one depressing draw to another, also conceding a pitiful 0–1 home defeat to the German Democratic Republic in November, which, coming on the heels of an equally pitiful 1–1 stalemate against Norway, confirmed that the European title France had won in such exhilarating fashion in 1984 would not be defended in the final phase of the next tournament. Meanwhile Bourrier's *Bleuets*, who dispatched Italy 2–1 in mid-March in the home leg of their European quarter-final, were a joy to watch, and a joy to be part of.

Two years later, in Montpellier, where Stéphane Paille and Cantona thought they could recapture the magic of those days, Éric would say: 'We had a good atmosphere to start with, which became a fabulous attitude, which enabled us to overcome unbelievable situations, because we went through great moments, important successes. When you live these emotions, you give everything again the next time, so you can live them again.' Paille felt just as strongly, and there was a great deal of emotion in his voice when we reminisced about these golden days, twenty years after the two friends had worn the blue jersey for the last time together. 'Our friendship was born on the pitch,' he told me, 'when we both joined the under-21s in 1986; and we took it from there. We got on well together when we were playing, we got on well when we were not. We both came from similar clubs, smaller clubs which had a tremendous reputation in terms of producing young players . . . I wouldn't say these academies were regimented, but it's true that being with the *Espoirs* gave us extra freedom. We were professionals, and we didn't abuse it.' Here, I could feel a smile creep into Stéphane's voice – it was obvious that many anecdotes could follow, but not at that time. We had touched on something very private, which I'm convinced was tinged with regret, pain even. He checked himself, and carried on. 'Marc Bourrier let us get on with it. From the beginning, it was all about the joy of being together and playing together, and Bourrier did nothing to take that joy away from us.' Could he tell me more about the nature of that joy? 'Éric and I shared a passion for *le beau jeu, le geste* [the beautiful game, the elegant piece of skill]. We just clicked. He missed the final because of a spat with Henri Michel, but he was still one of us; his contribution had been immense.'

When Bourrier, a lovely man, had to deal with the odd act of indiscipline, he sought an explanation, not an opportunity to administer punishment; he found his exuberant, generous, hard-working boys a dream to deal with. 'Cantona? He never gave me a problem,' he told me from his house in the south-west of France. 'He gave me pleasure. We trusted each other, and he didn't disappoint me. I don't know anything about the "difficult" side of Éric's character.'

So, by the spring of 1988, almost everything Éric had hoped for when he was smashing cans against the walls in Les Caillols had come to pass. He had become a professional footballer. He had scored for the national team. Under the guidance of two men who appreciated him for whom and what he was, Guy Roux and Marc Bourrier, he had become the leader of a new generation at club and *Espoirs* level. All that was left for him to do was to make the step up to a bigger club, to challenge for the trophies that were out of Auxerre's reach. Moreover, he could achieve this by coming home, to Marseilles. He eventually succeeded in doing just that, but the road that took him there proved far more tortuous than anyone could have expected.

4

FAREWELL TO AUXERRE

There wasn't a single club in the country that didn't dream of adding Cantona to their squad, but only a handful – four or five, as we'll see – could afford him now. The whole of the 1987–88 season had been a long, sustained crescendo for Éric, and his value on the transfer market had soared accordingly. He would cost in excess of FF20m, roughly twice as much as Manchester United paid Leeds for their outcast in November 1992. That he was not quite as prolific then as he had been the year before was an irrelevance. A return of 14 goals in all competitions for club and country (compared with 21 in the previous campaign) might suggest that he had withdrawn into his shell somewhat. This was emphatically not the case. Bernard Ferrer's injury had deprived Éric of his main provider at Auxerre, who were still in the process of finding a new balance after losing a number of key figures in the past couple of seasons: Andzrej Szarmach had retired, the sparkling Jean-Marc Ferreri had been sold to Bordeaux, and Patrice Garande to FC Nantes. Cantona was often switched from his natural position as a centre-forward to that of a playmaker, a role in which he excelled, but which was bound to affect his strike ratio. Moreover, Éric had a knack of shining on the big occasions.

He hit a magnificent streak of form in the spring, when such games came in quick succession. There was the Spanish side's visit for a friendly played in Bordeaux (whose Girondins were keen to secure his services), which France won 2–1 in convincing fashion. Three days later, on 26 March, the ambitious Paris club Matra Racing (another potential buyer) were dismantled 3–0 at the l'Abbé-Deschamps, with Éric orchestrating the slaughter, just as he had done five months previously when the other

Parisian team, PSG (who were also interested in him), had visited Burgundy. Nantes fell 1–0 in the French Cup. Then, on 2 April, it was Marseille's turn to come across a fired-up Cantona, who scored one of his team's two goals, to which OM could find no reply. At one stage or the other of the season, and especially towards its end, every one of Éric's suitors had been reminded of his capacity to raise his game further when the quality of the opposition warranted it.

Éric was now vital to his country's chances as well as to his club's. How much so was made plain by the comical manoeuvring which followed his on-field outburst in the return leg of the Nantes tie, on 5 April. The spectators of the Stade de la Beaujoire witnessed something extraordinary, even by Cantona's standards – the first public demonstration of Éric's *ossoto gari* flying kick, which would land him in far greater trouble when he launched into it again in south London, six-and-a-half years later.

Throughout the whole game (which ended in a goalless draw, sending Auxerre into the last sixteen of the French Cup), Cantona had been harried by Michel Der Zakarian, a player he had had previous disagreements with and with whom, according to Henri Émile, who was at the match, he had promised to 'have a word' at some stage. Actions speak louder than words, of course, and, on that day, Éric didn't speak so much as scream at the top of his voice. He gathered speed like a long-jumper on the track and hurled himself horizontally, studs first, at poor Der Zakarian, who had long since passed the ball. Fortunately for his victim, Cantona had spread his legs, which caught the Nantes player on each side of his chest. While Der Zakarian lay prone on the grass, apparently knocked out (which he wasn't), Cantona calmly walked away, making straight for the dressing-room. The referee brandished a red card at the back of the departing player. To be frank, despite the violence of Éric's judo kick, the whole episode was hilarious. It was clear that he had taken care not to hurt Der Zakarian – it would have been a different story if his legs hadn't been spread on impact – and that instead he intended to teach his tormentor a spectacular lesson. Once in the dressing-room, the comedy went on.

Auxerre's chief executive Gérard Bourgoin was there, together with a club attendant who, Guy Roux told me, 'had a right go at him'. A bad idea. 'Canto took the guy and threw him 15 metres away, against the wall!' A ban was unavoidable. But Roux, cunning as ever, had an ace in his hand, and played it shamelessly. 'The disciplinary commission had given Éric a three-match ban,' he recalls. 'Platini [*Roux might have meant Henri Michel, whom Platini would succeed later that year*] was there. He was furious. And he was even more furious when I told him: "If Canto is suspended, he won't play for France . . . because he's unworthy of the national team! I'll start a national campaign if need be!"' Eight days later, on 13 April, Marc Bourrier's *Bleuets* were playing the first leg of their European Championships semi-final in Besançon, and against formidable opponents – an England team in which a young Paul Gascoigne was accomplishing miracles.

Roux's arm-twisting amounted to blackmail, and he knew it. The French FA chairman Jean Fournet-Fayard phoned the manager of Auxerre and told him: 'You haven't got the right to do that!' Roux replied: 'Right or wrong, what about ethics? He won't play for France as long as he is suspended.' Shaken, Fournet-Fayard suggested an appeal. Roux purrs: 'And we appealed. There were cameras everywhere – Canto was delighted with that. They ask him: "What have you got to say, M. Cantona?" "But Michel Der Zakarian . . . he's from my neighbourhood! He's a friend! [*The two players were reunited at Montpellier a year later.*] We've been teasing each other ever since we were that high!" . . . and the ban was reduced to two games. Éric played for *les Espoirs* against England!'

Éric duly showed what France would have missed if the original ban had been upheld. Bourrier's irrepressible youngsters thrilled the whole country with a 4–2 win in Besançon, in which Cantona scored a vital goal. But nobody took a place in the final for granted. There was still a return leg to be played in the intimidating surroundings of Highbury. For Éric, it was a first visit to a country whose football he did not know much about and had little affinity with. Arsenal's narrow pitch was extraordinarily close to the stands, the crowd deafening. Right on cue, torrential rain beat down on the turf, while an unearthly fog settled in the old stadium. Everything seemed to conspire against Cantona and his teammates. Their bus was stuck in the London traffic, and the players entered the visitors' dressing-room a mere 45 minutes before kick-off. But what followed was unforgettable, one of the highlights of Éric's career. It had to be.

Five days earlier, Auxerre had exited the Coupe de France, losing out to Lille on the away-goals rule: the *Dogues* had hit the target in extra time after Cantona had scored. Éric could accept defeat, but the tone of his mentor's post-match talk rankled with him. Guy Roux had put their elimination down to a lack of experience, not of talent or of '*gnac*' (the French equivalent of bottle). They should not be ashamed of themselves, the paterfamilias said. Nobody had died. They had done their best. And they had won, dammit! Not well enough, that's all. To Cantona, this generous speech sounded like an admission of weakness. A professional footballer who had clocked 116 competitive appearances for club and country before his 22nd birthday couldn't be satisfied with excuses of that kind. He wanted out, and didn't hide it: he passed on a transfer request to the club on 25 April. The press got wind of it. In these circumstances, as Éric told Pierre-Louis Basse, 'it would be preferable for me to pass my English exam'. With more than a hint of self-satisfaction, he added: 'Live, in front of Canal+'s cameras, I came up with an excellent paper.'

In the England game at Highbury, Cantona's understanding with Sochaux's diminutive striker Stéphane Paille verged on the telepathic, much as his understanding with Ryan Giggs would at Manchester United. Twice, Paille sent him on his way to goal. Twice, Éric scored. A fine England team, which featured Martin Keown and Éric's future Leeds teammate David Rocastle (then at Arsenal) alongside Paul Gascoigne, was held to a 2–2 draw which had France enthralled, and Cantona was hailed as the hero of the '*miracle de Highbury*'. Éric might have already been thinking of what lay ahead of him. The *Espoirs*' English triumph was a glorious parenthesis in his career. The decision to leave Auxerre would open a whole new chapter. But where?

To start with, Éric was thrown off balance by the multitude of proposals that were made to his agent. Auxerre paid a high cost for this. When the French FA had handed a two-game ban to Éric for his assault on Der Zakarian, AJA still had a chance to qualify for the UEFA Cup for the second year in succession. But Cantona's disaffection had a destabilizing effect on the whole squad. Roux sighs. 'Canto's transfer exhausted me . . . He was impossible to live with at the end. He wasn't playing any more.' And neither were the friends he had made over the past five seasons. Auxerre, unsettled by the uncertainty surrounding Éric's future, collected a mere three points in their last eight league games – three draws, five defeats – a desperately poor return that gave them their lowest finish in the league (ninth) since the 1982–83 campaign. Followed by the cameras of Canal+, Éric had brought the French under-21s to the final of the European Championships, scoring three goals in two games against England. Were Trevor Francis, Howard Wilkinson and Alex Ferguson watching, I wonder?

To Guy Roux, qualification for the UEFA Cup in the previous season had represented a triumph – and Roux was right: it had been a personal triumph, and a triumph for the minuscule club he had built almost on his own, from not-for-profit association to finalist of the Coupe de France, and which now boasted the very best academy in the whole country. An older, wiser Cantona might have understood that, despite its old-fashioned, conservative image (which Roux spun in the media with something approaching virtuosity), Auxerre was the closest thing France had to an 'anti-establishment' club. The values he consistently claimed as his own – humility, loyalty, indifference to wealth – had a far greater resonance within the confines of the Stade de l'Abbé-Deschamps than almost anywhere else in France. Awash with television money, a number of the country's biggest clubs had become the playthings of powerful businessmen adept at bending the rules in their favour, some of whom were using football to further their commercial or political interests – the very men who were coveting the new superstar.

Nobody would have called Cantona a king at the time; a prince, maybe, a dashing cavalier, a poster boy for the *après-Platini* generation; but also a desperately naïve and easily impressionable provincial who was nowhere near as knowing in the ways of the world as he ought to have been. (It shouldn't be forgotten that Éric never lived in a capital city before his retirement, and that Manchester would have been the closest thing to a metropolis he had known in his playing days.) According to his former Auxerre teammate Michel Pineda, Éric had envisaged leaving France for Spain, to join his friend at Espanyol, the working-class club of a city – Barcelona – with which his mother's family had an old and cherished bond, and which Isabelle and he regularly visited during summer vacations. That particular dream would come back to him again later, as we shall see. Prompted by his Auxerre teammate Pascal Planques, and encouraged by Stéphane Paille, he had taken on an agent, Alain Migliaccio (Paille's brother-in-law), who would later become a prime mover and shaker in the football microcosm as Zinédine Zidane's key adviser. The sails of the rumour mill were spinning as if in a hurricane. It was universally agreed that Cantona seemed to have outgrown AJA in almost every respect, and huge pressure was put on reporters to find out which club he had picked to accommodate his ambitions.

My friend Jean-Marie Lanoé had been assigned by *France Football* the task of reading Cantona's mind at the time. 'It was insane,' he told me. 'It had become a competition between every single publication you can think of; the most contradictory rumours were leaked. There were constant denials, but you knew that, the evening before, Canto had been invited to this or that chairman's house – the very person who was swearing on his daughter's head that there had been no contact with the player. It was a circus. In the end, I decided to ignore all that, and follow my intuition.' It had become a case of calling heads or tails – Matra Racing and Olympique de Marseille were the last men standing – and hoping the coin would fall on the predicted side. Jean-Marie got it right. Very few others did.

Everyone who was anyone had wanted Cantona. Jean-Marie Campora of Monaco, Claude Bez of Bordeaux, Francis Borelli of PSG, Jean-Luc Lagardère of Matra Racing, Bernard Tapie of Marseille: a mix of old and new money, of the respectable and the objectionable, of hubris and true ambition, five men with eyes fixed on the same trophy. A helpless Guy Roux watched the tug of war from his tiny office at l'Abbé-Deschamps, reconciled to the idea of losing Éric one day – but not just yet: 'In 2008, [when] a guy sneezes, you let him go. Auxerre didn't at the time. We had a very strong argument: every time you play a game on a Saturday, it's as if you are taking a plane. If the plane hasn't gathered enough speed, it can't take off. Yes, you're internationals, you're going to multiply your salary by five or ten in a big club – but if you haven't gathered enough speed, you'll be in the reserves or on the bench. You'll wreck your career. But if you listen to us, you can be sure we'll let you go at the right time, because we need the money – but only when you're at your maximum value, and when you'll arrive in your new team like a nabob, not like a ball-boy.' Roux's wise words made absolutely no impression whatsoever on Cantona, who behaved like a satellite that has lost its orbit and is pulled this way and that between the attraction of various planets.

Characters appeared and vanished on the scene like cuckolds and lovers in a Georges Feydeau farce. Éric was paying frequent visits to Paris, where he and his most trusted friends set up camp in a hotel. Four rooms had been booked: one each for Cantona, Migliaccio, Paille and Didier Fèvre, who held war councils to discuss the proposals slipped under the player's door. Didier was in a very awkward position. Information his colleagues at *L'Équipe* were desperate for had to remain a secret that was getting heavier to carry every day.

'We were locked in there for three or four days to sort out the transfer, fielding calls from Borelli, Bez, Campora and the others,' he recalls. 'Stéphane [Paille] was managing the lot, as Éric wasn't as quick to seize on details as he was . . . whereas Stéphane was an ace at calculating bonuses. We went to Borelli's house, and you know what painting means to Éric? At one point, Éric tells Borelli: "Say, this picture is really something, isn't it?" Borelli wanted him so much that he said: "You like it? Take it!" Éric left with the picture under his arm! Stéphane was quick to react . . . he pointed at an object, and said: "Say, this is really beautiful!" – and he too didn't leave empty-handed.' But Borelli's gift was not sufficient to keep PSG in the race to sign Éric. Bez and Campora threw in the towel too. Their resources didn't enable them to come close to the offers made by Lagardère and Tapie.

The former, one of those captains of industry who amassed a colossal fortune by securing huge public contracts in France's so-called 'mixed economy', dreamt of creating a franchise which would make Paris one of the world capitals of football. But his Matra Racing, patched together by the merger between the old Racing Club de Paris and PSG's failing competitor, Paris FC, was far too artificial a creation to survive beyond a few years of lavish expense and underachievement on the field. The club he had purchased in 1982 recruited some first-rate players, such as the German winger Pierre Littbarski, the Uruguayan playmaker Enzo Francescoli and France's favourite midfield gladiator Luis Fernandez, paying them salaries only the richest Spanish and Italian clubs could match. But Lagardère's unpredictable collection of 'names' never attracted crowds big enough to earn itself a true club identity, and, within nine years of its inception, Matra Racing would – at its own behest, so precarious was its financial situation – be demoted to the the third tier of the French football league, with nothing to show for the millions spent by Lagardère but images that faded almost immediately, and few memories.

In the light of the club's eventual fate, the attempt to seduce Cantona can look like the gesture of a gambler playing his last hand. It was not so. In truth, for most outsiders, Roux included, Éric looked set to become another ornament in Lagardère's folly. 'One day, Canto comes to me and says: "M. Lagardère has invited me for dinner – how should I dress?" He had a pair of jeans on which looked as if he had slashed them with a knife. I told him: "You can't go dressed like that. Go buy yourself a suit." "A suit? Like yours?" "No, no – a young man's suit! Go to Patrick." Patrick was a Jewish-Tunisian tailor who ran a small shop in the Rue du Temple. He was gentle, very good at his job, and mad about football. He went to Patrick. "I've got my suit, M. Roux!" "And what about the tie?" "A tie? Like you?" "No . . . a leather tie, something for young people, you see!" So he bought it. I saw Éric and Isabelle after they'd met Lagardère. "Oh la la . . . it was like in the Middle Ages! The servants! They had wigs! And carried halberds! . . . and Mrs Lagardère . . . she's so, so beautiful!" So I thought – Canto is going to Matra Racing.'

What's more, Éric had noticed, hung on a wall of Lagardère's palatial home, a painting by Joan Miró, one of his favourite artists. An original. The 'man of taste and of culture' who had so impressed Cantona also presented him with two books, one about Pablo Picasso, the other an essay on the Catalan surrealist. Éric and Isabelle's home would soon become too exiguous for all these presents.

What Roux didn't know is that Lagardère's rival, Bernard Tapie, had a powerful ally in the person of Gérard Bourgoin, Auxerre's CEO. Tapie was in many ways an exact negative of Lagardère, in birth, character and social trajectory. Lagardère glided on deep, richly coloured carpets without a sound; the floor shook every time Tapie's feet (slipped into expensive Italian shoes) hit the ground. Lagardère spoke gently, each word accompanied by a smile; Tapie swore like a trooper, and one with a vivid imagination to boot. Few men could make as valid a claim to have made themselves as 'Nanard' Tapie, the Parisian prole who (after a brief stint as an unsuccessful pop crooner in the sixties) kicked off his business career by selling televisions door to door – introducing himself as an imaginary 'quality controller' employed by the state-controlled networks, who lent out sets free of charge for a week, then came back and, with genuine charm, convinced his preys to buy what was at the time an extraordinarily expensive piece of equipment.

If Lagardère was a product of his class, Tapie was entirely self-made. He became one of the most remarkably successful businessmen of his generation, building a portfolio of internationally renowned companies (Adidas, for example) which had fallen on hard times and could be bought for – literally – nothing; as soon as they became profitable again (thanks to some 'restructuring' which he blamed entirely on the previous owners), he would sell them, and move to another easy picking. There was genius in Tapie. He would become an MP, an MEP, a short-lived minister of cities in Pierre Bérégovoy's Socialist government. He would try his luck as an actor. He would try anything, apparently driven by a ferocious belief in himself (verging on recklessness) that some found mesmerizing, others appalling and which eventually led to his downfall.* The Tapie who courted Cantona was approaching the apex of his ascent. The boat he sailed in the Mediterranean, the *Phocéa*, was one of the world's most luxurious yachts.

---

* On 28 November 1995 (after an unsuccessful appeal), Tapie was sentenced to a two-year jail term (sixteen months suspended) and a FF20,000 fine for 'subornation of witness' in the 'OM–VA affair', which I'll come to in greater detail later in this book. He served six months in prison. Two years later, he was convicted of embezzlement by the Tribunal Correctionnel de Marseille on 4 July 1997, and sentenced to a three-year jail term (eighteen months suspended). The appeal court of Aix-en Provence reduced the sentence to three years (suspended) and a FF300,000 fine on 4 June 1998. Last, in December 2005, having been found guilty of tax evasion ('fraude fiscale') he was sentenced to a three-year jail term (twenty-eight months suspended) by the 11th Chamber of the Tribunal Correctionnel of Paris.

In 1986 Tapie had taken control of Olympique de Marseille, France's best-supported club. His instinct told him that, in order to further his political ambitions (which some say included winning the Presidency of the *République* itself), he needed to establish an impregnable base somewhere, anywhere, provided he could rule it unchallenged. It should be said that he had a genuine liking for and understanding of sport. When Bernard Hinault, then Greg Lemond, ruled the Tour de France in the early 1980s, they were wearing the colours of one of Tapie's companies, La Vie Claire. Tapie had also sent his manager, Gérard Banide, to Auxerre before making his big move; Banide's role was to explain to Éric which role he would play in the Marseille team: that of a '*numéro dix*', a goalscoring playmaker, a string-puller in the mould of Platini, rather than the centre-forward Célestin Oliver and Guy Roux had in mind. Cantona was strongly attracted to the maverick millionaire he would later dub 'a demon'. 'If everyone was as interesting as Tapie, I'd buy the papers more often,' he had said in 1987. One year later, his suitor announced himself in his customary dramatic fashion. Lagardère had invited Éric to his luxurious residence; Tapie would invite himself to Cantona's little house in the forest.

He chartered a private plane and landed in a small airfield at Branches, a few miles away from Éric's village, jumped in a car, and arrived at his destination in the middle of the afternoon. He only stayed for a few minutes to deliver his message. 'I'm speaking to you man to man,' he said. 'There's no need for big words. I want you. Whatever the other one is offering you, I'll give you the same – and you'll be at home! So long, Éric!' Then he left. Yes, there was genius in Tapie.*

---

* There was also a heart, as Tapie showed on the darkest day in OM's history: the tragedy of the Stade de Furiani, in Corsica. On 5 May 1992, a couple of minutes before a French Cup semi-final between SEC Bastia and Marseille was supposed to kick-off, a makeshift stand which had been erected to accommodate an extra 10,000 spectators collapsed, causing the death of eighteen people (a number of journalists among them), and maiming dozens more for life. The OM chairman spent the evening tending the injured and administering first aid when needed. One of the victims he helped had swallowed his tongue and, without his intervention, would have died that night. The man who owed his life to Tapie was my friend Jean-Marie Lanoé.

Cantona stood to multiply his salary not 'by five or ten', but by twenty, whichever club he decided to join. Figures of £4,000–5,000 a week were mentioned in the press, which apparently weren't that wide of the mark: Éric was about to be promoted to the super-elite of Europe's best-paid footballers. But money wasn't uppermost in his thoughts. In this as in so many other things, Isabelle's feelings and his own were perfectly attuned. He had been shaken by Lagardère's easy eloquence, and could see himself building a unique creative relationship with Enzo Francescoli at Matra Racing. But he had less than twenty-four hours to come to a decision. Alain Migliaccio advised him to sleep on it, and, during the night, Éric dreamt of Marseilles, not Paris. Not for the last time, he chose to trust his impulses.

That very morning, Éric and Isabelle made their way to Tapie's extravagant townhouse, the seventeenth-century Hôtel de Cavoye in the seventh *arrondissement* of Paris. Both felt incredibly nervous. Isabelle slipped on the marble floor, Éric caught her by the arm just as she was about to hit the ground. A bad omen? Then, as the contracts were laid out on Tapie's desk to be signed, the phone rang. Migliaccio's assistant was on the line: a close associate of Silvio Berlusconi wished to let Cantona know that AC Milan, Italy's champions elect, wanted him to partner the prodigious Marco van Basten at the head of the *rossoneri*'s attack. But Éric had given his word, and would not take it back. It was a noble gesture, in keeping with the persona Cantona wanted to assume for the outside world, but it would haunt him for a long time to come.

Auxerre pocketed 22 million francs – over £2m – for their academy graduate, which made Cantona's move to Marseille on a five-year contract the most profitable transfer in their history. But AJA's chairman, Jean-Claude Hamel, was furious. Éric had become even more uncontrollable since the news of his move to OM had been made public. Part of him already mourned the friends he was about to leave, and his way to deal with the grief was to seek their company at all hours of the day and night. The teams that roasted Auxerre in the last three weeks of the 1987–88 season faced a group of footballers who had hardly had a minute's sleep the night before. No matter how late it was, Éric drifted from room to room in the hotel where Roux's young men were supposed to gather strength before the Saturday game.

Cantona had a few accounts to settle, too, with a small group of supporters who had barracked him constantly since his departure from Auxerre had been announced. Éric had told his manager how he was intending to put an end to this: by giving them a good hiding after the last game of the season. Fortunately for Guy Roux, Tapie made a suggestion that would scupper Cantona's plan. Bernard Genghini, who had played such a pivotal role in France's epic campaigns of 1982, '84 and '86, was about to play his last-ever game for the Marseillais. Couldn't Éric take charge of a symbolic kick-off that day? That would be beautiful. The old passing on the baton to the new, in front of 60,000 passionate supporters . . . Yes, Roux thought, and that would happen 400 miles away from the guys he intended to beat up. A fine idea.

Hamel exploded. 'That's out of the question! He has to play the last game!' 'When Hamel is like that,' Roux told me, 'there's no point in talking to him. This time, I sat down in his office, which I never did, because he'd keep you there for an hour. "Mr Hamel," I said, "I will not leave until you've listened to me. Éric Cantona wants to have a good go at a few people in the ground, including one person who sits in the directors' box, not very far from you. Nobody will stop him – nobody. Either we tell these five people not to come to the game or . . ." "But we're paying him!" he screams. "Mr Chairman, they're paying us 22 million francs, we could consider that this is enough to give them an extra week." No answer. I think for a while, then tell him: "I might not be going to the game myself, you know." And in the end, Hamel relented.' And on this farcical note, Éric Cantona was gone from Auxerre.

THE *FRANCE FOOTBALL* INTERVIEW

Éric, you're welcoming us at the Stade de l'Abbé-Deschamps, apologizing for not doing so in your home, as you would have done normally. Why?

There are moments when I don't feel able to welcome somebody in my home. I do not have the strength for that. Because when someone comes to my home, generally speaking, he's made to feel welcome. At this point in time, I'd rather stay alone with my wife, with my dogs, to cut myself from everything in my mind. I haven't bought a paper since the game in Athens [*the 2–0 defeat to Panathinaikos, in which Cantona was uncharacteristically wayward in front of goal*], I've gone away from football as much as I could, to recharge my batteries.

Do you feel you do not have this inner strength any more?
I find it difficult to concentrate. Being aware of it is the hardest part. Then, you must have the inner strength to isolate yourself. I have that strength.

Do you lose this concentration when you speak to journalists?
I avoid journalists because, when I speak, I express a sensitivity, I give [a lot of] myself. A bit too much. It's energy, 'juice' – it's some of my strength I'm wasting. And twice: when I speak, then when I read the interview.

Your life seems to have changed a lot since you were pre-selected for West Germany–France, on 4 August . . .
There have been changes, but only around me. For example, people say 'hello', people I don't know. They have changed. I haven't.

Are you troubled by this notoriety?
My environment causes me problems. But in my head, I haven't changed, because sport is not the only thing in life. When I miss goals as in Athens, I come home, and there are so many things that make me feel good that I forget about such a bad moment. Even if I am a perfectionist and hate failure.

Do you find it normal to have been the object of so many solicitations over the last two months?
I am very much in demand because journalists have the feeling they've discovered a gold mine. They are under the impression they can make me say things which are out of the ordinary. As for me – saying these

things doesn't bother me. But you must know that I am not duped by it. I'm not a cretin, I say what I want to say.

. . . with the reputation of not mincing your words.
I do my job on the pitch, the journalist does his by asking me questions. If I don't play the game, I'm ruining his work. That's why I've made it a rule to be sincere.

Is that why people are seduced by you?
I don't think about consequences. These are impulsive reactions. I haven't the power others have to calculate everything they say. I haven't got the strength because I haven't got the desire to have it.

Guy Roux says that the media interest in you at the moment is twice as important as what he's known with [Jean-Marc] Ferreri or [Basile] Boli. Even magazines like *Paris-Match* talk about Cantona. How do you explain this?
People must have noticed through several press articles that I was not interested in football alone. By the way, I prefer to answer the questions of non-football journalists.

Why?
What can you invent in football? The only possible innovation is to say out loud what players think in silence. That's all.

But you have, in the space of three or four interviews, invented a new language for a footballer: frank, with no taboo or concessions.
I'm not making it up when I say things that all players feel. When I say that the French players' frame of mind explains why we've never won a European Championship [sic] or a World Cup, I'm not teaching anything new to the players. They're aware of it. They know that football is played in the head more than with the legs.

Has Cantona got more in his head than in his legs ?
I have [as much in the head as in the legs]. Fortunately so, because the day I won't be able to improve will also be the day when I stop. [*He*

would repeat these words verbatim at his very first press conference in Manchester.]

Talking about heads – it's shaving yours which really kicked off your career!
I didn't shave my head to attract attention or to make an ad for myself. It was just an impulse; we were in Brest, preparing for a game, and I felt like having my head shaved, there you go.

Did you do it yourself?
I went to the hairdressers. It took me half an hour to find one who'd agree to do it.

And if you had to do it again, knowing the impact this gesture had?
I'd do it again. I regret other people's reactions, but they'll never make me regret my actions, or prevent me from fulfilling my whims, my desires, my fantasies. It only proves that the milieu of football isn't that deep. If a great painter shaves his head, they'll say: 'That's normal, he's a creator, he's a bit crazy.' In football, people are too used to seeing healthy boys, with nice haircuts, who weigh everything they say . . .

A footballer has no right to be crazy?
A footballer isn't allowed to be crazy. And that is regrettable.

Would you like to be crazy?
But I am crazy! I need to have crazy reactions to be happy – and even to be good on the pitch. You must have the strength to be crazy. Not there and then, when sincerity is paramount, but afterwards, to claim one's originality. Football doesn't accept differences, that's why it disappoints me. Players are too banal. They are playing machines, they're not allowed to think for themselves.

Don't you fear being 'normalized' in the end?
I can't picture myself as anything but crazy, because I need to be happy. Crazy am I, crazy I will be.

Do you know the story of Jean-Christophe Thouvenel* who, when he started, had a very critical discourse on the football world, and today admits he was wrong?
I can't answer you. He's seven or eight years older than I am. Come back in seven or eight years and ask me the question again. But even if he doesn't speak out any more, I am convinced that, in his head, he hasn't changed. He's simply acquired the mastery of his self.

And you haven't?
I am too disappointed by the environment of football. People who come and watch the games have no sensitivity, no craziness, no capacity to think. I do not live the life I want to live in this milieu. It is only an approach to another life, another life which I'm waiting for.

A life without football?
Yes. Football is a minor art. What interests me is major art.

Painting?
Everybody now knows that I paint. But I have other passions. I want to live in the madness of the creative artist. What interests me is his suffering. Because a great artist is always misunderstood.

Is it how you would live if you weren't a footballer?
I'd have been a creator or an adventurer. But, above all, I'd be poor. When you're rich, sincerity is not what comes through. Many people would give their arse to earn money; I who have money, I'd like to be poor. Money doesn't make me happy.

Does it make you unhappy?
No. The money I earn at the moment is for my children, not for me. I put it all in a bank account so that they're happy, so that they don't suffer from my madness. But when football is over, I'll leave like someone who hasn't got money. I won't have more than two hundred francs in my pocket.

---

* French international defender, who was part of the gold-winning French team at the 1984 Olympic Games and would be Cantona's teammate at Bordeaux.

That's totally crazy.
But you need crazy things! You can't understand me, and that's normal: you're not on the same wavelength as I am. All I'm telling you is that I'll do that because, as a footballer, I am not completely happy.

Will you be happy one day?
Life is a big dream you wake up from feeling in a good or a bad mood; it depends. Happiness has to be found so that it is not a nightmare, [so] that it is a pleasant dream. That's what I'm looking for.

You have said that if you weren't a footballer, you'd be an adventurer. What is an 'adventurer' in 1987?
He is a traveller. But not a tourist like soccer players. I'll give you an example: in Athens, they'd organized a coach trip to the Acropolis. If I hadn't been a footballer, I'd have walked miles to see the Acropolis. In this case, I stayed at the hotel. It was too easy, it didn't interest me. The day I go there, I want the impulse to come from me. I'd say that, up to a point, I want to suffer in order to appreciate the Acropolis. Simple things give me no joy.

You'd said – when you were almost unknown – that players 'disgusted' you. Would you say the same thing today?
When I say something, I don't repeat it fifty times. What people must understand is that I am not a criticizing machine. I am a realistic man who says what he thinks.

People stick many labels on you. Do these seem justified to you: a rebel on the fringe of society?
Others see me like that. But it's true that I may be different.

Desperado?
I think that's . . . quite apt.

Provocateur?
Provocateur? . . . yes, yes.

Insolent?
No.

Haughty?
Who said that?

No one in particular. It's a label.
Never heard it. Haughty, haughty . . . yes, that's a word that suits me fine.

In the end, all of this makes you a media animal?
Probably. But I'm not trying to be one.

. . . and an icon for the young?
If I have a piece of advice to give to the young – as I am haughty! – it is to count on nobody but themselves to succeed. It gives me pleasure that ten-year-olds have my poster on their bedroom wall. But I ask those who, one day, will be contacted by professional clubs, to tear that poster up.

5

THE VAGABOND 1: MARSEILLES AND BORDEAUX

'When I was a little boy, what made me dream was the Stade-Vélodrome. And this love will never leave me. In Marseilles, I was happier than anyone else could have been in the whole wide world. My most beautiful memories are . . . my youth.'

Éric speaking to *L'Équipe Magazine*, April 1994

'Unfortunately, in Marseilles, there is a culture that glorifies cheats when they win. [. . .] The Marseillais is sometimes only proud of himself when he's managed to get something by cheating. Because it harks back to the image of the old Marseilles, of the Marseillais voyou *[lout]. Fake wide boys who think they're mafiosi. That's Marseilles. The cult of the mafia. The guy who steals a kilo of clementines, there he goes, he's a mafioso.'*

Éric speaking to *L'Équipe Magazine*, April 2007

Éric was not the only little boy who dreamt of the Stade-Vélodrome in the early seventies. The brittleness of the French national team exasperated its supporters. It suffered from staggering physical deficiencies, which nullified the technical excellence of what was otherwise a fine generation of players. *Les Bleus*, who did not figure in any major competition between the World Cups of 1966 and 1978, earned the dubious nickname of 'the world champions of friendlies', performing decently when the pressure was off, capitulating as soon as qualification for a tournament was in sight. Two clubs took it on themselves to produce football that didn't suffer from comparison with what could be seen on the English, Scottish, Dutch, Italian and German pitches of the time. These exponents of '*le football total*' were St Étienne, winner of seven league titles between 1967 and 1976 (as well as three Coupes de France), and Olympique de Marseille, the aesthetes' choice, who won the double in 1971–72, and were the only rivals of the *Stéphanois* in the nation's hearts. Fickle hearts they were, as they were bound to be in a country where club culture is yet to take root in 2009, thirty-three years after the Bayern Munich of Franz Beckenbauer pinched what would have been France's first European Cup from under the nose of St Étienne, on a still-lamented night in Glasgow. It's a story which is as deeply ingrained in the psyche of the French as England's disputed third goal in the 1966 World Cup final is in that of the Germans. If the goalposts hadn't been square, at least one of the two shots which rebounded on Sepp Maier's woodwork would have gone in, and the adventurousness of St Étienne would have been rewarded with a European title in May 1976. Or so it is believed to this day.

As a native of Marseilles, one of a handful of French cities where football is more than a stick-on patch in the fabric of daily life, Éric was bound to develop a powerful attachment to the white and sky-blue of OM rather than the green of St Étienne. St Étienne was a powerful, dynamic, efficient unit, not unlike the Liverpool team of the day. OM appealed to romantics much in the same way that Danny Blanchflower's Spurs had years before in England. In the Yugoslavian 'goal machine' Josip Skoblar, who scored an astonishing 138 goals in 169 games for the Marseillais between 1969 and 1975, and winger Roger Magnusson, 'the Swedish Garrincha', who cast his spell over the Vélodrome from 1968 till 1974, they possessed two of the most exciting players of that era. Their posters hung in Cantona's childhood bedroom, next to photographs of Ajax's gods, whom Éric had seen in the flesh on 20 October 1972, when they beat Marseille 2–1 in the European Cup.

Cantona, the matador, must have hoped that the shirt worn by Skoblar and Magnusson before him would be his mantle of light. But it turned out to be his tunic of Nessus. It consumed him, causing pain that the passing of years has done little to relieve. Marseille wounded the child in him, perhaps mortally, and it could be argued that his later career was an attempt to conjure back to life the youth he was stripped of by his home-town club. At Auxerre, he had rarely missed an opportunity to tell the world what he thought of the game's milieu (not much). But one could sense teenage bravado in his expressions of dismay at what surrounded him, and that a part of him wished his instinct to be wrong. Those who doubt it should cast their minds back to what he achieved for Roux and Bourrier: footballers never lie on the field of play. But Marseille was different. The fantasies he had entertained were cruelly shown to be mere daydreams. He craved innocence, light, splendour. What he got was betrayal, pettiness and what he called a culture of cheating, a perception that would be substantiated in 1993 two years after he had left the club, when OM was found to have suborned their way to success. In the summer of 1988, though, the talk on the Vieux-Port was of the rebirth of the *Phocéens*.

After a decade-and-a-half of turmoil, which had seen charismatic chairman Marcel Leclerc ousted by a boardroom coup in 1972, and OM being relegated to the second tier of the league four years later, the club had enjoyed a suitably chaotic renaissance. A team largely composed of *minots* (local boys) had earned promotion to the top flight in 1984, and the club had been further invigorated by the arrival of Bernard Tapie at its helm in April 1986, after some forceful manoeuvring by the city's elected monarch, Socialist mayor Gaston Deferre.

The Parisian businessman had grandiose plans for his club, which had finished the 1987–88 season with a sixth place in the league and a spot in the semi-finals of the European Cup Winners' Cup. Money was no obstacle for the boss of Adidas, as he proved by attracting Karlheinz Förster and Alain Giresse to the Vélodrome in the wake of the 1986 World Cup. Bringing back the prodigy of Les Caillols to his home town was, at first, a popular move. It satisfied the Marseillais' odd kind of clannish and unforgiving sentimentality, and made perfect sense as far as the team's progression was concerned, especially after the departure of playmaker Bernard Genghini. What is astonishing is the speed at which the crowd of the Vélodrome turned against their own. When I asked Célestin Oliver why Cantona had to suffer so much abuse so early on in his Marseille career, he replied: '*Il bouffonnait.*'

He 'played the buffoon'? Not quite. The habitués of OM perceived Éric's haughty demeanour on the pitch as a mark of disdain, of which they were the target. In contrast, they embraced the humble but demonstrative Jean-Pierre Papin, the Golden Boot of the previous campaign, with whom Cantona was to form a lethal partnership for the French national side, if not for Marseille. JPP made no claims to be an intellectual vagabond, and was mocked mercilessly in the French media for what could be euphemistically dubbed his rusticity. Papin and Cantona formed an odd couple: chalk and cheese off the pitch, they complemented each other beautifully on it, not in the way a Zidane and a Djorkaeff combined, as if they were the two hemispheres of the same brain, but by doing their utmost to dovetail each other's game. When Jean-Pierre's form was indifferent, Éric would raise his, and vice versa.* They functioned as a sort of two-man relay team, not unlike the famed duo that won the Ashes for England in 1956: 'If Laker doesn't get you out, Lock will.' But the Marseillais failed to see what was blindingly obvious for neutral observers. They closed ranks around the future *Ballon d'Or*, because he remained true to himself, while Éric was castigated – for exactly the same reason.

It is true that there have been more auspicious starts to a club career than Cantona's at OM. On 20 August 1988, on the day he had scored his second goal for the club in a 3–2 victory at Strasbourg, Éric's fuse blew in spectacular fashion in front of TV cameras. He had just learnt that the French manager Henri Michel hadn't picked him for a forthcoming friendly against Czechoslovakia. Cantona, a lynchpin of the national side since his debut a year earlier, had had no intimation that he would be rested for this largely inconsequential fixture. Michel had told his assistant Henri Émile that he 'wanted to try out a few things and let [Cantona] have a breather', and that he would call the player presently to inform him of this decision. But the call was never made. 'If Michel had picked up the phone, there would have been no incident,' sighs Émile. Instead of which an incensed Cantona earned himself

* In the 31 games they played together for France, Papin scored 22 goals, Cantona 10. But Éric provided 3 assists to JPP, and only received a single one from him.

a ten-month ban from *Les Bleus* with a tirade that demands to be included in its entirety, for the splendid robustness of its language as well as for the frequency with which it's been misquoted over the years, particularly in England.

'I will not play in the French team as long as Henri Michel is the manager,' he said. 'One day, I'll be so strong that people will have to choose between him and me. I hope that people will realize quickly that he [Michel] is one of the most incompetent national team managers in world football.' Then, infamously, 'I've just read what Mickey Rourke said about the Oscars: "The person who's in charge of them is a bag of shit." I'm not far from thinking that Henri Michel is one too . . . What will people think, whoever they are? I don't care at all.' You will note that Cantona stopped short of calling Michel a 'bag of shit' *sui generis*, preferring to invoke the authority of a Hollywood actor who shared his passion for boxing and motorbikes, and for whom he had developed an obsession at the time – but would later identify as a professional rebel who had exploited his image to earn fame and fortune.

In the furore that followed, hardly anybody noticed that, twenty-four hours after shocking the nation, a contrite Cantona had said: 'When I saw myself on television, I scared myself, and I was ashamed [. . .]. This rude, uncouth person wasn't me. Sometimes, when I have something to say, I express myself badly, very badly. I belittle people, I trample on them. It happens to me even within the family. [Michel's] announcement of the squad cut me to the quick. I panicked. I was afraid. I think it'll sort itself out – it is in everyone's interest. I need them and they need me.' His sincerity wasn't feigned, but the apology was by and large ignored, feeding Éric's feeling of injustice. Yes, he had made a mistake. But so had Michel. What was the use of wounding one's pride so publicly, when it was obvious to him that 'people' were out to crucify a maverick called Éric Cantona, regardless of the circumstances? 'People' wouldn't hear many other expressions of remorse in the years to come.

His ban – which had catastrophic consequences for France's chances of qualifying for the 1990 *Mondiale* – didn't extend to OM, for whom he played all but two of the first twenty-four games of the season, with greater success than local fans would have you believe today. But it prevented him from sharing in the *Espoirs*' conquest of the European title, in which he had hitherto played such a pivotal part. The first game of the two-legged final between France and Greece, held on 24 May in Athens, finished in a 0–0 draw, with Éric assuming his normal position in the side. The return match, held on 12 October, saw Bourrier's players run away with a 3–0 victory in their talismanic stadium of Besançon. This time, Éric, banned from the French national team until 1 July 1989, could only watch from afar. His six goals made him the competition's top marksman, and no one had done more to give France its first success in this tournament. But at the age of 22, he had come as close to international consecration as he would in his entire career.

Despite what the press suggested, Éric enjoyed a decent – if distant – relationship with his moustachioed manager Gérard Gili, another Marseillais who had been OM's second 'keeper in the early seventies, came back to the club in the eighties, and later showed his value as a manager by taking the Ivory Coast to the 2006 World Cup finals and the 2008 Olympics. Gili kept the Auxerre defector in the starting eleven despite a pronounced dip in his goalscoring statistics. Never the quickest of starters, Cantona had to wait until his sixth game, a 2–0 victory over Matra Racing on 17 August, to open his account. The brief flurry of goals which followed (three in three), perhaps fuelled by a desire to show Michel what he had been missing, suggested that Éric had found his feet at the Vélodrome, but he couldn't sustain this rhythm. Unsettled by the growing hostility of his home crowd, he would score only once more in the thirteen matches to come. In January 1989, the month in which Stéphane Paille had been voted French player of the year, way ahead of his friend and *Espoirs* teammate (something that would have been unthinkable six months previously), Gili admitted: 'Éric has a huge challenge to confront. He's a man of character, and I hope he can.' He meant it, but not everyone believed him.

Did Marseilles, the town, ever want Éric to succeed? Marseille, the club, has forgotten Éric Cantona. When I visited their museum, located under one of the stands of the Vélodrome, I searched in vain for a trace, any trace, of his stay there. None was to be found. It should be stressed, however, that the results of Éric's team didn't suffer much from his supposedly patchy form: OM only conceded three defeats in the twenty-two games he played before his dramatic departure for Bordeaux. One of these was a 1–0 reverse on Cantona's old ground at Auxerre, in November 1988, where he deserved to be named man of the match. By the time Éric's fuse-box short-circuited again, on 30 January 1989, exactly a month after Isabelle had given birth to their first child Raphaël, Marseille, chasing an effusive Paris Saint-Germain, had already built a platform from which they could spring to their first league title in sixteen years. But his indiscipline denied him a further part in OM's appropriation of *le championnat*, just as it had denied him a chance to partake in the under-21s' European triumph.

On the morning of 7 December 1988, the Armenian city of Spitak was reduced to ruins by an appalling earthquake which claimed over 25,000 lives. Hardly anyone in the vicinity of the tremor's epicentre survived. The French and Armenian peoples have long held a deep affection for each other; Marseilles, in particular, had been a refuge for the victims of Russian, Ottoman and Soviet persecution for over a century. Charles Aznavour, the most celebrated son of the Armenian diaspora, wrote a song on that tragic occasion, 'Pour toi, Arménie', which sold over a million copies in France alone. Tapie, who was also a warm-hearted man capable of genuine acts of generosity, proposed that OM play a charity match against a top side from the ailing USSR. The long French winter break allowed for such a fixture to be organized without detriment to Marseilles, who could field all their stars when they lined up to face – in front of national television cameras – Torpedo Moscow on a chilly night in Sedan, on 30 January.

The choice of Sedan was, to say the least, rather eccentric. The capital city of the Ardennes region is well known for two things: its place in French history books as the scene for one of the country's worst-ever military defeats, against Bismarck's Prussians in 1871, and its harsh Continental climate. In the month of January, Sedan usually froze, and in 1989 it did just that. Had the match been a league fixture, it would have been abandoned without a second thought. As Henri Émile recalled – Émile, the man who was seemingly fated to be present whenever Éric lost control of himself – the pitch was frozen, so dangerous that most of the players first refused to warm up on it. The organizers insisted; so did the networks, and both clubs' officials. Cantona 'missed two or three balls which looked within his reach, because they skidded on the ice', as Émile recalls it. Of course, Éric should have ignored the freakish bounces, pottered about, and waited for the warmth of the dressing-room. It was a *charity* game, for goodness sake. But no.

At one point, a ball hit the advertising boards and came back to him. Disgusted, he hoofed it into the stands. The referee, Monsieur Delmer, who had cautioned him when Auxerre played Marseille nine weeks previously, immediately came up to remonstrate with the player. Cantona replied: 'All right, don't fret, I know,' adding, with what the official felt was some menace, 'I don't need this.'

A worried M. Delmer walked up to the OM bench to have a quick chat with Gérard Gili. Émile, who was sitting alongside Michel Hidalgo just above the dugout, could hear everything. Gili thought Cantona was 'about to blow it', and decided to substitute him. As others did after him, the Marseille manager found out that it was not the wisest decision to take Éric off the pitch before a game was over, whether it was a friendly or not. Cantona's frustration with everything that surrounded him that night, the game, the referee, the icy field of play, swamped him. He took off his jersey and threw it towards his coach. Émile still pleads: 'It was just a misunderstanding that was blown out of proportion.' But millions were watching. Cantona was kicking a ball, or attempting to do so, to help raise money for widows and orphans. To him, however, at that moment, nothing mattered but a game of football, and an overwhelming feeling of injustice. 'I tell you what,' Gérard Houllier said in one of our conversations, 'when we coaches had to referee training games, and made a wrong decision, oh my god, Éric wasn't too pleased. In fact, we'd be looking for someone else to pass the whistle to!'

In no way did Cantona intend to demean the occasion. He had been wronged, and reacted without thinking. The image of Cantona's shirt lying on the frozen turf would remain as potent and enduring an emblem of Cantona's flaws to the French public as the Crystal Palace kung-fu kick would to the English.

A fidgeting Bernard Tapie, who had hoped for a better return on his FF22m investment over the first six-and-a-half months of the season, spoke of an '*inqualifiable* [indefensible]' act, and helpfully suggested that 'if we need to, we'll put him in a psychiatric hospital'. The honeymoon had long been over between the two men; the chairman's condemnation consummated the divorce. Michel Hidalgo, with some courage, went over the top to defend Éric: it was 'neither an affair of state, nor a public affair', he said, talking to everyone and no one in particular. The audience had already left. Where was Éric?

Cantona had disappeared. He had flown to Barcelona immediately after the game. His former Auxerre teammate Michel Pineda was playing for Espanyol and could shelter him for a few days. The wildest rumours started to circulate. He had no shirt any more? Johan Cruyff – his hero! – could provide him with one: the jersey of Barça. The French press agencies' reporters behaved as if they were paid by Pinkerton's. Vincent Machenaud and Didier Fèvre found themselves in the Camp Nou on match day, following a vague lead that Éric might be there. They circled the huge arena, looking at every face in the 90,000-strong crowd in the hope their eyes would meet the fierce black glare of the Marseille reprobate. Amazingly, they did.

Didier knew enough of Éric to refrain from taking any pictures of Cantona when they came across him by some miracle. The two hounds from *L'Équipe* had a drink with him instead. Then, when Machenaud asked Éric a question he didn't like, 'Canto walked out and lifted his arm,' says Didier. 'Just like in a movie, a taxi pulled by, and he was gone – pfft, like that!' To Éric's credit, when he learnt – through Paille – that the photographer had suffered a dreadful dressing-down from his employers because of his 'failure', he offered the hand of friendship. He and Didier would enjoy an even closer relationship over the next couple of years.

But what about OM? Éric had been excluded from the team on the spot, and fined a fortune. Insiders soon surmised that it was Marseille – Tapie – who had let it be known that an 'arrangement' with Barcelona could be worked upon. The Catalan club's chairman, Joan Gaspart, wasted no time in informing Michel Hidalgo that he had no interest in Cantona. What on earth was Tapie thinking about?

On 2 February Cantona was back in France, to meet the OM president in his other Xanadu, his company's head office on the Avenue de Friedland. According to carefully leaked 'information', the player showed contrition, his chairman forgiveness, so much so that Hidalgo could say: 'The incident is over and done with. Everything [has been] sorted to everyone's best interest. There will be no further statement regarding what is [*repeating himself*] not an affair of state, but a plain, private issue, which needs to be solved in a confidential manner.'

Back at the Vélodrome, most of Éric's teammates were supportive. 'There really are many things which have brought Éric to this situation,' said Klaus Allofs. 'That's why I can understand his reaction with a crowd that's been tough [on him].' Philippe Vercruysse added: 'I might have cracked myself if I'd been in Éric's place. Because he carries a heavy burden, and he's young.' Yvon Le Roux, the no-nonsense central defender: 'Éric's been victimized by the Marseille supporters for a few months. It's very difficult to play in a stadium where people are booing you.' Even Gili, the manager who couldn't manage the unmanageable Cantona, said of this incident: 'The playing conditions were too unusual for any lesson to be learnt.' Publicly, even the players who had been careful to distance themselves from Éric proffered a few words of encouragement. Philippe Thys was one such: 'What we want above all else is to be a tightly knit group of players and, in this case, I think he's put himself apart a bit. Maybe it's partly our fault. But no one's got anything against him.'

One man, and one man only, took it on himself to say the unsayable: Michel Hidalgo. 'Éric Cantona's career in France is probably over. The crowds don't want him any more.'

This was a sombre time for the Cantona clan. Éric's brother Joël's hopes to make it as a top footballer were more or less extinguished when, tired of playing for third division Meaux, he opted to sign for Belgian side Antwerp, just as his sibling was making himself scarce in Barcelona. Exile is a leitmotiv in this family's opera.

The usual flock of vultures began to circle. Seventy-two hours after he had passed judgement on Cantona as 'a basket case', Claude Bez, the chairman of Bordeaux, explained: 'My words shouldn't be taken literally.'

The truth is that Bez, who had wooed Éric when he made plain his intention to leave Auxerre seven months beforehand, was desperate. His team was sinking like a stone, lagging in 14th position, 20 points behind leaders PSG. No one could have predicted as severe a crisis as this at the start of the season. The Girondins had one of the country's finest coaches in Aimé Jacquet, who had given the club unprecedented success since he had become their manager in 1980. Bordeaux had no rival for the honorific title of France's team of the decade. They had won the league on three occasions during that period (in 1984, 1985 and 1987, the year of a historic double) as well as two Coupes de France (in 1986 and 1987).

But one obsession ruled Claude Bez: to make Bordeaux the first French team to succeed where Raymond Kopa's Reims and Jean-Michel Larqué's St Étienne had failed: in Europe. Jacquet came very close to fulfilling his chairman's dream, but not close enough, and paid the price for it. Bordeaux only fell 3–2 on aggregate in the semi-finals of the 1984–85 European Cup, losing out to Michel Platini's Juventus, who would go on to win a bloodstained trophy against Liverpool at the Heysel stadium. Two years later, Bordeaux exited the European Cup Winners' Cup at the semi-final stage again, on penalties this time, against a Lokomotiv Leipzig side which was there for the taking. A testimony to Bordeaux's then prominence was that no other French club provided as many players as they did for the national side that shone so brightly at the 1984 European Championships and in the World Cup that took place two years later.

Cantona's and Jacquet's paths would of course cross again, at Montpellier and in the national side, and we'll come to that in due course. It is not too early to say, however, that, contrary to what has been stated many times in speech and print, the two men had a great deal of respect for each other, and that their relationship was not as soured as some of Éric's 'friends' purported it to be after Jacquet left Cantona out of his Euro 96 squad. When Bez lost what little patience he had with his coach and sacked him, just before Tapie offloaded his rebel to the Girondins, Cantona was among the first to call Jacquet and offer him his sympathy.

That Bez and Tapie could 'do business' together was beyond the comprehension of most. The two men hated each other. To Bez, an old-fashioned bruiser who had made millions wheeling and dealing in property, Tapie represented the gravest threat to Bordeaux's domination of French club football. The league title of 1986 and French Cups of 1986 and 1987 had tasted particularly sweet to Bez, as they had been won by beating OM on each occasion. To celebrate one of these triumphs, he drove his Cadillac – bearing the '33' number plate of the Gironde *département* – up and down La Canebière, Marseilles' answer to Les Champs-Elysées, laughing his head off at the insults of bystanders. French football didn't want for characters in those days.

Bez doubled up as 'superintendent' of the national squad, a supervising position which carried few duties and practical responsibilities, but gave him influence at the highest level of the game. It had been created especially for him a few months previously, and he used it to facilitate Platini's elevation to the post of France's manager when Henri Michel's time finally was up, in November 1988. But he could sense that the grip he had on French football was loosening, despite the financial resources and the political leverage at his disposal. To hold on to his power (which also protected him from a number of investigations that would eventually precipitate his fall), he needed a strong, all-conquering Bordeaux, and what had he got? An admittedly superb collection of talents punching well below their weight. Shock therapy was required. Aimé Jacquet was replaced by the club's *directeur sportif* (and local boy) Didier Couécou, who had held his position since 1977, and enjoyed his chairman's absolute confidence.

The expression 'thick as thieves' might be used literally in their case. Gigantic holes would soon be discovered in Bordeaux's accounts, and, after a protracted court action, Couécou was finally sentenced in April 1999 to two years' imprisonment (eighteen months suspended) for his part in the embezzlement of Ff40m in a murky transfer operation. Bez had escaped punishment by dropping dead two months previously. If French football wasn't lacking in characters, it certainly didn't want for crooks either, which is well worth keeping in mind when assessing Cantona's condemnations of the 'milieu' at the time. Many thought him foolish then, or never forgave his breaking the prevalent rule of *omerta*: 'play, pick up your wages and shut up'. As Bez and Tapie still have their defenders in their old fiefs, it is worth repeating that Éric was right, and not just that: he also showed bravery of a kind that was all too rare then. In fact, no other active footballer dared to speak out as Cantona did. The 'chronic instability' that the English public would be reminded of constantly (four clubs in three seasons from 1988 to 1991, for goodness sake!) whenever he fell foul of authority at Leeds or Manchester United should also be seen in the light of the rejection he suffered from his employers when he denounced the compromises of French football. They would seize any opportunity he would give them to cut him down to size, none more so than Bernard Tapie, the very antithesis of the father figure Éric never ceased to look for.

But Cantona still had to do his job and, in February 1989, found himself under the aegis of a man he had worshipped as a child; for Couécou, whatever his faults may be, had been an abrasive but prolific forward for Marseille in the 1970–71 and 1971–72 seasons, in which OM had won the championship (he was also a member of the FC Nantes team which took the title in 1972–73, making it three titles in a row for himself). That he had won only one cap with *Les Bleus*, and that in 1967 against Luxembourg, was a mystery to the habitués of the Vélodrome, of which Éric's father Albert was one. As a manager, though, Couécou was at best unproven. One typical admission of his was: 'I have no tactics.'

He wouldn't last long – four months. Nobody would have in the mess that Bordeaux had created for themselves. The more Tapie needled Bez (which he did incessantly), the more erratic and vindictive the Bordeaux chairman's behaviour became. In the summer of 1986, OM had convinced Alain Giresse, a one-club man if ever there was one, to leave Bordeaux's Parc Lescure for the Vélodrome. No other player had exerted a more blessed influence on Bordeaux's game throughout the glory years of the Jacquet regime than he, and, at the age of thirty-four, the pint-sized playmaker could still dictate the play with his vision and the sublime range of his passing. Bez, however, recruited no less than three attacking midfielders of great promise, who would compete directly with the adored 'Gigi' for a place in the starting eleven: Jean-Marc Ferreri, Philippe Vercruysse and José Touré. Giresse, who had been at Bordeaux since 1970, was heartbroken, but felt he had to leave before he was pushed aside. One factor proved decisive. Michel Hidalgo, the national side's manager, had been named Marseille's sports director immediately after the 1986 World Cup. The international rejoined his mentor, sending Bez into an incontrollable fury; and when the 'traitor' came back to visit his former club, in March 1987, his name was replaced in the match programme with a question mark. Far worse, express orders were given from above to hack him from the first blow of the whistle. His man-marker, Gernot Rohr, was dismissed as early as the 22nd minute. Bez couldn't care less. He had made his point. He then decided to bring Giresse back into the family in the role of sporting director when Jacquet was fired – a position the player accepted. And Claude Bez was the man who would now sign Cantona's pay cheques. Éric had jumped from the frying-pan into a furnace.

Tapie's reasoning in setting a loan deal in motion made sense. If Cantona was the 'basket case' Bez had referred to, Marseille's boss could do worse than adding a rotten apple to his biggest rivals' already festering bushel. If – as OM's technical staff and his teammates believed – Éric only needed to cool down for a few months, a straight sale couldn't be envisaged: he was far too precious for that. But the manner in which an agreement was reached between the two clubs still defied belief. On the Monday, Éric had been brought back in Gili's group, and was supposed to play for Marseille against Laval at the weekend. On Tuesday night, Cantona was on a flight to Bordeaux, where he was welcomed by another 'child of Les Caillols', Jean Tigana. On Wednesday, he was training with Couécou's squad for the first time. On Saturday 18 February 1989, Cantona played his first game for the Girondins, a 2–3 defeat at Strasbourg.

During the warm-up, a few spectators shouted, '*Cantona, pourri* [scum]!' at him; all of them booed his name when it was announced on the tannoy; and some sang, 'Your shirt, Cantona!' They could abuse him as much as they wanted to: Bordeaux lost, but Éric was magnificent, in *France Football*'s report, the 'maestro at the heart of a team of stars': Jean-Marc Ferreri, Clive Allen and Yannick Stopyra were in the Girondins' line-up, the criminally underused Enzo Scifo on the bench, while a young Basque left-back still named Vincent Lizarazu, the future 'Bizente', world and European champion, crossed the ball that Éric volleyed for his side's first goal. The names of Jean Tigana and Jesper Olsen could be added to the list. What an almighty waste.

The three-and-a-half months Éric spent at Bordeaux, the 1,110 minutes of football he played there, the six goals he scored (twice as many as in his first season with Leeds) are not even alluded to in the autobiography he lent his name to in 1993. When you look at the list of 'past notable players' the club has posted on its website, his name is not deemed to be worth a mention. But Éric didn't sleepwalk to the end of the 1989–90 season. He missed training only once – on the morning he found his beloved dog Balrine dying of a seizure on his balcony. This was on 8 May, a bank holiday in France, and no vet could be found. But a distraught Éric was still at the afternoon session held at the luxurious Château du Haillan complex.

His teammates appreciated him, and would have liked him to stay beyond the end of the season. Clive Allen, whose excellent statistics during that campaign had a lot to do with the assists he got from Cantona, told reporters how Éric 'brings us his flair, his inspiration, the quality of his passing. He's already the conductor of our orchestra, and when we know each other better, he'll be an even greater asset for the club.' Couécou spoke of his recruit's 'huge influence on the team'. French fans had made their minds up, though. Cantona was there to be baited, regardless of his performance, giving weight to Michel Hidalgo's sombre prognosis that 'Éric Cantona's career in France [was] probably over', thanks to the same crowds who had been jumping out of their armchairs when, ten months earlier, Éric's two goals had taken the French *Espoirs* to a European final.

Proof of that disaffection was given on 25 February, when Bordeaux were eliminated from the French Cup by second division Beauvais. Cantona had been superb throughout the game, and could not be held responsible for the score being tied at 1–1 at the end of extra time. But he was one of two Bordeaux players to miss his penalty kick. He had tried a 'Panenka' with a cheeky chip down the middle but the Beauvais goalkeeper Eddy Caullery stood his ground and saved the shot. Cue boos, whistles, insults. Alain Giresse confessed his helplessness: 'He's blamed for everything and anything. He's an exutory. Maybe that's how people keep themselves warm?' Gigi left the journalists with these words: 'Why, we can talk about it as much as we want, it won't change a thing'.'

Cantona bore this admittedly well-paid walk to Calvary with commendable dignity and professionalism. He didn't demur when Couécou switched him from a centre-forward position to the role of playmaker, before changing his mind again. Bordeaux slowly, painfully, climbed up the table. By mid-April, they had reached ninth position in the *championnat*, after a splendid 4–1 victory over Metz, in which Éric was given a perfect 5 out of 5 by watching reporters. When his club faltered, as it did at Monaco (2–4) exactly a month later, on 12 May, he still shone, smothering the ball on his chest before hitting it on the turn with his right foot, bringing the score to 2–3, and being chosen as his side's best performer – 4 out of 5 this time. He cared. Few others did.

The bizarre circumstances of his move to Bordeaux meant that, on 20 May, the day the Girondins were beaten 3–2 at home by Caen (with Cantona scoring his team's first goal), Éric won the first major title of his career . . . as a Marseille player. It meant nothing to him. As he said later, 'I've never played at Marseille. Just the beginning of two seasons.' But he was still contracted to OM, and Tapie – who, entertaining a posse of journalists on the *Phocéa*, didn't mention Éric's name once when he talked about the forthcoming season – wouldn't let him go for less than FF19m. Very few French clubs could afford a sum that, taking football's peculiar rate of inflation into account, should be multiplied by ten to be compared to 2009 prices: close to £20m, a king's ransom, when Éric's throne would be built for a fraction of that in Manchester. One such wealthy club was the still-formidable Bordeaux, that was sucked ever deeper in a spiral of financial scandals, but clung on to its ambitions with the energy of a drowning man.

Bez had been impressed by Éric's professionalism and tried his luck, with the player's assent. Cantona had been in constant touch with his *Espoirs* teammate Stéphane Paille over a number of weeks, if not months, to discuss a future the two friends saw as a shared adventure. Both of them wanted a move away from their present club, for very different reasons: Éric wished to put as much distance as he could between the

Tapie regime and himself; Stéphane – the reigning French player of the year, no less – believed he had outgrown FC Sochaux-Montbéliard, even if the *Lionceaux* (the Lion Cubs) were on their way to achieve a very creditable fourth place in the championship. They were confident that, wearing the same jersey, they could rekindle the flame that had burnt so brightly under Marc Bourrier, and agreed that the Girondins could be that club. But Tapie wouldn't hear of it. It was one thing to get rid of a hot potato for a few months, quite another to enable his arch-enemy to field, game after game, and for heaven knows how many seasons, the striking partnership which had served the French under-21s so well and which most observers hoped would serve the seniors for years to come. Bordeaux conceded defeat.

This left Paris Saint-Germain as the only other potential suitor of the pair among the heavyweights of French football. Their urbane chairman, silver-haired Francis Borelli, who, as you will remember, had already wooed Éric in 1988, used his considerable charm to try to attract the two young men to the capital. PSG, the 1985–86 champions (under Gérard Houllier), still harboured the hope of another title at the time.* Paille and Cantona liked Borelli, and could see that his interest in them derived from a genuine appreciation of their talent, and not from a desire to cock a snook at Bernard Tapie. But the Parisian president failed to give them guarantees about the identity of the manager who would succeed the Yugoslav Tomislav Ivić, whose contract had come to an end. Was it because he had already chosen Henri Michel, and feared that Éric would turn his nose up at the idea of working for 'one of the most incompetent national team managers in world football'? In any case, Borelli's advances came to nothing. Another door had been slammed shut in the faces of the two friends. Nobody could have guessed which one would suddenly open wide to welcome them: Montpellier.

* PSG finished a mere three points behind OM in the end.

6

Two brothers: Stéphane Paille and Éric Cantona.

THE VAGABOND 2: MONTPELLIER

'I have this passion inside that I can't handle. It's like a fire inside which has to get out and which you let out. Sometimes it wants to get out and do harm. I do myself harm. It worries me when I do harm, especially to others. But I can't be what I am without these other things to my character.'

You could almost hear a collective gasp from the French footballing community when, on Sunday 28 May 1989, it was announced that Stéphane Paille and Éric Cantona had joined Montpellier-Hérault Sport Club, Stéphane on a three-year deal, Éric on a season-long loan from OM. Both the club and the players were felt to have taken a huge gamble. Despite its size – a quarter of a million inhabitants – Montpellier didn't have a record as a sporting town. Its old football team had only played a supporting role in the years following the Second World War, and its steady decline towards amateurism and near-oblivion had been viewed with indifference by the locals. It had regained professional status in 1978 under the colourful tutelage of Louis Nicollin, universally known as 'Loulou', who had assumed the chairmanship four years previously; but its team still struggled to fill the tiny, creaking Stade de la Mosson despite the club's promotion to the elite in May 1988. If one would have had to paint a picture of the Sport Club at the time, the arrival of the two celebrated internationals would have been the first brushstroke on a blank canvas.

There was still one more game to play in the *championnat* (in which Éric would shine, providing yet another assist for Clive Allen in a 1–1 draw at Auxerre), when Paille and Cantona had lunch with Nicollin and his sports director Michel Mézy on 22 May. Just as when Cantona was farmed out to Bordeaux, the operation was concluded with bewildering speed. A mere twenty-four hours later, all parties had finalized the small print of the contracts. Paille, in particular, had made a substantial sacrifice in order to play alongside his friend: Bayern Munich had sounded him out – but were not keen on Cantona. Fired up (blinded?) by the prospect of scoring for fun with Éric, Stéphane said 'no' to the German giants, and agreed to wages vastly inferior to what the Bavarian club (and quite a few others) was willing to offer him. As a player, he had reached the apex of his career at the age of twenty-four, and, tragically, didn't realize that he, the quick-witted, quick-footed matinee idol of French football, would be shot down in mid-flight as a result of following his instinct. Cantona himself saw his salary 'divided by two'. But, as he said, 'Some things are worth living for. You don't take your money to Heaven when you die.'

Nicollin was so besotted with his two young recruits – whose combined age was forty-seven – that he effectively gave them licence to run his sweet shop. Didier Fèvre was, again, a privileged witness to the surreal scenes which unfolded at the chairman's home. 'Stéphane was the originator of the move,' he told me, 'on the line of: "Either you take us both, or I'm not coming, as I have other proposals."' Didier boarded the plane with the two players and their agent Alain Migliaccio, who were then taken to Nicollin's house. 'Michel Mézy was there too,' he recalls. 'Éric and Stéphane recruited the team! Jacquet [now manager at Montpellier] didn't say a word, Mézy was just saying, "Yes, that guy's pretty good, yes, yes" . . . I'll always remember how Stéphane called Vincent Guérin – who was then at Brest – in front of Nicollin. "*Hé, Vincent, ça va*? We're in Montpellier, would you join us?" And Guérin did.' No wonder Nicollin called Paille a 'very determined young man'.

Since Cantona was still on OM's books, Tapie could have nipped Nicollin's quixotic plan in the bud; instead of which he did his utmost to encourage 'Loulou', reportedly telling him, 'Go for it!' when the Montpellier chairman showed his hand. For once, the OM boss was acting out of friendship – a little mutual back-scratching in accordance with his own idiosyncratic moral code. The French call this '*renvoyer l'ascenseur*': to send the lift back. The previous season, Nicollin had helped Tapie by giving him one of his players – midfielder Gérard Bernardet – on loan, for nothing. This was a chance for Nanard to thank Loulou, and he took it. Tapie always had had a soft spot anyway for the (much) larger-than-life Montpellier chairman, who described himself as 'a prick', drank like a fish, ate as if more than his life depended on it, and had an almost poetic way with language of the more robust kind.

For once, Tapie's and Cantona's wishes coincided. Montpellier agreed to pay the equivalent of £300,000 in compensation to OM, while Sochaux received four times that amount for Paille. For a club like Montpellier, this represented a massive investment, on top of the huge sums which had already been siphoned out of its coffers to recruit stars like 1984 Olympic gold medal winner Daniel Xuereb, Colombian *fantasista* Carlos Valderrama (the most famous hairdo in world football at the time), and, as a manager, none other than Aimé Jacquet, who, as we've seen, had been sacked by Bordeaux just before Éric joined Girondins.*

Nicollin wasn't coy about his ambitions for Montpellier. 'We'll finish in the top three,' he predicted at the end of June, somewhat rashly. 'With Jacquet, I thought we could build a good little "average" team, and then this crazy Tapie called me, and told me I should take Cantona and pair him with Paille. I was in Brides-les-Bains [*French papers cheekily*

---

* The Cantona and Paille transfers were financed – for the most part – by the City Council of Montpellier, then under the control of local Socialist panjandrum George Frèche, who topped up the FF10m grant the club received each year with another FF4m of taxpayers' money. The County Council of the Hérault *département* chipped in with an extra FF3m in exchange for a renaming of the club, previously known as Montpellier-La Paillade, and Nicollin himself plucked FF4m from his company's bank account (a company which specialized in the collection and recycling of domestic and industrial waste in the region and, yes, derived much of its income from the patronage of various institutional bodies). Such municipal involvement in French football was common at the time and entirely legitimate. It was a political gamble as much as anything else, not that Éric and Stéphane were aware of it.

reported on the number of kilos the famously rotund chairman was losing every week at the spa], I had nothing to think about except football, and, little by little, the idea made its way . . . I came back to Montpellier, talked to Michel [Mézy], to Jacquet. We didn't know then, but our mayor and MP, M. Frèche, was happy with this idea.' He then assured reporters: 'Both the boys have made an excellent impression on us from the very first time we met.' Everything was fine, then.

Loulou was not the only one to get carried away with his coup. As Stéphane Paille told me, 'The problem was that, immediately, it became the Paille and Cantona show. One month before the season started, every piece the papers printed about Montpellier was about us! That's why we decided we'd stop talking to the press. It was becoming detrimental to the group. There were many other wonderful players at Montpellier, who didn't get a mention. [Brazilian international] Júlio César was a fantastic defender, for example. We knew [the focus on us] would create frictions within the team.' It most certainly did.

In late June, however, the mood was one of wild optimism, understandably so. Éric shared it: 'I believe in this city, in this region and in this club. And I think that Montpellier is the best place to do great things. With Stéphane, there is a connection, sensations which we have in common. This goes back to the goal against England with the *Espoirs*, in London. What we felt then was really strong, and we promised ourselves to live it again as soon as the chance presented itself.'

The Montpellier squad had gathered in Aix-les-Bains, at the foot of the Alps, to prepare for the next season. No fewer than four of Marc Bourrier's heroes were there: Guérin, who hadn't wasted any time after the phone call mentioned above, Paille, Cantona (who, curiously, turned up for training sessions in a Tottenham shirt), and the supremely elegant Laurent Blanc, who could play in any position on the field with equal grace and efficiency. Wouldn't it be beautiful if these young men captured the country's imagination with their club as they had done with the *Espoirs*? French football, hobbling from scandal to scandal, desperately looked for some kind, any kind of redemption. The Paille–Cantona brotherhood provided journalists and supporters with a promise to focus on. Most of the hype was well meant, but both players were aware of the destabilizing effect it was having on the team as a whole, and attempted to deflect as much of the media attention as they could. 'I'd rather play *pétanque* [Provençal bowls] than answer your questions,' Éric retorted to a reporter who had been chasing him. Stéphane, who had roomed with his friend for the past two weeks, was more diplomatic in his answers. 'My role is not to "stabilize" [Cantona],' he said. 'I'm not his father. But I believe that it can only benefit everybody – him and me. For the moment, everything's OK.' On one of the rare occasions when Cantona agreed to talk to the press, his message conveyed a hint of the difficulties to come. '[Stéphane and I] don't think [our relationship] is incongruous, or surprising. What we find shocking is that people talk so much about it,' he said. 'We've all got friends. I have a friend in Marseilles who is a fishmonger. That doesn't mean he's going to play with me. [. . .] We get on well on the pitch, we get on well in life. That's all. Now, the ball is the priority.'

Still, the pressure increased. St Étienne were beaten 2–1 in a warm-up match. On 6 July Montpellier disposed of FC Porto in another friendly, in a Parc des Princes where Éric was barracked from the first minute to the last. Middle finger raised, he let the Parisian crowd know his feelings. The league championship had not started, but both Cantona's and Paille's unease was increasingly palpable. 'We're upset that people talk so much about us,' Stéphane said. 'We fear that it's going to ruin everything,' Éric added. 'I have travelled a bit; and I notice that when something works well, journalists aim to ruin it. Why should that be? Because you sell far fewer articles about trains when they arrive on time than when they come off the rails.' Cantona could feel what was in store for them. 'What I want people to understand is that we get on perfectly together. We have fun wearing the same kit, but we've got to stop talking about it. Because if people keep repeating the same thing, everybody's eyes will be on us, and it'll only take a mediocre game to be cut to pieces.' Such a game hadn't been played yet, but there was already a sense that nostalgia had proved stronger than common sense when the duo had listened to their hearts and chosen Montpellier. There could be, would be, no second 'miracle of Highbury'.

An ankle injury prevented Éric from featuring in Montpellier's first competitive match of the season, which his side won 4–1 against AS

Cannes on 22 July, thanks in part to a brace of goals by Laurent Blanc, whom Jacquet then thought of as a number 10. Cantona also missed the next game, which proved more of a harbinger of things to come, when his side surrendered 2–0 at Mulhouse. A blip, nothing more, was the verdict given at the time. For who could have guessed what a shambles the season of all hopes would turn into? The media, predictably, made much of Éric's comeback from injury, with headlines such as 'The Return of Hope' on the day he finally lined up alongside Paille on 1 August. Not for the last time, whoever wrote Éric's scripts showed a genuine feel for drama; for his opponents were none other than Bordeaux, the club which he and Stéphane had been so close to joining less than three months previously. Truth be told, Cantona had a superb game, but his teammates, Paille included, did not. Bordeaux left the Stade de la Mosson with a 2–1 victory, and when this scoreline was repeated in the following game, against a shockingly brutal PSG, Montpellier, everyone's outsiders for the title, found themselves last but one in the division. Éric had scored his first goal for the club that evening, but this didn't prevent those who wished him to fail from pointing the finger at the negative influence he and Paille allegedly exerted on Jacquet's team.

Their coach unwittingly gave ammunition to their critics by saying: 'Our idea was to create a group, a "club" with players who come from the area. Then we had the opportunity to get Paille and Cantona . . . Can you imagine me refusing Paille or Cantona? So we changed everything! We built the team around this duo. Their presence is a bit stress-inducing . . . but it is because of them in particular that [the team is] difficult to manage.'

Jacquet was right, especially as far as Paille was concerned. Stéphane's international career had taken off after Éric's scathing attack on Henri Michel had made the Marseille striker a pariah in *Les Bleus*' set-up. Paille had been selected seven times on the trot since, giving so-so performances that didn't make the watching public forget what (or rather who) they were missing. Michel's team had floundered dreadfully against Cyprus (1–1) in October of the previous year, a game in which the Sochaux forward had been conspicuous by his absence, and which triggered the replacement of the French manager by Michel Platini a few days later. The triple *Ballon d'Or* stuck with Paille, while saying quite openly that he couldn't wait to bring Cantona back into his line-up, a move that would effectively push Stéphane to the sidelines. As of 1 July 1989, the date when Éric's suspension would come to an end, the two spiritual brothers would be direct competitors for a place in the French team, as dropping Jean-Pierre Papin to the bench was highly unlikely. After the festival to which Cantona and JPP treated French supporters on 16 August, when they roasted Sweden 4–2 in Malmö, pairing Cantona and Paille became unthinkable.

France hadn't won away from home for five seasons, and the Swedes were no mugs. But Cantona, who had been fasting for well over a year – he hadn't played for his country since a 2–1 victory over Spain in March 1988 – seemed intent on delivering the most perfect ninety minutes of football he was capable of.

He characteristically said afterwards: 'I didn't miss the French team. I was following all its games, as a supporter. I was preparing for my return. That's it: I was getting used to my return [to the team]. I hadn't forgotten anything. I like *les gens rancuniers* [people who hold a grudge], it's a form of pride. I was thinking about the day when I'd come back.'

The game's last goal – Éric's second of the day – summed up his contribution to what was unanimously celebrated as the beginning of a new era. His astonishing flick, fully extended, wrong-footed one of the world's most experienced goalkeepers, Thomas Ravelli. Minutes earlier, one of his crosses, which Papin dispatched with his customary flamboyance, had prompted exclamations of 'Genius!' in the press box. Paille was watching this beautiful slaughter from the dugout. He didn't know it then, but not a single cap would be added to the eight he had won to date, partly because of his best friend's performances. Football can be a cruel game.

Paille, Blanc and Cantona flew back from Malmö in the private plane that Louis Nicollin had chartered for them. It was not a soft landing. Éric could revel in the praise that was bestowed on him. Platini gushed about the 'talent and the character' of the prodigal son. Henri Michel, who now assumed the function of National Technical Director of the French FA, nodded magnanimously in approval. The England manager Bobby Robson enthused about the 'awful lot of good' Cantona's return had done to *Les Bleus*. On the other hand, the glow Éric felt dissipated in a matter of precisely seventy-two hours. Montpellier travelled to Marseille, and fell 2–0 at the Vélodrome, leaving them with a haul of just four points after six games. The over-hyped fight for the title had turned into a struggle against relegation.

The manner of this defeat irked Cantona more than the result. Rightly or wrongly, he felt that some of his teammates hadn't been trying as hard as they should have done. He had seen Marseille's *modus operandi* from the inside, and would constantly allude to dark deeds in the years to come, to the point that he would describe Tapie as 'a demon' on the record. There is no evidence that Marseille bought their victory over Montpellier; but it was later established that they tried to buy one other league game, against minnows Valenciennes. The scandal erupted in May 1993 and led to OM being stripped of their championship title and relegated to the Second Division.* In any case, frustration was building up in Éric and would later turn to fury.

The seriousness of Montpellier's situation affected Paille's form far more than Cantona's. Both men were remarkable for their highly strung sensitivity, not the greatest of assets in the cauldron of professional football, which they dealt with in contrasting ways. Paille, the worldlier of the two when it came to business, didn't possess the more natural defence mechanisms which protected Cantona throughout his career. When Éric had to, he could overcome his shyness and deep-seated feelings of insecurity by harnessing his competitive instincts – what he described as his 'fear of losing' – whereas Paille's game suffered in proportion to the doubts others harboured about his abilities.

* '5m Francs were set aside each year to buy matches in the French League and the European Cup, that is 20m Francs from 1989 to 1993, including European games against Athens and Sofia.' This is a verbatim excerpt from the report submitted on 21 November 1995 by the prosecution service of Aix-en-Provence's Court of Appeal to the French National Assembly, in order to lift Tapie's parliamentary immunity. This document was leaked to French magazine *L'Express* in December of the same year. Even though they were raised in the courtroom, it should be stressed however that neither Tapie nor his clubs were prosecuted specifically for this alleged infringement.

Prompted by Éric, Jacquet's stellar but ill-balanced collection of individual talents finally found a common resolve for a few weeks. Lyon were beaten 2–0, Nantes held 1–1 at home, Toulouse vanquished 1–0 at the Stade de la Mosson, and Montpellier rose to eighth in the league. Cantona didn't score in those games, but could easily have been chosen as man of the match on each occasion, as he deserved to be when France all but blew its last chance of qualifying for the 1990 World Cup when conceding a 1–1 draw in Norway, at the beginning of September. Paille, meanwhile, was unrecognizable as the lightly built but elusive striker who had scored over a goal every three games for Sochaux between 1982 and 1989. But it would be grossly unfair to rest Montpellier's problems on his shoulders alone.

'I don't believe Montpellier had the structure or the management to deal with what was expected of us,' he told me. With some justification, Stéphane could identify his team's lack of equilibrium as one of the pivotal reasons for its failure. Laurent Blanc as a number 10, anyone? Éric's friend could see that Aimé Jacquet 'didn't fancy playing both of us [Paille and Cantona] together'. He could also see that the former Bordeaux manager – without malice – trusted another forward, Daniel Xuereb, more than he did a player who had taken responsibilities in the recruitment policy that aren't normally the prerogative of a twenty-four-year-old.

Little by little, Paille found himself pushed out of the picture, while Éric fought on like a man possessed. The golden age of the *Espoirs* was all but a forgotten dream, the hope to build a new Arcadia a hollow fancy. Montpellier briefly flashed in the pan with flattering victories (against Racing and Toulon), only to see every spark extinguished by disheartening defeats (Nice, Metz, Sochaux). Panic set in. There wasn't a plot to lose any more. Mézy was dispatched to South America to watch Carlos Valderrama in a Colombia–Israel friendly. The fuzzy-haired playmaker (whom Jacquet thought 'too slow') would be back by 3 November at the latest, two weeks after Montpellier had been beaten again, this time 1–0 by struggling Lille. Paille's display earned him 1 point (the lowest mark possible) in *France Football*'s report on the game, and the lid finally went off the pressure-cooker that was Montpellier's dressing-room. It was no surprise to find out that the explosion had been provoked by one Éric Cantona.

On Saturday 21 October, as the Montpellier players were trooping back to their dressing-room in the wake of their eighth defeat of their season, Jean-Claude Lemoult grumbled to Éric's old acquaintance Michel Der Zakarian (some sources say Gérard Bernardet): 'Can you believe it, they [Lille] only had one chance, and they put one goal past us! The problem is that we don't score ourselves.' Cantona misheard, or misunderstood, or simply gave way to his frustration. He sincerely believed that the diminutive midfielder (1.63m) had criticized his own strikers, the woefully out-of-form Paille and Éric himself, for not converting the opportunities they had. Four days earlier, an ugly argument between the 'stars' (Paille, Blanc, Júlio César, Guérin and Cantona) and the 'water-carriers' (Baills, Der Zakarian and Lucchesi) had already threatened to degenerate into fisticuffs. This time, Éric lost it. He hit Lemoult with his shoe, and threatened to punch his lights out. A scuffle erupted. Lemoult – rather bravely, given his size – defended himself. Once a semblance of order had been restored, Loulou Nicollin, clearly upset, addressed Éric in these terms: 'In my fifteen years as a chairman, this is the first time one of my players has hit a teammate. It's serious, it's unacceptable – you're fired.'

The next day – a Sunday – Nicollin was called at home by Tapie; someone (but who?) had informed the OM president of the fracas. All friendliness had gone from his voice. Marseille would not have Cantona back from loan under any circumstances . . . So, who spoke? A mole within the dressing-room? Cantona's entourage, out of spite? Or was it simply football's bush telegraph at work?

By Monday morning, Nicollin realized that the affair had become common knowledge, even if *L'Équipe* waited until Wednesday to publish the story. Surprising as it may seem, many journalists wished it to go away. A fight in a dressing-room? So what? There was one of those every weekend. Éric had been crucified before – couldn't we just forget about it this time? Cantona had enemies, but fewer than he thought. The club's supporters could not comprehend how Nicollin could cast away Montpellier's hardest-working, most effective player at the precise moment when his combativeness and his goals were most needed. The chairman's resolve wilted under pressure. He got in touch with Cantona and suggested they meet in the incongruous setting of Nicollin's company car park, where an uneasy agreement was reached.

On Thursday, journalists were told to arrive at the crack of dawn at the Stade de la Mosson, where the chairman of Montpellier would tell them which course of action the club had chosen to follow. Rumours were rife that a delegation of six unnamed players had demanded that Nicollin carry out his threat to dismiss Éric – even presenting him with a written petition – and that Cantona had only been saved from the chop when a counter-delegation, led by Laurent Blanc and Carlos Valderrama, issued threats of their own. Even leaving aside the fact that Valderrama had yet to come back from South America and would not play again for Montpellier until 25 November, this was a gross over-exaggeration of the storm that had engulfed Montpellier. The two days of embargo which had been observed by the press had only contributed to 'blowing the affair out of all proportion', as Paille, Kader Ferhaoui and Mézy all told me. The lack of reliable information only encouraged those who were, or wished to appear as if they were, 'in the know', to Chinese whisper allegations which everyone was inclined to believe and willing to disseminate. These would later be taken as gospel truth by British pressmen compiling catalogues of Éric's misdemeanours. 'Print the legend,' as the adage goes.

'Similar things happen everywhere,' Stéphane told me. 'In fact, there had been an almost identical incident in Montpellier the year before, and no one had said a word about it. But Éric was involved, and what happened afterwards was insane. I had to play the go-between, try and pacify everyone.'

Didier Fèvre too had to intervene. He received a call from Isabelle, who was (not for the last time) besieged in the Cantona family home, alone with the couple's newborn son Raphaël and a husband who didn't know what to do with himself. 'It's a mess,' she pleaded. 'Come over!' Didier obliged, with his paper's blessing: the photographs would be worth the trip. He expected something out of the ordinary, but not this. Every single French television station had dispatched a crew. Cohorts of reporters and cameramen were literally camping on the pavement of the only road that led to Éric's house, bored beyond words: there hadn't been a sign of life from the player for over forty-eight hours.

Didier bundled his way through the throng. 'Despite the results . . . and the stories,' he recalls with a smile, 'Éric was happy at Montpellier. We talked a lot, and devised a strategy to defend him. He was attacked everywhere.' Though this is not strictly true, as we've seen, there were still enough people after Éric to make him and his friend feel as if they would have to fight the whole wide world. Some of the most vicious gossip originated from the Montpellier area, where local politics and football were so closely entwined that the opprobrium lavished on Cantona couldn't fail to affect the city's Socialist mayor and *député*, George Frèche, who had so lavishly – and yet entirely legally – funded the player's loan from Marseille. 'The club simply couldn't afford the wages of the team,' Didier admits, 'and the huge amount of cash that had been spent couldn't be justified by its results.'

How to respond? Fèvre advised his friend to 'show them that you are at peace with yourself'. So Éric and Isabelle opened their door, emerged in the sunlight with Raphaël's perambulator, and had a stroll in their *quartier*, pretending not to notice the journalists who were pushing microphones under Cantona's nose. Éric couldn't resist a swipe at those who had called for his sacking. He hadn't talked to the press for four months now. 'What matters to me is playing,' he said, 'and if I must play in the street to do it, I will. It's not up to me to make the first step. It's not my fault if some players lack character.'

Another visitor would soon turn up at the Cantonas' home, presenting a letter in which Éric was informed he had been suspended by his club until 2 November. That is the decision Louis Nicollin wanted to tell the media at 8 a.m. on a weekday morning. A ten-day ban.

Interestingly, the general public's reaction to the whole affair was, this time, greatly in favour of Éric. Unlike David Beckham in another much-publicized incident, which English readers will be familiar with, Lemoult didn't need to have a few stitches sewn into his brow. Almost anyone who had played football had witnessed similar scenes in their own dressing-rooms, which would be joked about around a carafe of rosé a few hours later. The almighty fuss that had erupted revealed more about the faultlines within Montpellier than about any psychotic tendency on Cantona's part. The mediocrity of the club's performances grated with the players' pride: they knew, better than anybody else, how much had been expected from them at the beginning of the season. Jealousy played its part too. It was common knowledge that some of the foreign stars – Valderrama, Júlio César – were earning as much as twenty – twenty! – times more than teammates like Ferhaoui, who had helped Montpellier gain promotion in 1987 and was by then a respected captain of the Algerian national team. He got by on the salary of a train driver. Éric's violent quarrel with Lemoult crystallized tensions for which he could not be held wholly responsible. But then, that is another leitmotiv in Cantona's progress through his footballing life. Because he did act irresponsibly at times, and rarely showed a craving for forgiveness, it was easy and convenient to blame him for ills he was as much a victim of as anyone else.

Life without Cantona was short but eventful for Montpellier, who fought like cornered beasts against St Étienne, salvaging a 3–3 draw after being behind 0–1, 0–2 and 2–3. Could Éric's marginalization kick-start a new beginning in this rotten campaign? Aimé Jacquet issued a warning to the absent player: 'Either Cantona changes and comes back, or he stays the way he is, and it must be known that our life as a group will be different.' In other words: adapt or get out. Pronouncements such as this are invariably held as evidence that the future World Cup-winning coach 'had it in for' Éric. This, however, is a fallacy. Jacquet, understandably, was driven by his instinct for self-preservation: his grip on Montpellier had always been fragile and was becoming looser by the day. Mézy's Valderrama-checking mission in Colombia had rankled with him. It was a direct challenge to his authority, as was Nicollin's decision to bring Cantona back into the fold so rapidly. Jacquet respected Éric as a man and as a player, even if their personalities had markedly little in common. But his opinion hadn't been sought. He, too, felt pushed towards the periphery of the club.

Whether Jacquet liked it or not, on 5 November Cantona was playing with the reserves at Bastia, and three days later had regained his place in the first XI's starting line-up which played FC Brest. He scored in the 1–1 draw, with a superb half-volley. Well, he would, wouldn't he? Jacquet now expressed hope that it had all been for the best. 'I could have managed his absence as I am managing his return,' he said. 'I have a feeling that this story, in the end, is going to bring us back together. We thought that this incident was going to lead to the shattering of our team – and we see that, with a lot of goodwill from both sides [. . .] and, also, a good presentation of things by the chairman and Michel Mézy, it has given a new impetus to our squad.' The manager reminded his listeners that Éric had been 'one of the most satisfactory performers this season, especially at home', which was a very Jacquet-like way of saying he had been the best. The manager had much harsher words for the fast-disappearing Stéphane Paille, whom he hoped would soon show 'a truer image [of himself]', 'because,' he added, 'until now, it hasn't been fantabulous ['*mirobolant*']'.

Six days later, Paille was gone.

When Paille and I talked in 2008, he had just been sacked from his managerial post at Cannes, and it is possible that some of the sadness I felt in his voice then was related to the present rather than to what had happened almost twenty years ago. But did he still feel regret?

'Yes,' he replied, unequivocally. 'I left on a down note. I was angry with myself. With Éric, we believed [we could achieve something great], but Jacquet didn't. But it's all in the past. That's football.'

Probing that wound any further would have been like invading a very private grief, and I almost regretted asking the question in the first place. I knew what had happened afterwards. Paille left for Bordeaux, where Bez wanted him, but not the newly installed coach, Raymond Goethals, about whom much more later, as he was to wreck Éric's homecoming at Marseille just as he blocked his friend at the Girondins. Stéphane joined Porto, failed to settle, and spent the rest of his career freelancing for a number of clubs in France, Switzerland and Scotland, where he played his last competitive game in 1997, the year of Éric's retirement. But whereas Cantona left the game sporting yet another title with Manchester United, Paille finished fourth in the SPL with Heart of Midlothian. France never called him up again. And Éric?

'We never fell out with each other. We just drifted apart, as footballers do when they have to change clubs and, in both our cases, change countries. But we'll talk on the phone from time to time. And when we meet, it is as friends, always.' A failure it might have been, but not a betrayal.

Jacquet glumly admitted that Paille's absence 'made it easier to find a psychological balance within the group'. It also meant that the manager didn't have to choose between Cantona, Xuereb and Paille when he decided to play with two strikers. The arrival of William Ayache, who had been part-exchanged for Stéphane, stabilized Montpellier's defence somewhat, but the signs that the club would accomplish a stunning turnaround in the second half of the season took a while to become apparent. The only indication that something was stirring at La Mosson was the sustained quality of Éric's displays, as if Paille's departure had lifted him, and pushed him to claim the leader's role that the two friends could not play together. To his surprise, maybe, he found team-mates who were willing to let him show the way.

'At the beginning,' Kader Ferhaoui told me, 'Canto was a lone wolf, who kept himself to himself, and told others to fuck off when he felt he had to. But we learnt to tolerate and appreciate each other over time, and what we saw afterwards was *du grand, du très grand Cantona*.' Before Stéphane's departure, Éric had scored three goals in fifteen games; in the twenty-four which followed, he hit the target eleven times. His strike ratio more than doubled, from 0.2 to 0.46 goals per game. Statistics do not always lie.

Moreover, by mid-November, the faint flicker of hope that France had entertained of qualifying for Italia 90 was extinguished by Scotland (thrashed 3–0 by the French a month earlier, with Cantona on the scoresheet), who got their ticket for the *Mondiale* with a lacklustre draw versus Sweden. Until the end of the season, bar a handful of friendlies in which he invariably excelled,* Cantona would be able to focus exclusively on his club.

---

* One of these is worth a mention: a 2–1 victory over West Germany in February 1990, in which Éric scored the decisive goal. The *Mannschaft* would, of course, be crowned world champions in the summer. What could France have achieved, had Cantona not been suspended for over a year in 1988, when qualification was still within their grasp?

But the transformation of the fortunes of both club and player must, above all, be linked to the growing influence of Michel Mézy within Montpellier: 'the man,' Carlos Valderrama said, 'who made us play with more freedom, more joy'. It had been noticed that the 'general manager' had started turning up at every training session – wearing a tracksuit. It was inevitably inferred from that that Jacquet's position was threatened. Mézy didn't have Jacquet's pedigree as a coach, but he had overseen Montpellier's return to first division football in 1987, and collected 17 caps in little over three seasons in the early 1970s, until a managerial change at the top of the French team had deprived him of what many felt should have been a great deal more call-ups. Éric and he had felt an immediate affinity with each other, of a kind totally unique in Cantona's career. On to Oliver, Roux, Robert, Bourrier and, later, Ferguson, Éric projected his desire to find a father figure who could be admired – and trusted to defend him, whatever the circumstances. The easy-going, warm-hearted Mézy was, first and foremost, a friend. Had he been more than that, if I'm allowed to jump a year ahead in Éric's life, Cantona would never have left Nîmes in the manner he did. He would have feared rejection, whereas he expected understanding and support. The age difference between the two men, nearly eighteen years, didn't hamper the blossoming of their relationship, which must have puzzled Aimé Jacquet as it puzzled others. It was quite unusual for a boss (which Mézy was to Cantona) and his employee to hang out as the two men did. Neither of them saw anything odd or untoward in their complicity, and the bond they formed would be the foundation of Montpellier's resurgence and eventual triumph.

The worm hadn't turned yet, though, and a hamstrung Jacquet watched his infuriatingly inconsistent team drop to 18th place in the league after a 2–0 defeat at Bordeaux, on 2 December. Paille had played fifteen inconsequential minutes for his new side, whereas Cantona had been at the heart of anything of note that had been shown by the Montpelliérains, as he was again a week later when, this time, Sport Club prevailed 2–0 against PSG, in a half-empty Stade de la Mosson, Éric scoring one of the two winning goals. The traditional winter break couldn't come soon enough. The six weeks of hibernation French football had awarded itself that year would provide Nicollin with the time to sort out his shambolic club, which meant orchestrating Aimé Jacquet's exit and replacement.

Cantona, already the recipient of a meaningless championship winner's medal with Marseille, finished the calendar year by missing out (but only just) on another trophy: the *Prix Citron* [lemon prize], which was awarded by the press to the football figure who had been the most difficult, uncooperative and downright unpleasant to work with or, in Éric's case, without throughout the year. Bernard Tapie, always the favourite in that race, finished well ahead of him. The media had distinguished the duo who had provided them with more stories than anyone else, the difference between the two being that the OM chairman lived on publicity while his on-loan player had yet to learn how much he had to gain from it. England would teach him that.

Éric's holiday, which he spent in the USA, a country he had sometimes said he might settle in once he had retired from football, was a short one. Michel Platini asked him to join *Les Bleus* for a training break in Kuwait in mid-January, where a friendly had been arranged with the emirate's national side. He looked sharp in France's comfortable 1–0 victory, and did again three days later, on 24 January 1990, when he scored a double against the German Democratic Republic, who were brushed aside 3–0. Meanwhile, his Montpellier teammates had been recharging their batteries in the pleasant warmth of Algiers, and it was a transformed team which hosted Marseille when the league programme resumed on 4 February. The point they earned (the match finished 1–1) didn't flatter them, and not much could be read into the 1–0 defeat they suffered at Monaco shortly afterwards: the club was bracing itself for the departure of a manager on whom they had pinned unrealistic hopes.

The news broke on 13 February: as had been expected for several weeks, Jacquet and Montpellier had parted ways, without acrimony. The club's troubles had been caused by a casting error, not by the lack of quality of those involved, and Nicollin was generous enough to blame himself for Montpellier's disastrous first half of the season. But nobody could have predicted that the next four months would see an astonishing change in the Sport Club's fortunes that would take them to the first major trophy in their history.

It all started in low-key fashion. For once, Montpellier got lucky. Seven first division teams fell at the first hurdle in the Coupe de France, a competition that carries more prestige in my country than any other knockout cup in Europe, bar England and Scotland. Mézy's men scraped through thanks to a goal scored in the last minute of additional time by the unsung Kader Ferhaoui. As the opposition consisted of lowly Istres, few took notice. But when Montpellier started stringing together a fine series of results in the *championnat*, conceding just the one defeat in close to two months, French football woke up to the idea that the aggregate of stars Nicollin had assembled in a rugby town was, at last, shaping into a cohesive whole. The Lemoult incident? A catalyst, perhaps, rather than a catastrophe. Too many games had been lost to make the championship more than an exercise in survival, but there was still a cup to be won, and Montpellier showed their resolve by blowing away an admittedly poor Louhans-Cuiseaux side, 5–1, on 10 March, featuring Éric's only hat-trick for a French club at senior level. Cantona's personal festival consisted of a technically perfect chest control–volley sequence, a looping header, and a slalom through the opposite defence, concluded with a screamer in the top of the net. Mézy subbed him with one minute to go, and the Stade de la Mosson rose to applaud the Marseillais. Éric was enjoying himself all the more now that Mézy had brought back Valderrama in the picture; indeed, Ferhaoui pointed out that 'no one made Cantona catch fire like [the Colombian playmaker]'. France too benefited from Éric's purple patch. Two-and-a-half weeks after the French Cup tie, Hungary succumbed 3–1 in Budapest: two more goals for Cantona, who repeated the feat in the next game, for his club this time, a 2–0 success over Sochaux. Nantes were brushed aside in the last 16 of the Cup (2–0 again), Lille massacred 5–0 in the league on 14 April, all but guaranteeing Montpellier's safety, allowing Mézy and his men to concentrate on the Coupe de France.

The magnificence of what *La Paillade* achieved that year, the emotions that it stirred, have not been forgotten in Montpellier. If the English have a genius for spotting the mythical dimension of failure – provided it is heroic, of course – the French like nothing better than a triumph borne out of despair. In the space of ten months, Cantona's team brought an intoxicating cocktail of incompetence and inspiration to an ultimately successful resolution that one of Éric's closest confidants described to me as 'the encapsulation of his whole career, indeed, his whole life'. Montpellier – and this adds to the beauty of what they did – were by no means unbeatable; but every time questions were asked of their resilience, they won. On 2 May, Avignon, another lower-division side, fought like wild dogs at La Mosson before bowing out 1–0 in the Cup's quarter-final. On the 24th of the same month, Éric's 24th birthday, as it happens, St Étienne were beaten in the semis by the same margin, thanks to his 22nd goal of the season – quite a tally for a centre-forward who spent most of this campaign playing out of position.

That evening, as Michel Mézy told me, not without some emotion, the entire squad went to a local restaurant to celebrate their qualification for their club's first-ever final. Before coffee was served, Éric excused himself from the table. High on champagne and success, hardly anyone paid attention to his exit. 'But he hadn't gone to the bathroom,' Mézy said. 'He'd gone to pay for everybody else. That generosity, that's Éric.' This can't be a coincidence: each time those who loved him have tried to explain to me why they did, they always ended up evoking the same trait in his personality – his willingness to please, his delight in giving.

The final itself was a blur. Montpellier, playing without the suspended Valderrama, prevailed against Racing 2–1 in extra time, with all three goals scored between the 103rd and 109th minutes, with another of Ferhaoui's last-gasp efforts to settle the tie. Isabelle couldn't be there, so Didier Fèvre became Éric's 'wife' (his word) for a night nobody wished to end. Nicollin wined and dined everyone involved with the club on the Champs-Elysées. At 5 a.m., Didier snapped the last men standing: Loulou, Lolo (Blanc) and Canto, fighting to stand upright on the empty avenue. Please, let this moment last for ever. The party went on for three days: in Paris, back in Montpellier, in private, with the fans or in front of television cameras. Mézy: 'Canto made me cry. If, tomorrow, he is on the other side of the world and he has a problem, I'll go there. If he's sleeping in the street and knocks on my door, I'll open it. If there's nothing to eat, we'll share anyway.' What had he done that others hadn't? 'I listened to him. To know someone, you first must listen to that person. It's even easier with Éric: he's intelligent. By the end of the season, everyone loved him.'

The euphoria didn't last long. Within a few days, Mézy had left, to take care of the club he had always loved: Nîmes. Éric – who had known for a while that his friend was bound to go – would join him there him a year later, answering the call of friendship. But, for now, he was still a Marseille player. Bound by his contract, Cantona returned to OM, and to Bernard Tapie.

One man had particular reason to delight in Cantona's renaissance: Michel Platini. He had always stood by the renegade, one of the few men within the game's establishment to believe that a special talent like Cantona's warranted special treatment. More than that, as his then assistant Gérard Houllier told me, 'Michel adored Éric,' stressing the word 'adored' to make sure I understood that Platini's regard extended to the man as well as the player. The young French manager called Cantona 'a purist who looks for le beau geste *as a priority', adding a caveat which conveyed not frustration, but a deep desire to see Cantona fulfil his immense promise: 'the* beau geste *must be accompanied by efficiency. I think that Cantona doesn't use his physical qualities enough for a striker. And he has them! That said, he's improving steadily.'*

To Éric, the ideal manager should act as a surrogate father. Roux and Ferguson were avatars of Albert; Platini, the exception, of Jean-Marie Cantona. 'Michel acted towards me as . . . a big brother,' Éric said in 1991. 'If he gets the results he gets for the national team [France was in the middle of a record undefeated streak at the time], it is because he loves us, he loves the way we play, but, more than everything, he loves us for what we are.' The 'us' stood for 'me', of course. In the last few months of his stay at Montpellier, at ease with himself and his young family, at ease with his teammates, confident in his club's and national manager's ability to see beyond his occasional lapses into indiscipline, Éric could express another facet of his talent: his generosity. He revelled in the pleasure he was giving others.

Pleasure: what football was about, whether you were kicking a crumpled newspaper in your bedroom, juggling cans in the street, or having tens of thousands of people rise in unison when a backheel fell into the path of a teammate in full flow, with the unexpected delight of a perfectly placed 'wrong' note in a melody. Pleasure went hand in hand with simplicity and, together, conjured something like le bonheur, *a word I've always felt inadequate when translated into mere 'happiness', as* bonheur *conveys a sense of absoluteness (and physical joy) I can find no equivalent of in English. April, May, June, not a single defeat:* le bonheur. *Men playing like boys, egging each other on to greater things, remembering why they chose, or were chosen, to make others revive memories of their own youth. A trick of the imagination, a deceiving trap set by the inadequacies of age? Who cares? At the heart of every football supporter, and every football player, lies this conviction that, if only for a moment, a game can transport us all to Arcadia. Some will dismiss this as mere gesturing, baseless romanticism and, far worse, sentimentality. Éric strove to prove them wrong, and there lies his greatness. He could perceive the essential difference between a win and a conquest. He was given the talent to demonstrate it on a football pitch and he used it, out of personal necessity. The rest, the self-serving aggrandizement, the lapses into violence, the arrogance (not the insolence), came to the surface when he felt thwarted, and only then. 'Maybe, on the day I caressed a ball for the first time,' Éric said, 'the sun was shining, people were happy, and it made me feel like playing football. All my life, I'll try to capture that moment again.' That year, he did better than that: he caught the sun and offered it to others.*

7

With Raphaël in his pram, after the Lemoult incident.

THE VAGABOND 3: MARSEILLES, AGAIN, AND NÎMES

*'Tapie is a great manipulator. He's one of these people who really make me despair that any bond [*can exist*] between myself and a country I love: France. But it's not just him. All the politicians, all these people who make me hate a country that deserves to be adored.'*

Sunday 21 February 1993, Worsley. Éric was sitting in the lounge of the Novotel which had become his second home in Manchester, a bottle of lager and a bowl of nuts by his side. Facing him was the football-mad poet and essayist Bernard Morlino, who, a few days previously, had caught his attention at the end of a press conference by asking the most improbable of questions. 'Do you believe it is possible to succeed in the century of Buchenwald and Drancy?' It took some beating as an ice-breaker, it must be said. But it worked. 'We'll talk about it, next time, maybe,' Cantona answered. Morlino pushed his advantage further. 'You are the nightingale [singing] on the barbed wire . . .' Éric proposed to meet face to face with Morlino a week later. And when the time came for the two men to see each other again, it was Éric's turn to spring a surprise on his questioner.

'If I had four hours left to live,' he said, 'I'd jump on a plane and put a bullet in X—'s head.'

When Morlino recounted the anecdote in *Manchester Memories*, a book I've already mentioned and will mention again, he took the precaution of leaving out the name of Cantona's target. He had understood Éric's confession as a test of his own integrity. Could he keep a secret, or would he rather ruin a nascent relationship for the sake of a scoop – which Cantona could always deny? Perhaps – but only perhaps. In any case, when Morlino published the story, seven years later, he added a clue that made serious dents in X—'s anonymity. That individual 'used to write on the dressing-room's blackboard: "injection for everyone"'. No one denies that injections were routinely administered to Marseille players throughout the Tapie era. But of what? 'Vitamins', as was claimed by the medical staff? Or performance-boosting drugs? In Cantona's mind, obviously the latter. The belated 'revelations' of a footballer called Jean-Jacques Eydelie* gave credence to a point of view almost everyone within French football – players, managers (like Arsène Wenger), journalists and supporters – shared with Éric. Now, who at OM would have wielded enough power to impose injections on the players? Éric had three managers at the club. Gérard Gili? No. They may not have seen eye-to-eye on everything, but always spoke of each other with respect. Franz Beckenbauer? Most unlikely; the Kaiser appreciated Éric, who appreciated him in return. Raymond Goethals? The so-called Belgian Sorcerer's reputation could not be described as virginal, and, as we'll see, it was he who prevented Éric from playing in a European Cup final. But if Goethals is one of our two possibilities, the other is Bernard Tapie, whose control of everything related to OM verged on the absolute. Towards the end of his stay at Leeds, in the autumn of 1992, Cantona told Erik Bielderman

* Eydelie (whom Walsall followers may remember, as he briefly wore their club's colours in 1998) spoke to *L'Équipe Magazine* in January 2006, and later wrote a best-selling 'confession'(*Je ne joue plus* – I'm not playing anymore) in which the doping allegations (and numerous others) were reprised with a wealth of detail, including a full account of how, according to Eydelie, all OM players had to stand in line to receive an injection before the 1993 European Cup final, won 1-0 against AC Milan. Bernard Tapie strenuously denied the allegations, and immediately instigated a court action, which concluded that Eydelie's assertions could not be considered libellous. Tapie lost his appeal against the verdict in February 2008. Other doping allegations were also made in December 2003 by former Marseille player Tony Cascarino in his regular *Times* column, in which he also wrote that chairman Bernard Tapie 'made it clear my place in the team depended on me partaking'.

that it was a good idea to bring one's own orange juice to Marseille's training ground. A *France Football* reporter heard a similar story: 'At Marseille, it's better to come with your own cook, your own grub, your own drinks. But that's not all . . . it's better too if your chairman [Tapie] gives you a big bonus. That prevents you from taking money elsewhere . . .' Could he be clearer?

Yet when Tapie insisted that Cantona return to the Vélodrome for the start of the 1990–91 season, Éric complied without fuss. Another of my *France Football* colleagues, Laurent Moisset, caught up with him in mid-June, in the Pyrenees ski resort of Font-Romeu, where it was and is customary for the French national squad to gather for off-season physical conditioning. Cantona sounded thrilled at the prospect of rejoining 'the best club in France, the only one that corresponds to my ambitions'. It helped that since his forced errands to Bordeaux and Montpellier, OM had recruited a number of southern-born players who shared Éric's Mediterranean roots – and his passion for hunting: Bernard Casoni, freshly arrived from neighbouring Toulon; Bernard Pardo, who had just disembarked from Bordeaux; and the superbly gifted but mercurial 'keeper Pascal Olmeta, formerly with ill-fated Matra Racing, whom he had met with the *Espoirs* and who had been a friend for a number of years already. Olmeta, who hailed from Corsica, invited Éric to his native island on several occasions – which may be why Cantona is sometimes referred to as a Corsican himself.

The newly formed gang brought in another pure Marseillais, Éric DiMeco, to purchase a share in a large shooting syndicate in the Var *département*. 'It was true sport,' Pardo remembered, 'because Éric, purist as he is, refused to shoot game that had been "*lâché*" – that is, semi-tame, and freed from cages on the eve of the party.' ('I hunt for the beauty of the hunt,' Éric would say in his very first interview in England. 'I don't like killing for the sake of it. I kill only when there is beauty in it, otherwise it's butchery. Hunting, like painting, is an art.')

'On the opening day of the shooting season,' Pardo continued, '[Éric] arrived on a Harley-Davidson, with a gun slung over one shoulder. The old guys from the area thought they were hallucinating.'

*

The crowd at the Vélodrome was not as nonplussed as the 'old guys' of the Var had been, but the very sight of Cantona in an OM shirt was, in many ways, even more surprising. Many Marseillais thought they had seen the last of Éric as one of their own almost two years previously, on 17 December 1988, when he hadn't done much in a 2–0 victory over St Étienne. Only a few days before the season started – on 21 July – the talk in the bars around the Vieux-Port was of OM dispatching Cantona to AS Cannes on yet another loan. The rumours had no other basis than Tapie's close relationship with that club's chairman, Michel Moillot – and the *Phocéens*' refusal to believe that Éric and Nanard had agreed on a truce. But come the first day of the new campaign, Cantona lined up with his teammates on the pitch of the Vélodrome.

Was it the desire to finally prove himself in the city of his birth, the presence of like-minded friends, or simply the maturing of an exceptional talent? Cantona started the season in dazzling fashion. 'Who doesn't make mistakes?' he said. 'It happened to me, as it's happened to everyone. But I learnt my lesson, and I never make the same mistake twice.' And, for a while, it seemed as if a new player had, indeed, come back from Montpellier; a new man, too. 'I feel a desire to settle down somewhere,' Éric told Moisset. 'For good, and for a long time. Let's say I've had enough of packing my case every season.' So had Isabelle, who now had a child to look after and had tired of having to stuff the young family's possessions into cardboard boxes every six months or so.

Inspired by a splendid Cantona, Marseille opened the defence of their title with three consecutive victories: Nice were beaten 1–0, Metz vanquished 2–0 away from home, Caen edged 2–1 in a hard-fought game in which the team's eventual success was overshadowed by the Vélodrome's reaction to Éric's display. After he had scored the second of his two goals, both of them created by another future outcast of the Goethals regime, Dragan Stojković, a small section of the crowd started chanting his name. The whole arena soon joined in. A beaming Cantona shared his joy with the press afterwards. 'A game like this does a lot of good,' he said, 'especially now. I was happy to give pleasure to the crowd, I wanted to give them pleasure.' How could he explain this transformation? 'I find my place more easily in this team. It's good to feel the ball closer to you, to have a closer relationship with it . . . It's a bit like with women.'

Those who shared his life on the training ground spoke of a hard-working, dedicated professional with no airs and graces about him, and of their delight to see that, in Bernard Pardo's words, 'people realize that he's a man like any other, while remining a special player'. He had to be to earn a spot in Gili's starting eleven, given the richness of OM's attacking options at the time. The 'golden boot' Jean-Pierre Papin could be assured of his place as the leader of the strike force. The Ghanaian Abedi Pelé provided an explosive option on either flank, while Chris Waddle was reminding OM supporters (who nicknamed him 'Magic') of the great Roger Magnusson's gift for evading defenders at will. Philippe Vercruysse, the most naturally talented of a batch of 'new Platinis' who emerged in the late 1980s, vied for the role of *regista* with the newly arrived Stojković. Cantona's sparkling form, however, made him a fulcrum of the side, one of Gili's 'untouchables', together with Papin and Waddle.

The credit for this all too brief blossoming is universally, and wrongly, given to Franz Beckenbauer, who had left his position at the head of the German national team shortly after the *Mannschaft* had won their third World Cup in July. The Kaiser had joined the staff of Adidas (then owned by Tapie) almost immediately after celebrating victory in the *Mondiale*, and it seemed only a matter of time before his rather obscure role in that company led to an appointment at the helm of Marseille, despite the chairman's assurances to the contrary. But Gili, the 'dead man walking', remained in charge for two months, and it is with him and for him that Éric produced his best-ever spell at a French club, and almost convinced the fickle OM supporters that they had wronged the man who talked of them as 'brothers'. The statistics bear this out. Cantona played nine games for Gili, seven for Beckenbauer, scoring five goals for the unglamorous Frenchman, three for the impossibly debonair Bavarian. But, not for the last time, fiction would be accepted as truth, and Gili's faith in the player who had thrown his shirt at him that night in Sedan would be forgotten to make place for a more dramatic story: how one of the greatest defenders the world has ever seen formed an unlikely alliance with the 'bad boy' of French football and nearly rescued him, only to be torpedoed by the scheming of their powerful paymaster. That both of them were victims of Tapie's inconsistency, lack of nerve or impatience (all three descriptions are equally valid) cannot be denied. But luck, or the lack of it, played a far greater part in Éric's undeserved ostracism than is commonly admitted, and the prospect of playing for a legend of the game had little or no impact on the quality of his performances.

Up until 25 August (by which time OM led the league championship, ahead of Brest and Arsène Wenger's Monaco), when he missed a 1–1 draw at Nantes because of a slight injury, Cantona had played every single minute of every single game Marseille had been involved in. Nothing could stop him, not even the fires which ravaged the *garrigue* around Aubagne and Cassis towards the end of the month, and forced his family to be evacuated. Gili's day of reckoning was approaching with depressing predictability (Tapie now described Beckenbauer as his 'assistant'), but his squad held firm, and remained unbeaten. Lille were defeated 2–0, a scoreline repeated in the next league match, against Bordeaux, in which Papin scored the goals but Éric stole the show with an incredible shot from fully 50 yards, which rebounded off Joseph-Antoine Bell's crossbar – an even better version of the lob which he attempted in a later Chelsea–Manchester United FA Cup game, and which prompted BBC commentator John Motson to ask: 'Who needs Pelé?' In Marseilles, the question might well have been: 'Who needs Beckenbauer?' Three points (wins were worth two points then) now separated OM from their closest rivals, FC Brest.

Cantona's league campaign was interrupted by a trip to Iceland with the national side at the beginning of September, which is worth mentioning for two reasons. First, France made heavy weather of winning their first game of the Euro 1992 qualifying campaign 2–1 (Éric scored the decisive goal with a header from a corner kick). Second, with a quarter of an hour to play, Platini decided to protect *Les Bleus*' two-goal advantage and replaced Cantona with his old warhorse, defensive midfielder Luis Fernandez. Gérard Houllier witnessed what followed the substitution. 'Éric went to the dressing-room, seething with rage,' he told me. 'Michel [Platini] goes there too.

And we hear this almighty noise coming from below . . . White as a sheet, Michel comes back and tells me: "Gérard, I'll never, ever take him off the pitch again!"' True to his word, he never did.

While Éric was away on international duty, Beckenbauer was officially promoted to the rank of OM's technical director on 6 September. Still, the squad, the supporters (and many journalists) couldn't bring themselves to believe that Gili's tenure could be cut short when his team were playing with such spirit, verve and authority. PSG were the next visitors to fall at the Vélodrome (2–1), Cantona finding the target again. He celebrated the win by joining Olmeta and Pardo at dawn for a shooting trip in the Provençal hinterland, the three friends seemingly oblivious to the manoeuvring taking place in their chairman's office. Gili himself knew the writing was on the wall, though, and when his players brought back another success from Toulouse (2–0, on 14 September), he described it with a heavy heart as 'my last victory' to the media. That was not quite true: he survived long enough to see Marseille crush Dinamo Tirana 5–1 in the European Cup five days later, Éric finding the target for the seventh time since August. But within twenty-four hours, Gili's departure was confirmed in a club statement.

Beckenbauer inherited one of the strongest squads in Europe, a still united dressing-room, and a group of players at the top of their form. But Tapie had underestimated the extent to which Gili's death by a thousand cuts could affect the morale of the championship leaders. On the day the Kaiser first sat in the OM dugout, Cannes stunned the Vélodrome by inflicting a 1–0 defeat on the title-holders, their first of the 1990–91 season in any competition. Predictably enough, this was viewed as just retribution for the manner in which the club's previous coach had been ousted. But as so often in a situation of crisis – as he had done at Auxerre when their European aspirations were in danger, at Montpellier when his closest friend left him alone on the deck of a sinking ship, and as he would do time and again for Manchester United – Éric found new resources of willpower, and took it on himself to change the course of events. Chris Waddle is one of many to insist on the cordiality of Cantona's relationship with Beckenbauer. 'Cantona enjoyed training with him,' he told *L'Équipe Magazine* in 2007, 'and Beckenbauer was a big fan of his. We played Éric and JPP upfront, with me behind them or on the right-hand side and someone on the left. Beckenbauer liked him to get in the box a lot. He used him more as an English centre-forward, to get him to try and come in at the far post, to use his head and his height.'

The performance level of many Marseille players had suffered from the messy goings-on in the upper reaches of the club, but not Cantona's. After a fine display in a 3–1 victory at Monaco – one of OM's most dangerous rivals in the *championnat* – Éric played a stupendous game against St Étienne at the Vélodrome, adding two goals to his tally, which made him the fifth most efficient marksman in the league at the beginning of October. His new coach could not praise him enough: 'for me, Cantona–Papin is even better than Völler–Klinsmann, because they're a partnership that can better adapt to circumstances' – a partnership that shone again when France disposed of Czechoslovakia 2–1 in a Euro 92 qualifier in mid-October. Platini's France hadn't been beaten in nearly two years, and owed this record in large part to Éric's sustained excellence.

But three games later, disaster struck when Marseille played against Brest on the 28 October. OM needed to react after a 2–1 defeat at Sochaux and did so; in fact, they were cruising. Pascal Olmeta told me of an Éric who was then 'at the top of his game' and managed to put aside his disenchantment with the club when he had the ball at his feet. Cantona had opened the scoring with a header that afternoon, in front of a beaming Beckenbauer who was at last watching a performance worthy of his squad's reputation. But just before half-time, the Cameroonian midfielder Racine Kané launched himself in a wild tackle from behind which left Éric writhing with pain on the turf. He had torn the cruciate ligaments of his right knee. With Stojković, Vercruysse and Abedi Pelé already long-term absentees because of injury, OM had lost the last of its playmakers, and the glow of a 3–1 victory soon faded away. The wobble which had followed the German manager's appointment snowballed into a real crisis. Marseille fell 3–2 against Lech Poznań in the European Cup (a result they would cancel out in the return leg at the Vélodrome), then conceded a humiliating defeat to Nancy in the championship, which enabled Cantona's first club, Auxerre, to overtake them at the top of the league. But results only told part of a far bigger story.

Almost every day, it seems, France was waking up to the news of another football scandal. The Girondins of Bordeaux had been found to have a black hole of FF242m (£24m) in their accounts. The 'great treasurer of French football', Jean-Claude Darmon, was accused of having used phantom companies to siphon money out of both Toulon and Matra Racing. The ensuing investigation cleared him of any wrongdoing in the affair, but football's reputation within French society, which wasn't lofty to start with, sank a little bit deeper. Marseille hadn't yet been sucked into this quagmire of suspicion and financial irregularities, despite the rumours which surrounded the club; but this changed at the end of November, when a photocopy of Jean-Pierre Papin's contract was leaked to the press. It had long been suspected that OM used an undeclared slush fund to pay sweeteners of all kinds. Whilst the document which had just come to light – bearing the signatures of the player and of the club's then technical director Michel Hidalgo – did not provide conclusive proof of its existence, it nonetheless revealed serious irregularities in OM's accounting. JPP had been granted an interest-free loan of FF1m (about £100,000) in February 1988, 'to help him realize personal investments'. Compared to what Bez had done, of course, this was mere child's play. But everyone surmised that only the very tip of the iceberg had emerged. Previous OM bosses had unfortunately been susceptible to brokering 'arrangements' of that kind long before Tapie had taken control of the club: in 1972, Marseille's inspirational chairman Marcel Leclerc's downfall in a boardroom coup (dubbed 'The Night of the Long Knives') had been brought on by his use of OM's financial resources to prop up his media investments. In Cantona's eyes, though, the arrival of Tapie turned what the player called a 'culture of cheating' from an unsavoury trait of Marseille's character into a *modus operandi*, a superficial flaw into a full-blown disease which poisoned every nook and cranny of the club's management structure.

When I asked Olmeta how Cantona, who had been magnificent until his injury, could be first sidelined, then ostracized as he was in the second half of the season, he was quick to point out that football had little to do with it. 'Only three people dared tell Tapie what they thought of him,' he said. 'Éric, [Bernard] Pardo and myself. Éric told him he was an *enculé* [motherfucker] in front of the others. And that was that.' Cantona was disgusted by what he could see happening around him, and appalled by what he felt was the lack of courage of the great majority of his teammates, some of whom theatened to go on strike when their beloved chairman was threatened with disciplinary action after abusing a referee. The 'band of brothers' Éric had found at his return from Montpellier became a fractious dressing-room, and 'that's what really got to him', Olmeta recalled. 'Nobody had the balls to say *merde* to Tapie, and when you shit on Canto's head, he'll never forget it as long as you're alive.'

Another man had the 'balls' to stand his ground: Franz Beckenbauer, whom Cantona admired for his 'German rectitude' and his refusal to condone what Éric called 'southern dilettantism' – by barring hangers-on from the dressing-room, for example, which didn't go down too well with local journalists who had enjoyed 'access all areas' status for as long as anyone could remember. A World Cup-winning coach is unlikely to listen to the tactical advice of a failed pop singer, and when Tapie attempted to give a half-time pep talk to his players towards the end of the year, the Kaiser reminded his chairman who was in charge of the team. 'I'm the boss,' he said in front of an admiring Olmeta; but he wasn't for long. Many were of the opinion that Beckenbauer's fate was decided the minute he dared put Tapie in his place. In December 1990, speaking to the German press agency DPA, the manager had already admitted to 'differences of opinion between' his chairman and himself, and complained about 'the excessive outside influences on the players'. 'I'll meet Mr Tapie after Christmas,' he said. 'Either it'll all be over in five minutes, or we'll come to an arrangement.' A few weeks later, in January 1991, the arrangement had been found. The German World Cup winner was appointed 'director of the technical staff', a first step towards the door leading him out of Marseilles, and the team's future had been entrusted to a new coach, the third in a season that was just five months old: Raymond Goethals, whom Éric knew a lot about, as it was he who had made life a misery for Stéphane Paille at Bordeaux the previous year.

Goethals, the man who would effectively cut short Éric's career at Marseille, certainly didn't project the image of sophistication Beckenbauer was so keen for others to perceive. Garrulous, fond of outrageous metaphors, speaking with a thick accent that (depending on your outlook on what constitutes humour) accentuated your amusement or your embarrassment, the Belgian Sorcerer was a throwback to older, and not necessarily more innocent, times. He eked a decent career as a goalkeeper in the 1940s and 1950s for two of Brussels' lesser-known sides, Daring Club and Racing, before establishing himself as one of his country's most successful managers, guiding the national team to the 1970 World Cup finals and a superb third place in the 1972 European championships. Moving to Anderlecht, his three-year tenure there was highlighted by two European Cup Winners Cup finals, the second of which was emphatically won 4–0 against Austria Wien, in 1978. Having proved his worth, Goethals thought the time had come to be properly rewarded for it. He embarked on a peripatetic career that saw him look after Bordeaux (for one season only, in 1979–80) and, even more briefly, São Paulo, before taking over the venerable Standard Liège in 1981. He led them to another Cup Winners Cup final, narrowly losing 2–1 to Barcelona.

As a coach, Goethals had pedigree. He also had what police officers call 'previous'. He had to leave Liège in a hurry in 1984 when it was reported that the players of modest Thor Waterschei had been offered money to 'take it easy' in a league game played two years beforehand. Goethals was accused of having used his own captain, the fearsome Éric Gerets, as a go-between (at the time of writing, the same Gerets had just left his managerial post at Olympique de Marseille, of all clubs), and was banned from coaching in Belgium 'for life'. Goethals fled to Portugal, where Vitória Sport Clube Guimarães were happy to offer him a managerial position, which he kept for a year only, when the Belgian FA controversially pardoned Goethals and allowed him to go back to his native country. Amazingly, Standard were never stripped of their 1982–83 title. A couple of years with the tiny Brussels club Racing Jet, another two with, again, Anderlecht, and *Raymond-la-science* (a popular nickname in the underworld, which OM fans bestowed upon him almost instantly) was on his way again, to Bordeaux, at which point his eccentric trajectory joined that of Cantona.

This preamble is not gratuitous. If two men were ever born who were fated never to understand each other, it must have been Goethals and Cantona. 'The Belgian' (which is how Éric refers to him in his autobiography, where it doesn't come across as a complimentary or even informative epithet) changed clubs at the drop of a hat to serve his own, very material interests. Éric followed his instinct, with scant regard for the consequences. Goethals valued – *le mot juste* – victory so much that he was apparently prepared to buy it. Éric hated losing to such a degree that he would rather fail than admit that defeat was a possibility. The manager didn't rate the player ('he's not a modern striker'); the player despised the manager who put him on the bench. This, for Cantona, was the darkest hour.

The season had started well for him. Seven goals in twelve games. The Vélodrome chanting his name, at long last. Then Racine Kané launched into his tackle, ripping Éric's knee ligaments, Beckenbauer was gone, and by the time Cantona was fit again, Goethals had implemented a tactical system in which his striker's opportunities would be severely restricted. It would serve Marseille well, however, as two European Cup finals, one of them victorious, testify. Papin operated as a lone centre-forward, with Chris Waddle and Abedi Pelé jinking this way and that to attract defenders and create space for the dynamic striker. Both the Englishman and the Ghanaian were in magnificent form that season, providing JPP with chance after chance, which he gleefully buried. Did OM need Cantona? Not according to Goethals.

By the end of January 1991, Éric was ready to claim back a spot in the Marseillais starting eleven. In the 73rd minute of a routine demolition of FC Nantes (final score: 6–0), Goethals waved him on. On 1 February, he was given half an hour to jog around in a low-key 1–1 draw at Bordeaux. A week later, OM won 1–0 at PSG, without Cantona; he was back on the 23rd of the month (0–0 against Cannes); and was out again when OM beat Arsène Wenger's Monaco 1–0 on

1 March. To some footballers, the bench is purgatory. To Cantona it was hell itself.

Goethals was toying with Cantona, while Tapie contentedly smoked his cigar in the background. The other players found themselves in an impossible situation, 'between the hammer and the anvil', as the French expression goes. A full-scale rebellion was unlikely. Too many had too much to lose by siding openly with the outcast, even if, as Bernard Pardo insists, 'Éric was never ostracized from the squad by his fellow pros.' He added: 'Maybe, at the end of the day, it was for the better. If he hadn't imposed himself at OM, I am not so sure that he would have done so well in England.' It was a moot point at the time, to say the least. Goethals, for all his many flaws, knew how to organize the magnificent collection of talents put at his disposal. But it is hard to disagree with Olmeta when he says that 'with Éric, Marseille would have won the European Cup that year. To cut him out of the team was a lamentable thing to do . . . When I think of the final in Bari [*OM were held 0–0 by Red Star Belgrade and lost on penalties*], and what he could have done for us that day . . . lamentable is the word.'

What OM would miss was highlighted by the consistent quality of Cantona's performances for the French national team, of which he remained an essential cog. While Goethals was – at best – consigning him to the bench, Platini exploited Éric's versatility with great success, deploying him in a more withdrawn role in which he proved just as efficient as he had been as the spearhead of France's attack. Spain, the most dangerous of their opponents in the race for a qualifying spot at Euro 92, were dispatched 3–1 on 20 February, Cantona playing the full 90 minutes, as he did again six weeks later, when Albania were torn apart 5–0 at the Parc des Princes. France now headed their group with a perfect eight points out of eight. In the meantime, his Marseillais career had effectively been brought to an acrimonious end. The media had another 'Cantona affair' to report.

Incensed at being 'forgotten' for a crucial European Cup quarter-final against AC Milan, Cantona let Goethals know of his frustration and anger. He had demonstrated his fitness with *Les Bleus*, who now ranked among the very best teams on the Continent. What is more, his club manager was denying him the right to show that his partnership with Jean-Pierre Papin, so effective at international level, could benefit Marseille as well. But Goethals would have none of it. 'He refused to be on the bench,' he said. 'I don't care if he's on the bench or not . . . He doesn't care whether he's on the bench, so he won't play in Milan . . . I don't know how to use him against Milan. These are technical decisions. Full stop.' Goethals's disingenuity was plain for all to see. 'Technical decisions'? What technical decisions? Cantona was not just out of favour. He had to be humiliated, made to grovel. One week later, with a 1–1 draw in the bag, the Belgian manager carried on in the same vein. 'When a player comes to me and says: "I don't want to be on the bench, ever,"' he said, 'I can tell you, it's finished! Whoever you are, it's over!'

So Cantona was called to plead for forgiveness in front of the board; that is, Bernard Tapie and his yes-men. It must have cost him a great deal, but he complied, and asked to be 'put at the disposal of the group' again. Goethals threw him a couple of bones. A place in the starting line-up at St Étienne on 16 March, where Éric scored his side's only goal (1–1), and a walk-on part in a 0–0 draw versus Sochaux the following weekend. Then the carpet was whisked from under his feet one more time, and this time for good. Milan were beaten 1–0 at the Vélodrome in a farcical encounter: the stadium's floodlights failed in the 88th minute of the game, and the *rossoneri* refused to return to the field when power had been restored. UEFA awarded Marseille a 3–0 victory as a result. Cantona was nowhere to be seen. Neither was he when Strasbourg were crushed 4–1 in the French Cup. Or Dijon pushed aside 3–0 in the same competition, or Nancy atomized 6–2 on 12 April in the league.

The cruel crowd of the Vélodrome turned against the pariah. A few months previously, they had been singing 'Canto! Canto!' and now . . . 'They worshipped him,' Olmeta told me, 'but that's the nature of French supporters. In France, a player is a piece of meat. People chew them up and spit them out.' Crucially, Tapie had the local pressmen eating out of his hand. The champagne they were offered on the *Phocéa* went to their heads. There could only be one side to the Cantona story. In a nutshell: disgruntled player, successful manager, visionary chairman. There, you have it. Marseille won without Éric, Éric must be wrong.

The national dailies showed more understanding, which wasn't difficult. Cantona, who had kept a very low profile since he had been 'spat out' by his club, finally opened up in mid-April to *L'Équipe*. He needed to be trusted, he said, he wanted to be treated like a man first, a footballer second, he craved respect as a human being – and he was getting none of these things. 'I am sensitive,' he had said while at Montpellier. 'I need to feel warmth around me to be efficient in my job. I will not change.' He hadn't. He was not courting controversy, merely issuing a plea for understanding. For the first time in his life, he was losing heart, 'like a child who's been dreaming, and sees this dream taken away from him', as Olmeta put it to me.

Goethals ignored him. Marseille won surprisingly easily in Moscow, where Spartak were routed 3–0 in the semi-finals of the European Cup. Éric hadn't even been on the plane to the USSR, nor did he figure on the bench when the Soviet champions were beaten 1–0 in the return leg. OM were easing towards a third consecutive title in the *championnat*, and Tapie revelled in the plaudits he was receiving for his all-conquering team. French football, which had invented European competitions,* hungered for international recognition to such an extent that Tapie's shortcomings could be airbrushed in the name of expediency. PSG folded in the Cup (2–0 to Marseille), and Cantona's absence went unnoticed in the *Te Deum* which the media sang in near unison. Further Cup wins against Nantes and second division Rodez saw OM through to the final in June. A 1–0 victory over Auxerre ensured that the championship trophy stayed at the Vélodrome – then it was time to prepare for the coronation proper, in Europe this time. The crown was the 8-kilo silver trophy which the Spanish call *La Orejona* ('the big-eared cup'). Bari, at the top of Italy's boot heel, had been chosen as the venue to hold the final of the competition on 29 May, which would pit OM against rank outsiders Red Star Belgrade.

---

* Both the European Champion Clubs' Cup and the European Championship of Nations were born out of initiatives spearheaded by *L'Équipe*, *France Football* and the French FA, in 1955 and 1958 respectively.

Éric was invited to attend – but as a spectator only. Not unsurprisingly, he chose to remain at home, and watched a dreary game surrounded by his family. The Yugoslav side boasted a magnificently balanced midfield (the names roll off the tongue of any *connaisseur*: Jugović, Mihaijlović, Prosinečki, Savićević) and possessed in Darko Pančev one of the greatest strikers of his generation, but opted to channel this exceptional talent towards destroying Marseille's football rather than expressing their own. They rode their luck to reach a penalty shoot-out in which OM's world-renowned stars, deflated by their failure to engineer the expected triumph, would present Red Star with the trophy on a plate. This is precisely what they did that night, with arguably their most creative player 2,000 miles away, which is as close as he would ever get to lifting the 'Big Cup' in his entire career.

Ten days later, Marseille missed another appointment with what Tapie believed to be their destiny. Monaco prevailed 1–0 in the final game of the season, and it was Arsène Wenger, not Raymond Goethals, who left the Parc des Princes with the Coupe de France. I couldn't determine whether Éric watched the game or not. By then, he had retreated to Joseph and Lucienne's *cabanon* on the Côte Bleue, having added another title to his collection. He had played eighteen games in the championship, scoring eight goals along the way. Without him, OM wouldn't have had such a bright start to the season. Without him, there mightn't have been a medal around the neck of the teammates who said nothing when he was left to rot away for the best part of six months.

Cantona was kicked off the stage after the opening act, but had taken on one of the lead roles until then. His reluctance to associate himself with the successes of a man he despised, and despised perhaps more than any other he'd ever met, played into the hands of those who claim that he 'failed' at Marseille. His name has all but been erased from the club's history; that he himself wouldn't wish it to be different doesn't mean that his critics' verdict is fair.

'Me, I don't give a toss whether I'm playing for Marseille [or not],' he said in 2007. 'What I love is the game. There are people who want to win at any price, because their pleasure is not in the winning itself, but in showing off after the victory. My pleasure is in the moment.

I've never understood that some people could be proud of winning after having cheated.'

Cantona may have been many things, not all of them laudable. But a cheat? Never.

A departure from OM was now a certainty, with Lyon and PSG two possible destinations. But neither could satisfy Éric, who had been suffocating in the goldfish bowl of Marseille. He would go where he could breathe again, as far away from the noxious environment of football as possible, but without endangering his place in the national team, the only place he felt he could play the game as it ought to be played. Unsurprisingly, he chose to listen to his heart, and made a choice that was simultaneously logical and disastrous.

Upon leaving Montpellier, Michel Mézy had taken over the ailing club of his home town, Nîmes Olympique, which had spent the previous decade in the second division. Mézy, the *Crocodiles'* key player in their golden age – the early 1970s, when they twice took part in the UEFA Cup – proved an astute manager in his first season at the newly built Stade des Costières. The Nîmois finished the 1990–91 campaign as champions of division 2A, which gave them promotion back to the elite. Mézy had achieved this success with largely home-grown talent, but knew he needed reinforcements if Nîmes were to retain their status, and naturally turned to some of the players he had won the French Cup with when at Montpellier. Éric was the first name on his list. Once he had secured him, Mézy contacted William Ayache and Jean-Claude Lemoult, who accepted his offer, while another Marseille outcast, Philippe Vercruysse, followed Cantona to the ancient Roman city.

Nîmes clearly had no chance to challenge for major honours, but honours were not paramount in Éric's mind at the time. He had just won a bauble that meant nothing to him. He craved fresh air, he longed for football played without compromise, and Nîmes could provide him with both. Moreover, it held other significant attractions. As Didier Fèvre put it to me, 'Canto liked the louche appeal of that place.' Nestled between the Mediterranean Sea and the hills of the Cévennes, this medium-sized town punched well above its weight, not least because of the efforts of its charismatic mayor (a role which, in France, combines the power of a council leader and the prestige of a lord mayor) and MP, Jean Bousquet, the owner of the Cacharel fashion house, with whom Éric felt an immediate affinity. Nîmes' past could be felt at every corner of its stark, sun-drenched streets. The Tour Magne, the Maison Carrée, the Temple of Diana – no other French city boasted such an astonishingly well-preserved architectural heritage from the time of the Caesars. The jewel in that crown was the Arênes de Nîmes, built in the first century AD, in which aficionados gathered in their thousands to watch the *ferias*, the corridas on horseback of which Cantona was a devoted follower.* Bousquet had also invested considerable funds into a number of cultural initiatives, which had made Nîmes a leading centre of the contemporary arts scene in the south of France. Cantona could tick all the boxes on his wishlist.

Relating to the Nîmois was easy for Éric; like him, they were both exuberant and reserved, their natural warmth still checked by the rigours of Calvinism. In fact, when the football club had been created in 1901 under the name of Sporting Club Nîmois, its founder, Henri Monnier, had specified that only Protestants could wear its colours; the adoption of professionalism in the mid-1930s had caused much hand-wringing among the traditionalists, who feared the club might lose its God-fearing identity (which it did, but without altering many idiosyncrasies which can be felt to this day). Cantona sought to consummate his divorce from everything Marseille now represented for him; Nîmes, with its sparse crowds, humble ambitions and kind-hearted manager, could never compete with OM on equal terms, but this suited Éric to the hilt.

Goethals had mocked him; Tapie had suggested he should be sent to a psychiatric hospital. Mézy said: 'As a man, Éric has never disappointed me . . . as a player, he hasn't got the right to! But I'll always be here to support him.' Convincing Cantona to join the club had been easy. 'Maybe it is because he identifies himself so strongly with

* Éric's love of tauromachy inspired a series of photographs, which he exhibited in Marseilles in October 2008.

Nîmes,' Mézy explained, 'which is a passionate city, with passionate people.' He would give Éric 'the means to express himself fully and freely; he will have more responsabilities within the team than he's ever had before and will have to be an example to follow for our youngsters.' This was said without the least trace of irony – which is precisely how Cantona wanted it to be.

Money was a problem, as Éric wouldn't come cheap. Tapie asked for FF10m; fortunately, the club's chairman and the mayor of the city were one and the same person, Jean Bousquet, who released public funds to finance the acquisition of the player (again, entirely legitimate at the time). This arrangement did no favours to Cantona, whose purchase quickly became a political hot potato. The flamboyant Bousquet didn't want for enemies, who seized upon this opportunity to ask their electorate whether it was sensible to pay a fortune for a footballer when cash was needed to improve the city's sewage system. Should success prove elusive, Éric would be the first to feel the backlash.

Despite the controversy, the deal went through, and on 27 July Nîmes's new skipper made his debut at home, having missed the season's first game because of a slight knee injury. *Les Crocodiles* had drawn at Sochaux (1–1), and drew again – 2–2 against Toulouse – in front of little more than 10,000 paying spectators. Michel Platini had taken a seat in the stands, and left the ground a reassured man. Éric had coolly dispatched a penalty, looked fit and sharp, and pronounced himself 'fully satisfied' with his young team. He wouldn't be 'satisfied' for long. Two defeats and two 0–0 draws followed, in which Nîmes had created hardly any chances, and failed to score on each occasion. When they finally did, it was in a 4–2 drubbing by OM, of all clubs, a match Cantona missed because of a thigh injury which kept him out of competitive football for almost a month, from 17 August to mid-September. Nîmes now occupied 19th place (out of 20) in *le championnat*, which many believed was their rightful position.

Platini never lost faith in Cantona throughout this dreadful summer, and invited him to join the national squad for a crucial European qualifier against Czechoslovakia on 4 September, which France won 2–1 in some style, thanks to a magnificent brace by Papin. Platini's gesture touched Cantona a great deal. 'An international player is also a man,' he said, 'and, psychologically, it's comforting to know you haven't been forgotten, especially when you're not playing.'

Nîmes finally woke up in the eighth league game of the season. Cannes, for whom a certain Zinédine Zidane – then 19 years of age – was playing, were beaten 2–1. Still Cantona-less, Mézy's players fought out a precious 3–2 victory in Nancy. Fine results both, but not the kind that would stop tongues wagging in the provincial town. Nîmes, it seemed, were doing better without their star player – the striker who didn't strike, and who failed to do so again on his return when Le Havre were added to their victims (1–0) on 14 September.

When his team went through a purple patch of sorts in the autumn, remaining undefeated until late October, few attributed the club's newfound confidence to the influence of its skipper. In fact, Éric applied himself to the task of captaining a group of unproven youngsters with great diligence, despite his reluctance to take on the mantle of leader, for rousing speeches meant little to him. You only used your voice when you had failed to share information and feelings in a different, more profound way – instinctively, by exchanging a look, or by passing a ball.

Listen to Cantona speak. His delivery is halting, almost stuttering, in French as in English. He'll stop mid-sentence, swallow, pause again – unless he's acting, of course. What will eventually come out will read wonderfully off the page, but were you to transcribe faithfully what he said, the punctuation mark you'd use most often would be '. . .', as if verbal expression were an obstacle to communication. I'm wondering: for him, are poets the blessed few who have managed to go 'beyond words', something he was incapable of? Can it be what he admires so in them?

Cantona didn't lead by giving orders, but by example. He ran, and ran, and ran. He 'drenched the jersey', as the French say. This most selfless of egotists genuinely couldn't care less if another player came up with the goals. ('If I have a 49 per cent chance of scoring, against my teammate's 51 per cent, I'll pass the ball to him. That's normal.') Nîmes climbed up the table, at one stage coming within seven points of leaders Marseille, when Éric's penalty (his second and last goal for *Les Crocodiles*, for whom he never scored from open play) gave them a 1–0 win over Lille on 19 October. Michel Mézy had by now taken over from Bousquet as chairman of the Olympique, and France had won 2–1 in Spain (with Éric) and guaranteed *Les Bleus'* presence at the forthcoming European Championship of Nations, with seven wins in seven games in the qualification phase.

Apart from a fiery exchange of words with Robert Nouzaret, the general manager of Montpellier to whom he had 'jokingly' offered his captain's armband in a heated scoreless derby on 4 October, there had been little controversy on or off the pitch. Nîmes appeared to have welcomed him as one of their own. A couple of weeks after the draw at La Mosson, he attended the inauguration of a new playing field in a so-called 'difficult' neighbourhood of his adopted city, staying far longer than planned to please the autograph-hunters. 'There are places where you feel good,' he told a *France Football* reporter. 'Teams, players which enable you to express yourself. Fully and freely. Because when you give the ball, you know for sure that it'll come back where you expect it. Because runs actually serve a purpose. Because no one plays for himself. That's what football is for me, the best football.'

Too often, though, despite what Éric said, the ball didn't come back where he expected it. His devotion to Nîmes couldn't hide the plain fact that he, a player of the highest calibre, was surrounded with what was at best a half-decent squad of middling-to-average pros, untested youth team players and rejects whose skill and ambition could never match his. As happens with teams in which one individual clearly towers above the others in terms of ability, the excellence of a single player can push recipients of more moderate gifts beyond what is expected of them – but only for so long. Think of Maradona at Napoli, for example. The flipside of such a 'miracle' is that a single loss can be enough to precipitate a catastrophic series of results, as the ordinary mortals realize that their engine has been overheating. The wheels come off, seemingly all at once. Nîmes experienced this brutal awakening on the occasion of a not unexpected 2–0 defeat at PSG, on 26 October. Every manager at every level knows that it is only when you're bad that you find out how good you really are. To judge by what followed, Nîmes were decidedly poor.

First, Rennes ran out 2–1 winners at the Stade des Costières. Then Toulon blitzed the toothless *Crocodiles* 5–0. Caen inflicted on them their second home defeat in a row (0–1). Metz joined in the slaughter with a 4–0 win that didn't flatter the hosts. Fourteen goals conceded in five games, one scored and no points: Nîmes were heading for the drop at this rate. It mattered not one jot that Cantona showed exceptional form when playing for his country; it merely substantiated the sceptics' view that having Éric in your side was like having two coins in your pocket. When Platini flipped one of them, it landed on heads every time, whereas Mézy could only spin a dud.

On 20 November France established a new record in the history of the European Championship of Nations by winning their eighth and final qualifying match (their nineteenth undefeated game in a row – another record), to finish their campaign with sixteen points out of sixteen. In the absence of the suspended Papin, Éric had dazzled against Iceland in Reykjavík, revelling in the role of centre-forward in an ultra-attacking 4-2-4 formation. Two goals – one header from six yards, and a short-range shot following a superb one-two with PSG winger Amara Simba – rewarded one of his most devastating displays for the national team. A radiant Platini told the press how Éric 'sees things more quickly than the others, *understands* them more quickly . . . He's a very intelligent guy.' This was some praise, coming as it did from a supreme master of the game's geometry, Juve's greatest-ever number 10. Cantona found it almost overwhelming. 'This is the most beautiful compliment you can pay to a football player,' he said. 'The beautiful game recognized by someone who knows what he's talking about . . . It gives me incredible pleasure. These few words are more important than thousands of critical comments.'

They also came at a time when Éric needed them the most. While on a short break in the walled city of Carcassone, he had just learnt that his adored grandfather Joseph had passed away. It was a bitter sea that lapped on the Côte Bleue from then onwards. One by one, the threads that bound him to his Arcadian youth were cut away from him. As he told his biographer Pierre-Louis Basse, 'I should never have left the world of children.' Cantona's neverland is inhabited by many.

*

Éric, who had hidden his grief from all except those closest to him, still had to explain why he showed two faces to the world. 'At Nîmes,' he said, 'it's a different problem. It's a team of youngsters who have great qualities, but who are still finding their way in the first division. With the national team, we didn't reach that level in one day. We needed time. It'll be the same with Nîmes.' Time? But who was willing to give him time? It was so much easier to shoot him down. How did he feel about that? 'Criticisms hurt,' he admitted. 'But nobody has succeeded or will succeed in killing me. Nobody.'

Then, during an otherwise uneventful, scrappy 1–1 home draw with St Étienne, on 7 December, Cantona committed suicide on national television. 'He was fouled,' recalled Henri Émile. 'No free kick was given. He turned towards the referee and complained. The referee gave him a lecture. The game went on. Soon afterwards, he was fouled again. Still no free kick [*in Émile's view, because of the argument he had just had with the official*]. He took the ball, threw it at the ref, and went to the dressing-room without even looking back.'

The referee, one M. Blouet, was made to look rather ridiculous as he brandished a red card at the departing player, standing straight-backed in his black shorts. Éric confided to a journalist: 'It's me, so, people will talk about it for two or three days. Then things will calm down. Time should be given the time to work . . .' How misguided he was. Time was precisely what no one in the game's establishment was willing to give him. Cantona was hauled in front of the FA's disciplinary committee. He apologized for his action, and requested to be treated like any other player, expecting the customary two-game ban which punished any misdemeanour of this kind. But the response of the panel chairman Jacques Riolacci cut him to the quick. The apparatchik handed out a four-match suspension, adding, unforgivably: 'You can't be judged like any other player. Behind you is a trail which smells of sulphur. Anything can be expected from an individualist like you.'

Riolacci, who had been in place since 1969 and, at the time of writing, still held the post of chief prosecutor at the Ligue de Football Professionnel, was startled by Cantona's reaction to his comments. Éric walked up to every member of the commission and repeated the same word: '*Idiot!*' and left the room. The original punishment was extended to two months. That would teach him. Riolacci felt compelled to tell Agence France-Presse: 'This is a striking summing-up of the character of a boy who has chosen to marginalize himself, and whom no one can channel.'

Reprehensible as Cantona's behaviour had been, nothing could justify the harshness of the verdict and, especially, the condescending tone of the judge's statement. If Éric wanted proof that he'd been tried for being Cantona, and not for what he'd done, he had it. They couldn't quite push him off the cliff. So he jumped, and announced his retirement from football. Éric Cantona died for the first time on 12 December 1991.

'To move away, to change clubs and horizons wasn't something that worried me. I loved it,' he said shortly after his second coming to Marseille. He may well have felt that way. But I was struck by one of Éric's assertions that, when looked at more closely, made no real sense – certainly not when he talked to Laurent Moisset in 1990. Éric kept referring to his urge for constant change. 'I need to feel good in a club,' he said. 'With everyone. To have clear, untwisted relationships. Maybe that's why my adventures have been short-lived in some clubs. When you arrive, when you're at the stage of discovery, you tell yourself, "Everything is going to be just fine." Everything's beautiful. As time goes by, sometimes, you realize it's the other way round. It's better to leave.' True, at the age of 24, Cantona had played for five professional clubs already, and would join a sixth (Nîmes) a year hence. Howard Wilkinson would often refer to Cantona's nomadism to support his claim that Éric's departure from Leeds fitted a pattern of chronic instability rooted in the player's character, not caused by the circumstances he found himself in. In 2009 this shuffling of clubs would not be deemed exceptional, especially as three of Éric's moves were loans, not straight transfers. But nineteen years ago, when many footballers wore the same jersey for over a decade, Éric's zig-zagging trajectory jarred with the commonly held view that a player ought to 'bed himself in' to succeed.

Wilkinson's view (not so much an opinion as a consensus within football) superficially held water – until one realized that, contrary to his legend, Cantona had only instigated one *of his moves, when he felt, not unreasonably, that Auxerre had become too small for him, and decided to join OM. As he said a few months after returning to the city of his birth in 1988, 'I'd rather try to be good with the strong than bad with the weak.' But his other clubs? Roux and Herbet had plotted his stay at Martigues. Tapie had sent him to Bordeaux, and didn't want him back when the loan expired, which had enabled Éric to attempt the impossible with Stéphane Paille at Montpellier. And Cantona only sought to leave Marseille for good once his ostracism by Raymond Goethals had effectively erased his name from the club's books. Was Éric deluding himself, or – which makes more sense to me – was he claiming a kind of freedom he aspired to, but which the football world couldn't grant him?*

How tempting it was to portray himself as a bird going from branch to branch on a whim, a butterfly tasting flower after flower, and how convenient it was for others to take this claim at face value, when the truth was that Cantona's masters had disposed of him as a 'piece of merchandise', as he admitted to Moisset, but 'a piece of merchandise who is asked what his opinion is'.

Éric was a vagabond, at least by the standards of his time, but a vagabond who had been shown the door. Sometimes, as in Martigues and Montpellier, this suited his own aspirations, and he could convince himself that he alone had written these new chapters in his story. During his time at the Bataillon de Joinville, his colonel had sent Cantona to load bags of potatoes a long way away from the barracks in order to avoid a conflagration. Éric had won. But at Marseille, he dangled from a string in Tapie's puppet show. He referred to Tapie as 'a manipulator'. Is it any wonder that he despised him so?

This is another leitmotiv in the Cantona canon: Éric's peaks always coincided with the presence of a father figure at his side, a benign authority, but an authority nonetheless. Auxerre teammates like Prunier, Dutruel and Mazzolini used to tease him by exclaiming: 'You are Roux's son!' Yet he professed to hate any kind of regimentation. Following one's impulses sounded more poetic than following somebody else's orders. Think of what Rimbaud might have said to Tapie. But a poet only needs pen and paper to be a poet, whereas a footballer needs a club to become the artist of Éric's dreams. Players exist only in the present, even now that 'immortal' avatars of their selves are preserved through digitization, like figures in a stained-glass window. Despite what Éric repeated time and again, he couldn't be satisfied with going back to the street and juggling balls made of rags in the dust. To be a rebel, Cantona had to sign a contract first. To reclaim the joy which filled him in his youth, he had to accept the obligations of a pro. At times, he must have felt as if he were kicking the ball in the courtyard of a prison. Erik Bielderman's words keep coming back to me: 'Cantona sees everything in black and white, but no one is greyer than him.'

True, Éric always wanted to 'play'. And when you play, you don't cheat. Cheating is for those who pursue an ulterior motive, be it financial reward or power. But Éric's pursuit of purity was hampered by his excelling in a sport where transfers (aren't prisoners 'transferred' from jail to jail?) were handed out like sentences in court, and where calculation, in the form of tactical organization, is crucial to success on the field. Who does he consider to be the greatest player ever? Diego Maradona, of course, the only footballer who authored the triumphs of his teams, with Napoli and Argentina, and earned the right to sign his name in a corner of their masterpieces. Which team does he place above any other? The Netherlands led by Johann Cruyff in the first half of the 1970s, famous for their 'total football', which, at its most beguiling, looked like collective improvisation. Magnificent aberrations both.

Éric never reached their heights, but could at least cloak himself in the garb of a traveller, the wandering footballer whom nothing or nobody could tie down. He never did anything to discourage the myth-makers; in fact, he helped them write the legend. I'm the one who walks away, he told them, the hobo who answers the call of the road. As these confessions (or delusions) gave credence to the story journalists wanted to write, and their audiences to read, they were added to an almighty mess of half-truths and plain fabrications. The king's palace sometimes looked like a junk shop.

Then again, football can also be a redeemer. I'm thinking of Marco Tardelli running back to the halfway line after scoring Italy's last goal in the 1982 World Cup final, possibly the most exhilarating celebration ever seen on such a stage. What was the man-child screaming, as his whole body shook with the realization of what he had just done? 'Tar-del-li!' That's what – just like every schoolboy who has shouted his own name after imagining he had scored a World Cup-winning goal. I hope I can be forgiven this truism: in the chest of every sportsman beats the heart of a child. Cantona's pulsed more quickly than most and that heart, at least, was never tamed.

8

Éric salutes the Parisian crowd.

DECEMBER 1991: THE FIRST SUICIDE ATTEMPT

'It was over – but I wouldn't have died. I had the privilege to be a witness to my own funeral. That's everyone's dream: to know what will be said, how people will react.'

(Here's a game every child has played: let's pretend.

Let's pretend that the Japanese football season didn't end in March that year: Éric Cantona might never have come to England.

Let's pretend that a ski-lift did not stop 30 metres above the slopes of Val d'Isère in late December 1991: Éric Cantona might never have played for Leeds and Manchester United.

And now, let's see what really happened.)

Éric's decision to retire was made public in a statement to Agence France-Presse on the day the very first web page went 'live' on the internet: Thursday 12 December 1991, forty-eight hours after he had confronted the French FA's disciplinary commission, flanked by his manager and chairman Michel Mézy. Cantona had sent out invitations to his own wedding after Isabelle and he had tied the knot, but he made sure on this occasion that everyone was informed of his death as a footballer in good time. Whether he had committed suicide or been assassinated by the game's establishment depends on the degree of authorship one is willing to grant Éric for his career. I would lean towards the first interpretation, as there was no shortage of important figures throughout the game that were dismayed by the announcement and expressed their support for the outcast, including some at the very top of France's hierarchy. Michel Platini had long feared that Cantona's quixotic move to Nîmes would end in tears and had sounded out Liverpool manager Graeme Souness as early as the beginning of November, on the occasion of a UEFA Cup tie between the Reds and Auxerre. Would he consider making a bid for Éric at some point?

That brief exchange (which Souness owned up to many years later) led to nothing, of course, but showed that the French manager had already thought of England as the country of Cantona's rebirth. Without Éric, *Les Bleus* would have struggled to qualify for Euro 92, and would find it far more difficult to make an impression in the tournament proper. Their manager set the wheels in motion as soon as it appeared that Cantona was lost to football. He first tried to make Éric change his mind, without success. Then, unbeknown to Cantona, Platini and Gérard Houllier used their contacts within the English game to reach first base in the strange game of rounders Éric's rescue proved to be.

Eulogies poured in, as numerous as expressions of disbelief. One of his France teammates, goalkeeper Gilles Rousset, made this comment: 'Football has lost a great player. But life has just gained a super guy . . .' Cantona's brother-in-law Bernard Ferrer expressed his incredulity: 'He'll come back. He loves his job.' At Nîmes, all those involved in the life of the club closed ranks around Éric: Bousquet, Mézy, the new skipper too, Jean-Claude Lemoult – remember him? The same Lemoult at whom Cantona had thrown a shoe in Montpellier – who read out a very emotional statement written by the playing staff: 'Éric had nothing but friends here and hasn't lost them. We want him to know that he'll be able to find us any time he needs us. And that we'll always be here, with him, if, one day, he feels like playing again, if he changes his mind.'

But Cantona, touched as he was by the expressions of sympathy that came his way, had no intention of changing his mind. His decision was 'irrevocable'. If it hadn't been for Nîmes, a city he loved, and Michel Mézy, one of his most cherished friends, he said, 'I'd have chucked everything away, I'd have left [already]. I wouldn't have played football.' Why he had come to such a dramatic conclusion he didn't explain in more detail until a month-and-a-half later, when it looked as if he was about to settle at Sheffield Wednesday. 'I decided to stop because there had been many things which had been pissing me off for a while,' he told a French reporter. 'Many things I loved, too. But it had been going on for a long time. I've never said that I was in a milieu where I felt at ease, ever since I started playing [professionally]. But because I love the game, I decided to ignore what didn't agree with me. The decision of the disciplinary commission was the last straw . . .' Why hadn't he decided to pack up playing earlier, then, when Bernard Tapie and Raymond Goethals had done everything in their power to make him lose his hunger for football at Marseille? 'That would have been too easy. I wasn't playing. I'm a winner, not a loser. I'd just played a great game with the French team [*the 3–1 win against Iceland on 20 November, in which he scored twice*], it was the right time. It's precisely when everything goes wrong that you must find the strength to go on.'

To start with, 'irrevocable' seemed to mean just that, despite the dramatic consequences tearing up his contract with *Les Crocodiles* would have on his family's future. Mézy, deeply moved, explained that the club had accepted the compensation plan that Cantona had put forward – which was substantial, as there were still two-and-a-half years of his contract to run. Fully aware of the difficulties Éric would face in paying the equivalent of over £1m, Nîmes generously proposed a 'sabbatical'; but Éric would have none of that. His heart told him that agreeing to an extended holiday from football would be akin to lying to himself and to a club he had a great deal of affection for, and his pride baulked at the idea that he couldn't be a man of his word. This didn't prevent Mézy's conciliatory attitude from being subjected to fierce criticism, as Nîmes didn't have the resources to let Éric go and forget about the money they had invested in him. Legally and morally, Cantona himself was personally responsible for the whole of that sum, and paying it would bankrupt him, despite the huge salaries he had received since arriving at OM in 1988. The building contractor he had instructed to build a house on the outskirts of Nîmes politely asked if he would be able to meet the costs. A few weeks later, soon after arriving in Sheffield, he told a *France Football* journalist that he had 'a lot of money put aside'. That much was true, but there would have been very little left of it had he had to buy back his contract.

Maybe his wish 'to be poor', which had shocked so many when he expressed it four years earlier, was not just the idle, irresponsible talk of a born provocateur after all.

What would he do now? For the time being, he would enjoy his freedom. Draw. Walk along the beach of Le Grau-du-Roi, daydreaming of a future without football. Listen to music. The phone rang incessantly, but not once did he pick it up. This was a chance to become a painter, maybe. Or an actor? The celebrated French filmmaker Maurice Pialat, then at the height of his creative powers and commercial success, had thought of offering Cantona the role of Vincent van Gogh in a biopic of the painter, one of Albert's and Éric's heroes, but gave it to French pop singer Jacques Dutronc instead. So Éric went on holiday, as he and Isabelle had always planned to do. At which point Didier Fèvre must pick up the thread of the story, as he ought, as it is his story too, and a good one to boot.

'Éric really wanted to stop after Nîmes,' Didier told me. 'He'd had enough. He was absolutely serious, and Isabelle was sick with worry, with good reason. We'd planned to spend two weeks skiing in the Alps and had booked a big chalet in Val d'Isère. By we, I mean Stéphane [Paille], his wife and child, Éric, Isabelle and Raphaël, myself and my family. The atmosphere was quite oppressive in the first week of the vacation. Isabelle would leave the dinner table, and I could hear her sobbing upstairs. Ten days before we were due to get together, I'd heard that Éric had thrown the ball at a referee, and that nobody had managed to contact him since then. I did – and he told me: "Don't worry, we planned to go on holiday, we'll go on holiday." Every single sports journalist in France was on Canto's tail. We had to find a way to send the dogs on the wrong scent. So we struck a deal with the resort's radio station and the local media. No one was to know we were there – until the very last day, when Éric would give them a big interview. Believe it or not, they all kept their word.

'To start with, we met at the airport of Lyon-Satolas, and we got into two Renaults Espace. Stéphane and I laid down our strategy during the trip. "We've got a fortnight ahead of us," we told each other, "so let's just have a family holiday for a week – then we'll talk to him."

Éric's lawyer, Jean-Jacques Bertrand, managed to join us for a day, and explained to Éric and Isabelle the consequences of breaking the contract with Nîmes. Isabelle was crying. Meanwhile, the whole of France was wondering where he was and what he was up to. It was in late December – Christmas time. So Éric dressed up as Santa Claus and distributed the presents. Stéphane and I kept quiet for a week. Then . . . it was like something out of a movie.'

The three friends went skiing, as they had done most mornings. With his woolly hat and goggles on, no one could recognize Cantona on the pistes. With Éric safely seated between them, Stéphane and Didier made their way up the mountain in a ski-lift. Was there too much wind? Was it a mechanical failure? The ski-lift stopped midway, and remained stuck in the same spot for twenty minutes. Their feet dangling in the air, 30 metres above the snow, the two conspirators knew the opening they had waited for had come at last, and went on the attack.

'Éric, you can't do it. You don't realize what this means,' they said.

'We shook him,' Didier recalls, 'but he didn't say much there and then,' which he and Paille saw as a sure sign that Éric was wavering. Nothing more was said until the afternoon, when, back in the village, the trio passed by a telephone booth. This was the second opportunity they had been waiting for – no mobile phones were available at the time, of course, and no line had been installed in the chalet the three families shared. Didier counted the former St Étienne and France striker Dominique Rocheteau among his friends. 'The Green Angel' (as every journalist called him because of his almost babyish curls and the colour of the Stéphanois jersey) had tried his luck in music after his retirement from the game, before switching to the more lucrative occupation of football agent, a role he played for David Ginola and the FC Nantes international striker Reynald Pedros. Ringing him would be the first of many steps, but also a decisive one, as a 'yes' from Éric, who was standing outside the booth's open door, would mean that he also said 'yes' to football again. Cantona agreed to the call: 'OK, fine, let's do it.'

Luckily, Rocheteau hadn't left his office yet, and Didier could explain the whole situation to him. 'Éric is ready to resume his career,' he said, 'but he doesn't want to play in France ever again.' He wanted to play – in Japan.

Didier could see the expression of bewilderment on my face as he recounted these events in a London pub. 'I know, this sounds unlikely,' he laughed, 'but that is exactly what happened. Japanese clubs paid very good wages and, just as importantly, you can't go much further than Japan if you want to leave France behind you. *Non*?' Rocheteau took it in his stride, and promised he would make enquiries. Could they call him again in twenty-four hours, towards the end of the afternoon? Yes, they could. They would have to go down to the village anyway, to pick up an order from a local *charcutier*, who had been asked to prepare a huge dish of *choucroute* for their evening meal. 'I'll never forget the scene,' Didier said. 'The mounds of sauerkraut, the sausages . . . and the two of us cramped up in the phone booth, talking to Rocheteau . . .'

The agent had bad news and good news. The bad news first. The Japanese season was coming to a close in a matter of weeks, and no J-League club was looking to add to their squad at such a late stage in the football year. 'Wait a second, I'll tell Éric,' Didier said. And so he did. 'Really? Ah, *merde*!' was Cantona's answer. But Rocheteau hadn't quite finished: 'On the other hand, there might be something interesting in England.' 'Oh,' Didier went, 'Éric – there might be something interesting in England!' His friend's reaction was not exactly ecstatic: 'Oooohhh . . . well . . . *allez*. Yes.'

'I know it sounds crazy,' Didier told me, 'but I swear that this is exactly how it happened. Of course, Rocheteau must have spoken to *Platoche* [Platini]. He must have been behind it. But that's how Éric came to England.'

As we've seen, Platini had, indeed, been busying himself behind the scenes, as others had done: his assistant Gérard Houllier, who had taught in Liverpool after graduating from university and spoke fluent English as a result; Éric's worried adviser Jean-Jacques Bertrand, Jean-Jacques Amorfini, the vice-chairman of the French PFA, and Dennis Roach, the agent who had overseen the first £1m transfer in England when Trevor Francis was sold by Birmingham City to Nottingham Forest in 1979.* A meeting was hastily arranged on 23 January, at the headquarters of Cacharel in Paris, to which the fashion house's owner Jean Bousquet was also invited, as well as Sheffield Wednesday's club secretary Graham Mackrell. For Didier Fèvre, the time had come to retreat into the background and, unaccountably, out of Éric Cantona's life. Such a wonderful story deserved a happy ending, and Didier merited rather more than he got from the man whose life and career he had helped put back on the rails. There was no mistaking the sadness in his voice when he told me what follows.

'We left Val d'Isère in our two rented cars,' he recalled. 'We stopped at the last service station before the exit for the airport. We hugged and kissed each other. I was going back to Paris, Stéphane to Caen. Several days later, I left for Wengen on a skiing assignment for *L'Équipe*. A message was waiting for me. "Call the paper – it's urgent." I was told that Éric was taking part in a trial at Sheffield Wednesday. I left Austria on the spot. I called Éric and found him quite cold – but thought, "There must be people around him, let's not worry." I arrived at the Sheffield hotel with Vincent Machenaud of *France Football*. Éric was at the bar, with Bertrand and Amorfini. We go past. He has a faraway look in his eyes. He shakes Vincent's hand, who introduces himself. I joke and introduce myself, "Didier Fèvre" . . . and no reaction.

'I never had the least explanation of his behaviour. He hasn't talked to me since. I couldn't tell you why. Éric operates by breaking up. We were a band of mates, Lolo [Laurent Blanc], Gérald Passi and Laurent Roussey . . . they didn't understand either. It hurt me a great deal. People had been so jealous of my relationship with him. I ceased to exist in the eyes of those who saw me merely as the guy through whom they could get an interview with Éric. I came to Manchester on many occasions, and I made sure every time to position myself in a place where he couldn't miss me. But it made no difference.

'Recently, Éric went into an art gallery which is owned by my brother

* The actual fee was £999,999, as Forest boss Brian Clough didn't want the £1m tag to go his recruit's head, or so he said. When various taxes had been added to this sum, however, Francis had cost Forest over £1.1m.

Bertrand in Arles; he knew him. And my sister had tried to get him a role in one of Alain Corneau's films. Éric asked about me and said he'd like to see me again . . . But I don't feel like answering the whistle. We'd shared so much together. Heaven knows, it's difficult to be the friend of a famous footballer.'

So much happened so quickly. Éric had always felt a desire to run away from everything that tied him to the life of a salaried footballer. He aspired to a state of constant exaltation which the game he excelled at could only provide in bursts, whereas, in his naïve expectations, the poet, the painter, the adventurer inhabited a higher realm where instinct and desire ruled, not the impostures of wealth and success. Being cast away could be a blessing. The men he despised most, the panjandrums of the French FA, had presented him with a gift when they intended to punish him. He'd show them. He'd retire. Others would surmise he'd committed suicide; he'd merely have shed a self that didn't fulfil his aspirations. But he quickly realized that he lacked the powers to express himself in fields other than a football pitch. He also had a young family to feed. Yet such was the confusion in his mind and his life at the time that when I tried to unravel the affair by speaking to its main protagonists, and reading what Éric had told my *France Football* colleague Stéphane de Saint-Raymond in late January 1992, it was as if I had been brought into a conversation in which everyone talked over each other at the same time, a kind of Wellesian dialogue which went something like this:

Gérard Houllier: 'The idea of Éric going to England was Michel Platini's, whose assistant I was at the time. Michel asked me if I could use my contacts to find him a club in England, as he was suspended in France . . . I thought English football could suit him, because of his physique and his strength in the air. But I had no idea that he would be such a success there – in fact, nobody could have imagined what happened afterwards.'

Éric Cantona: 'I had other proposals. Many other offers came my way, things which were more interesting, financially speaking. But I liked

England. I liked life there, I liked rock music. And I felt like coming here, to learn the language, to allow my son to learn it. I felt like playing in packed stadia which "vibrate". And I – I need that buzz. As much as I love acting as a profession, I'm unable to be an actor on the pitch.'

Houllier: 'I called one of my contacts, the agent Dennis Roach, whom I'd been in touch with when I wanted Glenn Hoddle to come to PSG . . .'

Dennis Roach: 'Gérard was a good friend. The problem was that there wasn't a first division side in France which was able or willing to take on Éric, because he'd caused so many problems! It was a strange request . . . why wouldn't he cause as many problems over here? But because it was Gérard, I thought about it.'

Houllier: '. . . Hoddle went to Monaco instead; Dennis Roach then got in touch with Trevor Francis, whom he had represented.'

Trevor Francis: 'Yes, the trial was arranged by Dennis Roach, who was a friend of mine and organized something.'

Roach: 'Gérard and I had lunch with a couple of other guys from the FA. I'd already spoken to Trevor Francis, then manager of Sheffield Wednesday. Trevor told me he'd be interested in taking Éric.'

Éric: 'If I hadn't been married, if I hadn't had a child, I wouldn't have come to Sheffield. I would've gone to a place where nobody would have been able to find me.'

Roach: 'We were lucky that Trevor was a good friend, who believed he could rely on my judgement. That was the only way at this stage we could get Éric to England. Nobody would have taken him on, because of his reputation. But Trevor did, because I told him: "I've known Gérard for a long time, and he says that this boy can be a great player." This was the basis for his coming to England. I put that to Gérard, and we agreed to give it a go.'

Francis: 'I was given the opportunity to have a look at Éric Cantona, but, unfortunately, it was at a time when the weather was particularly bad in England. He was only with us for two days; and we couldn't train on grass, because there was a lot of ice and snow on the ground; so he trained for two days on astroturf; we wished he had stayed for a little longer . . .'

Roach: 'Éric came over and played in an indoor six-a-side tournament* – and he was absolutely fantastic. Unbelievable.'

Éric: 'Sincerely, I loved these few days in Sheffield. What a welcome I had! There were 10,000 supporters at the indoor tournament! 10,000 people who, like me, expected me to play against Luton at the weekend.'

Roach: 'The contract was supposed to be signed on the 30th of January. Trevor was a very good footballer but, unfortunately, as a manager, he hadn't yet learnt to make quick decisions . . . so he ummed and aahed . . . '

Éric: 'They wanted to put me on trial for two more days. I deserved respect. I was fifteen years old when I last did a trial. I am not "*une* big star", but I have my pride.'

Roach: '. . . and in the end, I got a phone call from Howard Wilkinson at Leeds.'

Houllier: 'I was in the West Indies, either in Guadeloupe or Martinique at the time, with a group of friends. I got in touch with my secretary in Paris, who said, "No, no particular message, except, ah, a Mr Howard Wilkinson would like you to call him urgently." She gave me the number, and I phoned Wilkinson from a phone booth at the airport of Fort-de-France – this was quite a while before mobiles took off!'

---

* Cantona played alongside Graham Hyde, Nigel Worthington, Chris Bart-Williams and Gordon Watson against an American touring team, Baltimore East. He scored a hat-trick.

Francis: 'I don't have any real regrets. The conditions were so bad. You didn't have to look too closely to understand he was a very talented footballer. I was aware that he had had some problems. But I don't think it could ever have been possible for Éric Cantona to stay with us.'

Éric: 'Francis was always clear with me, he never doubted my worth – but he had to be understood: he needed a 100 per cent operational player, right now. And he knew I hadn't played for a month-and-a-half . . . We trained indoors. He wasn't able to make a judgement for himself.'

Francis: 'At the time, he was a very, very big-time player, and we never got to the point where we were in a position to actually start negotiating. And if we'd ever got to that point, I don't think we'd have ever been in a position to bring Éric to Sheffield Wednesday, because he was too big at the time. We weren't like some of the other established clubs in the league, who could pay big salaries. He left Sheffield Wednesday very, very quickly. We were expecting him to stay for another couple of days, and the next minute, it was arranged that he would go to Leeds!'

Houllier: 'Wilkinson told me: "There's this player, he's French, name of Cantona" – "Yes, I know him quite well," I replied – "He's at Sheffield at the moment, but there's a problem, because they want to put him on trial, and he doesn't want to . . . what do you think?" I remember telling him – my very words – "Close your eyes and take him, you'll get a super-player. If you want to know more, I'm back in France tomorrow, and there'll be an *assemblée fédérale* at the Méridien Hotel in Montparnasse – Michel Platini will be there, and we'll talk about Éric again." The next day, Michel and I went to a phone booth in Montparnasse and talked with Wilkinson a bit . . . He had a bit of French, he could get along . . .'

Francis: 'We were very surprised at Cantona leaving so quickly. If my memory serves me right, I think he was a little disappointed that we didn't take a decision immediately when he was training with us. He wanted a quick decision. But if I understood what a talented player he was, I wanted to know more about Cantona the person. When you bring in someone who is such a big name, you've got to be 100 per cent sure he was not going to disrupt what was a very, very good team spirit.'

Houllier: '. . . and this is how Wilkinson signed Éric, following the recommendations of Michel and myself. Éric signed for Leeds – and became the champion of England.'

So it was that, little more than a week after the initial meeting between Roach and Houllier, Howard Wilkinson sat down with Cantona in a Sheffield hotel room to discuss his future.

Cantona himself was convinced that he had been hawked around to various English clubs (including a 'very, very big one' – possibly Liverpool, as Michel Platini had alerted Graeme Souness to Éric's availability in November) without his knowledge or assent over the previous three weeks. Paranoia? Maybe not. Some clubs were willing to pay a 'finder's fee' to agents who acted as mere go-betweens for players whom, strictly speaking, they had no legal right to represent. Cantona muttered that 'two English guys' (he later named one of them in an interview, which has evaded libel lawyers so far) had been 'on the take', but stopped short of revealing which clubs they had contacted. Wednesday agreed to pay a commission to Éric's representatives in case a deal was agreed. So far, so good, except that Francis was apparently unaware that Cantona had been told that the 'trial' he would be subjected to was supposed to be a formality. This ultimately ruined any chance of Éric settling in Sheffield. Éric had every right to point out that it would have been very unlikely for an established England international to go through a trial before signing for a French club (a point of view which his future Leeds captain Gordon Strachan publicly endorsed shortly afterwards). So, on 31 January, the day before his planned debut for the Owls, one hour before training was supposed to start, a fax bearing Cantona's signature arrived in Wednesday's office. In it, Éric expressed his regret that things hadn't worked out as hoped; but, in the present circumstances, he had no choice but to terminate the gentleman's agreement between the club and himself.

The news instantly filtered out of Hillsborough. It reached Manchester United, but too late (we'll come to that later on): Leeds United were the quickest to react. The England under-21s manager Lawrie McMenemy had alerted Leeds manager Howard Wilkinson to the goings-on in Sheffield, and, on his way back from the training ground, 'Sergeant Wilko' drove the few miles that separated his home from the hotel where Éric was staying.

Wilkinson's mind wasn't made up yet. Leeds had exceeded everyone's expectations by rising to the very top of the championship with a little over a third of the season to go. But their manager doubted that his squad possessed the necessary depth to remain ahead of a fast-chasing pack over a full campaign. An extra weapon had to be added to the armoury. Could Cantona provide the answer for the almost stereotypically English coach? Wilkinson telephoned Houllier, as we've seen, and also probed Michel Platini and Glenn Hoddle, who had seen Éric at close quarters over the three years he had spent in France, until a knee injury forced him to leave AS Monaco in December 1990. Wilkinson also sought the advice of a friend of his called Bobby Brown, for no apparent reason other than Brown's wife happened to be French. The feedback he received was overwhelmingly positive. Despite the problems he had encountered in his previous clubs, Éric Cantona remained an exceptional player, they said. His dips in form could be explained by disagreements 'which had resulted in him generally downing tools and walking out', as Wilkinson told Rob Wightman twelve years later. Éric's undeserved reputation for wilful instability preceded him, and his next manager didn't try and look beyond it. He had already formed an opinion of Cantona's strengths and weaknesses before he had had the chance to judge him on the training pitch, on the field of play or in the dressing-room.

As some of those who served under him have told me, none more forcefully than Gary McAllister, Wilkinson genuinely tried to act fairly towards his players, Cantona included, but, in this instance, perhaps allowed himself to attach too much credence to hearsay. It was hard for anyone at that stage of Éric's career to form a view of his character that was not tainted by prejudice, and Wilkinson, quite naturally, displayed a certain wariness towards the Frenchman from the outset of their delicate relationship. This wariness would later develop into mistrust, with disastrous results for the club.

Nevertheless, as January 1992 came to a close, Wilkinson took a deep breath and bravely dived in. He arranged to meet Cantona through Jean-Jacques Bertrand. Éric occupied a spartan single room at the Swallow hotel, two miles away from Sheffield city centre. 'His agent, Jean-Jacques, was sitting on the chair,' Wilkinson recalled. 'Éric was lying on the bed looking very dischuffed to say the least, with several days of growth on his face and looking as if the end of the world was nigh.'

In some ways, it was. Cantona might have scored a paltry two goals in sixteen games for Nîmes, but he knew that his talent hadn't waned; and just as he thought that Sheffield Wednesday might provide him with a springboard, the muddle-headed behaviour of the Yorkshire club's board had precipitated yet another crisis. It was not just a matter of 'Who will trust me? Where will I show I deserve to be trusted?' but of 'How will I pay the £1m I owe my former club?' Wilkinson wasn't just offering Éric the chance of a fresh start to his career, but also a way to keep the bailliffs at bay.

Cantona's customary bravado couldn't hide his fear. Upon arriving in Sheffield, he had told *France Football*: 'I give myself three years. Normally, I'd have five left [*he was twenty-five at the time*], but what I want is to play in the European Championships, to play them as well as I can, all together. If it works out well, [I want] to carry on with the World Cup in the United States, then *basta*. I'll be twenty-eight years old. That's another three years of my life, I'll have sorted out all these problems, I'll have tried to show the world what I am worth . . . If it works out fine, all the better; if not, at least I'll have tried. Then I'll go. But, this time, people will have had the time to prepare themselves for it.' There was a hint of callousness in another comment, which must have hurt Isabelle deeply. 'My parents, my family, my friends have found it very difficult to live through it,' he acknowledged. 'But me? Very easy.'

He concluded: 'I'll play out these three years in England. I've got money. In three years, I'll have even more. I will never play in France again, or anywhere else where a footballer's life counts for nothing.'

Cantona, Wilkinson and Bertrand spoke for over an hour in a mixture of broken English and schoolboy French. Éric himself remembered meeting 'an ex-cep-tio-nal man, a *grand monsieur*', which can be taken as an expression of gratitude as much as admiration – for Wilkinson was saving far more than his career by taking what he saw as 'a huge gamble, the biggest of my life'.

'Heaven knows, it's difficult to be the friend of a famous footballer.' Heaven knows it must have been difficult to be a friend of Éric Cantona. He gave many proofs of the generosity of his character throughout his career, but found forgiveness a more elusive virtue, even when there was nothing to forgive, except a misunderstanding that, more often than not, had been caused by his own confused appraisal of circumstances. Why did he blank Didier Fèvre in Sheffield? Had he suddenly seen a photographer rather than a friend? Had Fèvre become one of the seagulls following the trawler? Three years later, as he prepared to face the media following his appearance in an appeal court, Cantona noticed Erik Bielderman among a group of British tabloid writers at the back of the room. Of all the French journalists with whom Éric enjoyed a warm working relationship in Manchester, none had got closer to him than Bielderman. The reporter from L'Équipe *(a staunch Manchester United fan) had gained Cantona's trust when the two men had been involved in a heated exchange in which the journalist had refused to give ground to the football star. Mutual respect warmed into something resembling friendship. On several occasions (notably when Éric announced his retirement from* Les Bleus *in 1992, a comical episode we'll come to in a later chapter), Cantona dropped unguarded remarks which, had they been printed in the next day's paper, could have caused him a great deal of trouble. Bielderman knew when to check himself and resist the pull of a scoop.*

Still, that afternoon in Croydon, after Éric had been punished by British justice, Bielderman ceased to be a confidant of his. Cantona's eyes fell on the journalist, his face a living question ('What are YOU doing here?'), to which Bielderman answered by lifting his eyebrows and shrugging his shoulders with a sigh ('Well, I cannot be anywhere else, can I?').

And that was that. Their relationship had come to an end. Cantona, while remaining courteous when a perfunctory greeting had to be exchanged, never agreed to meet the journalist face to face again.

I remember Bernard Morlino telling how a friend must behave as an accomplice when wrong has been done. I also remember Éric himself confessing to his admiration of those who 'hold grudges', because it is a proof of 'character'. It's hard to find much that is admirable in this conceit. What is the worth of the unquestioning loyalty of a dog who sits when he's told to, and barks at a passer-by as if he were an enemy? Is subservience the acid test of affection between two human beings?

In truth, however, if 'heaven knows how difficult it is to be the friend of a famous footballer', heaven knows too how difficult it must be for a famous footballer to single out a friend among the courtiers of celebrity. Of all the obstacles that are laid in the path of friendship, none is harder to pass over than the unequal distribution of wealth and the attraction of vicarious fame. Erik and I went through the names of footballers we had spent a significant deal of time with over the years, and could find only one who had managed to retain his openness to others absolutely intact despite living in an environment where paranoia is the rule: Robert Pires.

Éric was no worse than the overwhelming majority of his fellow players in this regard. What made him stand apart was how he advanced through the stages of his life and his career by constantly stopping and starting again, as if breaking up with part of his past – a club, a friend – represented the only way to move forward, whether he had been the instigator of the break-up or not. He could always return to the womb of the family, the clan, if things turned awry. That at least could never change. His younger brother Joël could be relied upon when Éric craved absolute admiration. 'If Canto stood there with a turd on his head, Joël would say he's never seen anything so beautiful in all the world,' as a one-time member of the closed circle told me, without irony. To Albert and Léonor, he remained their child. To others, an enigma.

9

A footballer's home.

A STRANGE KIND OF GLORY: LEEDS, 1992

*'Maybe I'll play somewhere else in a year's time. If, in a year's time, I go somewhere else, then I'll tell you: now, it's there and nowhere else. Only cretins [*cons*] never change their minds.'*
Sheffield, January 1992

Of all the clubs Cantona could have ended up with after the Sheffield Wednesday non sequitur, he found himself at Leeds United, the pantomime villains of English football who, twenty years earlier, under Don Revie, had nonetheless managed to produce some of the most glorious football ever played in the country. They had also antagonized every single fan of every other club with their blatant cynicism and carefully orchestrated gamesmanship. After eight years in the second division, Leeds had owed their reinstatement to the elite to the organizational skills of Howard Wilkinson, who had already led Sheffield Wednesday back to the first division in 1984 and succeeded Billy Bremner at Elland Road in October 1988. The 'Whites' were then in real danger of sinking into the third tier of the English League for the first time in their history. His first decision was to take down the photographs of the Revie era from the clubhouse's walls, 'crutches', he said, 'for people who still basked in the reflected glory of those bygone days'. 'Sergeant Wilko' agreed with his predecessor Bremner's judgement that 'in football, yesterday happened a long time ago', and immediately embarked upon the rebuilding of his squad. The new manager had a 'nose' for players, and showed it when he persuaded Manchester United's goalscoring midfielder

Gordon Strachan to join the ailing club. A shrewd assessor of talent, he could also call in 'bruisers' like Vinnie Jones, who were ideally suited to the rough-house action of a lower division. As soon as promotion had been gained, much more rapidly than anyone would have thought possible, Jones was sold, and Wilkinson brought in from Leicester City that purist's dream, Gary McAllister. He could also take a bet on youth: David Batty and Gary Speed stepped out of the club's academy in the 1990–91 season to complete a formidable midfield quartet that had few equals in the country. Leeds powered to fourth place in the championship.

The days of the 'closed shop' and the 'Big Four' still lay a few years – an eternity, it seems – ahead, and other managers had achieved similar miracles in the recent past: Bobby Robson with Ipswich Town; Brian Clough, first with Derby County, then with Nottingham Forest; and Graham Taylor with Watford, albeit in a less pleasing style. What Wilkinson had done deserved praise nevertheless, not that many were willing to give it unless they read the *Yorkshire Evening Post*, and didn't buy it in Sheffield. His team could certainly match any opposition in physical terms – David Batty never claimed to be a poet on the ball – but in the context of early 1990s English football, to dismiss Leeds as a collection of brutes intent on destruction would have been grossly unfair. True, they scored most of their goals with headers, long-distance strikes and through creating mayhem in the opposition's box; but in Strachan, Speed and McAllister they also possessed footballers of genuine class and vision, not that anyone seemed to care outside Elland Road, where supporters took a twisted kind of pleasure in their vilification. To them, Revie's considerable success and the manner in which it had been achieved had never been celebrated as they should have been by a press in thrall to the teams Leeds fans most despised: Manchester United, of course, and London clubs such as elegant West Ham, glamorous Chelsea and classy Arsenal. This perceived injustice made them revel in their difference; they might as well give the others good reasons for hating them so. Cantona, the arch-maverick, the anti-hero par excellence, fitted perfectly with their vision of a world divided between 'them' and 'us'; that he belonged in the second category soon became clear.

The *Yorkshire Evening Post* informed its readers of Éric's arrival at the club on 1 February, and, judging by the reactions of some of those readers, that particular edition might as well have been dated 1 April. But a few hours after the newspaper went on sale, Cantona was sitting in the stands at Elland Road in person, watching his teammates put Luton to the sword 3–0. Leeds, who shared the top spot of the old first division with Manchester United at the time, but had played one game more, remained underdogs in the title race. The club's fortunes had improved so quickly since winning the second division championship in 1989–90 that many supporters could not bring themselves to believe that Wilkinson's thin squad could last the distance over forty-two games.

The manager spoke of 'the biggest gamble of his career', but was he really taking such a huge risk? How many proven international strikers could you get for a down-payment of a mere £100,000? Nîmes and Cantona were only too happy to agree to a loan rather than a straight purchase, desperate as they were to extricate themselves from their current situation. Wilkinson – who had never seen the player in the flesh before signing him – had until 15 April to make up his mind, by which time there would only be four games to play in the league. Should he decide to close a permanent transfer deal, Leeds would have to disburse another £900,000. But only then. And Wilkinson was a shrewd gambler, who already had a fair idea of how and when he would play his trump card. 'As far as I'm concerned,' he told the local press, '[Éric] doesn't have a reputation, because I don't believe what I read in the papers.' This was a slightly disingenuous statement, it must be said. As we've seen, Cantona's new boss had sounded out a number of people before driving to meet Cantona in Sheffield, not just to be reassured about the player's qualities (which all of Europe knew about), but also to establish how much of his 'reputation' was based on fact. None of those he had approached had pretended that Éric's behaviour had been a model of propriety. They had stressed, however, that when properly managed (that is, when his idiosyncrasies were not automatically construed as acts of rebellion), Cantona responded by repaying the trust put in him, sometimes beyond everyone else's expectations.

After a low-key presentation to the media, in which his interpreter had to keep a straight face when telling the journalists that 'the problems I [Éric] have had have been little ones that have been exaggerated', Cantona joined his teammates for his first practice match at Thorp Arch training ground, on 3 February. 'It took Éric a matter of minutes to impress the players,' Gary McAllister told me. 'During the warm-up, we already saw a few strikes, a few volleys, and it was obvious this was a very special player.' The Scottish midfielder sensed that Cantona could bring something that was lacking in an otherwise well-drilled and efficient unit: 'a bit of flair, a bit of imagination – in other words, what you need to create space to play in and open gaps in defences'. Leeds possessed a terrific goalscorer in Lee Chapman (one of the best headers of a ball in the league), while Rod Wallace provided coruscating pace and penetration on the wing; but, full of guile and running as Wilkinson's midfield was, it lacked a true *fantasista* and sometimes appeared devoid of solutions in the face of aggressive defending. David Batty played the role of anchorman, and tackled as if his life (and, sometimes, the life of the opposition players) depended on it. The twenty-two-year-old Gary Speed could be relied upon to 'cover every blade of grass' and pass the ball cleanly, without fuss, but not without skill. He could also strike the ball venomously with either foot. McAllister, the most elegant player in that superb quartet (which was complemented by ageing England international Steve Hodge), added threat in dead-ball situations and could alter the flow of play with the accuracy of his long passing. Last, Gordon Strachan, the club's diminutive skipper who had won seven major honours with Alex Ferguson's Aberdeen in the early 1980s, provided the experience of over fifteen years in the professional game, plus cunning and boundless energy. Together with Chapman, these four men had taken Leeds to the top of the championship table; but, to remain there, they needed a footballer who could make the difference on his own.

Éric was lucky. The tone of the Leeds dressing-room was struck by what the English call 'honest' players, decent, generous-minded men who did whatever they could to accommodate the brooding foreigner. What's more, the Scottish contingent which had long been prominent in the club of Bobby Collins and Billy Bremner, and to which belonged Strachan and McAllister, the two natural leaders of the squad, held no prejudice against a representative of the Auld Alliance, unless it was a favourable one. A moot point? Most certainly not, if one thinks ahead to the complicity that would be a hallmark of the relationship between Alex Ferguson and Cantona: together against *les Anglais*, the Auld Enemy.

According to McAllister, language didn't prove as much of a barrier as outsiders feared it might be. 'His English wasn't that bad, you know!' he told me. 'I think he chose his time to let you know that . . . but he joined in the banter. He understood the British dressing-room humour very quickly, the taking the mickey . . . The players made a big effort to put him at ease, and that's one of the reasons he settled in so quickly.'

Their support extended beyond the privacy of the training ground. Strachan used his regular column in the *Post* to defend Éric's decision ('quite a gifted player') to leave Sheffield Wednesday: 'He is of course a seasoned international, which, for me, makes it difficult to understand how anyone anywhere could really ask a player such as Éric to go anywhere for a trial. I cannot see a British player of a similar standing ever agreeing to go to an overseas club on a week's trial.' Gary Speed enthused just as publicly about the tremendous impression the recruit had made: 'he's big and strong, very dangerous in the air and packs a good shot' – quite a compliment coming from one of the fiercest strikers of the ball at the club.

The Leeds supporters lapped up the praise their Frenchman was receiving, and couldn't read or hear enough about the club's most exotic recruit since the arrival of black South African Albert Johanneson in 1961. Barely a day passed without a mention of Cantona in the *Post*, who were granted the rare privilege of a one-to-one interview with the player on 7 February, so rare a privilege, in fact, that this revealing article would be one of only two such pieces published in English until Éric left Manchester United and England in May 1997. I use the adjective 'revealing' with a caveat; for what was so revealing in the conversation Éric had with journalist Mike Casey was not so much his answers as the questions he was asked, only one of which had to do with football.

The interpreter was a young Yorkshirewoman named Julie Halford, who was predictably wowed by the Frenchman, and became the subject of an interview herself. Such was Éric's aura that even those who merely talked with him were deemed worthy of being talked to themselves. 'Speaking with Cantona,' she said, 'is more like taking part in *The South Bank Show* than in *Match of the Day*.'

How could it be otherwise? Éric's legend went before him. The *Post* and its readership were interested in this mythical creature, an accretion of second-hand anecdotes and unverifiable rumours, which Cantona did nothing to refute on that occasion. He philosophized ('I am only considered mad in today's society. I think in an ideal society, I would be considered normal'), lifted a corner of the tapestry that concealed him ('It bothers me if I'm recognized, and it bothers me if I'm not'), only to let it fold back in place with half-serious gnomisms about his personality ('I don't like looking at myself in the mirror. I always wonder who is the person I'm looking at'). The arrangement suited all parties. The press and the general public got the story they craved, while Éric retained his *quant-à-soi*, and could find some kind of peace in the bubble he had created for himself. Protected by his eccentricities, both knowing and sincere, he could position himself safely in the distance, aware that no one would seek to approach him too closely. Had they chosen to do so, they would have had trouble recognizing the chimera of their imagination in the flesh-and-blood Marseillais who traded dirty words with his teammates in the communal bath. Éric welcomed this cautiousness. 'I like the mentality of the English,' he said. 'They are warm and reserved at the same time. They give you respect. I like that.'

The relief Cantona felt at leaving the turmoil of the previous months behind alleviated the loneliness of his new life in Leeds. Isabelle and Raphaël had stayed behind in the South of France, and would only join him once it became a certainty that the club wished to retain him on a long-term contract. With the exception of Wilkinson and Chapman (who was considered an 'intellectual' of the English game, as he had passed an impressive number of O- and A-levels), the people who surrounded him spoke almost no French. Éric had met his captain Gordon Strachan once before, but on the field of play only, when France and Scotland had come head-to-head in a World Cup qualifier two-and-a-half years previously. Everywhere he looked, Éric saw the faces of strangers. Still, all did their best to put the newcomer at ease, with some success.

'Everyone seemed to take to him straightaway,' Gary Speed told Rob Wightman. 'The way the Leeds dressing-room was then, they would have welcomed anyone. That's one reason why we won the title, because of that. First of all he came over on his own and we socialized a lot – that was the way to get to know him. [. . .] We just tried our hardest to welcome him in and he seemed to thrive on that and it really showed on the pitch.'

The Leeds supporters played their part too. The excitement surrounding Éric's arrival at Elland Road was such that, on 8 February, 5,000 of them made the (admittedly short) trip to Oldham in the hope of seeing the debut of the player the *Sunday Mirror* had already nick-named 'Le Brat'. The result came as a disappointment to them – Oldham prevailed 2–0 – but their wish had been granted. A calf injury sustained by Steve Hodge in the first half led Wilkinson to usher Cantona onto the field after the interval, much earlier than his manager had planned. In truth, Éric did not see much of the ball that afternoon, and spent most of the game's last 45 minutes watching it sail above his head. He touched it less than a dozen times, still attempting a few of his party tricks (a backheel, a bicycle kick) when it finally got to his feet, but, apart from a weak header which hardly troubled goalkeeper Jon Hall-worth, failed to exert any influence on the encounter. Leeds's defeat had highlighted not so much what Cantona could bring to the club than what it was missing when Lee Chapman, who had broken a wrist in January, could not provide a focal point for his team's attacks.

'I found it physical to play in,' Éric told a *France Football* reporter at the final whistle, acknowledging that he had 'had a bad day. But the only surprise was that Leeds lost. After one week in Sheffield and one week in Leeds, I knew that the tempo was high here. I was expecting it. I had prepared myself for it.' The assessment he made of his own performance showed a Cantona who was able to take a step back and view his future with calmness and equanimity. 'I think I'll have fun here,' he said, and for two reasons: he believed that skilful footballers could create space for themselves despite the frantic pace of the action;

and, crucially, the bond between players and fans was closer than anything he had experienced before. 'I've never felt like playing in cold stadiums,' he said, 'where spectators are 30 metres away from the pitch. I lose myself in that empty space.' It would take time to adapt, of course, but he was willing to show patience and humility. 'I'll understand more with each day that passes. It's the same for the language. It won't be harder, it'll be just as difficult. To learn is always difficult.'

Éric applied himself to the task of 'learning' with a single-mindedness and a modesty that won his teammates over. His dedication in training (which, later on, would have such an impact on the youngsters coming through the ranks at Manchester United) provided another proof of his desire to blend in. Unusually for the time, a number of Leeds players, Gary McAllister among them, used to stay on the pitch after practice sessions to work on free-kick routines, shots at goal and the like, as Cantona had always done himself. 'Sessions' of a different kind regularly followed in various watering holes (preferably in the countryside, away from Wilkinson's gaze), in which Éric could relax all the more easily given that his drinking companions accepted that he sometimes needed to withdraw into his own world. He wanted to be left alone? So what? Let him do it. He wasn't sulking. He had just left his country and his family behind him, for goodness sake. As Gary Speed said: 'I don't think you'd ever pin him down. You couldn't say, Éric, come out for a drink, mate! Sometimes he was just there. He was his own person.' Cantona appreciated the attention he was given a great deal, but appreciated even more the freedom he was granted to be himself. As McAllister told me: 'Éric is a player who responds to being accepted; sometimes, it's about a bit of love, and he had that at Leeds United.'

Leeds then embarked on a short trip to Ireland, where they beat Irish champions Shelbourne 2–0 in front of 10,000 spectators, most of whom had bought their tickets to see Éric in the flesh. Cantona 'turned on the style', according to a fawning report in the local press, hitting the post with a fearsome 20-yard drive. But 'the wild man of French football' (another telling *Post* headline) still had to make his first appearance at Elland Road. He did so on 15 February, on the very day Isabelle unpacked her cases in their new home near Roundhay Park, where Éric would sometimes play football with his son Raphaël once the young family settled there for good later in the spring.* Leeds had invited Swedish champions IFK Gothenburg to take part in a friendly which attracted fewer than 6,000 spectators to a stadium that could accommodate five times that number. There would have been even fewer, of course, had Cantona not played. The game itself (which United lost 1–0) would have remained a dispensable footnote in the story of Éric's season, had not a solitary fan started chanting 'Ooh-aah, Cantona!' after a deft flick from the new folk hero. Part of the crowd (some of whom had turned up wearing Breton shirts, berets and the obligatory string of onions) joined in spontaneously, and one of the most famous terrace songs of the 1990s was born.†

Cantona fever spread at a barely credible speed within two weeks of Éric's arrival at Leeds. New words were put to the old Leeds anthem 'Marching on Together'. '*Marchons ensemble*' didn't scan perfectly, but was great fun to sing. A young couple was said – in all likelihood apocryphally – to have christened their new-born with the middle name Cantona. The fervour displayed so dramatically in the stands (and which turned to hysterical hatred once Éric left for Manchester United) intrigued a sociology PhD student from the University of Salford named Anthony C. King to such an extent that he published a paper on the topic of *The Problem of Identity and the Cult of Éric Cantona* several years later (in 1995). Deconstruction in football would normally be a jocular euphemism for tackling *à la* Joey Barton. King, now head of the Philosophy and Sociology Department at Exeter University, applied this methodology with rather more finesse. He made a strong

---

* The club had found him a discreet, somewhat ramshackle house in this leafy but unremarkable suburb, where West Indian and Pakistani immigrants lived side-by-side with dyed-in-the-wool Yorkshire natives. The very ordinariness of his surroundings pleased Éric, who had no taste for the trappings of footballing success, and the friendliness of his neighbours helped to forge a genuine bond between the exile and his adopted city. In fact, Roundhay remained the Cantonas' base in north-east England long after Éric had been sold to Manchester United.

† This was an adaptation of an earlier (and much less famous) chant, originally created in honour of Manchester United's Irish defender Paul McGrath. For Mancunian supporters, singing it for Éric was a re-appropriation, not a theft.

case for understanding the 'cult of Cantona' as a collective crystallization of a number of frustrations, urges and fantasies peculiar to the working class of that part of England, which were then externalized through ritualistic channels familiar to anyone who inhabits the football world. The fans clad in replica shirts and Leeds scarves repeating the simple but insistent rhythm of 'Ooh-ah Cantona' ad infinitum on their way to Elland Road . . . give them orange robes, and they may as well chant the Hare Krishna *Maha Mantra* down Oxford Street.

I put some of King's insights to Leeds supporters, and was surprised by how willing they were to accept them as valid (but not demeaning) interpretations of their own behaviour. 'Leeds fans did not merely admire Cantona's manliness or his style,' for example, 'but loved him in the way that someone might love their partner.' (In some cases, *more* than their partner, as the story of one such fan, Gary King, will show later in this book.) The Salford student argued that this emotional transfer was facilitated by the stereotypical view the English held of the French as red-hot lovers, as I found out to my embarrassment when I arrived in England myself ('Oh, I *do* love your accent!').

More intriguingly, as King rightly remarked, some groups of Leeds fans (whose opinions were echoed in the fanzine *Marching on Together*) had launched a number of anti-racist initiatives in the late 1980s and early 1990s. They saw in Cantona's Frenchness a means to assert their own aspirations to cosmopolitanism. This was not the easiest of tasks in a city still reeling from the effects of Thatcherite vandalism, and which had a long way to go before it reinvented itself as a thriving service centre, complete with the first branch of Harvey Nichols outside London. The left-leaning terrace dissidents aimed to achieve supremacy over the hooligan element that had tarnished the club's image for two decades already. Thanks to Éric, King wrote, 'the fans were able to distinguish Leeds as a team, symbolically represented by Cantona, that was different and superior [*more skilful, more seductive*] to the rest of the English league'. It was an extraordinary reversal of the xenophobic values which were and still are attached to the Leeds support, in which Éric played a function he had no control of whatsoever. I've often referred to the mythical dimension of Cantona, but a psychoanalyst might rather use the word 'fantasmatic', as the object of adoration was idealized to such a degree that his performances became – almost – incidental to his worshippers. Howard Wilkinson might not have put things in quite these terms, but was nonplussed all the same. He could live with the aggrandizement of one of his players (which Cantona did absolutely nothing to encourage) as long as his own authority remained unchallenged. It would take a matter of months before he felt it was endangered to the point that a parting of ways presented him with the only opportunity to carry on doing his job as he saw fit.

Éric had played 45 minutes of competitive football since throwing the ball at a referee in December of the previous year, but such was the regard Michel Platini held him in that he did not hesitate to field him from the start in a prestigious friendly held in, of all places, Wembley Stadium, where goals by Alan Shearer and Gary Lineker gave England a flattering 2–0 victory over France on 19 February. Cantona featured for the full 90 minutes, and should have won a penalty when Mark Wright stopped his very first shot at goal with both hands. Most observers agreed that his return to international football had been a success; the one-eyed *Yorkshire Post* even went as far as illustrating its match report with a photograph of the Frenchman that dwarfed the picture of Lineker scoring his 47th goal for England – which put the Spurs centre-forward within two strikes of Bobby Charlton's all-time record for the national team. And when the players made their way out of the dressing-room, English or French, the gaggle of journalists converged on just one of them: Éric Cantona, who else?

Hardly any questions concerned the game itself, which is all the more surprising since both teams had been drawn in the same group in the forthcoming European Championships. But journalists, British as well as French, were after Éric's *impressions d'Angleterre*. 'England is just as I expected after watching your game on television in France,' he told the former. 'It's very quick and positive, and the ball is moved to the forwards as fast as possible. Most French players wouldn't like that, because they prefer to play through midfield, but for a striker like me, I like to get the ball early, and that's what's happening, so I'm enjoying myself.'

In truth, Éric had not yet adjusted to the pace of English football, as was shown when Leeds drew 1–1 at Everton the following weekend, an encounter which also marked Cantona's first live appearance on national British television. Howard Wilkinson sought to temper the expectations of the public when facing ITV's cameras after the match. 'Éric has a lot in his favour,' he said. 'He's big, strong and fit and has a terrific build so he can compete easier [*sic*] than, say, someone of five foot nought. And, most important this, it seems he wants to succeed. I'm sure he will. But it's up to him.' It was a fair assessment of Cantona's contribution. A goal had eluded him – just – after he had skipped past the challenges of Dave Watson and Matthew Jackson to find himself with just Everton's 'keeper Neville Southall to beat, only to see see his shot shave the Welsh international's far post. But apart from that, Cantona hadn't posed a real threat to the visitors.

Wilkinson was understandably reluctant to alter his system for the sake of a late recruit, and feared that throwing the footballer-artist into the cauldron of first division football head first would lead to burn-out. In fairness, the manager had informed the player of his intentions from the outset of their relationship. Later on, once Cantona's match-winning ability had become obvious to all, the Yorkshireman's reluctance to deviate from his plans would bring accusations of pig-headedness. In late February, however, it simply demonstrated that he was coherent enough in his thinking to make Cantona's introduction to English football as smooth and trouble-free as possible. Éric himself seemed happy with the walk-on parts Wilkinson gave him; he realized that, following his two-month suspension, he still lacked match fitness and couldn't be expected to waltz in and lead Leeds to victory through the sheer magnitude of his talent.

The goal he and thousands of Leeds fans had been praying for came six days later, against Luton Town at Elland Road, when Cantona stepped off the bench after Tony Dorigo sustained an injury on the half-hour mark. Éric was told to move upfield and position himself alongside Lee Chapman, whose convalescence had ended at last. McAllister pierced the Hatters' defence and side-footed the ball, which Cantona coolly placed in an empty net. Late in the game the finisher turned provider as he headed the ball towards the unmarked Chapman, who rifled his shot past Steve Sutton. Two–nil to Leeds. Gordon Strachan spoke for the whole of the Leeds dressing-room when he said: 'We do not really mind who scores the goals for us just so long as someone does, but in this case, we were really just as delighted for Éric himself.' He added: 'It cannot have been easy for him trying to settle in a completely different environment while attempting to come to terms with a different style of play as well as having a language problem. But we have a lot of time for him and we have been very impressed with the way he has tackled the problems.' Éric would play more spectacular games for Leeds, but would rarely prove as decisive as he was on that Saturday, 29 February 1992. The maverick had chosen the rogue day of a leap year to open his account in English football.

The media's response to that performance ('Stuttering Leeds Lifted By Cantona' was one headline among many in the same vein) did not alter Wilkinson's view that Éric was best used when the opposition lacked the physical freshness to close down space as rapidly as in the opening stages of a game. Not unreasonably, he also reminded the doubters: 'I have not been down a championship road before, and neither have most of my players. So at this stage of the season, with every game like a cup tie, I tend to fall back on the team which started the season and has got us so far.' So, when February turned into March, Cantona found himself in the dugout again, and had to wait until the 65th minute to take part in a goalless home draw against Aston Villa. The ploy nearly worked, when Éric forced 'keeper Nigel Spink to make a couple of outstanding saves in the last quarter of the match. Leeds had relinquished the lead in the title race to Manchester United by then. Ferguson's men, who led by a single point, had the advantage of a game in hand, and many Leeds fans found it difficult to understand why their flamboyant Frenchman had not become an automatic choice in Wilkinson's starting eleven. As Gordon Strachan reminded the fans, while praising Cantona's 'first-class attitude', and regretting that 'we could not have him at Elland Road from the start of the season': 'You have to remember that when [Éric] joined us, he had not played for six weeks – so it was really like pre-season for him, and we have to break him in gently, though hopefully he will be a big help to us in the final weeks of the season.' These considered words did little to alter the growing perception that Wilkinson's measured approach was too rigid by half. The manager, however, would not bow to fan pressure.

When Leeds travelled to Tottenham on 7 March, Éric found himself on the bench again, to be waved onto the pitch with a quarter of an hour to go when defender Mike Whitlow suffered an injury. Leeds, leading by two goals to one at that stage, faced a nervous conclusion to the game. A victory would see them overtake Manchester United in the league table by two points. When, less than sixty seconds after walking onto the turf, Éric laid the ball in the path of Gary McAllister, who doubled Leeds' advantage, pandemonium erupted in the stand reserved for visiting fans, who had been chanting Cantona's song non-stop since he had been warming up on the touchline. 'No one in France gets that sort of reception for running up and down on the side of the pitch,' a visibly touched Éric confided afterwards. What made it all the more special was that the Cantona clan – his father Albert, his brothers Jean-Marie and Joël – had come from Marseilles to see him play that afternoon. Éric's heart must have swelled with pride. It hardly mattered that Wilkinson had yet again resisted the temptation to do what a whole city willed him to do and send him on from kick-off. 'He's subjected to less pressure when he comes on once the game has started,' the manager explained, somewhat befuddled that a magnificent away victory could be overshadowed by a perfectly sane selection choice. But overshadowed it was.

Éric had conducted himself irreproachably on and off the pitch since his arrival at Elland Road. No complaints. No tantrums. No yellow cards. Frank Worthington, a free spirit who had plied his trade at no fewer than fifteen clubs (Leeds among them) in a career which spanned twenty-three years, called him 'a breath of fresh air on the English scene'. 'In this country,' he said, 'we've long had a mistrust of genuinely talented footballers; that's why I'm glad to see Cantona here.' But come the next game, Éric could only watch from the sidelines as Leeds folded 1–4 against QPR at Loftus Road. He played the last twenty minutes that time, taking Gary McAllister's place long after the white flag had been hoisted: Rangers already led by two goals.

Then, at long last, Wilkinson relented. On Saturday 14 March, on the occasion of Wimbledon's visit to Yorkshire, he deployed the three-pronged attack fans had been clamouring for. Rod Wallace provided width and crosses, Lee Chapman battered the opposition's centre-backs into submission, Éric Cantona added his *je ne sais quoi* in the 'hole', positioning himself just behind the target man. The Dons suffered their heaviest defeat of the campaign, and the final score (5–1) hardly flattered their victors. Chapman beat 'keeper Hans Segers on three occasions to walk away with the match ball. Éric pounced on a mistake by John Scales to run sixty yards and make it 4–1 to the hosts. It was a slaughter; and when a solitary strike by Nigel Clough gave Nottingham Forest a 1–0 win over Manchester United four days later, Leeds found themselves two points clear again at the top of the first division table.

This splendid exhibition convinced Wilkinson to field an unchanged side for what promised to be one of the toughest games of the season: a trip to Arsenal, who remained formidable opponents at their Highbury home despite a mediocre defence of their title. A brutal confrontation was expected and that is exactly what millions of ITV viewers got. The game, played in atrocious conditions, ended in a 1–1 draw that satisfied the visitors rather more than their hosts. Chapman scored his 19th of the season, and Cantona was a few inches away from gaining all three points for his club, only for David Seaman to produce a stupendous one-handed save and deny him at the very last second. Leeds had passed a stringent test that many thought they would fail, and so had Cantona. With seven games to go before the curtain fell on the 1991–92 season, he had finally established himself as one of the key players in the United squad – in the minds of Leeds supporters, that is, even if Howard Wilkinson was yet to be convinced. One Mr A. Bradley won £5 for submitting the prize-winning letter in the *Post*'s sports mailbag at the beginning of March. 'Cantona's ball skills,' he wrote, 'allied to his obvious liking for the English game, have made him a great hit with the Elland Road crowd. Even during the pressure of the push for the First Division title, Cantona has proved there is still room for a little Continental flair.' There was indeed – but a couple of disappointing results made the Leeds coach rethink his strategy.

Leeds first drew 0–0 with West Ham at Elland Road on 28 March, three days after Éric had played 90 minutes with the French national team against Belgium (3–3). Cantona showed no signs of tiredness, though. A dubious offside decision deprived him of a goal in the first half, and later on in the game, he tested the Hammers 'keeper Luděk Mikloško with a fine chip, after gracefully evading a couple of tackles. Then, on 4 April, Leeds' hopes of a first title in eighteen years were dealt what many thought was a mortal blow by Manchester City, who simply walked over Wilkinson's team 4–0 at Maine Road. Starved of service, Cantona had sunk like all around him. Bookmakers now rated Leeds' chances at 9/2, while Manchester United's odds had been cut to 8/1 on – roughly what could be had for Neil Kinnock's Labour Party in the forthcoming general election. But whereas the bankers and brokers of the City were panicking at the thought of a 'socialist' government, Wilkinson was merely 'weighing his options'. He had held talks with Éric's adviser Jean-Jacques Amorfini, as the 15 April deadline to finalize a permanent transfer from Nîmes was fast approaching. A statement was passed on to the press: 'both parties are hoping for a satisfactory outcome'. Wilkinson's mind was made up in that respect: he wished Cantona to commit himself to Leeds for the three seasons to come. But which role would Éric play until the end of the present one?

Manchester United had – on paper – a far better chance than Leeds to capture the trophy that had eluded them since 1967. The next four fixtures that awaited them (Southampton and Nottingham Forest at home, Luton and West Ham away) should have held no fears for the recent winners of the League Cup (won 1–0 against Forest, on 12 April). Leeds would have to travel to Liverpool and face Sheffield United at Bramall Lane, while hosting Chelsea and Coventry. Wilkinson decided he would trust the players who had taken Leeds to the top of the championship by Christmas, which meant that Cantona, though in no way personally responsible for his team's stuttering progress, would revert to the role of 'supersub'. And rarely was this epithet better deserved than when Chelsea turned up at Elland Road on 11 April.

Éric watched Rod Wallace give Leeds a 1–0 lead before replacing him with twenty minutes to go. And what a twenty minutes they were. First, he presented Chapman with his 20th goal of the season. Then . . .

BBC pundits awarded the honorary goal of the 1991–92 season trophy to a spectacular Mickey Thomas effort for Wrexham against Arsenal in the FA Cup. But Éric's strike against Chelsea was on a different plane altogether, the kind of goal that is dreamed of and remains scorched in the memory. Gordon Strachan took a quick throw-in on the right wing. Cantona ran to the ball just outside the area, and, seeing that Paul Elliott had committed himself to the tackle, flicked it over the Chelsea defender's head with his right boot. Elliott regained his balance, only to see the ball loop beyond his reach again. As it fell, in slow motion it seemed, Cantona's right foot connected with the sphere on the volley and sent it soaring into the top corner of the net. Elland Road had seen nothing like it for more than twenty years, not since Eddie Gray, starting from the corner flag, had ghosted his way past five Burnley defenders before slotting the ball home. Elliott, the reigning Scottish footballer of the year, freshly acquired by Chelsea from Celtic, had spent two seasons with Pisa in Serie A. 'I can honestly say that I haven't seen anything like it since I was in Italy,' he said afterwards. 'And then it came from Marco van Basten. That should tell you everything.'

Gordon Strachan, with one eye on the confrontations that laid ahead, tried to temper the wildly enthusiastic reaction of Leeds supporters. 'That goal came when the game was won,' he said, 'and maybe just now it suits Éric to come on when the heat of the battle has died down a little. Not because he physically cannot take it, but because coping mentally with the demands of the English game at this particular time might be a bit of a problem for him.' Try telling that to thousands of famished fans who had waited for a generation to be treated to such splendour again. Nor were the Elland Road season-ticket holders the only ones to stand up and notice. Across the Pennines, a teenage Welsh winger who had made his debut for Manchester United in the previous season was enthralled by the beauty of a goal 'that any player would have been proud of': Ryan Giggs.

Two days later, Wilkinson announced that Leeds intended to take up their option on Cantona's contract, 'subject to agreement on personal terms'. Éric's salary was rumoured to approach £7,000 a week (far more than his manager was paid), a huge outlay for a club like Leeds United, which could not yet rely on television money and European games receipts to balance its books. Prudent by nature, gambler by instinct, Wilkinson felt he could not afford to lose a player who had given substance to his team's ambitions by his presence alone. Éric Cantona did not win the title single-handedly, as it could be argued he did for Manchester United in 1995–96. When Leeds fought out a crucial goal-less draw at Anfield on 18 April, the hero of the day was 'keeper John Lukic, not Cantona, who couldn't summon the verve he had displayed against Chelsea the week before. Gordon Strachan would, quite rightly, be voted Leeds player of the year, a distinction to which McAllister also had a better claim than the Frenchman. But Éric, as so often in his career, was a catalyst. When I asked Gary whether he thought Leeds could have become champions without their 'supersub', his answer was as unequivocal as the view expressed by every single fan I've spoken to.

'He played a vital role in our winning the championship,' he said. 'It's not about the statistics. When you're going for the championship, you get a bit nervy towards the end, the pressure starts to tell. Certainly when Leeds played at home, the visiting teams tried to park the bus in front of the goal, and play ultra-defensively. Éric would come on when we struggled to find a way through, and more often than not, he'd get the crowd going with a little bit of magic, and the crowd would lift us – and we'd score an important goal. Strachan, Batty, Speed . . . they were the engine of the team, but, when it came to winning the championship, Éric played a pivotal part, and his role grew as the season went on.'

If nerves were frayed at Elland Road, they were exposed raw at Old Trafford. Manchester United's progress in the League Cup had led to the postponement of a number of their league games, five of which had to be played between 16 and 26 April. Wilkinson compared his team's situation to that of Mary Decker in the 1984 Olympic 3,000 metres final, when the American favourite's heels were clipped by Zola Budd as she was about to kick for home in the back straight. No one was fooled. The title was Ferguson's to lose. Much depended on his skipper Bryan Robson's fitness – a recurrent theme in this magnificent footballer's career – but even 'Captain Marvel' couldn't cope with the accumulation of matches, and neither could his teammates. On Easter

Monday (20 April), Leeds took the field against Coventry knowing that their rivals had been beaten 2–1 (at home, no less) by their bogey team Nottingham Forest. Fired by this unhoped-for result, Leeds strolled to a 2–0 victory over the Sky Blues, in which Cantona played his now customary cameo. He jogged on the pitch with fifteen minutes to go, and induced a penalty when Lloyd McGrath appeared to block his shot with a hand on the goal-line. Two days later an exhausted Manchester United then proceeded to lose 1–0 at already relegated West Ham, which prompted Alex Ferguson to 'concede' the title. With 76 points to the Mancunians' 75, and a substantially better goal difference than their rivals (+35 against +30), Leeds were now 3/1 on to become champions of England.

The pressure on both title contenders was increased by the Football League's decision to bow to television's wishes and hold their next games at different times on Sunday 26 April. Neither side relished the trips that a sadistic schedule had set for them. Leeds had to go to Bramall Lane, knowing that their neighbours Sheffield United would like nothing better than to derail their campaign at the very last. Manchester United had to perform in the noxious atmosphere of Anfield, where Liverpool fans would celebrate a victory by the home team as if it had brought them another championship crown. Wilkinson's men had the support of 5,000 of their fans, who could not have felt that confident when the game was locked at 2–2 with fifteen minutes to go. McAllister made way for Cantona at this point. A few seconds later, Éric and Rod Wallace closed down on Brian Gayle in the Sheffield United penalty area, hurrying the panicking defender who comically managed to loop the ball over his 'keeper Mel Rees with the strangest of back-headers. Somewhat fortuitously, Leeds had taken all three points, and could now sit back and watch Manchester United try and bring the title race to the wire.

Sit back is precisely what Éric did, in Lee Chapman's living room, where ITV had installed a camera to record the reactions of the Leeds players to the events unfolding at Anfield. David Batty and Gary McAllister also perched themselves on the sofa, literally on the edge of their seats. It soon became clear that Manchester United's tank was running on empty. Demoralized by the result at Bramall Lane, their bodies drained by the insane schedule that had been forced on them, Ferguson's players barely put up a fight. Once Ian Rush had scored his very first goal against Manchester United, the Kop cruelly sang: 'And now you're gonna believe us/You'll never win the league' to the tune of 'For He's a Jolly Good Fellow'; and when Mark Walters put the result beyond doubt late in the second half, thousands of jubilant Kopites joined in an impromptu conga: 'Let's all laugh at Man U, let's all laugh at Man U, ha haa ha ha'. As Ryan Giggs walked back, broken-hearted, to the team coach, he was accosted by a fan who asked for his autograph. The player complied – only to see the sniggering Liverpool supporter tear up the piece of paper in his face. It wouldn't be too long before Cantona found himself the subject of such visceral hatred.

Back at Chapman's home, Walters' title-clinching goal had been greeted with an explosion of joy; but while his teammates embraced and danced a victory jig, Éric remained impassive throughout, his arms folded, his eyes staring at the television screen, with the face of a child stumbling on an incomprehensible scene of adult celebration. True, some of the events of that afternoon verged on the surreal. The ITV presenter Elton Welsby tried to get a comment from Cantona, but in vain, and ventured in desperation: '*Magnifique*, Éric!' to which the player answered – in English – 'Oh, do you speak French?' '*Non*,' came the reply, bringing an immediate end to one of the most bizarre interviews ever aired on British television.

It's not that Éric felt he didn't belong – he most certainly did, and would overcome his shyness in the days to come; but he must have found it difficult to believe that he, the outsider, the rebel who had been cast away five months previously, had just won the third championship title of his career and perhaps the first that meant anything to him, even if he had spent far more time on the pitch when Marseille were crowned in 1991. As the magnitude of what he and his new friends had achieved began to sink in, a different Cantona emerged from his shell. He opened himself fully to the extraordinary outpouring of pride that lit up the city and, by his own admission, barely slept over the next few days. He had never encountered such devotion to a club. Everywhere he looked, windows were now festooned with blue and white flags. Fans climbed up the statue of the Black Prince in City

Square and sang his name (two of them had to be taken to hospital when they fell). Another supporter, one Christopher Bromage, told the *Yorkshire Post* that he had travelled 50,000 miles to follow the Peacocks in the 1991–92 season, timing his business trips so that they would coincide with football fixtures, as he worked in Japan. One of his most cherished moments was 'being there' when 'Éric made his debut at Oldham'. What can you say to fans like these? Precisely what Cantona said to tens of thousands of revellers from the balcony of the Town Hall: 'Why I love you? I don't know why, but I love you.'*

In the midst of the parties and civic receptions that followed, Éric still managed to play another two games of football, including, rather oddly, a 7–2 trouncing by Liverpool of the reserves which Howard Wilkinson had added to his programme for reasons only known to himself. And twenty-four hours after attending a well-oiled lunch at which the championship winners of 1974 and 1992 sat down together, Cantona and his teammates summoned enough professionalism to end the season on a high on Saturday 2 May. Norwich were gracious enough to let a sleep-deprived (and hungover) Leeds trot to a 1–0 victory, during which the Elland Road Kop bawled out a tuneless version of '*La Marseillaise*'. It had just been announced that the Frenchman had agreed to sign a three-year deal with the champions, and the whole crowd rose to their feet when he was subbed with fifteen minutes to go.

The match itself was a mere sideshow to the triumphant parade the following morning. An estimated 150,000 people – over one-fifth of the city's entire population – lined the streets where the team's open-top bus proceeded at a snail's pace. The closer it got to the Art Gallery, where a temporary stand had been erected, the thicker the crowd, the louder the songs, until, finally, one by one, the champions were introduced to their fans. Huge cheers greeted the appearance of Strachan and Wilkinson, but reached a fortissimo when Éric's turn came to salute the multitude. The now familiar chant of 'Ooh-ah, Cantona, say ooh-ah Cantona!' filled the Headrow. Éric, stunned, raised his arms

* A local dance music outfit, Ooh La La, used a sample of Éric's 'love' speech on a single which achieved moderate success in the Leeds area.

and clapped. Who was applauding who? Who was the star, who was the admirer?

Later that evening, the heroes gathered with 400 guests in Elland Road's banqueting suite, where they received their championship medals from the hands of Leeds chairman Leslie Silver. Cantona, sporting a 'psychedelic multi-coloured shirt', listened to the speeches, smiling when the *Post*'s editor Chris Bye opened his allocution with a few words in French. Cantona's teammates didn't mind the praise lavished on the single member of their squad who didn't carry a British passport, even though Éric had taken part in only fifteen of forty-two league games (nine as a sub) and scored the same number of goals as left-back Tony Dorigo: three, which gave him equal eighth place in Leeds's scoring charts. Most of them agreed with journalist Mark Dexter, who wrote that 'Wilkinson's best move of the campaign [had been] the signing of Éric Cantona on loan'. His presence had nourished the belief, both on the terraces and on the pitch, that, after eighteen trophy-less seasons, this could be Leeds' year.

Wilkinson's attitude was more ambivalent. Feted as 'the future of English football' (both a bleak prospect and a less-than-prescient prediction, as no other English manager has lifted the championship trophy since he did), he revelled in the plaudits he received at the hour of his greatest achievement, but was puzzled by the importance attached to Éric's role in the conquest of the title. Less charitably minded observers suggested that Wilkinson resented having someone else steal his thunder. Had he not been the director, and Éric a mere extra? For the time being, with a city 'living on champagne' (as a player's wife put it), and Leeds about to take part in their first European Cup since a bitter loss to Bayern Munich in the 1975 final, such interrogations could be left aside. They made no sense for Cantona himself. The French public struggled to understand how he had accepted a glorified substitute's role with good grace at Leeds when he wouldn't have (and didn't) at Olympique Marseille, for example. The answer was simple. 'I have always been implicated in the adventure of Leeds,' he explained shortly before the start of Euro 92. 'The manager always trusted me. He brought me in little by little. He didn't want to "burn" me. People managed to make me understand the reality of English football, the life of the club . . . Remember that I had so many things to discover.'

To him, England had represented a means to an end – literally: the end of a potentially catastrophic dispute with Nîmes, which could have left him penniless. Four months on, not only had he settled that matter once and for all, but also discovered a country in which his 'difference' was cherished. 'If things had not worked out at Elland Road, I would have quit the game,' he assured Mike Casey in the second (and last) of his heart-to-hearts with the British press. But the Leeds manager and players 'have taken me at my face value and ignored the stories about me being a bad boy. The fans too have made me so very, very welcome. I love them. I'm flattered by the way they have treated me. The English have a great sense of respect for people and that has been very helpful to me. Despite the language barrier, I know they like me. And that feeling is mutual.'

On 5 May, a couple of days after sending his love letter to the *Post* readers, Éric packed his bags and made his way back to Paris, where Michel Platini and his squad were waiting for him. The first French player to receive a championship winner's medal in England now had to get himself fit and ready for Euro 92 (shedding the four kilos he had put on in a single week of celebrations in Yorkshire would be a start). Cantona's progress in the English league had been documented in great detail by the French media, but Wilkinson's cautious handling (if not wariness) of his charge had not gone unnoticed either. Not everyone was convinced that a reformed character would step off the plane at Roissy. There would be trouble ahead, they said, in which they erred. What lay ahead was in some ways more hurtful than trouble: disappointment.

Researching this book entailed going through hundreds of match reports and viewing hours upon hours of tapes of games that have been forgotten, and not without reason. It's not paying a great compliment to the British press to say that, nine times out of ten, reading the account of a match brought more reward than watching it. It is easy to forget the rut into which English football had fallen at the time Éric Cantona arrived at Elland Road. The post-Heysel exile from European competitions had made

English football fold back into the worst of itself, a perverse mixture of fear – of the outsider, the foreigner, the eccentric – and glorification of 'manly' virtues in which the detached observer could see little but crudeness and brutality. What happened on the pitch mirrored what took place in the stands. Football of the late 1980s and early 1990s was a drab, sometimes vicious affair. There was no shortage of hard-working, hard-tackling, box-to-box one-footed midfielders. In almost every team could be found what is regarded as a 'typical', or 'old-fashioned' centre-forward, all forehead and elbows. Some were fine pros, the heirs of Nat Lofthouse, keepers of a respected tradition. Éric's Leeds teammate Lee Chapman belonged to that family; but too many others were bullies who would have been refereed out of the game on the Continent. Central defenders hoofed the ball away from the danger zone with the blessing of their coaches. Everyone was running at a hundred miles an hour, saturating their jerseys with honest sweat, kicking and being kicked, negating what skill they might have had in the relentless pursuit of victory.

More delicate birds like Glenn Hoddle and Chris Waddle had flown south, to Monaco and Marseilles respectively, and both had been welcome in the country Cantona had vowed never to play in again. Clive Allen, Trevor Steven, Ray Wilkins, Graham Rix and Mark Hateley also flourished in France. In any case, at least since Stanley Matthews' retirement, and despite the brief regency of gifted rogues à la *Rodney Marsh and Frank Worthington in the early 1970s, dashers had always been thin on the ground in England. The few who had surfaced had rarely been trusted by managers influenced by the noxious theories of the long-ball merchants who wielded a great deal of influence within the FA. The name of Charles Reep should still send shivers down the spine of anyone who cares about football. In fact, more often than not, the entertainers came from Scotland, the land of the passing game, Ulster or the Republic: Kenny Dalglish, George Best, Liam Brady. Those who did not frequently ended up on the scrapheap, like the tragic Robin Friday, hacked to oblivion after shining so brightly, so briefly, for Reading FC.*

In the eight years between the butchery of Heysel and Manchester United's first championship title since 1967, English football seemed to be played in the deep of winter, on windswept, rain-soaked fields of mud. It could still hold a visceral appeal for the Saturday crowds; but these crowds were dwindling, despite the cheapness of tickets, and not just because the so-called ordinary fans wanted to avoid trouble. The poison of hooliganism was a symptom, not necessarily a cause, of the game's sorry decline. It was Cantona's paradoxical luck that he drifted to England precisely when the game he loved was played there in an environment and a fashion that ran against his deepest-held convictions and feelings. Should he fail, it would be a confirmation that a player for whom self-expression was paramount had better pursue personal fulfilment elsewhere; the failure would not necessarily be his. Should he succeed, he would become Éric Cantona as England remembers him.

Of the twenty-two teams which then comprised the old first division, only three or four could claim to play entertaining football. Spurs clung on to their aristocratic reputation with varying degrees of success or justification. Ron Atkinson's Aston Villa, infuriatingly inconsistent though they were, at least put on a decent show for their fans. Norwich's combination play, with its simple elegance, its emphasis on passing to feet in neat triangles, could remind a Continental connoisseur of another team clad in yellow, the 'canaries' of FC Nantes. Alex Ferguson held on to his belief in the more expressive, more vibrant brand of football that had brought him success with Aberdeen – but with players who did not quite possess the technical ability required to fulfil his ambitions. And that's about it. Nottingham Forest was fast becoming a shadow of its former, admirable self, and so was Liverpool, who could still summon some of their old verve, but too fleetingly to equal their previous incarnations. Sheffield Wednesday held promise, but did not have the financial resources to rise above the fray for long. This is no exaggeration. Watching English football in 1992 might have been exciting – for some – but it certainly wasn't pretty.

There is little to indicate that Cantona himself was aware of Leeds' role of villain in the pantomime of English football. England was not his spiritual homeland; Brazil, yes, where, to him, 'passing the ball [was] like offering a gift', the Netherlands too, whom he had wished to beat France when they met in a crucial World Cup qualifier in 1981. What little English football was shown on French television when he grew up (and believe me, it was very little) came in infuriatingly short snippets of Liverpool cutting the opposition to shreds in the Sunday evening sports programme. From time to time, before 1985, a European game featuring an English team might dislodge a TV drama from its evening slot, and a great deal was made of the ritual known as the FA Cup final, in which many saw the sporting equivalent of a coronation, an arcane, quasi-mystical ceremonial so far removed from our own experience that the less we understood it, the more pleasure we derived from its pomp and circumstance. In international tournaments, England kept on under-performing with bewildering consistency; in fact, when Éric signed his first professional forms for Auxerre, in 1986, the heirs of Bobby Moore had not been in serious contention for a major title since the 1970 World Cup – when Cantona was four years old.

True Anglophiles like Gérard Houllier, the exceptions rather than the rule, tended to come from the north of France, where strong links had been forged between footballing cities from each side of the Channel. My home team, Le Havre Athletic Club, which had borrowed its colours from Oxford and Cambridge universities, had taken part in semi-serious summer tournaments with the likes of Portsmouth and Southampton in the 1960s. It felt natural to confess an allegiance to, say, Peter Osgood's Chelsea, just as it felt natural to listen to The Kinks, The Clash or Doctor Feelgood. The more adventurous would book a trip on the ferry to stand in the terraces of Fratton Park or The Dell, or listen to Ducks DeLuxe at the Hope and Anchor, but such visitors were few, and Cantona certainly didn't belong to that micro-culture. He himself had trodden on English soil just once before flying to Sheffield. That was in 1988, when he played that splendid game against the England under-21s at Highbury. English football still carried an aura, now tinged with real menace after its travelling supporters' innumerable excesses. Our national team invariably lost against the rosbifs *(our 1986 campaign, which saw* Les Bleus *play one of the greatest games of this or any tournament, a 1–1 draw with Brazil, had started with their customary defeat against Bryan Robson's team), and French clubs rarely fared better when drawn against the English in Europe.*

The fanciful souls who had crossed the Channel to seek some kind of footballing glory before Cantona could be counted on two fingers. In the early years of the twentieth century, a goalkeeper named Georges Crozier had been employed by Fulham – but he was an eccentric rather than a pioneer. More recently, the failure of Didier Six at Aston Villa exemplified the irreducibility of our footballing differences. A strong, speedy winger of established international pedigree (he played in the 1982 World Cup semi-final), Six could cross the ball beautifully from both flanks. His direct, determined play should have suited the English game; instead of which, following a handful of promising performances, he foundered and left after a single season (1984–85). Platini and Houllier knew this, but, partly out of desperation, they trusted their instincts, and their instincts told them that no clear alternative presented itself to save the career of the most gifted French player of his time, in their eyes the only one who could fill the huge void left by the final eclipse of the 1978–86 golden generation. England was the choice of a gambler down to his last few chips; the last-chance saloon.

10

The acrobat at work: at Clairefontaine with the French squad.

FAREWELL TO DREAMS: EURO 92 AND EXIT FROM LEEDS

The 1992 European Championships are now remembered for the astonishing triumph of Denmark, and little else. The Danes had been drafted in at the eleventh hour (nine days before the start of the competition, to be precise) to replace the team they had finished behind in their qualifying pool. The soon-to-be 'former Yugoslavia',* then torn apart by civil war, had been excluded by UEFA in accordance with United Nations resolution no. 757. Denmark, perennial makeweights of international competitions (one participation in the final phase of the World Cup until then), then qualified ahead of France and England in the Euro 92's group phase before dispatching Dennis Bergkamp's Netherlands and Jürgen Klinsmann's Germany en route to the biggest shock witnessed in a major tournament since Uruguay beat Brazil 2–1 at the Estádio do Maracanã in 1950. The Danish squad's preparation had been minimal, so much so that many of the players were said (wrongly, it seems) to have cut their summer holidays short to rejoin the squad in Sweden, where the championships took place. Their coach, Richard Møller Nielsen, had stayed at home: there was a new kitchen to be installed, apparently. Michael Laudrup, the undoubted star of a team in which there weren't many – not yet, anyway – had announced his retirement shortly before UEFA informed the Danes that they had qualified by default. The rank outsiders

* This was the Yugoslavia of Prosinečki, Savičević, Pančev, Boban and Stojković, potentially one of the greatest sides to have emerged from beyond the Iron Curtain, which many felt would have gained European supremacy just as Red Star Belgrade had done at club level a year previously.

dropped their buckets and spades and, with all the odds stacked against them, had their day in the sun. It made for a heartwarming story, which, unfortunately, the football played in the competition didn't live up to. Denmark, with an exceptional Peter Schmeichel in goal, set out to nullify what little threat their opponents dared to pose, and succeeded beyond their wildest expectations, while their Viking-helmeted supporters popularized face-painting and drank Sweden dry. Goals were scored at the pitifully low rate of 2.13 per game, an average inferior to that of the most dismal World Cup of modern times, the Italian 1990 *Mondiale* (2.21). And for the French, it was even more miserable than that.

Les Bleus hadn't taken part in a major tournament for six years, but made most observers' short list of favourites. No other team had ever sailed through the qualifiers with such ease: eight games, eight victories, a record that still stands. Before England had prevailed 2–0 at Wembley in February, Platini's men had remained undefeated for over two years. A couple of hiccups against Belgium (3–3) and Switzerland (1–2 in Lausanne) prior to the championships didn't worry their supporters unduly, as Michel Platini had used these friendlies to try out new players and tinker with tactical formations (no less than six substitutes had been introduced against the Swiss, another European record in internationals for Platini). When, five days before the start of the tournament, France drew their last warm-up game 1–1 with the Netherlands, the satisfaction of having contained a redoubtable opponent obscured the negativity of the performance. It was almost universally thought that, once the tinkering had stopped, the true visage of France would appear.

Sadly, it was a sullen face that Platini's team showed to the rest of Europe. This most inventive of players adopted a negative strategy that would have been anathema to his mentor Michel Hidalgo. For France's inaugural game against Sweden, Platini ditched the 4-3-3 that had served him so well during the pre-tournament phase in favour of a lopsided system in which Cantona was required to play in a withdrawn position behind Jean-Pierre Papin, and Pascal Vahirua alone provided a measure of width. The Swedes were well worth the 1–0 lead they held at half-time, and were entitled to feel disappointed when JPP equalized from fifteen yards on the hour. Éric had been at best subdued, at worst transparent. Some wondered whether the calmer, more mature Cantona who had emerged from four tremendously successful months in England hadn't lost some of his old bite. Judging by his next game, they might well have had a point.

The ninety minutes of that goalless draw between England and France must rank among the most tedious ever suffered by the fans of both teams. Platini asked his veteran midfielder Luis Fernandez to drop so deep that *Les Bleus* took the shape of an inverted pyramid, a grim 5-3-2 in which Cantona and Papin, with no support to speak of, watched the ball being tackled to and fro in midfield by the likes of Carlton Palmer and Didier Deschamps. Come the end of the most depressing anticlimax of the competition, Graham Taylor's and Michel Platini's teams found themselves with two points from two games – in other words, perilously close to the elimination their displays so far merited. And to every neutral's satisfaction, they exited the tournament three days later, Sweden taking care of England by 2 goals to 1 and Denmark, astonishingly, seeing off France by an identical scoreline. No French or English player featured in the Group 1 XI selected by the French press after three games. Cantona? Not a single goal. No assist. His only contribution of note had been in France's equalizer against Denmark, when his cross from the right was controlled, then backheeled by Jean-Philippe Durand for the on-rushing Papin. A few hours after their defeat, a lugubrious French team boarded a private charter plane and left Sweden in silence.

What on earth could have gone so disastrously wrong? The individual qualities of the players were not in doubt. A number of them had stepped up from Marc Bourrier's successful *Espoirs* (though not Stéphane Paille, by then marooned in Caen), Laurent Blanc among them, who now played in Serie A (with Napoli). Jean-Pierre Papin too had gone to Italy, where he counted Ruud Gullit and Franco Baresi as teammates in Milan. No less than seven of the thirteen players who had fired blanks against the English were in Bernard Tapie's employment at all-conquering Marseille, who had just won their fourth consecutive *championnat*: Manuel Amoros, Basile Boli, Bernard Casoni, Jean-Philippe

Durand, Franck Sauzée, Jocelyn Angloma and Didier Deschamps. OM, runners-up in the 1991 European Cup, which they would win two years later, now belonged to the pantheon of European club football. Other French teams such as Auxerre, PSG, Monaco and Bordeaux had recently featured in the latter stages of UEFA competitions. Never had French football been in such rude health at international level – as far as clubs were concerned. Awash with television money, they were able to attract the best talent available on the Continent and beyond, while retaining a strong French core. There was something incomprehensible, then, about the fear that had suddenly gripped the national team in Sweden. Platini was criticized for his timorous approach (with some justification) and for his eagerness to switch systems from one game to the next (a less fair charge, as tactical adaptability had been long been a strength of *Les Bleus*). Many also suspected that the dressing-room unity made much of beforehand by Cantona among others was a façade, and that deep faultlines ran within the camp, which was dominated – at least numerically – by Marseille players. Éric probably sensed them more acutely than any other, but only alluded to them much later on and then rather obliquely: he was aware that France's failure was partly to be blamed on himself.

Some individuals he found difficult to relate to, particularly those who played for his former club Marseille. Reminiscing in 2007, he had damning words for Didier Deschamps in particular. '[He] is not a man,' he said, 'and the gravest thing is that there are guys who've won beside them [*a 'them' by which Éric made clear he meant Didier Deschamps and Marcel Desailly*] who despise them as much as I do.' When *L'Équipe Magazine* pressed for more detail, Cantona replied, 'I don't hold anything against them. To each his own.' Then: 'Honestly, would these people save you if you were drowning?'

Éric could hold a grudge, as we know, but why would he focus his anger on someone – Deschamps – who had only arrived at OM *after* he himself had left for Nîmes? DD, or Dédé, represented everything that jarred with Cantona's belief in the primacy of self-expression on the football field. Deschamps seldom ventured beyond the halfway line, and revelled in the functionality of his own role. It was easy, not to say convenient, to feel that he had ultimately placed the game at the service of his career. That he was an apparatchik, a civil servant looking for promotion after promotion, in short, a water-carrier (*porteur d'eau*). This expression was in common usage in French football parlance before Cantona made it his own a few years later, but it only acquired its derogatory connotation once Éric had directed it at Deschamps.* That the holding midfielder was remarkably good at what he did, and won everything a footballer of his day and age could have won, including the Champions League, European Championships and World Cup titles that all eluded Éric, undoubtedly struck him as an injustice. But there may have been another, simpler explanation for the dislike that Cantona expressed in such forceful terms over the years. At the time of Euro 92, Deschamps was only twenty-three and keenly aware of the seniority of other squad members, Cantona among them. The problems would arise later, and would only be proposed as an explanation for the 1992 failure in hindsight, when Aimé Jacquet, who enjoyed a close relationship with his defensive midfielder, made Deschamps his captain in 1995. This was little over three months after Éric had been stripped of the armband, in the wake of the infamous Crystal Palace 'kung-fu kick'. Jealousy there may have been at the usurper's elevation, as well as a feeling – shared by many Cantona supporters – that Deschamps actively campaigned against Éric's reinstatement to the national team once he'd served his ban, and deprived him of a chance to take part in the 1996 European Championships and the 1998 World Cup. DD vehemently denied that this was the case, and, in the view of what would happen in January 1996 (the time of Éric's second 'suicide', as we'll see), if he'd tried to undermine Cantona's position within the French camp, he'd failed. When I contacted him to get his side of the story, his reply was courteous but firm: he had no wish to revisit that part of their common past. Many of the dark corners in Cantona's career become even darker when you try to shine a light on them.

*

* I've since wondered whether Éric was familiar with his hero Diego Maradona's famous quote deriding Real Madrid's obsession with star players: 'You need someone to carry the water to the well.' One sees what he meant by that, but only just.

The unravelling of France's aspirations in Sweden is only alluded to in Cantona's autobiography. All that can be found is an eight-line paragraph which lists 'bad luck' and 'inexperience' as reasons for the desperately poor performances of Platini's team. Neither explanation holds water. *Les Bleus* created very few chances, and were punished for their timidity; referees had officiated fairly; no injuries had disrupted the team's preparation; and it was the same group of players who had torn through the opposition all through the qualification phase. Éric must have realized that Platini had failed to galvanize his charges when it most mattered, but couldn't bring himself to admit that responsibility could be laid at his manager's door. How could he condemn the 'big brother' who had shown so much faith in him when everyone else had abandoned any hope of a future for Cantona? The gratitude and loyalty he felt towards his saviour forbade him to side with those who, quite reasonably, believed that Platini should resign his position. And when the time came for the manager to step down later in the summer, Éric would make himself a target for ridicule with one of the most quixotic decisions of his whole career. He announced his retirement from international football at the age of twenty-six, and was fortunate that no one was prepared to take his words seriously.

Éric and Isabelle could only enjoy a few weeks' rest away from football before the Leeds squad set off to Ireland in the penultimate week of July, a trip which passed without incident – unless some late-night high jinks can be considered 'incidents' in the life of a professional footballer. On one occasion, while Wilkinson slept in his Dublin hotel room, Cantona and one of his teammates broke the curfew, slid down a drainpipe in the small hours of the morning, and went in search of entertainment in the centre of the city. According to my source, their search was not unsuccessful. His integration was proceeding apace, and proving to be fun, too. Not for the first (or last time), English football in its many guises would provide Éric with a welcome break from the vicissitudes he endured serving his country.

This Irish interlude was brief, dominated by the news of David Rocastle's arrival at Elland Road. Many observers were baffled by Wilkinson's willingness to pay £2m (twice Cantona's transfer fee) for an attacking midfielder who had suffered a serious knee injury two seasons previously at Arsenal, and scored a goal only every nine games or so for the London club. 'Rocky' Rocastle, adored as he was by the Highbury crowd, had never established himself at international level. It was later felt that George Graham had exploited the midfielder's selflessness, bravery and enthusiasm with a degree of callousness, and sacrificed the most naturally gifted player at his disposal to serve a vision of the game in which endeavour, organization and ruthlessness must prevail over fluency and skill. Rocastle's reward had been a right knee reduced to pulp, and what amounted to a summary dismissal. Heartbroken at the idea of leaving the club he had played for since leaving school at the age of 16, the player never settled in Yorkshire.

Wilkinson saw Rocastle as a long-term replacement for Gordon Strachan, who, as it happens, would still be playing at the top level after he had passed his 40th birthday, by which time the Londoner was rotting in the Chelsea reserves, having played a single season at Elland Road. The Leeds manager was right in one respect: far too many of his players were on the wrong side of thirty to sustain another title-chasing campaign. No team had successfully retained the trophy since Liverpool in 1983–84, and the bookmakers agreed with the pessimistic appraisals of most columnists: Arsenal, the 1989 and 1991 champions, were 9/4 favourites, ahead of Liverpool (7/2), with Manchester United and Leeds both quoted at 4/1. Wilkinson's thin squad would also feel the strain of taking part in the European Cup, and Éric, like all around him, anxiously waited for reinforcements – which never came, with dire consequences for his relationship with the Leeds supremo.

For the time being, all was still sweetness and light in Yorkshire. The champions were fitted with new suits for the forthcoming Charity Shield, a far bigger occasion back then, and rounded off their pre-season with warm-up games against Nottingham Forest, VfB Stuttgart (their future opponents in the European Cup) and the Genoan club Sampdoria in the so-called 'Makita Tournament'. This competition, if that's the word, was organized over a single weekend at the start of August, and was the first occasion on which the new FIFA 'no back-pass' rule was implemented. Éric, who only played nine minutes of Leeds's 2–1 victory over Stuttgart, replaced the newly arrived Rocastle at the interval of the tournament's final (against Sampdoria), and missed three decent chances before Leeds were beaten 1–0 in front of 15,000 spectators who didn't seem to care much more than himself for the game. Two days later, he looked far sharper in a 2–0 defeat of Norway's 1991 champions Strømsgodset IF, scoring a virtuoso goal that gave a better indication of what was to follow at Wembley, when Leeds would face FA Cup holders Liverpool in the Charity Shield.

No fewer than five Liverpool first-teamers – John Barnes, Michael Thomas, Steve McManaman, Rob Jones and Jan Molby – were missing from Graeme Souness's squad through injury, while a full-strength Leeds United could be assembled by Wilkinson, with Cantona wearing the no. 7 shirt for the first time in a competitive match. With 26 minutes of the game played, Rod Wallace found himself in acres of space on the left wing, and had all the time in the world to cut the ball back to Éric who, from the penalty spot, drilled the ball between two Liverpool defenders, high into Grobbelaar's net. An Ian Rush header cancelled out the advantage, but not for long: as half-time loomed, a deflection put Tony Dorigo's free kick out of the Liverpool goalie's reach. Dean Saunders brought the scores level in the 67th minute, only for Cantona, again, to score a sumptuous goal. He first leapt to claim a Gary McAllister free kick, the ball falling into Rod Wallace's path in the box. The winger, by accident as much as on purpose, laid it back to the Frenchman, who thumped a glorious angled shot across Grobbelaar, and celebrated by kissing his shirt in front of delirious Leeds supporters. That was 3–2 to United – then 4–2 four minutes from time when Wallace, claiming his third assist of one of the best and most competitive Charity Shields ever staged at Wembley, chased a ball that was kept in play after bouncing off the corner flag on the left flank. His deep, floated cross found Éric, who outjumped his marker at the far post. Grobbelaar had left his line, and heading the ball beyond him was an easy task for Cantona. There was still time for a comical own goal by Gordon Strachan, who took no less than three touches to ensure Mark Wright's shot crossed the line, but not enough to deny Leeds United the second Charity Shield in their history.

No one had scored a hat-trick in the season's curtain-raiser since Tommy Taylor (who lost his life in the Munich air crash) helped

Manchester United demolish Aston Villa 4–0 in 1957. Cantona had registered a number of firsts on that glorious summer afternoon. He was the first Frenchman to feature and score for an English club at Wembley, the first to be named man of the match in England, earning his highest-ever rating to that point in his career (9/10) in the *Post*; he was also the first Leeds player to score three goals in a single game in the old stadium. The significance of these achievements didn't escape him. Could there be a greater contrast to the destruction of France in Sweden eight weeks previously? As he walked up the thiry-nine steps to Wembley's Royal Box, the voices of tens of thousands of fans chanting his name told him that he wasn't an exile any more.

'In just two months in England [*Éric was referring to the signing of his permanent transfer contract in May*], I feel more at home than I ever did in France,' he said. 'Now that I have mastered the perils of driving on the wrong side of the road, I can cope with everything.' He struggled to express how much it meant to him, a Frenchman, to have taken part in 'such a big occasion', but fared better when his future was discussed. 'Right now,' he said, 'I'm like a singer who goes to number one in the charts but has only one hit. I can't say I've arrived yet. I've got to go on now and prove myself every weekend and convince everyone I can play in English football. It's a completely different style and it has been every bit as hard as I thought it would be to adapt – but I have always been convinced I could get used to it.' He also had kind, measured, respectful words for his beaming manager, words which must, however, be understood in the context of Éric's own appreciation of his progress. He believed that his apprenticeship had ended, and that he had earned the right to start Leeds games instead of having to wait on the bench for an hour to go by before removing his tracksuit. Moreover, as Gary McAllister assured me, the majority of his teammates were of the same opinion. 'I must take my hat off to Howard Wilkinson for helping me to integrate,' Éric said. 'He could have played me after I arrived last season, but it would have been very difficult for me to get used to it. But he made me wait. He told me I had to think about the English game and observe it, study it. I have done that, and I have worked hard in pre-season training because my target now is to get a regular first-team place.'

Wilkinson concurred with the latter part of this statement. 'The hallmark of a good player is to consistently produce the level of which he is capable, week in week out,' he said. His cautiousness was understandable. The Charity Shield remained a glorified exhibition game, and Leeds had had their share of good fortune against a severely depleted Liverpool side. Some of Wilkinson's words nonetheless revealed more than prudence, betraying a deep-seated suspicion of a footballer whose qualities he could see, but whom he still doubted possessed the steel necessary to achieve greatness. In his twenty years in the game, he conceded, he had never dealt with a player of comparable ability, with the exception of John Barnes and Glenn Hoddle. But he couldn't help but add a rider to his praise. 'Éric was always the sort of player that you would step back from signing,' he said. 'I knew that and people kept telling me "*non, non, non*" when I was looking at him. They said you couldn't trust him. *They may be right yet.*' The italics are mine, of course, but the words were Wilkinson's; not only that: he spoke them as Leeds fans were still making their way back to Wembley Park tube station. The Yorkshireman's call-a-spade-a-blooming-shovel approach had its virtues. Cantona knew where he stood in his manager's estimation, and could accept it, but only for as long as it was obvious to him that he also had his trust. Éric's elevation to the rank of demigod at Elland Road jarred with Wilkinson's team ethos.

It was all about the Frenchman as far as the *Post* and its readers were concerned. When their customary pre-season supplement was published on 10 August, a photograph of Éric holding the Shield aloft occupied most of its front page. 'The best [of Cantona] is yet to come!' proclaimed the paper. The *Post* was right – but the best wouldn't come at Leeds, despite the hopes of a whole city.

The champions started their title defence with a nervous win over Wimbledon (2–1) on 15 August, with Cantona starting alongside Chapman and Wallace in an attacking set-up. He didn't repeat his Wembley heroics, and only played a modest role in his team's success. One of his crosses should have brought Lee Chapman a goal in the first half, but the Dons' goalkeeper, Hans Segers, saved well from the tall centre-forward. This undistinguished performance – his seventeenth appearance for Leeds United – also saw him earn his first caution in English football for a clumsy foul on John Scales. The 'wild man of French football' had shown remarkable self-control until then. As Gary McAllister told me, 'He never got in trouble with referees, really. Occasionally, we'd see he could be touchy.' And intimidating: 'People who don't know Éric Cantona are always surprised by the size of the guy when they first meet him. For somebody who's got such a lovely feel for the game of football, he's a giant man! Six foot plus, and close to 90 kilos . . . But we didn't see the 'bad boy'. We were aware of some of his tackles back in France, but we never saw anything like that at Leeds United.'

Éric's almost exemplary disciplinary record demonstrated his eagerness to be accepted into the fold, as did his work rate, which was in evidence again when Leeds brought a 1–1 draw back from Villa Park in the second game of the season. Wilkinson had by then opted for a policy of turnover which resulted in Rocastle, Strachan and Hodge being left out of the starting eleven. Only thus, he thought, could Leeds make the most of their slim chance to keep the championship trophy at Elland Road. Reporters questioned the wisdom of this approach. Had not Leeds' previous success been based on continuity? How would his squad accept the manager's constant chopping and changing? 'Players will have to get used to that disappointment,' he grumbled. Wilkinson's already perceptible doubts about his team's qualities deepened into gloom on the occasion of Leeds's next sortie, a stinging 4–1 defeat at Middlesbrough that marked Éric's fourth consecutive start since his brilliant display in the Charity Shield. Cantona had been the best of a very poor bunch on Teesside, and deserved the fine consolation goal he scored late in the game. Somewhat to his surprise, Wilkinson realized that Éric could sustain a high level of performance despite the strenuous schedule he was subjected to. The visit of Tottenham would be his fourth game in ten days and, by all accounts, the high watermark of his nine months in Yorkshire.

The game was played late in the evening, on Tuesday 25 August, and the floodlights added to the majesty of Cantona's masterclass. Spurs were swept away from kick-off. Éric could have scored as early as the sixth minute, when his bicycle kick nearly eluded Tottenham's 'keeper Éric Thorstvedt. It fell to Rod Wallace to open the floodgates a quarter of an hour later. Spurs panicked. Justin Edinburgh fumbled, Éric pounced, 2–0 to the hosts; then 3–0, when David Batty's clever chip allowed Cantona to place a header into Tottenham's net. The pattern of the game remained unchanged after the interval. Both teams had barely restarted play when Éric was on hand to show his poacher's instinct after a goal-bound Lee Chapman header had been half-cleared by the Spurs defence. This was his second hat-trick for Leeds in less than three weeks – but also, ironically, the last of his career. Éric hadn't quite finished with Tottenham yet, however. Put through by Batty, he squared the ball to Chapman for a training-ground tap-in.

No one was calling him 'the King' just yet, but the Elland Road crowd could justifiably claim to have witnessed a coronation, and the *Post* published a suitably ecstatic panegyric about France's 'greatest entertainer since Maurice Chevalier trod the boards', a footballer who had 'more time than a clock when the ball comes to him'. Gary McAllister extolled his friend's qualities in more sober terms: 'When Éric first came, there was a suggestion that he was more of a provider than a goalscorer, but he has slung that one aside in no uncertain manner.' Even Wilkinson allowed himself to drop his guard – by an inch or so – and added his tuppenceworth to the praise lavished on his striker 'who feels at home now' and 'is coming to terms with English football', though the Eeyore-ish manager couldn't help but qualify his judgement thus: 'Hopefully he will make the transition complete because he has a lot to offer.'

In fairness, Wilkinson's appreciation of Éric's contribution may have been tainted by his frustration at having to release his striker immediately after Tottenham's rout. Bizarrely, Cantona was to fly to Paris the very next morning to join the French national team, which was playing against Brazil that very same day. Cantona's call-up was pointless to the point of absurdity. He could not be expected to figure in the game, and his presence in Paris could only be explained by the desire of new French manager Gérard Houllier* to have the whole of

* Michel Platini left his position on 2 July, the day FIFA announced that France had been awarded the privilege of hosting the 1998 World Cup. Houllier, until then Platini's assistant, officially succeeded him a week later.

his squad by his side when he took his bow. Éric reluctantly agreed to travel to France, only to change his mind at the very last minute – and change it again, after he had missed the flight he had been booked on originally. He took his seat at the Parc des Princes seconds before Careca and Bebeto kicked off, wearing a sphynx-like expression that indicated that trouble was brewing. As indeed it was.

As Leeds were to play one of the title favourites – Liverpool – over the coming weekend, Éric immediately returned to England, wondering why on earth the French FA had thought it necessary to disrupt his preparation for such a crucial encounter. He had to vent his anger somehow, and decided to do it as spectacularly as he could, by granting an interview to Erik Bielderman of *L'Équipe*. Fortunately for him, this interview was never published, at least not in its original form. As we know, Cantona had been dismayed by Michel Platini's removal from the position of national manager after the debacle of Euro 92 ('Platini has gone, and the disappointment of what happened in Sweden was particularly difficult to accept'), so much so that he told Bielderman that he would rather make himself unavailable for selection than associate himself with those who (in his opinion) had masterminded the coup. 'Take your pen and write,' he told Erik, pompously enunciating every syllable like a schoolteacher addressing a class of five-year-olds, '"E-ric Can-to-na says: 'I'm through with *Les Bleus.*'"' A shocked Bielderman retired to his hotel room to file the story. This was dynamite. *L'Équipe* would be flying off the shelves with a headline like this one. But Erik could not bring himself to do it. He called Cantona and tried to make him understand what the repercussions of his decision would be. A long pause ensued. Then Éric broke the silence. 'Take your pen, and write: "E-ric Can-to-na says: 'I'm through with *Les Bleus* . . . for the time being.'"' The old Cantona was back, but as a comedian this time. Maybe the *Post* had been right to liken him to Maurice Chevalier after all?

Houllier himself had some explaining to do. Éric's 'retirement' had been taken with a large pinch of salt in France. His newfound popularity there was based on his success in England, naturally, but also on the general public's appreciation of Cantona's public gesture of loyalty towards Platini. Its very awkwardness highlighted its sincerity;

in short, France was at last warming to the rebel, which put the new national manager in a delicate situation, as Houllier himself held his 'difficult' player in great esteem. 'Éric is mentally tired,' he said, which was the truth. As Cantona explained, 'Things are different [in England]. I play in a different team, in a different context. With the French team, I am someone else. At Leeds, I am English in my soul, whereas when I am in France, my memories take over. I've talked it over with Gérard [*note the use of Houllier's first name – no such affection was ever shown for 'Monsieur Wilkinson'*]. It would be easy to play badly [for France]. No, I'm really not sure I can give 100 per cent of myself for my country [in the circumstances].' France's loss should be Leeds' gain, at least in theory. And for a while it was.

Cantona excelled against Liverpool (2–2, on 29 August), drawing three superb saves from a young David James, and bettered that display with a brace of goals at Oldham (2–2 again) three days later, Leeds' sixth league game in eighteen days. The sustained quality of his performances made a return to the bench unthinkable to anyone: anyone, that is, but Howard Wilkinson, who could see his side sliding towards mid-table, but couldn't quite fathom why this was, still less how to remedy it. Leeds were then soundly beaten at Old Trafford (0–2, on 6 September), and Aston Villa held them 1–1 at home a week later. Éric was still playing, coming off the bench to have a superb game in Manchester – a bicycle kick nearly brought him one of the finest goals of his entire career – but the very fact he stood out perversely worked against him in his manager's mind. The togetherness of his squad was questioned in the media, who made unflattering comparisons between the 'commando spirit' shown during the previous season with the uncertainties of the present one. The point wasn't lost on Wilkinson, whose hesitant acceptance of Cantona's idiosyncrasies hardened into distrust of the striker who had scored nine goals in as many games since that glorious afternoon at Wembley.

The camel's back started to break for good on 16 September, when Leeds surrendered 3–0 in Stuttgart. This wasn't the triumphant return to the European Cup a whole city had been hoping for, seventeen years after their club's undeserved loss to another German club – Bayern Munich – in that competition's final. The circumstances of the rift which ensued between player and manager epitomized their incapacity to communicate. Éric first told Wilkinson that a hamstring injury would prevent him from taking any further part in that game, before assuring his bench that he had recovered. He still felt some discomfort, but, as his team's top goalscorer, was willing to play through the pain, as his departure from the pitch would not only weaken Leeds's attacking options, but also provide encouragement to their opponents.

Unfortunately, one of his trademark cross-field passes was intercepted; Stuttgart counter-attacked and scored their opening goal. Two more followed without answer. Leeds' prospects were grim: no English side had ever recovered from a three-goal deficit in Europe. For Wilkinson, Cantona had committed the cardinal sin of making his team pay for an individual error of judgement. Éric himself believed he had acted in the best interests of his club. The truth lay somewhere in between, but neither man had it in him to accept it. It didn't help that Cantona's injury prevented him from taking part in Leeds's next two games, a colourless draw at Southampton (1–1) and an anodyne 4–1 victory over lower-division Scunthorpe in the League Cup. The adulation that the fans lavished on Éric didn't assuage his coach's discontent; in fact, it played to Wilkinson's increasing wariness of his striker. For the manager's allies, the supporters were deluded; they were forgetting that the title they had craved for nearly two decades had been won by harnessing 'traditional' British virtues (doggedness, stamina, aggression and so on), not thanks to the exotic tricks and flicks of a Continental import. But Wilkinson was also aware that, should he decide not to call on Cantona, he would incur the wrath of an uncomprehending crowd – another irritant for the proud Yorkshireman.

In fairness, Wilkinson's head was still ruling his heart at this stage, and Éric rejoined the squad as soon as he had regained fitness, to help Leeds gain their first victory in six games, against Everton on 26 September (2–0). Four days later, it was Stuttgart's turn to visit Elland Road, in a game that was billed as 'Mission Impossible' by the national press. This pessimism was shared by the Leeds fans: only 20,457 of them passed the turnstiles, far less than the stadium could contain;

there couldn't be a starker indication of their disenchantment with the team they had feted in May. But the doom-mongers missed an unforgettable night. If the 5–0 win over Spurs had marked Cantona's most accomplished display for Leeds, this 4–1 triumph over the German champions rivalled – and not just for the intensity of the drama – the greatest displays of the Revie era. No fire burnt more brightly than Gary McAllister's at the heart of this collective incandescence. Within 15 minutes of kick-off, the Scottish midfielder had produced three fizzing strikes at goal. Stuttgart held on as best they could until two minutes later, when Cantona and Strachan combined to set up Gary Speed, whose sweet left-foot volley found the target. They couldn't do it, could they? But just as belief started to swell the crowd's hearts, Andreas Buck equalized in the 34th minute. The away-goals rule meant that Leeds would have to score four more to qualify, and over a third of the game had already been played. But Strachan and his teammates carried on battering the Stuttgart defence, and were rewarded with a penalty shortly before half-time. Gary McAllister stepped up to the spot and made it 2–1. A host of chances had come and gone for Leeds when they doubled their advantage in the 66th minute; Strachan, again, lofted the ball towards Éric, whose looping shot could only be deflected into the net by defender Gunther Schafer. Ten minutes before the final whistle, Lee Chapman, who had led the line with even more vigour and purpose than usual, surged at the near post and beat the German 'keeper with a header. One more goal and Leeds, incredibly, would be through.

But Stuttgart, overpowered as they had been for so long, regrouped and were not breached again. And as the curtain fell on one of the greatest games ever played by an English side in Europe, the Germans collapsed in a heap on the Elland Road turf. Buck's goal had sent them to the next round. A defiant Gordon Strachan told a *Post* journalist: 'You can talk all you like about Italian and Spanish football, but there is no better spectacle than a British team, going at it as we did against Stuttgart.' The bittersweet chord of gallant failure strikes the British heart more poignantly than any other, of course, but Strachan wasn't fooling anyone with his noble speech. Wilkinson was truer to the emotions felt by his players when he said: 'Most of them would wake up feeling that their stomach was eight feet deep and that they had a pain somewhere near the bottom of it.'

Leeds were out – or so they thought until the following morning, when the phone rang in the *Post*'s office. A German voice asked to be put through to someone on the sports desk of the paper. Their football correspondent Don Warters picked up the phone and very nearly dropped it when he heard what the caller, a journalist himself, had to say. Fans of a rival German club had watched the game on television and spotted that Stuttgart's coach, Christoph Daum, had fielded four 'foreign' players in total, rather than the three then allowed by UEFA regulations. VfB could be thrown out of the tournament! This astonishing development was relayed to the club, which immediately contacted the organization's headquarters.

UEFA hummed and hawed. They knew, as everyone did, that Daum's mistake was not part of a sinister plan to rob Leeds of victory. His oversight could easily be explained by the chaotic nature of the game. Nonetheless, Stuttgart had derived an unfair advantage from their infringement of the rules; whether inadvertently or not should have been beside the point. But the wise men of European football decided against excluding the German club from the competition, and awarded Leeds a 3–0 win instead (the customary punishment for teams forfeiting a game). As Wilkinson's team had been beaten by the same margin in the first leg, it would be necessary to play a third match, which UEFA wished to stage in a neutral venue: Barcelona's Camp Nou. Leeds fans didn't quite know whether they should feel relieved or hard done by. But by the time the decider took place on 9 October, they were too worried to bother.

Wilkinson's exhausted team had sunk 4–2 at Ipswich four days after that splendid hurrah at Elland Road, adding substance to the fear that his squad was too thin, and too old, to be seriously involved in more than one competition. The champions had yet to register a single victory away from home when the leaves had long turned in Roundhay Park. Drained as much by emotion as by physical exertion, Cantona saw his form dip for the first time since he had joined Leeds United. Never had he played so many games on the trot, even allowing for his injury. A return to France's national team also beckoned. More importantly, he found it more difficult by the day to decipher Howard Wilkinson's attitude towards him on a personal level. He still enjoyed his manager's trust when it came to representing Leeds' colours on the field, but could not gauge how firmly rooted this trust was from their exchanges off it.

A friend recently told me about a line he had found in an unpublished diary of novelist B. S. Johnson: 'It's not so much that I am thin-skinned; I have no skin at all.' The writer's confession could easily pass as a comment on Cantona the footballer-artist. And, as ever, Éric's uncertainties translated into a (probably unconscious) weakening of his commitment to the club, imperceptible at first, and a degradation of his play which grew clearer as the weeks went by. There were rumours of late arrivals (and even no-shows) at training sessions, and of less than fulsome comments made by Wilkinson in private about his star player. I have been unable to ascertain whether the gossip had a basis in fact or was nothing more than extrapolation made in hindsight, once the squabble had degenerated into open conflict. Judging by Éric's performance in Barcelona, however, Wilkinson's frustration had more objective roots than the ill-matching words and deeds of two men.

Leeds overcame Stuttgart 2–1 in their winner-takes-all decider but, for once, Éric had been a mere passenger on someone else's train. It fell to the unsung journeyman Carl Shutt to deliver the blow that ensured the Yorkshire club's passage into the next round. The eerie atmosphere in which the game was played might have accounted – at least in part – for Cantona's ineffectual showing. Only 7,400 spectators were dotted around the gigantic arena. Cantona 'lost himself in the empty space', to paraphrase what he had said earlier that year. Celebrations were strangely muted back in England, as if too much energy had been exhausted in the useless victory earned nine days previously, and while all Leeds supporters can recall with tellling precision what happened on 30 September, what followed on 9 October has all but faded from their collective memory.

In an ironic reversal of the situation Éric had found himself in after Euro 92, *Les Bleus* brought him the solace he needed. The deepening sense of malaise that permeated his club evaporated once he slipped on the blue jersey for the first time since Denmark had kicked France out of the European championships on 17 June. Houllier's team waltzed past Austria 2–0 thanks to strikes by Papin and Cantona, a scoreline that would have been more emphatic had not four French goals been disallowed, and JPP not missed a penalty.* France had ended a dismal nine-game winless sequence in emphatic fashion.

Éric brought back some of his revived form to England, where he made a solid contribution to a rare Leeds victory (3–1 against Sheffield United) in mid-October. But this result failed to spark the reaction Wilkinson had been hoping for. Cantona would never find himself in a winning Leeds side again and, within a month, would sit beside Alex Ferguson in Manchester United's press conference room. The next round of the European Cup would act as the detonator of a full-blown crisis that could only be resolved by a parting of ways, as no unhappy marriage can end otherwise in football.

Leeds' opponents in the second round of the European Cup were Rangers. The Scottish champions were a far more formidable force then than today, as they would prove by remaining unbeaten in the competition and missing qualification for that year's final by a single point (Marseille pipped them to the post in the tournament's second phase). Whoever prevailed in this two-legged encounter would earn a coveted spot in the so-called 'group phase', a mini-league in which the eight survivors slugged it out in pools of four teams each. A club's mere presence in one of these two pools guaranteed millions of pounds of income in gate receipts and sales of broadcasting rights.

Wilkinson knew by then that winning the inaugural Premier League title was an unattainable ambition. But provided his team could ensure safety in the first tier of English football, the huge revenue derived from Europe's top club competition could give him the means to rebuild his squad for a fresh assault on the championship a year hence. Leeds first had to win what every single newspaper in the country, north and south of the border, dubbed 'The Battle of Britain'. Rarely was

* Of the 20 goals Éric scored for France (in 45 games), only one was scored from the penalty spot or from a direct free kick.

the use of a clichéd headline more strikingly vindicated than on this occasion.

The tone of the clash was given by the decision to bar away fans from both legs of the tie. Anglo-Scottish confrontations had been marred by crowd violence since the 1960s, and the regular outbreaks of hooliganism that accompanied fixtures of that type had contributed to the abandonment of the British Home Championship at the end of the 1983–84 season. The Heysel tragedy and the subsequent ban inflicted on England's clubs had prevented sides from the two countries from facing each other since 1985. Judging by the sheer brutality of what ensued, the ban had been no bad thing.

Unfortunately for Éric, thuggish behaviour did not stop on the touchline. The Ibrox 'walls of hate' enclosed what could almost be called a killing field, if the victim were football as Cantona wished to play it. Gary McAllister – a native of Motherwell with a broader outlook on life than sectarian Glaswegians – has vivid memories of those two European nights. 'The Rangers players knew Éric very, very well,' he told me with a knowing smile. 'They gave him some . . . special attention. Their centre-backs were very physical with Éric in both games . . . Éric is a strong guy and can look after himself, but he did get some proper treatment those nights.' Delicately put; Cantona was kicked off the park.

Wilkinson, no shrinking violet himself, had an inkling of what was in store for his Frenchman. It started well for Leeds – too well maybe. Two minutes were on the clock when McAllister unleashed a superb volley that was greeted by what I can only describe as an explosion of silence. Then the crowd's roar rose again around the stands like goosebumps. The Leeds 'keeper John Lukic was forced to punch a corner kick into his own net, and obliged. Ally McCoist then doubled Rangers' tally with a typically opportunistic goal from close range, leaving the visitors with the task of scoring once without reply at home to go through.

Most observers thought that, once they had emerged from the cauldron of Ibrox, Leeds could summon the coolness required to do just that, but Mark Hateley had other ideas. As in Glasgow, two minutes had elapsed when the first goal was scored; this time, though, it was an Englishman playing for a Scottish club who struck, not vice versa. When Hateley pierced the Leeds defence on the left to provide a perfect cross for McCoist to head into the net, the hosts found themselves three goals in arrears, needing to score four themselves to avoid going out of the competition. Leeds responded by hurling balls in the direction of Chapman and Cantona with predictable results. They laid siege to the Rangers goal, in which Andy Goram was having one of the best nights of his life. It was like lobbing oranges at a wall. Éric managed to reduce the deficit after a scramble in the penalty box, but far too late to save his side. Rangers won 4–2 on aggregate, and Wilkinson's plans lay in ruins.

English football hadn't known many darker days in Europe. While Leeds were vanquished in the 'Battle of Britain', Liverpool were dumped out of the Cup Winners Cup by Spartak Moscow, losing 2–0 at Anfield, while Sheffield Wednesday's first European venture (in the UEFA Cup) ended with a 3–5 defeat on aggregate against Kaiserslautern. England still played in the shadow of Heysel.

The scene now shifts forward sixteen years. I am sitting with Gérard Houllier in a plush Neuilly restaurant which seems to cater only for a clientele of impossibly well-connected businessmen, Paris Saint-Germain footballers and cosmetically enhanced beauties. We'll be joined by one of Arsène Wenger's advisers later on, but for the time being, France's present national technical director is talking about Éric Cantona with some passion. We've now reached a pivotal point in Houllier's narrative. Gérard had made the trip to Glasgow to assess the striker he hoped to deploy when Finland visited le Parc *four weeks later, on 14 November, and flew to Leeds for the return leg. Shortly before that game, Howard Wilkinson invited him to watch a video cassette in his hotel room. The Leeds manager inserted the tape in the VCR, adding three words: 'Look at Éric.' It was a recording of Cantona's reaction to being substituted at Ibrox. He'd made straight for the dressing-room.*

Houllier was at pains to explain that such behaviour was commonplace (if not the norm) in France, and that Wilkinson shouldn't take Éric's silent exit as a snub directed at his coach. But 'Howard saw it as a mark of disrespect towards the other players, and I could feel there was some tension between the two'. It so happened that when the substitution took place, Gérard was sitting between Andy Roxburgh (then manager of Scotland and technical director of the Scottish FA) and Alex Ferguson, whom he'd known since 1986. 'I turned to Alex,' Houllier recalled, 'and said, "Oh, big problem . . . maybe I'll have to find another club for him." And the day after that, Éric's adviser Jean-Jacques Amorfini called me and told me, "Gérard, it's a right mess at Leeds, Éric wants to go."'

This version of events differed so markedly from the account Alex Ferguson would give later on – according to which the prising of Éric Cantona from Leeds occurred almost by chance – that I got in touch with Dennis Roach (who'd been at both the Rangers games) to see if he could vouchsafe Gérard's story. No football agent wielded more influence in English football than Roach at the time. He was adamant: yes, Manchester United 'had already made several enquiries about Cantona' weeks before the transfer was concluded. What's more, 'Wilkinson agreed that if Éric didn't want to stay at Leeds, he could go to United'.

Wilkinson didn't lose – or jettison, according to whom you're listening to – Cantona without doing everything in his power to try and keep him at Elland Road, but he had never had to tame as weird and unpredictable an animal as this one. Éric had become 'unmanageable' as far as he was concerned. Sometimes, Howard would pull the carrot out of his bag; at others, Sergeant Wilko wielded the stick, only to find out that his player didn't respond to either. To Cantona, Wilkinson's increasingly desperate attempts to rebuild bridges over a widening chasm demonstrated incoherence on the manager's behalf. 'One moment he would tell me that he wants me to know that I owe everything to him,' he confided to his ghostwriter a few months later, 'that I am only a Frenchman lost in the English league and at other times he would say to me that without me the team is nothing and that I am the essential part.'

Cantona's teammates didn't know what to make of the meltdown between Éric and Wilkinson. Lee Chapman, for one, didn't doubt that Cantona's performances so far demanded his regular inclusion in the starting line-up. But he also felt that his manager's favoured 'direct' tactics did not exploit the Frenchman's qualities to the full. As Éric enjoyed dropping off behind the first line of attack, play more often than not passed him by. Chapman's head, not Cantona's feet, acted as a magnet for the ball when Leeds were in possession. A frustrated Éric didn't attempt to hide that he longed for a more measured approach – to which Wilkinson seemed to be receptive for a while; but when results went against him, the manager reverted to the tried-and-tested formula that had brought him two titles over the past year. Subbed against Stuttgart in Barcelona, subbed again in Glasgow, Cantona didn't even leave the bench when Leeds travelled to Queens Park Rangers three days after their defeat at Ibrox. By then, the camel's back had been well and truly broken.

The team had arrived in London on the eve of the game, and set up camp in the Royal Lancaster hotel, a few paces away from Hyde Park. Gary McAllister and Cantona sat in the lounge that evening and talked about what the future held for their ailing club, and what role the Frenchman would play in it. According to Gary – Éric's closest friend at Elland Road – both agreed that Leeds could only progress if a means could be found to make Cantona 'the focal point of the team'. They went further, and discussed 'how the team should maximize his ability to get the ball in the right area' – hardly the kind of subject that would be raised by a footballer desperate to find a new club.

But this was not the last conversation Éric had that night. Howard Wilkinson couldn't have known how ill-timed his intervention was, but its impact on Cantona was all the more dramatic for that. One minute, Éric was sharing his worries, but also his hopes, with a trusted teammate. The next, a man he regarded with a mixture of respect and incomprehension was informing him that he had been dropped. Wilkinson might not have been the subtlest of psychologists, but had always endeavoured to act honestly, which is why he told Cantona: 'Look, we're struggling, you have certain qualities, but we are very much a team that has to have a pattern. People have to do jobs, we have to think in terms of what is the overall shape and strategy, and at the moment it is not possible to have the consistent team and selection [I] would like.' The manager's honesty was commendable, and might have been rewarded by another man; but Éric's pride prevented him from seeing in those words anything but an abandonment. If

Wilkinson couldn't trust him in an hour of need, how could he, Cantona, trust Wilkinson? According to the manager, Éric refused to accept his decision, which led to a surreal scene the next morning, once the players had returned from a light training session in the nearby park.

The squad assembled to hear who would and who wouldn't be selected for the afternoon game at Loftus Road. All knew that Cantona had requested and been granted a few days' leave to return to France, as Leeds wouldn't be playing again for a week. But nobody expected Wilkinson to rise from his chair and say: 'Éric, here's your passport, off you go!' In full view of teammates, who didn't know where to look, Cantona collected his travel documents from the manager's assistant Michael Hennigan. Gary Speed, one of Wilkinson's most loyal lieutenants, still sounded bemused when he recounted the incident to Rob Wightman over a decade later. 'Éric took his passport and had to stand up and walk out of the room. [. . .] We had to just sit there and watch him go out. We wanted to say goodbye to Éric but no one did.' Speed, who admired his manager's straightforwardness, believed Wilkinson couldn't have staged this public humiliation without a good reason, but was at a loss to say what this reason could have been. 'It was weird, really, really weird,' McAllister told me; but was it so 'weird' that Leeds went out to lose 2–1 at QPR as Éric was driving to the airport?

Leeds' fortunes didn't improve much with Cantona sulking on the periphery of the first team. Rod Wallace was preferred to him when Wilkinson's men fought out a 2–2 draw at home with Coventry. Éric was given half an hour to show his worth, far too little to make an impression. Brought back into the fold on 7 November for a trip to Manchester City (0–4) three days after United's midweek exit from Europe, he cut a helpless figure on the pitch. He had barely seen the ball that John Lukic stooped at depressing intervals to pick out of his goal.

The malaise had turned into a full-blown crisis: Leeds had by then the worst defensive record in the Premiership; in fact they had lost more games by the end of October than in the whole of the previous campaign. They were showing signs of imploding just like title-holders Arsenal had done the season before. Very few pundits pointed the finger at Cantona's diminishing influence to explain the champions' freefall. Instead they concentrated on Wilkinson's reluctance or inability to breathe new life into an ageing squad: captain Gordon Strachan was in his thirty-sixth year, Lee Chapman and John Lukic would be thirty-three and thirty-two respectively in December, while Carl Shutt, Mel Sterland and Chris Whyte were on the wrong side of thirty. Leeds, 'too old to regroup', were written off in the title race, just like Manchester United (who had been beaten 1–0 at Villa Park on the day of the City debacle, and hadn't found the net once in their last four games).

Cantona's own performances suffered accordingly. When Watford kicked Leeds out of the League Cup on 10 November (1–2), he was guilty of two dreadful misses, heading wide a pinpoint cross by Gordon Strachan and, unforgivably, freezing in a one-to-one with opposing 'keeper Perry Suckling. With the nearest defender ten yards away, he prodded rather than struck the ball: he had lost belief in himself just as he had lost belief in Leeds United.

'At times,' Lee Chapman said, '[Éric] looked almost suicidal as he moped around the dressing-room area. From my time in France [*Chapman spent a few months at Niort in 1988*], I knew just how isolated he felt. Being dropped is bad enough, but when it is in a strange country, and you don't speak the language, it is considerably worse.' As if he had to prove that his environment was to blame, and not his form, Cantona scored (with his shoulder!) France's second goal in their 2–1 victory over Finland, four days after Leeds' defeat at Watford. And when he returned to England, Wilkinson kept him out of the eleven which, against everyone's expectations, halted Arsenal's run of six wins with a resounding 3–0 win on a muddy, windswept Elland Road pitch. A diplomatic 'groin strain' was alleged to have forced Cantona's late withdrawal, not that many were fooled. This unforeseen result (which future events would show to be a fluke: Leeds would win just one of their next six games) was held up as a vindication of the manager's choice by a minority, to which Wilkinson naturally belonged. The smouldering Cantona, by now incensed, responded by refusing to report for training on the following Tuesday. A transfer request was faxed to the club's office, in which Éric apparently stated that he wished to join one of three English clubs: Manchester United, Liverpool or Arsenal. The date was 24 November 1992.

11

On the catwalk for Paco Rabanne.

MANCHESTER UNITED, AT LAST

'Cantona simply does not fit in well in English soccer in my view. Leeds produced by far the best team performance of this season by any club last Saturday at home to Arsenal – and Cantona was not in the side. It's no coincidence. I don't think Cantona has really produced for Leeds.' Johnny Giles

'I really can't understand what all the fuss is about. We have three million unemployed people in this country, and there is all this upset about a Frenchman going to Manchester. People are saying what a blow it is to Leeds, but it would be a much bigger blow if either Gary Speed or David Batty wanted to leave the club.' Billy Bremner

'I think Cantona's transfer is sound business. He is a good player, but I still have doubts about him. He has not played all that well in the last few weeks. He cannot have settled down all that well if he has been in to ask for a transfer, as is widely suggested. You do not get that sort of thing happening if you are a genuine good clubman and especially after he had been so well received by United supporters.' Norman 'Bite Yer Legs' Hunter

Two weeks had passed since the release of Ooh La La's single 'Why I Love You, I Don't Why, But I Love You' when *Post* readers picked up their copy of the paper on Friday 27 November. The headline was bad enough: 'Ooh-er! United idol becomes a red devil – CANTONA FANS FURY'. But the photograph that illustrated the story was even worse: Alex Ferguson shaking hands with the idol of the Leeds Kop. Leeds fans had not so much received a slap in the face as a kick to their tenderest region.

The chemistry experiment that Howard Wilkinson had attempted with that strange new element, Éric Cantona, had ended in an explosion. Given that rumours of the deterioration in their relationship had been filtering out of the dressing-room for over a month, this shouldn't have come as the shock it undoubtedly was for thousands of Leeds supporters. Tears were shed, however, and anger flowed in the messages that swamped the dedicated phone line the *Post* had set up as soon as the player's departure had been confirmed. Of the 1,337 fans who rang the paper that day, 1,065 opposed the sale of Cantona to the club they hated more than any other. Were they listening to their heads or to their hearts? To both. And they provided another example of one of English football's more captivating truths: the verdict of supporters may sometimes lack eloquence, but is often sounder than the opinions of professional pundits, particularly when the experts have been professional footballers themselves. The above-quoted Giles, Bremner and Hunter were joined by Emlyn Hughes ('a flashy foreigner'), Eddie Gray ('a fair deal') and Jimmy Greaves ('Cantona is not the man for [Manchester] United') in their appraisal of Leeds' decision to offload Cantona for a pittance. A rare instance of foresight was provided by the *Daily Express* ('Leeds has handed the title to Manchester United on a plate'), while the *Daily Mirror* sub-editors had fun with 'Oo-aargh Cantona'. What the old warhorses of Revie-era Leeds and dinosaurs like Hughes failed to understand was that, following the birth of the Premier League and the emergence of Sky Television, the game they had played with distinction (if not always without malice or cynicism) had already changed beyond recognition. Their distrust of anything foreign would soon belong to another era, even if, approaching the end of the twenty-first century's first decade, some of their successors still cannot bring themselves to admit it. Leeds fans knew better than anyone what an impact Cantona's daring and sense of adventure had had on their own faith in the club; they had responded to his flamboyance with such fervour that not just Éric, but all around him, had been lifted to a higher plane of performance – a two-fold catalysis, if you will.

The strength of feeling within the Leeds fan-base startled Howard Wilkinson. Season-ticket holders threatened to boycott Elland Road. Ray Fell, the chairman of the Leeds supporters club, said: 'I am amazed and stunned. I am certain the reaction of most fans will be one of bewilderment.' One of these bewildered fans, Vivienne Olbison, told a local reporter: 'I think it's absolutely disgusting. Éric is the best player there's been at Leeds for ages. To sell him makes no sense at all – particularly to Manchester United!' Wilkinson's critics had a field day in the climate of fury which surrounded the announcement of Cantona's sale. He had just parted with his most skilful player, and who had he brought in? David Rocastle and Mel Sterland: an Arsenal reject and a thirty-something right-back who couldn't command a place at Rangers.

The manager first tried to justify himself by explaining why, in his view, 'a deal was struck which was in the best interests of all concerned'. The move would, 'perhaps, give Éric a better chance of first-team football than he would have had at Leeds United'. Leeds remained an ambitious club, a club 'with aspirations to establish itself as one of the top names in the game'. Its manager must therefore rotate his squad, and players who couldn't live with the disappointment of finding themselves on the bench had no place in his project. He used his column in the *Post* to hammer home his argument. 'The long-term interests of our club have to be served at all times,' he wrote, 'and on this occasion this is the case. What happened yesterday [*Thursday the 26th – the deal had in fact been struck twenty-four hours earlier*] produced a situation which left everyone sitting round a table feeling satisfied. Alex Ferguson got a player and Éric Cantona has got a transfer which on the face of it offers him a greater opportunity of first-team football than which he had here.' Such equanimity wouldn't last.

Leeds chairman Leslie Silver unequivocally supported Wilkinson. 'Éric was upset that he had not been used as often as he would have liked this season,' he said, 'so it was sensible for him to go. He made a major contribution last season but was not entirely happy this time and was keen to move on. Éric thought he would be an automatic choice this season. But the manager picks the team and reserves the right to select the players he wants. Éric was a cult hero for the fans but the team is judged on results and Éric was not even on the bench when we beat Arsenal last Saturday.' The chairman made no further comment when Chelsea beat Leeds 1–0 two days later, however; nor did he say a word after Nottingham Forest humbled them 4–1 at Elland Road in the following league match.

Wilkinson, his common sense perhaps affected by the hostility of the fans, advanced another reason for letting Manchester United get hold of Cantona for a paltry £1.2m – only £200,000 more than Nîmes had been paid for handing over the striker's registration in May, and half of what Arsenal had received for David Rocastle. Leeds, he said, 'were skint', as 'they had come up a very long way in a very short time'. The second assertion was a statement of fact; the first was rather confusing, as Leeds' turnover had reached a record £8.5m at the conclusion of the 1991–92 season, and the club's operating profit stood at a very healthy £500,000. The terraces soon proposed their own (totally fabricated) explanation of Éric's dramatic exit: Cantona had been having an affair with Lee Chapman's wife, actress Leslie Ash,* causing discord in a previously united dressing-room. The unfounded allegations caused far more pain and upheaval than they purported to report, as, despite Wilkinson's not entirely innocent suggestion that his players found it increasingly difficult to relate to Cantona, Éric's

* 'He's French, he's flash/He's shagging Leslie Ash/Cantona' was an especially popular chant with Manchester United fans seated in the Stretford End. The Leeds fanzine *Square Ball* published a photo-montage of Éric in the shower, wearing bra and suspenders, and linking the whole thing to the Leslie Ash rumours: 'Mrs Chapman [. . .] noticed that her underwear drawer had been tampered with and found several ladders in her fishnet stockings. Suspicious, Lee placed a hidden camera in the Chapman bathroom and was astonished when confronted by the photograph shown here. This proved too much for the Elland Road players who approached manager Howard Wilkinson demanding Cantona's immediate removal.' A cartoon published in the same fanzine (called 'The Temptation of Cantona' and attributed to one Fra Filippo Magsonioni) depicts the crucifixion of 'Leeds Pride' with 'Judas' Cantona being led off, with his thirty pieces of silver, by Alex 'Beelzebub' Ferguson to 'Sodom and Manchester'. 'Pontius' Wilkinson is shown having his hands washed, a kneeling disciple beside him saying: 'Forgive him Lord for he knows not what he does.' What 'Beelzebub' Ferguson tells Cantona had something prophetic in it: 'Behold – I shall make thee master of all thou surveys.'

popularity within the squad had not been dented by the breakdown of his relationship with the manager.

Cantona wasn't and couldn't be everyone's best friend, but even players whose outlook on life differed markedly from his – Gordon Strachan, for example – stressed that 'nobody had anything against him personally' and that 'he wasn't a problem to get on with', despite the reservations he and others might have had over his contribution to the team's performances, particularly in the previous couple of months. Strachan felt that Éric 'found it hard to understand how Chappy [Lee Chapman] played and Chappy found it difficult to understand him', and believed that the Frenchman could have done more to ingratiate himself to his fellow players. For the captain of Leeds, Cantona had retreated into his shell instead, and his play had suffered accordingly, particularly in Europe. Strachan balanced his criticism with an avowal that Éric had been frustrated by his side's inability to embrace a more flowing style, in which his vision would have been put to better use. With more time, he said, 'we might have been able to bring in some better players to play with him' – but 'he had just made up his mind he wanted to leave; there was no way he wanted to stay'.

Had he stayed, what might have been? Sixteen years on, Gary McAllister still harbours regrets shared by every Leeds fan I have spoken to. 'Don't forget that Leeds is a one-club town,' he told me. 'The title should've been a massive catalyst for the club. We could've moved on, especially now we'd beaten our biggest rival to the championship. If we'd got the right players, it might have been the start of something big.' But the 'right players' didn't come. Instead, 'the money that Howard Wilkinson got to spend was used to recruit footballers who couldn't necessarily command a place in the team, and there's no doubt that Éric felt frustration because of that.' Judging by McAllister's tone, Éric was not alone in feeling that frustration. 'After a few months, we were more or less back to the team that was playing at the same stage of the season before! And we found it very difficult to replicate what we'd done. We were a good team – but we were not a great team. A great team wins year after year, and we failed.'

Let's hear one last voice, that of Gary Speed, for whom Éric's playing style was 'off the cuff and [. . .] a bit of a luxury', words that show plainly enough that he couldn't be suspected of bias towards his moody teammate. But the Welsh midfielder refused to blame Cantona for the unravelling of their club's expectations. 'We were that kind of side where everybody had to be working as hard as one another to be successful,' he said. 'The year after [winning the title] when Éric was in the team and things weren't going well, we weren't good enough to accommodate him and Man United were.'

'We failed'. 'We weren't good enough'. Not good enough to keep the man who would engineer Manchester United's renaissance. But it would be under the guidance of a manager who had found a key Howard Wilkinson had looked for without believing it really existed.

Accusations and counter-accusations kept flowing over a number of months, years even, and would be rekindled by the publication in Britain of Cantona's autobiography in 1994. By then, adulation had long turned into hatred at Elland Road. Some supporters – a tiny minority – retained their affection for the hero who, to them, had only been guilty of putting his proud manager in the shade. But within a few weeks of Éric's startlingly successful introduction to the Manchester United line-up, the initial wave of grief that had engulfed a whole city was but a distant memory. The pitifully small amount of money Leeds had received for Cantona – which could and maybe should have served as an illustration of Wilkinson's managerial shortcomings – was taken as proof that the decision to get rid of the 'mercurial Frenchman' had been forced on the coach by the player's behaviour, ill discipline and flouting of club rules (charges that Wilkinson repeatedly brought against Éric with little outside encouragement). Cantona saw this as a Machiavellian trick played on public opinion by his former manager. Wilkinson wanted him out, whatever the cost might be, and selling him on the cheap was a way of saying, 'But what else could I do?' and thus draw some credit from a catastrophic decision.

Questions were bound to be raised about Wilkinson's competence as Manchester United's star rose spectacularly in the wake of this oddest of transfers, while Leeds got sucked into the quagmire of a struggle against relegation. The manager naturally sought to defend himself, sometimes fairly, sometimes less so, as we'll soon see. But before rejoining

Éric in Manchester, I cannot resist adding another quote of Wilkinson's. Having alluded to unspecified events ('[Cantona's] life off the pitch was sometimes colourful and required assistance'), he added: 'Once you cut away all the myth and all the dressing-up and all the manufactured stories, he was fairly straightforward.' Once you cut away all the myth, and . . . Not an easy thing to do.

Let's go back (or sixteen years forward) to Le Murat in Neuilly, where Gérard Houllier hasn't quite finished his Dover sole – or his surprising account of how Alex Ferguson secured the best transfer deal in Manchester United's history. Leeds United had already been sounded out (at least indirectly, though at what level isn't absolutely clear), but no formal proposal had yet been made. Let's accept that. What about the famous phone call, then?

'I remember very clearly,' Houllier tells me. But it is another phone call he has in mind, one he had made himself once Éric's adviser Jean-Jacques Amorfini had advised him of the irretrievable breakdown between his client and Howard Wilkinson, not the astonishing conversation which took place in Martin Edwards' office (of which more presently). 'Alex had a carphone, to which calls to his office were redirected,' Houllier says. 'I apprised Alex of the circumstances, and he told me: "I'll have him" – meaning Cantona, of course. "It'll cost you about a million pounds," I said. "No problem – and they want a full-back, Dennis Irwin. What do you think of Cantona yourself?" I replied – using the same words I had used with Wilkinson, "Close your eyes, and take him. The only thing you've got to be careful of is [man-]management. He's a good guy, who loves his work, and needs to be trusted, and not messed about."'

I feel utterly confused at this point. If we accept that Ferguson had had his eye on Cantona for a while (and that, I believe, is more than likely, especially since Steve Bruce and Gary Pallister had raved about him to their manager after United's 2–0 victory over Leeds in early September), who said what to whom on that day – 25 November – and in what order?

The story of how the deal was closed has become part of Manchester United's folklore, one of Alex Ferguson's best, which he's always told with the glee of a canny horsetrader pinching the next Grand National winner from his biggest rival's stable, and for a bag of oats at that. The role of the then general manager of Leeds, Bill Fotherby, is sometimes played by Howard Wilkinson (this was the case at the press conference that accompanied the unveiling of Éric Cantona as a Manchester United player), or vice versa. But Alex Ferguson remained true to his thread: Cantona was signed almost by chance, on a hunch, an afterthought.

This is how the story goes. Desperate for a striker – United had failed to score in four of their last five games – Ferguson was sitting in his chairman Martin Edwards' office, remarking what a shame it was that Manchester United had missed out on Cantona when he was available. Right on cue, the phone rang. It was Bill Fotherby, enquiring about the availability of Dennis Irwin, Manchester United's Irish left-back who had started his career at Leeds. Edwards's straightforward 'no' didn't end the conversation; he seized this opportunity to tease Fotherby about some of his players, including Lee Chapman, a proven goalscorer he must have known Leeds wouldn't get rid of. Then, on Ferguson's prompting, Edwards moved on to Cantona, whose name the manager had scribbled on a piece of paper. The rift between Wilkinson and his Frenchman was common knowledge at the time, even if its real causes were a matter for guesswork. Edwards showed some surprise when Fotherby confirmed that some serious turbulence had hit the precarious relationship between coach and player. Edwards made it clear that he wanted a quick deal, and there the conversation ended – but not for long. A few minutes later, the phone rang again: the deal was on. Fotherby had consulted with Wilkinson, who had given his blessing to the transfer. By that time, Ferguson had left his chairman's office and was given the news on his carphone. Mischievously, Edwards asked his manager to try and guess how much they would be paying for the catalyst of Leeds' success the season before. 'Like a TV quiz,' Ferguson would say, several years later. Of course, he didn't get the exact figure. Who could have? At £1.2m, Cantona was a steal.* So much so that doubt could justifiably creep into the manager's mind.

---

* That same afternoon, Ferguson contacted his assistant Brian Kidd and asked him if he'd like to see Cantona play for United. Kidd said yes. When told that this would be the case – and for little over £1m – Kidd gasped: 'For that money? Has he lost a leg or something?'

Had he been too hasty? Would this prove to be another of these signings he had been caned for before in the press? He had looked for the missing piece in United's jigsaw puzzle for a while, and believed he had found it on several occasions, only to be proved wrong every time.

It was at this point that he talked with Erik Bielderman, to seek advice from perhaps the only journalist he would trust in such circumstances. Erik remembers what he told Ferguson on that day. His words echoed those of Gérard Houllier's: 'Éric can only work with a coach who'll be a substitute for a father, who will stand by him in public as he would stand by his son, regardless of what he does; in private, he'll be able to chastise him if he thinks he must, and the "son" will respond.' Cantona, by nature so quick to confuse displays of authority with bullying, later explained this side of his character thus: 'In fact, I've always had problems with people who can't take decisions. I want to be given directions, but I want to know where I'm going. I have to be persuaded that a certain path is the right one. Otherwise, problems start.'*

No one can doubt that the exchange related in Ferguson's 1999 autobiography (*Managing My Life*) really took place. I finally got a chance to put a couple of teasing questions to Sir Alex about this episode late in the winter of 2008–09, which he answered with the candour that is part of his character, and which he's rarely given credit for. Yes, Houllier had alerted him of Cantona's availability on a couple of occasions (this much I never doubted); moreover, he had been told about Éric's problems at Sheffield Wednesday – but he'd been 'caught on the hop', and Howard Wilkinson had been quicker to react, perhaps because of the close relationship he enjoyed with Trevor Francis and his advisers. Had Ferguson been able to pounce then, in January 1992 (as he would have wanted to), Éric Cantona would have become a

---

* Ferguson's perception of Cantona's 'unmanageable' character would evolve over the years Éric spent at Manchester United. Comparing him with another player, Sir Alex told my friend Marc Beaugé: 'You could reach Éric, because there was a common thread of humanity you always felt you shared, whereas X— was beyond it, beyond everything.'

Manchester United player several months before he did. When the opportunity presented itself, not to correct what can hardly be described as a mistake, but to exploit the circumstances, Sir Alex seized it with impeccable timing. The phone call, the slip of paper passed on to Martin Edwards, all this was true. What no one knew was that Cantona had been a target for Manchester United for a while already. In my opinion, Houllier's, Roach's and Bielderman's accounts actually add to the tale rather than detract from it, and show a Ferguson who was not only able to trust his instinct, but also had the clear-mindedness to seek advice and, more importantly, take heed of it.

Manchester United could easily afford Cantona, but whether Ferguson could afford a failure was less obvious. His once fragile grip on the manager's position had been strengthened by wins in the 1990 FA Cup and the 1991 European Cup Winners Cup, but the feebleness of United's title challenge in the last few weeks of the previous season had led some to wonder whether, given the means at his disposal, Alex Ferguson really had it in him to deliver the championship craved by the club's followers since their 1967 triumph. That albatross had hung heavily around the neck of Manchester United managers since then, and his team's mediocre start to the 1992–93 campaign made it heavier still.

The fee involved in Éric's transfer represented a negligible outlay for a club which had already broken the £1m barrier on eight previous instances since Ferguson had taken over in 1986. Moreover, of the players involved in those deals, only one – Dion Dublin (purchased for £1m from second division Cambridge United in August 1992) – had cost less than the French international. Ferguson had been willing to part with far more money to lure Alan Shearer away from Southampton during the summer, until Blackburn Rovers broke the English transfer record to bring him to Ewood Park instead. The name of Peter Beardsley (then at Everton) had also been frequently mentioned and, a few days before Éric's arrival was officially announced, Ferguson had failed in his second attempt to buy the superbly gifted (but troubled) Sheffield Wednesday centre-forward David Hirst. The Yorkshire club had rejected an offer believed to be well in excess of £3m, another figure that highlights the derisory nature of the amount Leeds were prepared to accept in exchange for their most gifted footballer – the man of the match of a sumptuous Charity Shield which had been played little over three months previously. In that context, the reassurance Ferguson sought maybe had as much to do with the questions he was asking about himself as about his new recruit. It would be excessive to speak of a 'last roll of the dice', but how long could he hold on to the keys of power if this latest gamble didn't pay off?

Regardless of Ferguson's long-standing interest in, if not active pursuit of his recruit, events had unfolded at tremendous speed: the deal had been struck just four days after Cantona's exclusion from the Leeds squad for their game at Arsenal. Forty-eight hours later, on the morning of 27 November, Éric passed his medical and was treated to the traditional stadium visit by his new manager. Cantona wandered on to the pitch on which he had played half an hour of football with Leeds twelve weeks previously. As he approached the halfway line, Ferguson stopped him and, with a sweeping gesture to the stands, asked: 'I wonder if you're good enough to play in this ground . . .' to which Éric replied: 'I wonder if Manchester is good enough for me!' As it is no secret that players with an inflated sense of their own worth rarely last long at Old Trafford, it might surprise some that Alex Ferguson rather enjoyed this show of bravado. But the Scot could distinguish pride from cockiness, and was looking for a protagonist big enough for the 'Theatre of Dreams'. Any Manchester United fan can name footballers of undoubted talent who failed to live up to their billing at their club. An incontrovertible sense of self-belief is crucial for those who wish to survive and flourish in an environment where myth has tended to be out of step with actual achievement. Cantona's reply, for all its mock arrogance, at least manifested a genuine desire to succeed, and a refusal to be intimidated.

The two men then made their way to the press room, where Éric was to be formally introduced to the British media as a Manchester United player. Alex Ferguson opened the proceedings in his idiosyncratic French: '*Mon plaisir à présenter Éric Cantona*' – bringing a faint smile to Éric's lips. Like most great managers, Ferguson has used and continues to use the press to relay a message to the only audience he really cares for: his players; on this occasion, he was addressing the Frenchman who was sitting by his side, interpreter in tow.* 'Éric is the goalscorer we have been looking for,' he said. 'He is a very exciting footballer, the type Manchester United fans love. He is one of the best entertainers in the country.' Ferguson couldn't resist a small dig at Éric's former club: 'I do believe he was instrumental in Leeds winning the championship last season. He has flair, he has class, and we have now provided him with the biggest of stages upon which to perform.'

From the outset, Ferguson was implementing the policy from which he would never deviate throughout Cantona's stay in Manchester: talk Éric up, reassure him, shore up his fragile confidence at every possible opportunity. Houllier and Bielderman had advised him to become a surrogate father to Cantona. It is a tribute to Ferguson's considerable gifts as a psychologist that he immediately felt that no other course of action was open to him. He later wrote: 'I had resolved when he [Éric] arrived that I would ignore all past attempts to present him as an *enfant terrible*, I would judge him on what he was like in his dealings with me, making my aim to communicate with him regularly and to try and understand him. He was not, I soon discovered, the overwhelmingly confident person many perceived him to be. He needed nourishing.' Éric's first day at Old Trafford provided Ferguson with a chance to do just that, in public, and set a pattern that would transform the player – and, ultimately, the club.

It helped that both men took an instant shine to each other. Cantona would not hesitate to talk about a case of 'love at first sight', and confided to his friend Bernard Morlino: 'Ferguson fills us with a joy of living. Either you enter the *tourbillon* [whirlwind], or you're thrown outside the hurricane.' Note the violent undertones to Cantona's metaphor; note, too, how little room is left for reason in this appraisal – what matters is the 'joy of living'. The young footballer of Auxerre had said: 'Maybe, on the day I caressed a ball for the first time, the sun was shining, people were happy, and it made me feel like playing football.

* This interpreter had very little to do. When asked if he'd submitted a transfer request to Leeds, Éric replied, '*Non*,' and that was more or less that.

All my life, I'll try to capture that moment again.' The twenty-six-year-old wanted to believe that the time to do so had come at last.

Howard Wilkinson had lost his way when attempting to read the confused map of Éric's character. All he could see was a tangle of roads whose destination was unclear. He might have understood that the firebrand he had brought to Leeds needed to be cajoled into abeyance; but he was unable to bring himself to define a space that Cantona and Cantona alone could occupy in his team, as this jarred with both his instinct and all he'd learnt in his own tough ascent from lower-league pro to champion of England. It would have gone against what had made him a successful manager – his organizational skills, his ability to instil discipline in a group, his rigorous (some would say rigid) approach to the game of football. Football, an art form? Not bloody likely! A battle, yes.

Ferguson was cut from a different cloth. To him, discipline was a means to an end, not an inflexible imperative of man-management. He knew how to instil fear in a player's eyes, but he also had an intuitive grasp of other people's insecurities and how best to exploit them; kindness and understanding, which came naturally to him, were other weapons in his arsenal. I have only spent a few hours in Ferguson's company, but, like so many before me, I was struck by his easy charm and his genuine ability to listen to the interlocutor of the moment. What time he had given me felt like a gift, presented without affectation; though it's also true that I was kept on my toes by a sense of imminent danger. I most certainly didn't want to cross that man, and realized it wouldn't be very difficult to do so.

Ferguson knew how all but a very few professionals are inhabited by a sometimes overwhelming sense of anguish, how much doubt preys on them, and how what differentiates the great from the good can also be the capacity to conquer a deep-rooted feeling of inadequacy, rather than an unshakeable self-belief in one's ability. So, how best to deal with Cantona? Ferguson's secret was of the utmost simplicity: tea. As he told Gérard Houllier, 'Every day, I had a cup of tea with him. Every day.' We now know how Éric responded to that, as he had responded to Guy Roux's grumpily affectionate guidance, and to Marc Bourrier's gentler, but still father-like rule. Ferguson also realized – again, from the very beginning, which is why the point must be made at this stage in the story – that he would have to allow his recruit far more leeway in the day-to-day life of the club. At first, some of the other players found it difficult to believe, and accept, that such a notorious hellraiser could be forgiven lapses in United's code of conduct which would have earned them a severe reprimand and, in some cases, more serious punishment. Éric showed admirable dedication on the training ground, often staying behind with a couple of youth-team players to practise his scales when others had long since closed the piano lid. But he also turned up late on a few occasions, without incurring the wrath of his coach, who equally tolerated various infringements to the club's dress code by the Frenchman. Lee Sharpe has told how he was the subject of a verbal lashing by his manager when turning up at a civic function dressed in a snazzy silk suit, whereas Cantona, wearing T-shirt and trainers, had waltzed in without so much as a peep from Ferguson.

Éric was a man apart? Treat him like one, and see what happens. And what happened was that, out of respect for and gratitude to a manager who was treating him with the kind of empathy and kindness he had longed for, Cantona learned to conform to United's rules and regulations. Docile, perhaps not; accommodating, certainly. And as the effect his presence had on the team's performance grew more obvious – and this was clear to see in a matter of a few weeks – professional footballers who could have felt jealousy, even rancour, towards the teacher's pet accepted that a different man could be treated differently, all the more so since Cantona never sought to aggrandize himself because of the special status he enjoyed at The Cliff, Manchester United's training ground.

It also helped that the Glaswegian had a genuine liking for all things French, and not just the *grands crus* of Burgundy he stocks in his cellar. 'If Alex had been English,' Erik Bielderman told me, 'I'm quite sure things wouldn't have worked out as well as they did. Their non-Englishness created a bond between them.' On the day Éric faced the press for the first time in Manchester, Ferguson had made a point of mentioning the Auld Alliance (and promising a new one). Many years later, long after the promise had been fulfilled, he added: 'Cantona is the man who had "*La Marseillaise*" sung from the stands at Old Trafford. Can you imagine more than 60,000 Englishmen singing "*La Marseillaise*" with a single voice?'

12

Cantona's return to Elland Road.

THE HOMECOMING: 1992–93

'If there was ever a player in this world who was made for Manchester United, it was Cantona. I think he had been searching all his life for somebody who looked at him and made him feel that a place was his home. He had travelled around so many countries; there is a wee bit of the gypsy about some people. But when he came here, he knew: this is my place.' Alex Ferguson

Isabelle and Raphaël – who was now two years old – had stayed behind in their Moortown semi near Roundhay Park, where many of the family's possessions remained in the sealed cardboard boxes that had been sent from Nîmes at the beginning of the previous summer. Éric had lived like a soldier who is billeted wherever his regiment is sent, not like the vagabond of his youthful dreams. For Isabelle, there was no sense of adventure in being pulled this way and that in the wake of an unsettled player; only tedium and uncertainty. In the seven years they had lived together, the young couple had moved their belongings from Auxerre to Aix-en-Provence, Martigues, Marseilles, Nîmes and Leeds (Éric lived on his own in Bordeaux), but not once had they settled. Only Guy Roux's house in the forest had felt like a real home, at a time when there was no child to find a school for and fame was just a rumour.

Isabelle had grown fond of Leeds. She had found a job which suited her, running French conversation classes at the local university. Her neighbours, cautious at first, had taken to the unassuming Frenchwoman, just as she had taken to their simplicity and warm-heartedness.

The Cantonas' small garden often filled with Raphaël's schoolmates on evenings and weekends, and the children were soon followed by their parents, whom Isabelle came to rely upon more and more to guide her through the apprenticeship of life in another country. 'Where I come from,' she told a passing journalist, 'people live outdoors, so we try to do the same thing here. We just take an umbrella.' And umbrella in hand, Éric and Isabelle set out to explore the countryside of Yorkshire. They discovered Bridlington, Scarborough, Bolton Abbey, Haworth and walked the galleries of Leeds City Museum. Éric's still imperfect command of English made their visits to movie theatres less frequent than they would have wished (once in Manchester, when it had improved, he would be a regular visitor to the Cornerhouse, a *cinéma d'art et d'essai* beneath the railway arches by Oxford Road station); but, all in all, their life passed pleasantly enough. Elland Road would become a bowl of hate when Cantona returned there in his new colours, but the crowd's venom had not brimmed over the stadium walls at that stage. In Isabelle's presence, 'people were sad,' she said, 'but not nasty or aggressive' – not yet, anyway. She preferred to remember the extraordinary welcome the fans had given her husband, which had brought tears to her eyes. For all these reasons, Isabelle decided to stay put. Leeds would remain their home, to which Éric would return whenever he could.

It was an odd arrangement – or so it struck me, when I realized that the hotel in which he decided to set up his home from home (the Manchester West Novotel, in Worsley Brow, not the Mottram Hall hotel where new United players usually found a temporary base) was only a twenty-five minute drive away from Leeds on the M62. Many commuters with far less free time on their hands than a professional footballer routinely travel over far longer distances, day after day. But a room was booked in his name – throughout the year. Cantona explained his choice to a journalist from *L'Humanité* a few months later. 'It suits me,' he said. 'I do not need to give three months' notice, or to organize moving out, with all the time it takes. A credit card is all you need to say goodbye.' This flippant remark might have been meant to shake his questioner a bit, another variation on the 'Cantona the adventurer' theme, but there's no denying its underlying callousness.

Then again, the borderline between independence of spirit and plain egotism can be a very thin one, and it could be argued that Éric's integration into United's squad would benefit from his being as close as possible to the two nerve centres of his club – The Cliff and Old Trafford. What's more, the Novotel was conveniently located just round the corner from Ryan Giggs' new house, and the Welsh prodigy (a few days away from his nineteenth birthday at the time of Éric's arrival in Manchester) could give Cantona regular lifts to the training ground and to the stadium. Like Gary McAllister before him, Giggs discovered that Cantona's English gained a great deal of fluency when fellow footballers surrounded him, not journalists.

In the beginning, Cantona naturally did most of his talking with the ball, and a short training session arranged on the morning of United's game against Arsenal, on 28 November, provided his new teammates with proof that this was a language he spoke more fluently than most. Steve Bruce was among those who had been puzzled by the news of Éric's arrival; but the central defender later admitted that he 'didn't realize the quality [Cantona] had'. 'I'd never really seen that at Leeds,' he said. 'We knew he was a good player, but I didn't realize the skills, the balance and the vision he'd got. As soon as I'd seen him in training, I knew he'd give us another dimension.' Éric had been registered with the Premier League too late to figure that day, and watched from the stands as Mark Hughes gave United a 1–0 victory over the 1991 champions. Ferguson's team now stood sixth in the championship table, nine points behind the unexpected pace-setters, Norwich – and six ahead of Leeds, who suffered their sixth League defeat of the season a day later at Chelsea.

The events of the previous week had created quite a stir in France, even if only the most dedicated readers of *L'Équipe* and *France Football* could gauge how much of a shock the news of Cantona's transfer was for Leeds and Manchester United supporters. It shouldn't be forgotten that Premier League highlights were still a novelty in French TV schedules at the time, and that they only gained prominence because of Éric's growing stature on the other side of the Channel. English football and Éric Cantona would remain synonymous for a majority of the French audience until Arsène Wenger took charge of Arsenal in November 1996. Claims that Éric 'invented' English football in France are not too wide of the mark; until then, you would tune in to the Sunday evening sports programmes in the hope of seeing the nation's favourite maverick in action, surrounded by Anglo-Saxons whose names were routinely butchered beyond recognition by commentators. A change of club for Éric Cantona would not normally have been news in France – just another twist in an increasingly convoluted tale. But with *Les Bleus*' next World Cup qualification game two-and-a-half months away (a trip to Israel), everyone wanted to know exactly how Gérard Houllier's key player was getting on. *L'Équipe* duly dispatched my colleague Jean-Philippe Bouchard to find out. It made for interesting reading.

He joined Éric in St Albans, where United had set up camp before their match at Highbury. Some of Cantona's comments must have caused astonishment in Yorkshire. No, he'd never had any problems at Leeds and, had Manchester United not made an offer, he'd have been quite happy to stay there. He'd had enough of these 'rumours' about being angry with substitutions. He hadn't been subbed, merely 'rested'. He'd been injured before the Arsenal–Leeds game, nothing else. Wilkinson was making gratuitous accusations. 'You only have to look at my performances for Leeds to be convinced I was worth my place,' he said. 'Eight goals, eight assists – I was a hit with everyone. I had become the leader.' On the other hand, he admitted, 'I like change. I need it more than most people. I like to live for the moment. It's as true for my game as it is for my career and my life. I've always been like this; I need to fill up my tank with energy, to start from zero again. That's what gives me the most pleasure. What's more, that's what enables me to improve, to go up one level after another, like a mountaineer who climbs up the small peaks in his area before confronting Everest. You see a lot of civil servants in football. This type of behaviour doesn't agree with me. I become bad. Moving on excites me, and only excitement allows me to play well.' Is it any wonder that Elland Road soon learnt a couple of new songs? 'He's gay, he's French/He's always on the bench/Cantona, Cantona' was one. 'He's French, he's dumb/He'll do fuck all with scum [*i.e. Manchester United*]' the other. It would get worse.

Much to Bouchard's surprise, he ended up staying with Cantona for two weeks. The Manchester United squad had left England immediately after the Arsenal game for a golfing break in Portugal, where a testimonial match with Benfica had been arranged in honour of that club's – and that country's – greatest-ever player, Eusébio. Cantona and Bouchard, footballer and journalist, made their way to Lisbon under their own steam. Jean-Philippe's most salient memory of that trip – apart from serving as an impromptu translator at a press conference – is of Cantona wolfing down his airline meal, then picking up the tray his travelling companion hadn't finished yet. When Bouchard protested, Éric simply answered: 'I'm still hungry,' and ate the lot.

The match itself was a non-event. The Estádio da Luz, bathed in pale autumnal sunlight, was barely half full when Éric took the field in the jersey of Manchester United for the first time. Ferguson's players trotted on to the pitch and lost 1–0, having posed close to no threat. Brian McClair, with whom Cantona had been paired upfront in the first half, was invisible; Mark Hughes, who took the Scot's place after the interval, merely subdued. Éric kicked defender Abel Silva – and earned a caution, quite a feat in a game of that nature. The poor quality of his team's performance didn't worry Ferguson unduly: this brief escapade to Portugal was designed to strengthen the bond between his players, and according to Ryan Giggs, proved a success in that respect. The whole squad descended on a casino 'for a laugh and a few beers', in other words, to get drunk, and found in Cantona a willing companion. According to Giggs, Éric took an instant liking to goalkeeper Peter Schmeichel, with whom he later roomed on trips. He liked the Dane's fiery temper on the field, and his far more relaxed attitude off it. Schmeichel was a bit of an artist too, an accomplished amateur pianist who entertained his teammates with renditions of West End musicals at parties.

Just as in Leeds, Éric enjoyed his English teammates' tolerance of a man who kept himself to himself when he wanted to, provided he was also able to let his hair down from time to time. And just as at Leeds, Cantona got on with almost everyone. 'Straight away, he mucked in with the rest of the boys,' Gary Pallister recalled in his autobiography, *Pally*, 'fitting in socially and clearly relishing our "team meetings"'

– a euphemism that no reader should have much trouble deciphering. Pallister could sense that Cantona's supposedly poor command of English was akin to the deafness from which elderly family members miraculously recover whenever they're talked about at the dinner table.

Paul Ince too fell under Éric's charm. 'He was a lovely, lovely man,' he said. 'We used to spend a lot of time together, go out for a few drinks together. It was always all about him, the way he walked in, his charisma. He was one of the best, perhaps the best I've played with. It was his awareness. He seemed to know where anyone was on the pitch at any given time when he had the ball. He used to say to me, "Treat the ball like you treat a woman – caress it." I'd say, "I'd kick the ball over the fucking bar! I couldn't kick my wife over the bar." He just loved the ball, didn't he? His little touches, flicks . . . he was just unbelievable. A fantastic player and a lovely, lovely person, the most gentle gentleman.' Not everyone, though, agreed with Ince's and Giggs' opinion that Éric was 'just one of the lads' who enjoyed joining in the lager-fuelled banter.

Steve Bruce, an older and perhaps more perceptive man, later told Lee Chapman that the Frenchman had 'hardly said a word' in his first few weeks in Manchester. This chimed with the Leeds striker's recollection of Cantona as a loner who 'would often arrive, train and leave . . . without uttering more than a few words', and this despite the fact that Chapman was one of the very few people Éric could converse with in French. Everyone, it seems, had 'their' Cantona; garrulous with some – Gary McAllister, for example – he would shut up like a bad clam with the rest. He could switch from one persona to the other at will, with the paradoxical ease of one who is convinced of the worthlessness of outsiders' judgement yet nonetheless craves their approval. How much he delighted in being the centre of attention was demonstrated a few days later, when, leaving his teammates in Lisbon, he headed for Paris, where France's answer to Terry Wogan, Jean-Pierre Foucault, had asked him to be the star of a one-hour prime-time television special.

Here was more proof of how his status had been enhanced by the quality of his performances for *Les Bleus* and his largely unexpected success with Leeds United. The broadcast revealed little about Cantona, who was happy to engage in a sentimental, almost mawkish, celebration of his Marseillais roots, crowned with a 'surprise' appearance by his grandmother. This made for excruciating television, not that Cantona seemed to be aware of it. The attention devoted to him flattered his vanity and more than made up for the embarrassment many of his admirers felt at the time. Moreover, on 3 December Éric's *starisation* was completed by the first appearance of his puppet (nicknamed 'Picasso') on France's answer to *Spitting Image*, *Les Guignols de l'info*, a spasmodically amusing programme in which Cantona's party trick was to throw his shirt at whoever happened to be on the set with him. Unsurprisingly, Cantona loved his latex alter ego and was later seen sporting a promotional cap for that popular programme.

A subtle change had occurred. Éric had always provided good copy, in his interviews as well as in his regular brushes with authority, but, within a matter of weeks, the rebel in exile, now covered with an exotic veneer, underwent his transformation into *un people* (a celeb), the first French footballer to enter the age of celebrity. He was a willing protagonist in this metamorphosis, and would be richly rewarded for it, with some of the most lucrative commercial endorsements ever offered to a European sportsman. The self-confessed loner who 'would love to be poor' did nothing to discourage the creation of a Cantona brand. Shortly after the end of the 1992–93 season, he appeared on the catwalk modelling Paco Rabanne's suits. The *couturier* had been attracted by the 'sincerity, sensitivity and authenticity' of 'a passionate, excessive, generous human being who symbolizes a whole generation'. For Éric? 'Just another experience.' Another experiment, rather. If he had yet to transform Manchester United, he was now well on the way to transforming himself.

Four-and-a-half years later, one of the reasons he advanced for his decision to retire from the game was his unease at how his image had been exploited by Manchester United. I would argue, however, that, whilst Cantona might have had reason to feel that United had 'betrayed' his trust – something that still stirred his anger when he spoke to *L'Équipe Magazine* in 2007 – he was not quite the innocent victim of a ploy hatched by others to 'exploit' his increasingly powerful image. He was, by and large, a willing actor in the campaigns designed to turn him into a commodity, and I can't help but feel that his main bone of contention at the time was United's reluctance to give him a fair share of the profits; in which, by the way, he may well have been in the right. 'Shrewd' and 'businessman' make a lazy couple in the prose of journalism, but could be used in tandem with good reason in Éric's case. While George Best – the only footballer who had benefited from similar opportunities before him in England – just went with the flow and, quite literally, got drunk on fame, Cantona had more than a measure of control over his reification in the media. Not only did he sell himself, but he helped define what would be sold, and found in Manchester United a club of immense potential in that regard. Crucially, his departure for England had also provided him with a unique opportunity, as French League regulations prohibited professional players from striking sponsorship deals on an individual basis. In other words, had he not been forced into exile, he would probably never have been in a position to enter the enduring relationship with Nike which shaped his image and – to a significant extent – his career to the last. As it is, the sportswear manufacturer (who already had John McEnroe on its books) courted and won the rebel as early as 1992, almost as soon as Cantona had put the Nîmes charade behind him. In this, as in so many other ways, he was the right man in the right place at the right time, or, as Alex Ferguson puts it, 'the perfect player, in the perfect club, at the perfect moment'.

Meanwhile, in Leeds, Howard Wilkinson was fuming. Some fans backed the manager, and their number would grow in parallel with Éric's influence in his new team. One of them came out in support of Cantona's sale in a letter to the *Yorkshire Evening Post*, in which he produced a set of 'damning' statistics, such as: none of the three goals Éric scored in the 1991–92 championship-winning season helped clinch a single point; or: when Cantona made three consecutive starts after the 5–1 demolition of Wimbledon in that campaign, Leeds failed to record a single victory. No mention was made of his hat-tricks in the Charity Shield and against Spurs. Consolation had to be sought where it could be found. Wilkinson too went on the attack, his anger fuelled by the loss of any hope that his Cantona-less team had of retaining its title. He passed on his programme notes to the *Yorkshire Evening Post* on the eve of Nottingham Forest's visit, which would take place on 5 December, twenty-four hours before Éric's competitive debut for United. 'Éric Cantona left because he wanted to go,' he wrote:

> . . . to put it another way, he wasn't prepared to stay and abide by the rules for everybody at the club. I have categoric proof of that. It has never been my policy to keep a player once he has expressed a strong desire to leave. Look at the facts. He has stayed only a short time at any of his seven previous clubs. By his own mouth, he is the sort of person who, in order to survive needs change, a new environment and new surroundings. He was very disillusioned with football [when I took him to Leeds], his international career was in serious jeopardy. He was good for us, we were good for him. For the first time at a club, he acquired a cult following. The easy way to avoid disappointing his fans would have been to stay here working within the rules of the club as they apply to everybody else, but he felt he couldn't do that. So be it. He can't have his cake and eat it. I cannot guarantee anyone that they will play every week.

In private, Wilkinson was even more scathing, as the now travel-weary Jean-Philippe Bouchard found out when he managed to blag his way into the Yorkshireman's office, the door to which had been repeatedly shut in the face of British journalists. 'He was guarded at first,' Bouchard told me, 'then something snapped, and I couldn't stop him.' Wilkinson assured him that he had spent more time and energy talking to Cantona than he ever had with any other player. His voice rose. 'I cannot tolerate the whims of a kid.' What whims? Turning up late for training was one. Sometimes, not turning up at all. Wilkinson was on a roll. 'I do not have to put Éric in the team just because he cannot bear being a sub. Nobody likes it. But you first have to prove you're worth your place in the team, at training and in the games. Éric wasn't doing it any more. He took advantage of his image with the fans and thought he was the best, like many players who've fallen into the same trap before. The saddest thing is that I don't think he's aware of it himself. That is why I didn't think he was a good player any more.' Then: 'Éric wasn't indispensable. The fans are the victims of media overkill. My own son cried when Cantona went. But I cannot be influenced by anyone.'

The interview – which somehow escaped the attention of the English press – was concluded by two short sentences which showed how profoundly upset the old-style coach had been by Éric's behaviour. 'Let him have [his] fun in Manchester. If Leeds play well, it'll be enough for fans to forget him.'

The next day, Leeds were humiliated at home by bottom-of-the-table Forest (1–4), a defeat which saw them drop to 15th in the League, 18 points adrift of leaders Norwich, and prompted Wilkinson to say: 'We've been so bad that people will spend the weekend talking about this rout and not about Éric Cantona.' As to 'forget him', how could they?

Take Gary King, a lorry driver (some say a plasterer) who had given up his Leeds season ticket when Éric had been sold, and told Bouchard that he hadn't slept for three days afterwards. He confessed he had felt less pain when his wife had left him, and that he was ashamed of this. One comment King made at the time struck me: 'Éric was putting [Wilkinson] in the shade. He was too popular. That's why he sold him on the cheap, for £1.2m, when Ferguson was willing to pay £4m. To devaluate him.' These words appear almost verbatim in the autobiography Éric and others cobbled together during the following summer, but were then attributed to anonymous 'fans'. These 'fans' were, of course, King himself. He had played the role of self-appointed gopher for Éric and his entourage at Leeds. When the player left for Manchester, he felt that the only way he could assuage his grief was by following his god, and fulfilling the same function in a city he hated. Work, family, friends – King turned his back on everything that had composed his life up to then. He had five children, three of them boys who showed no interest in football whatsoever, and couldn't comprehend their father's social suicide.

King acted as a chauffeur, or as a minder whose presence reassured Isabelle, especially after death threats started to arrive at the Cantonas' home in Leeds shortly before Manchester United were to play at Elland Road. He turned into a shadow within a shadow, enduring what must have been a nightmare, in order to live some kind of a dream. Wherever Éric turned up, Gary King could be seen, throughout the four-and-a-half seasons the footballer played for United. Then the most fanatical of all Cantona's worshippers disappeared without a trace. Erik Bielderman phoned almost every King he could find in the Greater Manchester directory when preparing the Cantona special published by *L'Équipe Magazine* in 2007, without success. My luck was no better than Erik's. No one seems to know where Gary King lives today. When Éric left football, King was erased like so much chalk on a blackboard. The Cantonas moved from Manchester to Barcelona, and he was left behind. I've often wondered whether this tragic man feels betrayed now, or finds solace in the memory of having been someone Éric trusted. To him, Cantona must have died in May 1997. And I've also wondered if, in that, Gary King wouldn't be closer to the truth than anyone else.

The Cantona circus rolled on. Éric was readying himself for a Manchester derby in which Alex Ferguson had suggested he might play a role, and the 5 December edition of *The Times* devoted its traditional Saturday profile to the '*enfant terrible*' (of course) of French football. The expression made its appearance as early as the first paragraph. 'Gallic flair' in the second. 'Maverick' in the third. His taste for 'Rimbaud's surrealism' popped in later (the poet died five years before André Breton was born), together with comparisons with James Dean and Alain Delon. Alain Delon? Cantona had a knack for sometimes bringing out the worst in those who wrote about him. Here, the player was casually described as 'slimly built' and his height was given as '6ft', when he had the body of a light-heavyweight boxer and was a good two inches taller. 'Print the legend', as Neville Cardus is supposed to have said, and the temptation to do just that becomes irresistible when the subject of the mythmaker's distortions does nothing to dispel the untruths. Éric rarely disappointed in that respect.

Moreover, his new coach was of the opinion that his recruit needed to be talked up in public as well as in the almost daily heart-to-heart conversations he had with him. 'The most important thing is that he has tremendous ability,' Ferguson told the press after barely a week spent with the Frenchman on the training ground. 'I hope we can add to that, because at this club I think he has the potential to become a real giant.' What sounds now like the prediction of a visionary was then also possibly more of a psychological trick played by the best man-manager in the business.

The Old Trafford crowd was introduced to Éric Cantona on 6 December, which happened to be the date of the 117th Manchester derby, an occasion on which Éric would nearly always shine in the future.* Not that day, though. Wearing the no. 12 jersey, he came on as a substitute for Ryan Giggs after the Welsh winger had damaged ankle tendons. Cantona judged his performance 'average', and most summarizers spoke of a 'negligible contribution'. Paul Ince was the catalyst of United's 2–1 victory, chipping in with a rare goal, and the most remarkable aspect of Éric's debut, bar a couple of decent passes, had been the restraint he had shown in the face of his man-marker Steve McMahon's constant provocations. Cantona ignored the hand extended to him by the defender after the latter had hacked him for the umpteenth time, and that was all.

Most habitués of the press box thought that Alex Ferguson would take his time to bed his recruit in, but they were soon proved wrong. The United manager knew how much his player had been frustrated

* One of Cantona's closest friends in Manchester, Claude Boli, remarked in a much later interview that Éric 'was particularly successful against the clubs which United supporters despise the most: Man City, Liverpool, Arsenal, Leeds United, which led fans to say: "He's close to us, he understands us, he knows it's far more important to win at Anfield than in the European Cup; [more important to win] against Liverpool than against Barcelona, that's very English! He's the man we needed." Claude Boli PhD (in history and sociology) was the brother of Éric's former Auxerre teammate Basile Boli and had come to Lancashire to write a sociology thesis about football which later formed the basis of his book *Manchester United, L'Invention d'un club (Deux Siècles de Métamorphoses)*, to which Cantona contributed a foreword. Another excerpt from this interview, given to *France Football*'s Xavier Rivoire in 2003, is worth quoting: 'From the very first day [with Manchester United], Éric told himself, "I'm going to learn; I can succeed here, but I've got to take my time, to adapt, and people will have to adapt to me." Éric was very humble. He wasn't there to change United's style, but to bring something extra. The rapport between him and Alex Ferguson meant that they gave each other time to succeed.'

by Howard Wilkinson's refusal to make Éric the lynchpin of his team, just as Henri Michel's failure to inform Cantona he would be rested for an international friendly had led, quite unwillingly on Michel's side, to France missing their most potent striker in the qualifiers for the 1990 World Cup. Cantona needed proof of his manager's trust, which meant being given a place in the starting line-up, no matter what. And on 12 December, the date of Norwich's visit to Old Trafford in the League, Éric's name featured in United's starting eleven for the first time. Remarkably, in this season as well as the three to come, unless he was rested for a minor game or had picked up an injury, Cantona would be substituted for tactical reasons on two occasions only: when he came off the field in the 73rd minute of a 3–0 thrashing of Wimbledon fourteen months later – after scoring perhaps the most famous goal of his Manchester United career (the game was sewn up by then, and a League Cup semi-final lurked on the horizon) – and in March 1994, when, under the shadow of a five-game ban, he sleepwalked through the first 75 minutes of a 1–0 win over Liverpool. Alex Ferguson had never shown such trust in a player, and never would again.

If Éric's undroppable status would never be questioned by his mentor, his role would change markedly over the coming months. He had been identified as the man who could revitalize United's attack and revelled in Ferguson's expectations. 'I knew that Manchester United were looking for a striker,' he told Bouchard, who hadn't yet taken leave of his subject. 'When you play for a team that finds it difficult to score goals, you really have the feeling you're working for something.' How he would best work hadn't yet been ascertained. Against leaders Norwich, who were beaten 1–0 thanks to a Mark Hughes goal, he excelled in a link-up role, playing in the hole behind the Welsh centre-forward and Brian McClair. Paul Ince, the self-styled guv'nor, grumbled about Éric's unwillingness to track back and share in defensive duties ('it's all very well doing the flicks when you're winning, but when you are losing, it's more important for someone to put their foot in'), but also remarked upon the quality of his short passing and his clear footballing vision, which Ferguson too singled out for praise: 'the most important ingredient he has given us,' he said after the game. 'Éric starts attacks out of nothing.'

Ryan Giggs, watching from the sidelines, was astonished by another of Cantona's qualities: his deceptive pace. 'Once he got going,' he said, 'nobody could outrun him.' Éric's magnificent close control also enabled his teammates to use him – and Mark Hughes – as a *point de fixation* (another French expression for which there is no equivalent in English, despite the fact that Kenny Dalglish was perhaps the greatest exponent of that role), a forward who could dictate and orientate the play under pressure, and give his wing-backs or wingers time to rush down their respective flanks and overrun the opposition's full-backs. 'Éric would receive the ball, turn in one movement and lay it off,' Giggs said. 'Because of his vision, you just knew he'd read your run and play you in.' What's more, he could also score himself, as he did, vitally, in United's next league game, a 1–1 draw at Stamford Bridge. Chelsea's biggest crowd of the season so far had little to cheer, but the travelling support did, despite the atrocious weather: Cantona was magnificent. The players could be forgiven for registering a mere two shots on target throughout the 90 minutes as the rain arrowed on to the muddy pitch; but Éric flew over the puddles, unerringly finding another red shirt with his subtle flicks when all about him hoofed the ball like frustrated schoolchildren. Paul Parker rushed to congratulate him when he found the net to give United an equalizer that propelled United to fourth spot in the League – despite the absence of their injured captain Bryan Robson.

The 'flashy foreigner' had shown how he could master what were supposed to be alien conditions. 'I've always had this feeling I was protected by something, I don't know why,' he said afterwards. 'And confidence brings the freedom to express yourself, and freedom to express yourself brings genius, euphoria, fire.' You could read that euphoria on Éric's face after he netted the first of his 82 goals for Manchester United. And he had another gift: the capacity to share the pure joy of scoring, so obvious, so fresh in these first games. Come the next training session, fans were queueing up at The Cliff, where Éric made it a point of honour to sign autographs for everyone present. 'You have to do it,' he said. 'It's not like that in France. The fans are not like that either. I sometimes refused to sign autographs in France; I have criticized the [French] public violently, because there is no love, no passion. They never give anything, and want you to give in return.'

In Manchester, as they had done in Leeds, they gave a lot, and it would take Cantona the best part of quarter of an hour to walk the few yards that separated the exit of the training facilities and the players' car park. Things have changed since then. A fan turning up at the gates of the Carrington complex today will be ushered off none too gently by a security guard, while the stars drive away in ostentatious anonymity behind black-tinted car windows. Cantona, in so many ways a herald for the cult of football celebrities, still belonged to a more innocent age.

It couldn't be a coincidence that United's fortunes had taken a turn for the better since Éric's arrival. Norwich's surprising 2–0 loss at home to Ipswich on 21 December gave the Reds a chance to emerge during the Christmas period as serious title contenders for the first time. On Boxing Day, Cantona helped salvage a miraculous 3–3 draw at Sheffield Wednesday, for whom his former Marseille teammate Chris Waddle had been on fire. Twenty minutes before the final whistle, United were as good as dead, trailing by three goals, before the Frenchman engineered a late, desperate rally, offering two goals to Brian McClair and scoring the third himself at the second attempt. Lee Sharpe had given a superb exhibition of wing play, but all the talk in the dressing-room was of Cantona, who had transformed the game, and was already well on his way to transforming the team.

Many were surprised by how well Mark Hughes, a very intense man with a keen (but not inflated) sense of his own worth, was connecting with a player who was supposed to be in direct competition with him for a place in Ferguson's starting line-up. When Coventry were crushed 5–0 at Old Trafford forty-eight hours later, the Welsh centre-forward, who couldn't buy a goal before Éric's transfer, had scored his third in as many games since the Frenchman's arrival. Cantona himself (who also laid on a perfect pass for Lee Sharpe to tap in from six yards) had been chosen to take a penalty for the fourth goal after Phil Babb had handled the ball, and dispatched it with remarkable coolness, given that it was the first time he had been granted such a privilege in England. It said a great deal about his growing influence on the team and the regard in which his manager held him already.

Describing those early days at Old Trafford and the immediate impact he had on those around him, Cantona later said:

> I loved to pass the ball where nobody expected it, provided it produced a result. The game becomes more fluid, more surprising. When you know how to do that, you have ten times more possibilities, because the players around you know that you can put the ball anywhere at any time. So, they look for spaces. Mark Hughes loved to receive the ball with his back to goal and give it back – we could combine in small places. Roughly speaking, Manchester's game plan was: use Hughes as a focal point, I get the ball back, and before I've even received it, the two wingers have already started their run.

But Éric could just as easily have spoken of himself as his team's focal point, and not only on the field of play, where his teammates would look to him to provide the beat of their attacks; the press too – quite literally – focused on the big, fast, skilful Frenchman: every single United report *The Times* had printed since his arrival at Old Trafford featured an action shot of Éric. When Ferguson's men opened the 1993 calendar year with a relaxed 2–0 win over third division Bury in the FA Cup, it had been a young Northern Irishman named Keith Gillespie who had provided them with inspiration and goals, but it was still Éric's frame that loomed the largest in the accompanying photograph – as it did when Tottenham were added to the list of his victims five days later. This time, no one could doubt who had been the catalyst of a 4–1 victory that sent United to the top of the league on goal difference. 'Ferguson's team boasts many outstanding individuals,' wrote the reporter of a London daily, 'but only one genuine star: Cantona, of course.' A header gave Éric his fourth goal in six league games, after which he set up Dennis Irwin with a superb pass, and United strolled to the finishing post.

His exhibition had been witnessed by the only British player whom Éric counted among his footballing heroes: George Best, whose path he crossed for the first time that day. The two men exchanged a glance, a smile and a nod; neither needed words to acknowledge the presence of a kindred spirit. Best, a much sharper judge of the game than he was sometimes credited for, naturally devoted his next column to Cantona. 'If he keeps doing it, this club is going to win the title,' he predicted. 'That's how important he is to United. He has given this team a brain. I honestly had my doubts about him fitting in, but he has convinced me that – at just £1.1m [*Éric actually cost £100,000 more*] – he is Alex Ferguson's shrewdest signing.' Statistics bore this judgement out. Before Éric's arrival, United had managed just four goals in nine games. In the nine since he joined, they had scored twenty-two. Cantona had unlocked his team's attacking potential; he had also given them an impetus that was carried through to their next fixture, a 3–1 win at QPR on 16 January, despite his missing the trip to London through injury. His absence was brief: he didn't feature in a routine qualification for the fifth round of the FA Cup at the expense of another modest team, Brighton & Hove Albion, and resumed playing eleven days later, as if he had been there all along at the heart of United's purring engine.

Nottingham Forest conceded only two goals, the second of which Éric had created by volleying a pass to Mark Hughes, but it could have been many, many more. 'Our game was superbly tuned,' Cantona later said of the first of his many purple patches. 'We didn't have to adapt to the opposition. [Before the games], he [Ferguson] spoke more about details, whether a 'keeper didn't like the ball on the ground, what was the weaker side of a defender. But he always ended up his talks by saying: "And now, enjoy yourselves." Have fun. It's a magnificent thing to say, because you've worked throughout the week, and everything has been done for you to have fun.'

And what fun they were having – their fans, too. Just as Leeds had fallen in love with Éric at first sight, Manchester, or at least half of it, took to its French talisman from the outset, re-appropriating the Kop's famous 'Ooh-ah Cantona' (one supporter, Giorgina Williams, even took the trouble of teaching the chant to her parrot Rodney; another named a yearling after it – the horse won a race at Redcar in June 1993 despite odds of 12/1) and unfurling the tricolour in the Old Trafford stands. Twelve games had passed since United had last conceded defeat, and bookmakers had now installed them as joint favourites for the title. Only Ron Atkinson's flamboyant Aston Villa possessed the strength in depth to pose a real threat over the four remaining months of the season. Norwich, for all their neat interplay, were felt to lack the steel required to be champions. Moreover, United were ready and willing to strengthen an already formidable line-up and, come February, Alex Ferguson was alerted to the possible availability of a twenty-one-year-old Irishman who had made himself the fulcrum of Brian Clough's Nottingham Forest: Roy Keane. Keane was dallying over extending his stay at the City Ground, and insisted on adding escape clauses to a new contractual agreement. It was not a question of if, but when United would pounce with an offer Forest could not refuse. In the end, Ferguson would have to wait until the summer to get his man, but another seed of his club's future dominance had been sown.

United stuttered briefly at the very end of January, dropping three points at Ipswich (1–2), where Cantona was subjected to the kind of all-out assault that led a fast-diminishing group of doubters to reflect that he could still wilt under the physical pressures of English football; but he had also added another assist to his collection (for Brian McClair this time), and when Sheffield United visited Old Trafford a week later, the scoreline was reversed, Éric getting his fifth goal in nine starts for Alex Ferguson. Not much attention was given to that game, however. The talk was already of the next fixture, which would pit the Mancunians against another Yorkshire side. Cantona was coming back to Elland Road.

Éric had some idea of what was in store for him – but even the threatening messages that had been delivered to his Roundhay home (and caused Isabelle to fear for her family's safety) failed to make him realize what vicious hostility his name now inspired in Leeds. Had he done so, he mightn't have bothered writing an open letter to his former fans (according to a contemporary report), in which he assured them that he still cherished the club, its manager and its supporters. His emergence from the United coach seventy-five minutes before kick-off sparked a torrent of insults, which carried on unabated throughout the day. As *The Times* put it, 'Hatred in this guise – pure, fist-clenching, foul-mouthed and incessant – required no translation.' Two days previously, on the thirty-fifth anniversary of the Munich air disaster, Leeds had travelled to Selhurst Park to play Wimbledon. To many of the travelling supporters, the game had meant very little; they were already thinking of Manchester United's visit, rehearsing for the hatefest of Cantona's return. A chant went round: 'Happy Birthday, dear Munich.' Then, on 8 February, shortly before the two teams lined up on the Elland Road pitch, an inflatable plane was bounced round the Kop. The banner that greeted Éric – 'FOUTRE LE CAMP, CANTONA' ('Fuck off, Cantona' in schoolboy French) – looked tame in comparison, and in truth, Cantona was far more shocked by the Munich chants than by the abuse he had to suffer personally. Several years on, when asked what he had felt during these ninety minutes of unending abuse, it is the ugliness of the Munich chants that came back to his mind. They had had a numbing effect on him. 'Nothing could touch me,' he said. 'I knew I would get a hot reception. I expected it. If I'd been a Leeds suppporter, I would probably have reacted the same way. It was not a surprise.' But other Manchester United players – Ryan Giggs was one – had far more difficulty coping with the experience: 'The crowd's hostility towards him was evil, and we were all just happy to get away from the place safe and sound,' the Welshman said.

Typically, Éric felt compelled to show how little effect the insults had on him. Was he provoking the crowd? Not necessarily. Expressing a lack of concern was a means to defend himself. So, during the warm-up, and with the Kop already in full, filthy voice, he had been the last Manchester United player to leave the field. My friend David Luxton – a Leeds fan – was in the stands that day, directly behind the goal at which Éric was aiming his shots in practice. When the moment came to return to the dressing-room, drowned in an ocean of noise, a sewer in full flow, Cantona took the ball, juggled it for a while and signed off with a volley to the top corner. The jeers redoubled in ferocity but, as David remembers it, intensified by the admiration the crowd couldn't help but feel for such arrogance ('We had to admit it – this guy had balls'). His former teammates – who felt no animosity towards him – had been impressed too. 'He was like he had always had been,' Gary McAllister told me, 'his shoulders back, and his chest forward, with the arrogance of a gunslinger.'

The gunslinger fired blanks, though. The game petered out to a goalless draw, the result the police (and the management of both clubs) had hoped for. Éric contributed little himself, save a dribble past two defenders followed by a shot which goalkeeper John Lukic easily parried with his legs. He was also shown a yellow card – a 'soft' caution, which punished a nudge off the ball on John Newsome. The wall of hate of the Kop rose a bit higher for a few seconds, and that was that. He could now turn his mind back to football, which had been a mere sideshow in Elland Road's theatre of hate. This meant rejoining the French national team, which was due to play Israel in Tel-Aviv in a World Cup qualifier nine days later.

Éric's call-up couldn't have come at a better time. He badly needed some fresh air after breathing the poisonous atmosphere of Elland Road. His absence was undoubtedly detrimental to United, who were surprisingly dumped out of the FA Cup by Sheffield United while he readied himself to celebrate his thirtieth cap. Euro 92 was by now but a bad memory, pushed further back in his mind by the very real hope of achieving qualification for the 1994 World Cup. A relaxed Cantona found time to mix with journalists in the familiar environment of Clairefontaine. At peace with himself, he also expressed himself fully on the field of play. Gérard Houllier deployed an enterprising 4-3-3 formation in which Éric, positioned slightly deeper than usual, supported striker Jean-Pierre Papin with Patrice Loko and David Ginola occupying the flanks. This was a role not dissimilar to the one he had been given by Alex Ferguson at United: he had the freedom to roam wherever his instinct took him, and scored a superbly judged opening goal, sliding in at the far post to volley home Didier Deschamps' long, raking pass. The only blot on a near-perfect copybook was a caution that would prevent him from taking part in France's next game, a trickier trip to Austria in March (*Les Bleus* would indeed struggle in Vienna without Cantona's vision, and only just prevailed thanks to a strike by Papin).

It's true that some indiscipline was creeping back into his game. Back in England, another booking (his third in three matches for club and country) in a 2–1 win over Southampton triggered an automatic two-match suspension, which forced him to sit out two crucial away games in March, of which United won the first – against Liverpool – and lost the supposedly easier second against a sprightly Oldham. This was Cantona's first ban in English football. Hardly anyone noticed it, though: the challenges that had been punished were clumsy or petulant rather than malicious, and by the time United had whipped Middlesbrough 3–0 on 27 February, the talk was of another stupendous performance of which my friend Michael Henderson, a journalist with the *Guardian* at the time, was an admiring witness and an inspired laudator. 'Cantona will never look natural in English football,' he wrote. 'Craftsmen rarely do. There is something of the poet in his disdain for the clutter around him, and he is selfless enough to furnish others with many of his best lines.'

I reminded Michael of the aptness of his remarks many years later. This 'unnaturalness' has often been mistaken for an inability to adapt, I told him, and he had been one of the only Englishmen I had met who understood that so early in Éric's United career. 'Did I write that?' Michael chuckled. 'That was quite good.' Yes it was, and so was what followed. 'No ball is too difficult either to stun or to lay off,' he continued, 'so he is an ideal conduit for others to play through, seeing the possibilities earlier than they do and having the facility to achieve these aims.' That day, had it not been for the excellence of Stephen Pears (a Manchester United reject) in the Boro goal, Éric would have finished with the third hat-trick of his English career. He had to be content with a solitary goal instead, United's third, his last contribution to his team's pursuit of the title before his ban was activated.

When he returned to action, on 14 March, two clubs shared the lead in the league table: United – and Aston Villa, whose next game was to be played at Old Trafford, to the delight of the satellite broadcasters. Andreï Kanchelskis made way for Éric, whose majestic performance drew comparisons with the way Dennis Viollet used to orchestrate United's attacks when Matt Busby was at the helm. Ron Atkinson's team exuded confidence to start with and took the lead through Steve Staunton, before Cantona headed a Dennis Irwin cross towards Hughes, who obliged with an equalizer; 1–1 it stayed despite Cantona's displaying tremendous stamina and imagination, only to be stifled by an inspired Mark Bosnich in the Villa goal. Perhaps as a consequence of their superiority going unrewarded on that occasion, a subdued United couldn't shake off their collective torpor when a strangely passionless Manchester derby finished with an identical scoreline. Éric, as profligate as any of his teammates in the first half, redeemed himself with a fine equalizing header towards the end of the game, but United's run had been checked, and a third consecutive draw – 0–0 at Arsenal, where David Seaman did well to deny Cantona when he swivelled and shot at goal in a single movement – brought fears of a repeat of the previous season, when Leeds had been able to exploit United's nervousness in the final furlong. Fortunately for Alex Ferguson, Norwich did his team a good turn by beating Villa 1–0 on the same day. United hadn't won in four matches but were still very much in contention, trailing the Norfolk side by a single point with a game in hand – and their next game would take place at Carrow Road, where a victory would see them leapfrog the leaders once again.

The radio was on in the coach taking United to the stadium, and brought them news of Villa's win at Nottingham Forest shortly before their own kick-off. 'We had no choice but to win in Norwich,' Éric explained later, 'otherwise we'd be four points behind. That was the turning point. We played a perfect game. We played perfect football.' This could have been a royal 'we', as Cantona, 'so marvellously cool in control, so rapid of eye', to quote one of many mesmerized reporters, engineered United's resurgence with his eagerness as well as his artistry. The first Mancunian goal demonstrated Éric's ability to set and alter the rhythm of play as a conductor induces legato in a musical phrase. He held the ball just long enough for Ryan Giggs to move onside, receive what was not so much a pass as an offering, and round the Norwich keeper to establish a lead. The third saw him in the guise of a finisher, converting a straightforward chance from Paul Ince's selfless lay-off: his eighth successful strike in seventeen games for United. Norwich lost 3–1 and, with six games still to play, it came down to a single question: who, of United and Villa, could best withstand the pressure?

The track record of the two managers involved boded well for neither. Alex Ferguson had suceeded Ron Atkinson at Old Trafford in November 1986 after a catastrophic start to that season had seen United feel the first glows of heat from what the Italians call football's *inferno.* 'Big Ron' had lasted a little over five seasons in Manchester, long enough to win two FA Cups and throw away a championship title in 1985–86 after his side had strung together ten victories on the trot. Ferguson's own record in domestic competitions was better than Atkinson's, but not by much: one FA Cup (in 1990), one League Cup (in 1992) and two runners-up spots in the top division (in 1988 and 1992) which, in the eyes of many, made him a 'choker' when it came to the prize all Manchester United fans had their eyes on. A tremendous success over Barcelona in the 1990–91 European Cup Winners' Cup final had given him the breathing space that Atkinson had been denied. Luck, sound judgement and Éric Cantona helped him to exploit it to the full, in proportions that it would be foolish to ascertain. But luck definitely came first, and on two occasions.

On 10 April, a valiant Sheffield Wednesday seemed destined to bring back a point from Old Trafford with the score locked at a goal apiece after 90 minutes. That result would have given Villa (who drew 0–0 against Coventry) a two-point cushion over their rivals, but referee John Hilditch – who'd replaced another official, Mike Peck, when the latter had to be treated on the field of play for an Achilles injury – allowed an extra 7′ to be played that afternoon, Steve Bruce scoring the winning goal with a header seconds before Hilditch at last brought the whistle to his lips. Alex Ferguson could afford to make a joke of it. 'We didn't start playing until the 99th minute,' he said. United now led Villa by 69 points to 68. Two days later, not so much luck as a miracle or two enabled them to win 1–0 at Coventry, cancelling out Villa's remarkable win by the same margin at Highbury. Éric played with a sprained wrist for which the team doctor refused to administer a painkiller, until the excruciating pain forced him to hand his place to Bryan Robson – who was so unfit that he had decided to drop himself to the bench in the first place and give the skipper's armband to Steve Bruce. A bad goalkeeping error by Coventry's Jonathan Gould gifted Dennis Irwin a goal, while a Roy Wegerle shot cannoned off Peter Schmeichel's upright and rolled along the goal-line without crossing it. Disaster had been averted – just.

But luck had no need to intervene when Chelsea turned up at Old

Trafford on 17 April to be turned over 3–0. The London club had last succumbed in Manchester in August 1987, and it may be that this barely credible statistic (mentioned in every match preview) had helped Ferguson's players concentrate on their task rather more intently than had been the case in their previous outings. It may also be that they remembered how, almost a year to the day, their failure to overcome Chelsea in similar circumstances had opened the door for Leeds to win the trophy. Lee Sharpe danced on the wing, Cantona executed the final pirouette, signing off with his eighteenth goal of the season in English domestic competitions, an astonishing return for a player whose future had been in the balance during the autumn. Still, Villa, who were in action the next day, responded in kind, and beat Manchester's other team 3–1 – to the delight of some City supporters. United, who boasted a vastly superior goal difference (+31 v. +22), kept the upper hand but remained one slip-up away from catastrophe.

But it was Villa who imploded, conceding two goals within the first fifteen minutes of their visit to Blackburn Rovers, to end up losing 3–0 at Ewood Park. United didn't put on the most convincing of shows either, at relegation-threatened Crystal Palace: the teams were still tied at 0–0 in the sixty-fifth minute, when Cantona and Hughes combined to break the deadlock, the Welshman concluding the move with one of his trademark volleys. Éric also provided the pass that sent Paul Ince through for United's second goal, which effectively ended the game as a contest, and virtually gave his team the title, as a single victory in their last two games would be enough to ward off Aston Villa. In fact, just as had happened the previous season, when he'd watched himself win the championship from Lee Chapman's sofa, the trophy fell into Cantona's lap before he'd had time to lace his boots. The Oldham midfielder Nick Henry sent a left-footed shot past Mark Bosnich at 15:30 on 2 May, and his team held on to their slender advantage in front of 35,000 dumbstruck Aston Villa fans. The long wait had ended: when Manchester United took the field twenty-four hours later against Blackburn Rovers, it would be as champions, for the first time since 1967.

A few years ago, I started compiling what I hoped would be an English–French/French–English football glossary, which would help me in my work as a translator, and for which I had a vague hope of finding a publisher. It was a revealing task. I couldn't have wished for a clearer illustration of the chasm between our footballing cultures. It seemed the French (and, indeed, the Spaniards, the Italians and, believe it or not, the Germans) had at their disposal an arsenal of descriptive words and phrases which my English press-box colleagues had yet to coin. I first encountered a problem when trying to find an equivalent to 'l'amour du geste', *an expression Éric has always been fond of using.* 'Geste' *has no equivalent, unless you accept 'piece of skill', which lacks the (maybe excessive) nobility of the French noun, whose semantic history encapsulates both sleight of hand (or foot in this case) and tales of chivalry (which we call* 'chansons de geste'; *Cantona as Sir Lancelot – now there's a casting idea). The British had 'nutmeg' for* 'petit pont' *('small bridge', a self-explanatory expression); but no* 'grand pont' *('big' or, rather, 'long bridge', when the attacking player, typically a winger, kicks the ball past the defender on one side, and races on the other to get hold of it). Everything else was a 'flick'. I couldn't find an approximation for* 'aile de pigeon' *('pigeon's wing', of course), a marvellously evocative semantic shortcut for one of football's most elegant* 'gestes': *running forward, the player receives the ball slightly behind him, and by shaping his leg as a trussed bird's wing, 'flicks it' in front of him with the outside of the boot. We've also got the* 'madjer', *named after the delightful Moroccan player Rabah Madjer, a backheel behind the standing leg – only used when it is an attempt at goal. And the* 'coup du sombrero', *a Patrick Vieira special, which involves lifting a ball – generally on the volley – above an opponent's head (hence* 'sombrero'*) before resuming control of it on the other side. For a perfect example of this, watch Cantona's famous cracker for Leeds against Chelsea at the end of the 1991–92 season, when poor Paul Elliott did a convincing impersonation of a hat-stand – twice. Or watch Paul Gascoigne fooling Colin Hendry to score the most famous of his England goals at Wembley. There are many other such words –* 'feuille morte' *('dead leaf' – a shot struck with very little power, which relies on precision and surprise to float into a goalkeeper's top corner, used almost exclusively of free kicks), and the* 'coup du foulard' *('kerchief's trick') being just two of the most popular in my home country. Even as basic a skill as a* 'déviation' *(a first-time pass in which the course of the ball is merely altered by contact with the outside of the foot) is referred to as a 'flick',* *again. What surprises me most is that it's not as if these were outlandish 'pieces of skill' that had proved beyond the talent of British-born footballers. All of them were in George Best's repertoire, and Robin Friday's, and Chris Waddle's. Pelé's sublime* 'grand pont' *– without even touching the ball – on Uruguayan goalkeeper Ladislao Mazurkiewicz in the 1970 World Cup has been played umpteen times on the BBC, not that Barry Davies or John Motson would have known how to describe it without resorting to paraphrase. But we are not talking about unique inventions such as Fernando Redondo's 'forward backheel', which led to one of the greatest goals in European Cup history when Real Madrid beat Manchester United 3–2 in the first leg of the 1999–2000 Champions League semi-final. These are skills which are attempted by every street footballer in the world, be they from São Salvador da Bahia, Sheffield or Les Caillols. What is astonishing is that the English never developed a vocabulary that would enable them to refer to some of a footballer's most balletic and, sometimes, efficient expressions of his talent on the training ground, in match reports or in pub conversations. Could it be that such fancy flicks were and still are considered unfair play, 'not cricket', if you will? Could they be perceived as too arrogant, against the true spirit of the game?*

During Éric's first two seasons in particular, on the rare occasions when he failed to ignite Manchester United's play, reporters and columnists were quick, often ridiculously so, to point out the eccentricities of the 'flashy foreigner' (an expression used by Emlyn Hughes, you'll remember, to characterize Cantona the day after he moved from Leeds to Manchester United); these, they implied, had been the undoing of his team, which needed 'last-ditch tackles' (no equivalent of this in French, by the way), not backheels and, yes, 'flicks'. Now that British-born footballers account for less than half of the starting line-ups in the Premiership, it is worth recalling how, in the early 1990s, suspicion, not expectancy, accompanied the arrival of so-called 'imports' in the English League. Cantona played up to every single prejudice held by the traditionalists who ruled, played and watched the game; he reinforced these prejudices as much as he demonstrated their shallowness; and, through his success, proved them utterly devoid of judgement by behaving precisely as his fiercest critics would expect him to do. He was unpredictable, undecipherable, manifestly untamed; he also brought four championship titles to a club that had spent twenty-six years in the desert.

The verbal abuse that greeted him in every ground in England, save Elland Road and Old Trafford, of course, did not differ much from the opinions of many commentators: it was a brutal and brutish magnification of their pronouncements. Such supporters probably agreed with Emlyn Hughes's characterization of Cantona as the 'dark, brooding Frenchman' of Manchester United. His comment was – if I can be forgiven this oxymoron – a coarse distillate of the pundit's instinctive rejection of a Frenchman who embodied all that is the most foreign in a foreigner. Those who question Cantona's greatness would do well to remember who had the last word in this particular battle.

13

The night it all went wrong in Galatasaray.

THE WORST NIGHT OF ÉRIC'S LIFE

'I'm not interested in the image people have of me. When I'm on the catwalk for Paco Rabanne, for example, there's no ulterior motive, I'm just giving pleasure to my own body. The most important thing is to feel at ease within your body, without cheating yourself. To pose for a beautiful photograph is a selfish pleasure – but in life, nothing is innocent. "Tout est égoïsme" *[everything is selfishness].'*

Éric had come back to Manchester from Paris on the morning's first flight three days before the BBC opened its evening news programme with images of crowds assembling on Piccadilly to celebrate the title. His mind was still swimming with images of the previous night's celebrations – France had beaten Sweden 2–1 at the Parc des Princes, and seemed poised to achieve qualification for the 1994 World Cup, in no small part thanks to him. He had struck a penalty shortly before half-time to cancel out Martin Dahlin's opening goal, the first spot kick he had been entrusted with since his debut with *Les Bleus* nearly six years previously. Then, with eight minutes remaining on the clock, he had met a hopeful punt by Jocelyn Angloma with the tip of his boot to make it 2–1 to the French. With Papin injured, much had been expected of him in the lone striker role, and he had responded magnificently to that expectation. Dizzy with the champagne that had been flowing until 2 a.m. in a Champs-Elysées nightclub, he was already thinking of what lay in wait, which he didn't doubt would be another celebration. For the third year running, Éric Cantona would be a national champion. No other player had ever achieved this with three different clubs. He had said – and would say again – how little he cared for the trophy won under the aegis of Tapie and Goethals with Marseille in 1991 (though he had played a crucial part in establishing a platform for its conquest); but those collected with Leeds and, especially, Manchester United, were a different matter altogether. He, a Frenchman, once a pariah in his own country, had taken the English title twice in two years for two clubs. The feat was unprecedented, and brought tangible proof that England had not been the destination of an exile desperate for a new home. He belonged there – and how.

As Albert Square filled with the songs of supporters drunk with joy, he lay on his bed at the Novotel, answering phone call after phone call, somewhat apprehensive (as he later admitted) of the tidal wave of fervour that was sweeping through the city – even there, in the suburb of Worsley. One of Éric's callers was Steve Bruce, who told him that all the United players were expected to turn up at his home in Bramhall that evening. Alex Ferguson had given his blessing to the party. The last of the newly crowned champions to arrive was Andreï Kanchelskis, at midnight, by which time beer and champagne had already been consumed in prodigious quantities. Éric's new friend Bernard Morlino was there too, watching Mark Hughes (wearing the Frenchman's red cap) and Cantona mimic memorable passages of play from the title-winning season, encouraged by the whole team. More drink was fetched in the early hours of the morning. As Gary Pallister put it, 'We were all steamrolled.'

Éric loved these heady moments of alcohol-fuelled bonding – not that he was a heavy drinker himself. He'd still be nursing his first flute of champagne while others were beyond counting which pint of lager they were on. Despite Alex Ferguson's concerns and efforts to stem the culture of 'drinking schools' (which led to United getting rid of talented but uncontrollable characters such as Paul McGrath), it was still customary for United players to hold 'sessions' that baffled non-English observers such as Henri Émile, who often visited Cantona in England to pass on messages from Gérard Houllier and, later, Aimé Jacquet. Some evenings he spent with Éric's family ('Wives have a huge influence on players in football. They often get married when they're very young, and I knew I could use this as a lever in certain areas – and I did'), others in the company of Cantona's teammates. 'What I discovered in England,' Émile told me, 'was the pleasure shared by the players. Éric was in the thick of it. He was the catalyst of the group. He commanded a great deal of respect. The English had really adopted him, even when things went a bit mad, as they do in England, with the beers, the cigars and the rest.' This is not to say that French professionals never let their hair down; but their celebrations – generally held in far more salubrious surroundings than the country pubs favoured by the United players – never reached a similar pitch. They also lacked the communal dimension Éric relished so much, which gave him a sense of belonging to another family, a family united by its love of football and its delight in success. Something like paradise. Heaven knows how the hungover players managed to gather enough strength to beat Blackburn 3–1 later on that afternoon, but they did, in front of 40,447 delirious spectators, at least one of whom, a student, had walked all the way from London to be there. A poignant touch was added to the occasion by the presence of Gérard Houllier and Michel Platini in the stands; Éric knew better than anyone how much of the joy he felt was due to their unremitting efforts on his behalf. Touts quickly ran out of tickets, which had been changing hands for up to £150 before kick-off. Éric, playing with a broken wrist, heard the Old Trafford crowd sing his name to the tune of *'La Marseillaise'* and paraded the Premier League trophy around the pitch at the final whistle, arm in arm with Peter Schmeichel (his son Raphaël's hero), the top of the trophy balanced with one hand on his head, the most fitting of crowns for the new king of Manchester.

The title, United's first in twenty-six years, was also a victory for what the press misguidedly described as Ferguson's '4-2-4'. But the romantics could be forgiven, as this triumph marked the rebirth of wing play in English football, more than a quarter of a century after Ramsey's 'wingless wonders'. A twenty-first-century analyst would describe United's organization in that 1992–93 season as a fluid 4-4-1-1, a lethal counter-attacking machine in which Mark Hughes, the lone frontman, would hold the ball long enough for Cantona, the withdrawn striker, to play it into space on the flanks, where Giggs and

Kanchelskis could be expected to bomb forward, by which time the team's formation could indeed be described as a 4-2-4 – but this 4-2-4 bore no relation to the revolutionary tactical set-up that Brazil had dazzled the world with at the 1958 World Cup. Though most United players were comfortable on the ball, their game was not based on keeping possession, with the patient build-up and exhilarating changes of tempo that were a hallmark of the *Seleçao* – not yet, anyway, as a number of unsuccessful European campaigns would soon demonstrate. More often than not, when faced with Continental defences more adept at keeping their shape than their Premier League counterparts, United's coil would fail to spring. Nevertheless, Cantona's contribution to the evolution of the English game towards a more 'modern' type of football remains grossly undervalued in my view. He was the first to demonstrate the value of the so-called '9-and-a-half' – in practice, an old-style no. 10 who positions himself further down the pitch, and combines a playmaker's vision with the finishing of a high-class striker – against the classical British flat back four. Dennis Bergkamp, possibly the greatest-ever exponent of that role, would only be signed by Arsenal two full years after United had become champions again. When the question of Cantona's greatness is raised, his pioneering role in defining a new playing position (at least in England) is overlooked too often. In that sense, he can be talked of as an innovator, even if he was not driven by a desire to create something radically new. What is true is that he could best express himself in that transient and ambiguous space behind, and created by the movement of, the front man between the lines, as it were. He had the immense stroke of luck to play for a manager like Alex Ferguson, who was a born pragmatist in the best sense of that word, and therefore ready to alter the shape of his team to accommodate an exceptional talent.

On this at least everyone agreed: Cantona had made the difference, indeed 'he *was* the difference between this season [1992–93] and the last', as Peter Schmeichel put it. 'English strikers are predictable,' the big Danish 'keeper said, 'and Éric brought the element of surprise from French football: it wasn't just the goals he scored himself, but the way he created openings for other players to score.' Statistics bore Schmeichel's point out. Once United had concluded their campaign with a 2–1 win away at Wimbledon on 9 May, their seventh victory in seven games, ensuring that the record of the 1992–93 season would match exactly that of the famed 1966–67 side (24 wins and 12 draws), Éric not only had the best goals-to-games ratio of any United player in the championship (9 in 23, plus 2 in the FA Cup, compared to Hughes's 15 in 41 and Giggs's 9 in 40), but also topped the assists chart, with a quite phenomenal 13. Ferguson's team had lost only one of the games Cantona had been involved in; and he had played a decisive part in 22 of the 46 goals his team scored during that period. This was a stunning return on United's paltry investment of £1.2m a little over five months previously; but, despite what hindsight tells us, it was then still too early to infer from that success that Cantona had at last found a permanent home.

Laurent Chasteaux, a French reporter from the communist daily *L'Humanité*, had paid Éric a visit in mid-April, when, with United four points ahead in the league table and two games to go, Cantona was all but assured of his second consecutive English league title. This is what the journalist was told: 'All United supporters wonder if I'll stay at the club. That's a question I also ask myself. My only clue to an answer is, as ever, pleasure. The day I'm bored going to the training ground, I'm off. I come, I go, I'm only passing through.' Tempting as it is to read remarks like these as mere gesturing for the gallery, it's worth keeping in mind that Alex Ferguson took them very seriously. In the book that was rush-printed immediately after the capture of the championship (with the self-explanatory title *Just Champion*), Ferguson wrote: 'I think if Éric is here today, tremendous. But if he is gone tomorrow, we just say: "Good luck, Éric. Thanks for playing with us. You've been absolutely brilliant." Honestly, we just don't know what's going to happen. How do we cope without Éric? By switching off and not actually expecting anything at all beyond the next twenty-four hours.' Or expecting the unexpected, which, after a while, became as predictable as Éric's attire at the civic dinner organized by the city of Manchester in honour of its trophy-winning team: while his teammates turned up in club-crested blazers and matching trousers, Cantona waltzed in wearing an expensive designer silk jacket over a T-shirt. Joking demands of 'Fine him!' were met by a benevolent smile from the manager. The devil could get away with anything, it seemed.

The lack of a major tournament enabled Éric and Isabelle to take an extended break that summer, which was spent visiting their families in France and Spain and holidaying in the Tunisian beach resort of Djerba with one of Cantona's closest friends in football, his former Montpellier and *Espoirs* teammate Laurent Blanc. Snapshots from that trip show a remarkably relaxed Éric, able to overcome his shyness, grab a microphone and entertain fellow guests of the Club Méditerranée with a song or two. Footballers head for Dubai or Florida nowadays; but Éric had remained unaffected by his wealth and preferred the lack of pretence of that upmarket (but only just) French version of Butlins, when he could have afforded the priciest hotels on the planet. Another manifestation of having achieved some sort of peace, perhaps.

This happy parenthesis was closed in mid-July with the resumption of the international schedule; in Éric's case, this meant heading for Clairefontaine, rather than for South Africa, where his United teammates were playing a couple of pre-season games. This was in preparation for a friendly against Russia, which would have serious consequences for his involvement with United over the first month of the new domestic season. The match, played in the small D'Ornano stadium in Caen on 28 July, pitted him for the first time against his clubmate Andreï Kanchelskis (one of three Ukrainians who, following the break-up of the Soviet Union, had pledged their future to the new Russian team). Remarkably, Cantona scored for the fifth time in a row for the French: he had found the target in every single encounter since the debacle of Euro 92, this time with a deflected strike from fifteen yards. But he also sustained a hamstring injury that prevented him from playing any part in United's warm-up games against Benfica and Celtic, and it was a half-fit Cantona who walked up Wembley's thirty-nine steps to collect his second successive Charity Shield winner's medal on 8 August. He had been instrumental in United's win over Arsenal, on penalties, after a forgettable game had ended 1–1, in stark contrast to the previous year's scintillating season opener. As early as the eighth minute, his lobbed pass had been volleyed home by Mark Hughes. United, however, had struggled and would have walked away the losers had Ian Wright, who had previously scored a magnificent equalizing goal, not missed his kick in the penalty shoot-out. But after Bryan Robson had found the net and Peter Schmeichel kept out David Seaman's attempt, another trophy had been added to Éric's and United's collection. United fans that I spoke to only remembered this Wembley win because it was the first time that Roy Keane wore their club's shirt, having finally been prised away from Nottingham Forest under Blackburn's nose for £3.75m, a British transfer record at the time.

Fielding Éric in the Charity Shield had been a risky, not to say rash decision, as he only lasted thirty-five minutes of United's next game – a friendly against Danish side Brondby – before suffering a recurrence of his hamstring injury. The champions (15/8 favourites to retain the title) nevertheless managed rather well in the absence of their talisman, who was forced to sit out wins against Norwich and Sheffield United, as well as a 1–1 draw against newly promoted Newcastle; and when Éric returned to competition, it was with France, in Sweden, where a 1–1 draw brought them within touching distance of qualification for the World Cup. Next would be a trip to Finland, followed by visits by Israel and Bulgaria. Four points would surely see *Les Bleus* achieve the redemption a whole country was praying for. Meanwhile, United were faced with a punishing schedule (four games in eight days!), earning a precious win over Aston Villa two days after dropping two points against Newcastle. It was only then that Éric eventually joined the fun, for fun it most certainly was.

First, Southampton were beaten 3–1 at St Mary's on 28 August (with a majestic Cantona scoring his first Premier League goal of the new season), after which West Ham lost 3–0 at Old Trafford (Éric doubling his tally with a penalty). Liverpool, whom most observers believed would be their strongest challenger for the 1993–94 title, already trailed Manchester United by three points. It was almost too easy. The season wasn't even a month old, yet bookmakers cut their odds to the extent that punters hardly bothered to put their money on the champions any longer. Cantona, it seemed, just had to turn up to win, be it with club or country.

On 8 September France squeezed the life out of a modest Finland team in Tampere, scored a couple of goals without reply and serenely waited for the Israelis to come to the Parc des Princes a month later, hoist the white flag and provide them with a ticket to USA 94. One point would be enough. France were already spoken of as potential World Cup winners. They had (everybody thought) all but achieved first place in one of its most awkward qualification groups, adding considerable style to a great deal of substance, and proving that the generation of players on which so much hope had been pinned when they claimed the under-21 European title in 1988 had acquired the will to win that had been conspicuously absent from their flop in Sweden six months previously. Their time, Cantona's time, had finally come.

The Manchester United juggernaut was checked at Stamford Bridge three days after the French stroll in Finland. With the score still tied at 0–0, Éric nearly produced what would have been one of the most spectacular goals of his entire career. It started with a long pass-cum-clearance from Gary Pallister. Had Roy Keane collected this hopeful ball, the Irishman would have found himself one-on-one with Chelsea's 'keeper, Dimitri Kharine. The Russian, playing as a sweeper, rushed from his line and bravely headed the ball back towards the halfway line. Danger averted? No. The ball fell to Éric who, with his back to goal, swivelled and hit it on the volley from fully 40 yards as Kharine was still frantically trying to get back to his line. The ball dropped a couple of yards shy of the goal, bounced and rebounded off the crossbar, to end up in the arms of a relieved goalkeeper. The BBC commentator John Motson exclaimed: 'Fantastic! . . . Ha! Who needs Pelé?' This 'goal' would have, he said, 'been etched, I think, in Stamford Bridge history'. But it was a match of near-misses for Éric, who was constantly harried by Dennis Wise and relentlessly barracked by the crowd. Chelsea took the lead through Gavin Peacock in the first half, and seemed destined to keep it through sheer determination when a glorious move involving Bryan Robson, Dennis Irwin and Lee Sharpe should have been finished off by Cantona's diving header – instead of which the ball missed the open goal by a couple of inches, and United had suffered their first defeat since 9 March. But as Liverpool fell at home to Blackburn a day later, it could be brushed away as an inconsequential blip.

A far more significant occasion was fast approaching: United's return to the European Cup, or, to give it its proper name at the time, the European Champion Clubs' Cup, the trophy that had brought George Best a *Ballon d'Or* in 1968 and had helped lay the ghosts of Munich to rest. Manchester United, who had become the first club from England to win the trophy on that occasion, had been envious bystanders when their domestic rivals Liverpool, Nottingham Forest and Aston Villa had crushed Continental competition from 1977 to 1984, Hamburg (in 1983) being the only non-English side to claim the title during that period. Alex Ferguson's self-proclaimed aim was, famously, to 'knock Liverpool off their fucking perch' – a wish that could only be fulfilled if a European trophy (and one weightier than the Cup Winners Cup won in 1991) was added to the Mancunian roll of honour.

Éric too had some unfinished business to take care of. In 1991, still a Marseille player, at least nominally, he had been robbed of a final by his manager Raymond Goethals. Two years later, the same OM had finally won the trophy – now called the Champions League – and it can euphemistically be said that Cantona derived no particular satisfaction from seeing his home-town team give France its first success in a competition Frenchmen had invented thirty-seven years previously.

English representatives had performed dismally in the past season's international competitions,* their failure giving a lurid illustration of how far behind they had fallen since the Heysel ban. UEFA regulations, which specified that any one team could not field more than three 'foreigners' and two 'assimilated' players (i.e. players who had lived in the country for five years and been part of that club's youth squad), had a disproportionately hampering effect on English clubs,†

---

* Leeds had been knocked out of the Champions League before the group phase, Manchester United had been thrown out of the UEFA Cup by Torpedo Moscow in the second round, Sheffield Wednesday in the third (by Kaiserslautern), Liverpool falling against another Muscovite team, Spartak, in their second tie of the Cup Winners Cup.

† The European Commission had that regulation scrapped in 1996, following the celebrated 'Bosman ruling' ('*arrêt* Bosman') of the European Court of Justice (15 December 1995), which redefined a player's right of movement within the European Union.

as Irish, Scottish and Welsh 'foreigners' naturally gravitated towards the more prestigious (and more lucrative) Premier League. Andreï Kanchelskis told me that, had it not been for the imposition of this quota, it was his conviction that 'we would have gone to the semi-finals [in 1993–94], maybe the final, even'. Manchester United's first XI sometimes contained no less than eight 'foreign' or 'assimilated' players: Schmeichel (Denmark), Kanchelskis (Ukraine/Russia), Cantona (France), plus Hughes, Giggs (both of them Welsh, at least as far as football affiliation was concerned), Irwin, Keane (Ireland) and Brian McClair (Scotland). Alex Ferguson would have some tough choices to make in the following months, starting with United's first European Cup tie for twenty-five years, an admittedly undemanding trip to the Hungarian champions Kispest Honvéd FC, who were but a distant echo of their magnificent former selves. The old army club of Ferenc Puskás, Sándor Kocsis, József Bozsik and Zoltán Czibor had enjoyed a resurgence in the late 1980s, but their failure to hold on to their best players prevented them from asserting themselves on the international scene as they did in domestic competitions.

Two thousand Manchester United fans – over a fifth of the total attendance – took their seats in the Bozsik stadium and witnessed an untidy performance by their team, who could thank an on-fire Roy Keane for their 3–2 win. The twenty-three-year-old midfielder scored a brace of goals, while Cantona notched one with the easiest of tap-ins; it hadn't quite been the glorious night of football that had been hoped for, but a 3–2 victory away from home would certainly suffice to ensure qualification for the next round. In any case, there was hardly time to reflect before coming face to face with the Premier League's in-form team, a reinvigorated Arsenal, who had strung together a series of five wins and a draw since capitulating 3–0 at home to Coventry on the opening day of the season. George Graham's Gunners were now right behind United at the top of the league table.

A bruising encounter was guaranteed, in which the foul count would greatly exceed the number of chances, and it was no surprise that a single goal decided the issue of the game. But what a goal it was: a shot from 28 yards by Éric, hit from an indirect free kick which Paul Ince put in his path. The ferociousness of the strike – no swerve, no bend, just a rocket of a ball – left David Seaman bewildered. But the brutal beauty of that goal was not the only thing that struck me when I watched it again and again on my video. Cantona's hand was bandaged, a reminder of the fractured wrist that was still causing him pain. And could it be? . . . yes, the collar was up, for the very first time.

'It happened by chance,' he told *L'Équipe Magazine* in 2007. 'One day, I put on my jersey and the collar stayed up. The game must have been a decent one. But I can't remember when it took place.' Was it on 19 September 1993, then? Very possibly, even if images of the matches that took place immediately afterwards are inconclusive. Sometimes it is up, sometimes it is not, because of the wind, possibly, or of material that was not rigid enough. It is only from the Manchester derby which took place eight weeks later that the collar remained defiantly up for good. As Cantona told his friend Bernard Morlino, 'Nature made me stiff. My neck and my lower back often give me pain. But I haven't suffered as much of a stiff neck since I began to play with an upright collar.'

His United shirt was now a part of King Éric's regalia. 'It became a superstition,' he said in the same interview. 'It wasn't part of a marketing ploy, or to make me stand apart from the others. Many people wondered why I did it. Some said: "He's pretending to be the King, he thinks he's Elvis Presley." One day, a Liverpool player even tried to provoke me, to make fun of me: Neil Ruddock. He put his collar up and did a dance step *à la* Elvis. But he was the only one who found it funny.'

Some United fans still believe that the actual reason for Cantona's mannerism was to ensure that cameras caught the sponsored 'swoosh' that had been embroidered on the back of his collar (wrongly: Umbro, not Nike, were United's kit manufacturers at the time). Others spread the mischievous rumour that Éric had had 'I LOVE LEEDS' tattooed on his neck and understandably wished to hide it (in fact, the only time Cantona visited a tattooist's studio was to have the head of a Native American chief drawn above his left breast). Sifting through the history books, it is difficult to think of other players who claimed part of their equipment as an extension of their individuality (which Éric must have known it was), and turned the customization of a piece of kit into a trademark. Johann Cruyff teased defenders with the sight of his padless shins and rolled-down socks, inviting the challenge he would skip like a *torero* – but so did the great Juve forward and playmaker Omar Sivori long before him. George Best let his red shirt hang over his shorts in an era when the proper thing was to wear it neatly tucked in – but many players of the 1920s and 1930s had done exactly that without anyone taking notice. Denis Law, the first 'King' of Manchester United,* made sure his cuffs were buttoned before he walked on the pitch, and clasped them with his middle fingers when he raised his arm in celebration. ('Don't know why I did that,' he told me a couple of days after Cristiano Ronaldo had been given his *Ballon d'Or* in December 2008. 'I hated playing in short sleeves, that's all.') But other, less celebrated footballers of his era shared this affectation: it was Law's genius on the field of play that drew attention to this eccentricity – whereas Éric appropriated one of the most emblematic jerseys of world football with the simplest of gestures, one which was familiar to the *blousons noirs* (leather-clad 'black jackets') of his generation and mine, instantly identifying you as a 'bad boy' in France. There was more defiance than met the eye in the iconic upturned collar. Cantona had also, by luck more than by design, added a brick of gold to the wall that his sponsors were busily building around him.

Éric, however, claimed not to be one of those footballers who are slaves to what the England goalkeeper David James has called a 'mental machinery' of preparation – players like John Terry, who inserted the same battered shin-pads in his stockings for ten years before mislaying them in the Nou Camp (Chelsea were beaten on that night). But, if Cantona didn't stick to obsessive routines (except maybe when exchanging passes with Steve Bruce in the warm-up, which he invariably did), he developed a quasi-mystical affinity with

* Pete Boyle, the unofficial 'bard of Manchester United' (and Cantona's most passionate fan), reminded me that his most famous creation, 'Éric the King' (which is still sung at Old Trafford), was based on an earlier chant, 'Denis the King'. Both borrow their tune from The Scaffold's 'Lily the Pink', a huge hit in the winter of 1968–69.

the number printed on his shirt. He had good reason to do so, as this number – 7, of course – had a unique resonance in Manchester United's history. Its stewardship imbued the recipient with a unparalleled sense of responsibility: in Éric's case, it represented the passing of the baton from one great no. 7 – Bryan Robson – to himself. In truth, Cantona probably did more than any other to give a magical aura to that number at Old Trafford.

Éric's timing was perfect, as that season – 1993–94 – saw the introduction of squad numbers at Manchester United. Before that, a player's position on the pitch dictated which number he was given, according to strict rules that had been in place since the days of the old 2-3-5 and had survived the abandonment of this system in favour of the 'WM' formation in the 1930s. This explains why, to the great confusion of Continentals, the no. 6 is associated with central defenders like Bobby Moore and Tony Adams in England, whereas it conjures up images of hard-tackling midfielders and precursors of the 'Makelele role' in France and Italy. For the English, a no. 7 played on the right wing and, later, in midfield, when it was surmised that the right-winger had dropped from the front line to the engine-room of the team – one of the more curious legacies of Alf Ramsey's reshaping of the English game. This makes it all the more surprising that George Best could be considered to be the founder of United's quasi-biblical genealogy of number 7s: Best begat Robson who begat Cantona who begat Beckham who begat Cristiano Ronaldo. In fact, Best, who wore that jersey for the first five years of his career at Old Trafford, passed it on to Willie Morgan in 1968 and played two-thirds of his games with United wearing the no. 11 shirt – as befitted a left-sided winger. It has been all but forgotten that Steve Coppell, a distinguished recipient of the no. 7 between 1975 and 1984, wore the number he had inherited from Morgan on 236 occasions in league matches, more than twice as many as the Irishman, and that Cantona himself only comes in eleventh position in the all-time appearances chart of United number 7s (143 games). And who remembers that Andreï Kanchelskis had the honour of donning the legendary jersey on twenty-five occasions in the early 1990s? The legend was constructed *a posteriori*, once Cantona had imbued the sacred digit with an aura that only grew with his retirement, to the extent that it acquired fetishistic qualities for his successors David Beckham and Cristiano Ronaldo, who tattooed, etched, marquetted and embroidered it wherever possible, on their skin, coffee tables, bed cushions and lines of ready-to-wear. Their obsession can be understood as a desire to inhabit a myth at the so-called 'Theatre of Dreams', but it primarily remains, consciously or not, an *hommage* to the myth-maker himself – Éric Cantona.

With Arsenal beaten, Cantona could project himself four weeks ahead, to 13 October, the date of Israel's visit to Paris, as United's schedule mostly comprised games they were expected to win with some ease: Honvéd never threatened to halt United's progression to the next round of the European Cup, despite a frustrating performance at Old Trafford in which Steve Bruce had to provide both goals in a 2–1 victory.

When Sheffield Wednesday were beaten 3–2 at Hillsborough on 2 October, Arsenal were now trailing by five points, and most bookmakers had installed United as odds-on favourites to retain their title, with a growing number of punters gambling on a domestic treble. Wednesday's manager Trevor Francis went so far as to say that 'United [were] the best team in Europe' after seeing Éric craft the visitors' second and third goals with perfectly weighed passes. Such hyperbole had no justification other than United's dominance of the English game and, in hindsight, seems slightly ludicrous; but it was felt by many at the time that Alex Ferguson – in no small part thanks to Éric Cantona – was drawing ever closer to solving this conundrum: how to reconcile the sophistication of the Continental game with the intensity and physicality for which English football was renowned. Increasingly, United offered a template for other ambitious Premiership clubs, who were shown week after week that it was not just possible, but also desirable to graft the artistry of a Cantona to the still robust spine of predominantly British teams.

Éric, the pioneer, the trailblazer, rejoined his French teammates in the second week of October. With two games to go before the end of the qualifiers, France was sitting pretty: one draw would be enough to guarantee them safe passage to the USA. Both their opponents, Israel and Bulgaria, would have to come to the Parc des Princes, where *Les Bleus* hadn't been defeated in a competitive game since November 1987.

Qualification seemed a formality, so much so that a short-lived French weekly magazine called *Le Sport*, not wishing to miss the party, decided to ignore the most basic rule of reporting (i.e. wait until something happens before writing about it) and dispatched tens of thousands of copies bearing the headline 'QUALIFIED!' to newsstands everywhere in the country in the early hours of Thursday 14 October.

The only problem was that France had contrived to lose the previous evening.

But how could anyone have predicted it? Israel had been walloped 4–0 in Tel Aviv seven months before, and the Parisian crowd was in fine voice at the kick-off of what was supposed to be a procession. Even Ronen Harazi's opening goal in the 21st minute failed to silence them. France created chance after chance, shots raining down on 'Boni' Ginzburg's goal, and it only took eight minutes for Atalanta's midfielder Franck Sauzée to put the scores level. Six minutes before the break, David Ginola gave the lead to the French with a stupendous curler from the left corner of the box, and the celebrations began in earnest. Cantona then played Papin through after evading a couple of challenges, but the Milan striker pulled his shot just wide. Éric himself came close to giving France a 3–1 lead with a header at the far post. How they would rue those missed chances. Israel, who had played with spirit and skill throughout, equalized with seven minutes to go. The Liverpool player Roni 'Ronny' Rosenthal bundled his way through a series of tackles and drew a stupendous save from Bernard Lama, whose parry fell sweetly for twenty-one-year-old Eyal Berkovic to volley the ball home with the outside of his right foot, despite Marcel Desailly's last-gasp intervention. It didn't matter. Seven minutes to go plus added time without conceding, and Houllier's team would have achieved qualification.

The lanky Israeli number 10 Reuven Atar had other ideas. A few seconds before the final whistle, he met a miraculous Rosenthal cross on the half-volley, and France were beaten.

A late reversal as dramatic as this one must have had an explanation. The post mortem conducted in the French media concluded, not illogically, that *Les Bleus* had suffered a disastrous collective lapse of concentration. Just as the Milan players sang victory songs during the interval of the 2005 Champions League final and then collapsed, throwing away a 3–0 lead against an apparently ragged Liverpool, Cantona and his teammates were already mentally on the plane to the USA as they walked out on to the Parisian pitch. Once Ginola had put them 2–1 ahead, they were convinced they had landed safely. And when they were shaken from their dream by the Israelis' late equalizing goal, panic set in. This explanation did no favours to the ability of the managerial staff to keep the squad's feet on the ground, or to Houllier's *coaching*, a term the French use to describe the real-time tactical changes a manager implements as a game unfolds. Still, if this shock defeat had made qualification for the 1994 World Cup more problematic, France surely couldn't lose the ground they had gained since the disaster of Euro 92, as they would play the crunch game at home – against Bulgaria. A share of the points in that game would be enough.

England wouldn't have minded being in that position. While the French rued the missed opportunities and swore to themselves that this wouldn't happen again, Graham Taylor's team fell 2–0 in the Netherlands, ensuring that Éric's United teammates Paul Ince and Gary Pallister would be on holiday when the 1994 World Cup was played in America.

Three days later, some kind of normality was resumed when United and their beaten internationals made Tottenham pay for their frustration. Spurs wilted almost embarrassingly against the champions. The 2–1 final scoreline was achieved at a canter; Cantona hardly broke sweat. After eleven games, his team had extended their lead to seven points in the Premiership, and that with players intent on preserving as much energy as possible before their next European engagement, against Turkish champions Galatasaray.

The Red Devils' lack of European experience was cruelly exposed when the Turks swept past a naïve United in the second half. It took a Cantona volley a few yards from the goal-line nine minutes from time to rescue a 3–3 draw and spare United their first-ever home defeat in a European competition. All the same, it had been a thrilling game in which Éric, while not quite at his best, nonetheless held his rank against fine Continental opposition – in retrospect, one of a handful of performances which can be offered in his defence when his admittedly poor record in Europe is questioned by critics.

What cuts and bruises United had suffered to their self-esteem against Galatasaray could be appeased by the balm applied week after week in England, where their opponents were developing a pleasant habit of rolling over. Everton (1–0 at Goodison), Leicester City (blasted away 5–1 in the League Cup, Éric rested) and QPR (2–1) obliged them in quick succession in the second half of October. United's supremacy was such at the time that when Les Ferdinand opened the scoring in the third of these games, they only needed to accelerate on a couple of occasions to restore the natural order. First, Cantona raced 40 yards to beat goalkeeper Bradley Allen for the equalizer, Mark Hughes poaching a second goal from a corner kick to claim a victory that had never been seriously in doubt. As Norwich and Arsenal had only achieved a draw on the same day, the champions now led the league by a huge margin: 11 points – after just 13 games.

Unfortunately, Galatasaray refused to follow the script written by English teams when the second leg of their tie was played on 3 November. The atmosphere in which the game was played was shocking, even to players used to the 'Munich aeroplanes' which crashed sickeningly in the stands of Anfield and Elland Road. The United squad were greeted on their arrival at Istanbul airport with banners reading 'Welcome to hell' and 'You will die'. A bell boy working in the palatial hotel where United were staying scowled at Gary Pallister and ran a finger across his throat. Bricks were thrown at the team bus when it crossed the Bosphorus. The game itself was worse. Cantona missed United's best chance in the 55th minute, when Parker lobbed a ball into the box. Twice he snatched at the ball, twice he failed to connect properly. Anger and anxiety had got the better of him. Then, in the 77th minute, incensed by Bulent feigning injury, he ran off the field across the perimeter track and kicked the ball out of the gloves of Nezihi, elbowed the 'keeper in the ribs in the ensuing scuffle and had to be rescued from a swarm of Turkish players by the referee, who – showing surprising leniency – decided not to caution him. It didn't stop there. After the game had finished 0–0, sending the Turks through on the away-goals rule, with all kinds of missiles raining on the United players, Cantona walked towards the official, shook his hand, and said a few choice words in French – which happened to be the language that Mr Roethlisberger taught to earn a living when UEFA didn't require his services.* This time, a card was shown, and it was red.

'He had gone, mentally,' was how Ryan Giggs later described Éric's behaviour that night in the Ali Sami Yen stadium. Cantona was manhandled in the tunnel by a police officer, and snapped; the policeman struck him on the back of the head with a baton. Bryan Robson, trying to defuse the situation, was hit by a shield, and needed two stitches. Chaos ensued, with the whole United squad, it seems, joining the mêlée, before their own security men finally managed to usher them into the dressing-room. An unrepentant Cantona addressed the press in these terms: 'Tonight was a scandal. I was punched on the back of the head by a policeman. I don't care about the red card. I just went to the referee and told him he was a bad referee.' But he also revealed the true cause of his frustration when he added: 'Galatasaray is a little team. Equally, tonight, so were Manchester United.'

He would make sure they were great again the next time they played, at Maine Road.

Manchester City was one of Éric's 'lucky' teams over the course of his career. He scored in every single one of the seven Manchester derbies he took part in – eight goals in all – and never finished on the losing side, though he nearly did on 7 November 1993. United fell 2–0 behind. Then Éric, collar turned up, erupted into life shortly after the pause, and almost single-handedly rescued a losing cause. Vonk's misdirected header opened a clear path to goal: 2–1. Then Giggs, who had been one of United's most disappointing performers in Istanbul, came off the bench to provide a perfect cross for Éric to tap in. Two each. Keane consummated a redemption of sorts by snatching the winner. A frustrated Cantona was a dangerous animal, as City had found out – and Bulgaria undoubtedly would as well. But Bulgaria didn't.

---

* The UEFA dispensed with Mr Roethlisberger altogether in 1997, striking him with a life ban when it was established he had approached Grasshoppers Zurich in 1996 to 'sell' them the referee of a forthcoming European game against Auxerre. The referee in question, Vadim Zhuk, happened to be a friend of his, and the price would be Sw.F100,000. The ban was upheld on appeal. Mr Roethlisberger's performance on the night Cantona was sent off had been the subject of a number of rumours immediately after the game.

No one saw it coming. The front page of *L'Équipe* bore a single word: 'INQUALIFIABLE', which meant: 'unable to qualify', but also 'impossible to describe' and 'disgraceful'. Any sub-editor would have been proud of this witty example of self-inflicted *Schadenfreude*. The shame was that a picture of Éric Cantona had been chosen to illustrate France's footballing Waterloo – and that *France Football* followed suit a few days later. He most certainly didn't deserve to be made a symbol of failure. Cantona had put France in front with his sixth goal of the qualifiers. With 32 minutes on the clock, fed by Papin, he volleyed from six yards to open the scoring, and 48,402 spectators were booking a trip to America. They still had their tickets in their hands when Emil Kostadinov equalized five minutes later from a poorly defended corner. France controlled the game, and a draw was good enough. But with twenty-three seconds to go, from a free kick which had been awarded to the French (!) within touching distance of the Bulgarian right corner flag, David Ginola opted to send a wild, deep cross to what the French call 'the third post' which sailed over Cantona – the only French player present in the opposition box at the time – landed on the other wing and was quickly, beautifully worked upfield. Three passes later, the same Kostadinov found himself running towards Bernard Lama's goal in a tight angle, and, despite Laurent Blanc's desperate lunge, arrowed a magnificent strike under the bar, so emphatic that it almost screamed: 'WE'RE IN THE WORLD CUP!' to the silenced ground. The power of the shot was such that Bernard Lama didn't stand a chance. France were out. Houllier, chin down, hands in pockets, walked a few desultory steps on the touchline, where his assistant Aimé Jacquet held his head in his hands. It couldn't be. But it was.

The French manager tore Ginola to pieces in his post-match press conference. 'He sent an Exocet missile through the heart of French football,' he said. 'He committed a crime against the team, I repeat: a crime against the team.' Houllier, a very emotional man, was factually correct, of course. Had the PSG winger not given away possession in the dying moments of the game, France would have qualified and Bulgaria would never have reached the semi-finals of USA 94. But what Houllier didn't mention was the statuesque reaction of the French midfield and defence to the Bulgarian counter-attack. Didier Deschamps,

Reynald Pedros and Emmanuel Petit had switched off, jogging when they should have been running for their lives, and watched the ball go from the other end of the park to the back of their own net in nineteen seconds. Neither did the soon-to-be former national coach explain why it was Pedros (5' 8") rather than, say, Sauzée (6' 2") or even Cantona (6' 2") who had been put on the goal-line for the corner kick that led to Kostadinov's headed equalizer. Everyone knew who would be the first loser in this game of ifs and buts. Houllier fell on his sword, and was replaced by Jacquet.

Gérard's anger had not abated when we relived this catastrophic moment fifteen years later. 'It was a pleasure to have Cantona in your team,' he told me. 'He was a gem, a loyal man, a player who gave everything. But Ginola? . . . I'll never say anything good about Ginola.' He broke his bread like 'Tiger' O'Reilly broke a match when asked how he rated Don Bradman. 'As a cricketer? The best. As a man? Not worth *that*,' the leg-spinner had said, snapping the stick in his powerful fingers. What Houllier could never forgive was not so much a temporary moment of madness than what had preceded it: Ginola had publicly questioned the soundness of his coach's decision to give preference to Papin and Cantona rather than to him in his starting eleven – and intimated that Papin and Cantona could do as they wished in the French set-up, that they had forced their manager's hand. Against Israel, it was he, Ginola, who had provided the assist for Sauzée's opening goal, and who scored a superb second; but Houllier kept him on the bench until the 69th minute against Bulgaria, when the score was still level at 1–1. He certainly wished he had kept him there.

The next morning, as France awoke in a state of shock, an unshaven Cantona, wearing a dazzling white suit, was the last to board the Air France shuttle that took passengers of the earliest Paris–Manchester flight to their plane. By pure chance, my *France Football* colleague Jean-Michel Brochen – then at *L'Équipe* – found himself sitting just behind Cantona on the Airbus. His mission was to extract a pearl or two from the clammed-up star of the humiliated national team. Jean-Michel, who had first met Cantona on the night he shaved his head in Brest, six years earlier, knew that the safest policy was to resist the temptation to tap on Éric's shoulder. As the plane landed, footballer and journalist exchanged a polite greeting, nothing more ('No, I don't talk [to the press],' were Éric's parting words), and went their separate ways – except that their destination was the same: Éric's home from home, the Worsley Novotel, where the French-speaking staff (who adored Cantona) were used to welcoming a variety of pressmen who had come from the other side of the Channel. What followed over the next few days was hardly spectacular, but quite comical all the same, and highlighted a certain streak of innocence in Éric's character which I believe is worth mentioning here.

Every morning, Jean-Michel, accompanied by another French journalist, Geoffroy Garitier of *Le Journal du Dimanche*, walked down to the breakfast room where, every morning, Éric Cantona could be found sitting down to a bowl of cereal. And every morning, the same exchange: 'Good morning' – 'Good morning' – 'Éric, could we have a chat with you?' – 'No. I don't talk.' Then, every morning, the two reporters would drive to The Cliff, the ramshackle group of buildings and primitive pitches which couldn't really be described as a 'training complex'. Security was lax, consisting of a handful of ageing stewards who had probably brewed tea for Duncan Edwards, and didn't mind strangers wandering around the car park. How things have changed. For four days, every day, Jean-Michel and Geoffroy placed slips of paper under the windscreen-wiper of Cantona's Audi ('Éric – can we have a chat later?'), adding their room number more in hope than in expectation. The next morning at breakfast time, Éric would appear in the hotel's restaurant, make his way to the journalists' table, shake their hands, say the customary '*Ça va?*', and when they inevitably asked: 'Can we talk to you later?', just as inevitably reply:

'No. I don't talk.'

This game of cat-and-mouse lasted for the full duration of Jean-Michel's stay; beyond that, in fact. A year later, he was at The Cliff again. Éric had kept his room at the Worsley, but was also renting a house which had been occupied by Mark Hughes before him. More slips of paper placed on the windscreen, blank following blank, a routine which had become hilarious to the journalist himself. Nevertheless, one day, he wandered into the training ground's main building, where a kind soul directed him to Alex Ferguson's office. The manager, a Francophile, as we've seen, happened to cross his path on the stairs and asked him whether he would like to have a chat. How times have changed. Jean-Michel was deep in conversation with Ferguson ('I'd pay to watch Cantona play' was one of the manager's most vivid quotes) when a rap was heard on the door. It was a sheepish Éric who had come to apologize for arriving late for training (not for the first time, it seems). He had spent the night at his Leeds home and been caught in an almighty traffic jam on his way from Yorkshire. Ferguson gently chided him, and recommended an alternative route. Jean-Michel popped the usual question ('Éric – can we have a chat later?'), and, as you've guessed already, got the usual answer.

'No. I don't talk.'

Comical? Certainly. There never was any animosity in Cantona's stubborn refusal to speak, just an almost childish – quite endearing, in fact – will not to give in to defeat. The night of that game against Bulgaria had been 'the worst in my life', he had said – and meant it. Disciplinary problems had prevented him from helping France to qualify for the 1990 *Mondiale*. Euro 92 had seen a collective collapse for which no one could remember a precedent. The 1994 World Cup, which he had been so close to, had turned away like a woman offering her lips, then slamming her bedroom door shut with no explanation.

But Cantona was also a brave man. Some of his unfortunate (or guilty) teammates had thrown in the towel. Laurent Blanc, Jean-Pierre Papin and Franck Sauzée, destroyed by the failure of *Les Bleus*, announced their international retirement with immediate effect. Fortunately for France, only Sauzée stuck to his word in the end. Papin rejoined the national team in March 1994, Blanc two months later, while Ginola carried on as if nothing had happened, despite Éric siding with his sacked coach in forthright terms. 'Who is Ginola?' he asked. 'He played five times for France, and lost on three occasions. I'm angry with him because he's manipulated people, because he talked bullshit to journalists so that their readers would believe him. [. . .] If he talks to the press rather than to us, it's because he hasn't got any balls. Fuck it, if I was choosing the team, we'd play with twelve strikers!' When his interviewer, Jean Issartel of *France Football*, expressed some surprise at Cantona's choice of words, Éric made sure that his message to the PSG would-be model was as unequivocal as possible: 'He's got the technical ability. But there's the head. You must write this down. When you let yourself be influenced like that, you're an ass. The head doesn't follow. He's got every quality except this one. He's too weak.'

Cantona himself could not be accused of weakness. Pilloried as he had been, he applied himself to the task of salvaging as much as possible. Henri Émile, by then a trusted member of France's coaching staff, was a privileged witness to this act of rebellion, for an act of rebellion it was, but a selfless one, for which Éric never got the credit he deserved. 'Aimé Jacquet took the lead on what was supposed to be a temporary basis,' Émile told me.

> Gérard Houllier and the president of the federation had gone, but all of the technical staff remained in place. Aimé and I did the rounds with the the older players, to find out who had a desire to carry on. Their disappointment was huge. Why? Because the American World Cup would be something grandiose for players who were nearing the end of their career. They could find a new stage for themselves in the USA, as we thought that the World Cup would bring on an explosion of the professional game there. And the two teams which finished above us [Bulgaria and Sweden] reached the semi-finals. We could have gone as far as that ourselves. Aimé wanted to find out which of these older players would have the motivation to pick up the challenge to qualify for Euro 96. And the first one who said: 'We'll go to the European championships' was Éric – who was immediately chosen as France's captain. Why? Because of his allure, and of how he'd been the first to accept the challenge of qualification. We needed men of courage.

There was more to France's astonishing defeat against Israel than was made public at the time. Embarrassing rumours had been circulating for a while in and around Clairefontaine, the superb estate which had become the national team's headquarters five years previously. They were substantiated, but remained whispers within the upper circle of the sporting press, and, to the best of my knowledge, appear in print for the first time here. Houllier's *squad had its fair share of flamboyant characters, for whom it had become customary to slip out of the training camp under cover of night, and meet up in Chez Adam, a VIP club situated near the Champs-Elysées, whose owner was one of France's most successful producers of pornographic videos. Footballers formed a substantial share of Chez Adam's clientele, and it had become a tradition of sorts to organize after-match parties there – which the players called '*dégagements*', quite an amusing term, as it turns out, since it can be translated both as 'letting off steam' and 'a goalkeeper's clearance'. These* dégagements *normally took place after the games, and the unwritten code of misconduct seems to have been broken on that occasion. Some of* Les Bleus *were said to have acted as if Israel had already been beaten, and visited Chez Adam on not one, but several consecutive nights before the match was played. They didn't expect to be turned away at the door. Admission criteria were at the same time vague and strict, but helping a footballer to stick to an energy-saving lifestyle was not one of them. You needn't be famous to get in, but had to know the right people, or be accompanied by one of them. Discretion was guaranteed. The girls with whom most (but not all) of the players ended up were not interested in gathering material for kiss-and-tell stories that could be sold to newspapers – French privacy laws saw to that. What's more, journalists too were regular visitors to the club's dimly lit salons and suites, and were unlikely to risk their own marriages or careers to find themselves on the wrong end of a libel action.*

By pure chance, I talked to a couple of former patrons of Chez Adam as I was completing this book. I was having breakfast with a Marseilles restaurateur I'd been told could put me in touch with a couple of Éric's friends. His eyes lit up at the mention of the 'good times' he'd had in their company. Numerous stories followed, all of them unprintable. 'Don't misunderstand me,' he said. 'There was no violence, nobody was forced to do anything against their will, and certainly not the girls. If you talk about Chez Adam, be sure of this: there was no harm done to anyone. It was young, healthy, successful people enjoying life, laughing, drinking, joking and, yes, OK, sometimes taking one of the girls upstairs . . . but what was fascinating was that you saw these guys [the players] in situations where they had lowered all of their defences. X— was a grumpy old sod. Y— was just fantastic fun . . .'

'And Éric?' I heard myself say. 'Did you see him there?'

'Yes, once. He was different. People were doing the most outrageous things on the first floor, but he couldn't have cared less. He remained himself. Imperious, you know, the chest like that, upright, very dignified. What he did he did with class . . . or, rather, he acted as if he wanted people to say, "Ha, he's got class!" – there's a difference, you see.'

British tabloids would have paid a small fortune to find an eyewitness of the goings-on at Chez Adam. In fact, one of them got wind of the rumours at the time of Éric's fictitious dalliance with Lee Chapman's wife, Leslie Ash, and approached a journalist friend of mine, who turned down their offer of £5,000 for a detailed account of Cantona's visits to the club. That Éric had – just like his father, 'Le Blond' – an eye for the ladies was hardly a secret. He was being himself, sticking to his oft-declared 'principle' of going wherever his impulses told him he should go, whatever the cost may be to himself and to others. In the video Éric the King, *which Manchester United released in November 1993, he said: 'I have a kind of fire inside me, which demands to be let out, and releasing it is what fuels my success. I couldn't possibly have that fire without accepting that sometimes it wants to come out to do harm. It is harmful. I do myself harm. I am aware of doing myself harm and doing harm to others.' These quotes resurfaced later, in the wake of his moment of madness at Selhurst Park. But Éric was not just talking about football. It was the confession of an egotist* malgré lui, *who had found that the only way he could live with and, yes, control his raging desires was to give vent to them. That it led him to feel remorse is beyond doubt. Éric was a genuinely generous person, who derived great joy from pleasing those he loved, the 'good man' that so many of those who knew him best talked to me about. His spontaneity absolved him of mere callousness – until he used it as justification for the unjustifiable. Here, as in so many aspects of his personality, the man who saw the world in black and white became a blur of grey.*

And that is why what Cantona did or did not do at Chez Adam does not matter. What is far more significant is that it gave me more proof that, contrary to what Éric has claimed so often, he couldn't live without the football environment he despised or the players he had nothing good to say about. He might not have liked it, but he was one of them. Many teammates – Ryan Giggs, Roy Keane, Gary McAllister, to name but three – have expressed surprise at the idea that the 'true' Cantona was some kind of desperado who only felt at ease away from the crowd, with his dogs, his easel or a shotgun slung across his shoulders. He had been the ringleader of Auxerre's pranksters. He organized hunting parties with OM players. He treated his Montpellier teammates to a birthday dinner, and celebrated their French Cup triumph late into the night. He climbed down a gutter to spend a night on the town in Dublin with a Leeds United teammate. He joined Manchester United's drinking club (on his terms: champagne, rather than beer). He behaved like a seigneur *at Chez Adam. Solitary and gregarious, forgiving and implacable, by turns loyal and cruel to his friends, he had barely changed from the little boy who watched Ajax, perched on Albert's shoulders. He still longed for reassurance and warmth, and craved the togetherness that football, despite its faults and its hypocrisies, had provided him with since he could walk. When he rejected it publicly, he was also admitting a double failure. He couldn't find a balance outside of the game. And he couldn't bring himself to admit it. He would have to kill the footballer to become a man, a prospect he had every right to be terrified of. What and who could that man be?*

14

The other Cantona: a dream for advertisers.

THE CONSECRATION: 1994

'Doubt? Me? Never. But I'm different. I'm a bit of a dreamer. I feel I can do everything. When I see a bicycle, I'm sure I can beat the world record and win the Tour de France.'

Éric Cantona celebrated the first anniversary of his arrival in English football in the most appropriate manner: with another goal, his eighth in the league that season. It was at Coventry on 27 November, a game in which United's dominance was such that they only played for fifteen minutes before shutting up shop and driving away with as emphatic a 1–0 victory as could be wished for. Phil Neal, who had just been named head coach of the defeated side, had an unusual compliment for Éric, whom he called 'one intelligent beast of a footballer' – an inspired oxymoron that captured the feeling of confidence oozing from his performances. A week earlier, Wimbledon had been the victims of that intelligence when he had supplied Andreï Kanchelskis and Mark Hughes with goalscoring opportunities they couldn't miss. The Dons lost 3–1, giving United their eighth consecutive win in the league and extending their lead to 11 points. With Coventry beaten, the gap grew to 14.

'[Éric] has completely confounded the critics who said he was trouble,' Ferguson said. '[He is] the fulcrum of our side.' The manifest superiority of his team didn't reflect well on the standard of the recently formed Premier League, but said a great deal about Cantona's capacity to spring back from France's heartbreaking elimination from the World Cup. On the last day of November, Everton were brushed aside 2–0 at home in the fourth round of the League Cup, despite United having three goals chalked off in the last 15 minutes of the game. And when those around him were having an off-day, Éric shook them from their apathy: two more assists, the first for Giggs, the second for McClair, the culmination of a stupendous nine-pass move, ensured United salvaged a 2–2 draw against a combative Norwich at Old Trafford in early December. The only worrying sign for Ferguson was a resurgence of Éric's indiscipline, first noticed when he was lucky to escape dismissal after kicking at Norwich defender Ian Culverhouse, who had been harrying him by fair means and foul for most of the game.

Fans were beginning to forget when United had last lost in England. Sheffield United – destroyed 3–0 at Bramall Lane, Cantona making the most of a 'telepathic' pass from Ryan Giggs to conclude the scoring. A 1–1 draw at Newcastle. A 3–1 demolition of Aston Villa, the previous season's most resilient challengers, which prompted Ron Atkinson to say: 'The only way anyone will catch them is if the rest get six points for a win and they don't get any.' By 19 December United had amassed 52 points, a 'ridiculous' total with only half of their games played. A jubilant Cantona could claim he was now in 'the best team [he'd] ever played for'. Atkinson had given Earl Barrett the task of following the Frenchman's every move, the very first time an English manager had tried to negate Cantona's influence by placing a shadow in his trail. The ploy failed, dismally. Éric scored twice. 'He was unbelievable,' Ferguson said. 'Ron Atkinson has always played 4–4–2, but he changed all his principles to man-mark Éric Cantona, and you can't get a greater accolade than that.'

There could've been one, of course. Late in December, it was announced that *France Football*'s *Ballon d'Or* had been awarded to Roberto Baggio, winner of the UEFA Cup and scorer of 21 goals in 27 games for Juventus in Serie A. The European jurors had placed Éric third in their votes, the only time in his career that he ended on the podium of the most prestigious of football's individual awards. Cantona's pride at having been considered one of the worthiest pretenders to the trophy was obvious, but his response was remarkable for its genuine humility. He extolled the beauty of Dennis

Bergkamp's play (the Dutchman, who had just left Ajax for Internazionale, had narrowly lost to the Italian playmaker), focusing on the collective ethos of the *Oranje* 'who work like crazy'. 'The team makes the individual,' he said. 'It's an exchange. You need a lot of personality to accept putting yourself at the service of someone else. The creator doesn't exist without this tacit agreement.' If the *Ballon d'Or* jury had failed ('gravely', according to Éric) in one regard, it was in ignoring the claim of players in the mould of Paul Ince. 'Guys like him make people like me shine,' he said.

Shine he did. It wasn't a competition any more, but a procession, a litany. A 1–1 draw against Blackburn on Boxing Day brought United's unbeaten run to 20 games, then 21 with a 5–2 atomization of Oldham three days later. In the 1993 calendar year, United had scored 102 points, 26 more than the second best, Blackburn, scoring 2.13 goals per game in the 1993–94 season. Statistics like these augured a long supremacy, the like of which English football hadn't seen since Liverpool collected seven titles between 1977 and 1984, and it was confidently predicted that 1994 would see a confirmation of that trend. That wasn't quite the case, however.

A drop in form had to check United's progress at some stage, but it's fair to say that no one saw it coming. The 0–0 Leeds United took back from Old Trafford on New Year's Day didn't constitute much of a surprise. Five of the six 'Roses' derbies which had taken place since Leeds regained elite status in 1990 had ended in draws and, after dicing with relegation in the months following Éric's departure, Howard Wilkinson's side had rediscovered some of its former grit and efficiency, and spent most of the autumn solidly installed in the pack chasing United. Cantona was given the reception he could expect from the crowd, as well as a robust welcome by Chris Fairclough, who frustrated him so much that Éric was very lucky not to be dismissed for a stamp on the defender. Another bad foul forced referee David Elleray to caution him, but Cantona was by then playing with a persistent, silent fury. The official chose to give him a lengthy lecture when he could easily have produced another yellow card later in that game. Not all his colleagues would be prepared to show the same leniency in the coming months. Éric's bad-tempered display gave Wilkinson a chance to have a dig at his former player: 'He is the same player on a different stage, in different circumstances,' he said. 'When he was on my stage, we were losing football matches. Those were not performances conducive to the way he played, so I left him out, he didn't like it, and he asked to go.' In other words, put Cantona in a winning team, and he'll look like a world-beater; but don't count on him when the wind is not blowing fair any more.

Three days later, it was a gale that swept through Anfield, on a raw night that signalled that some complacency was creeping into the leaders' performances. United contrived to lose a three-goal lead at Liverpool. But as every single one of their rivals took it in turns to lose when they looked poised to challenge, Alex Ferguson could console himself with a look at the table: his team still led by 13 points. In truth, the fluency of the preceding months seemed to have deserted United. They were scrapping for results: 1–0 against Sheffield United in the Cup, Éric missing an open goal; then 2–2 against first division Portsmouth in the League Cup, their fourth draw in five games.* Even if the champions were scarcely in danger of suffering the kind of physical and mental decline that wrecked their 1991–92 season, the fact remained that their standards had been slipping for several weeks. They needed a performance that would reassert the emergence of a new order in English football. Éric, who had just recovered from a heavy cold, took it on himself to make sure it would be in their very next game.

The majesty of Cantona's play in United's 1–0 victory over Spurs on 15 January was such that the White Hart Lane crowd joined the travelling supporters in applauding him off the field. *The Times* saluted Éric's 'flair, fitness and enthusiasm bordering on fanaticism' and already installed him as favourite for the title of 'Footballer of the Year'. United now needed just 23 points from 16 games to be champions again, and, whatever Howard Wilkinson might have had to say, it was primarily

* Alex Ferguson had initially decided to rest Cantona for that tie, but changed his mind when he saw the look on his player's face when the news was broken to him. 'If I left him out,' the manager said, 'I would probably never see him again.' Some were fooled by the jocular tone of Ferguson's remark. Éric, typically, responded by scoring his 15th goal of the season.

thanks to the prodigious imagination, coolness in front of goal and stamina of the Leeds reject. Ferguson's gamble had paid off, and handsomely.

On 22 January a lone piper playing 'A Scottish Soldier' slowly led the footballers of Manchester United and Everton on to the field of play. Flags were flying at half-mast, and one seat was empty in the directors' box – that of Sir Matt Busby, whose long struggle with cancer had ended two days previously. The architect of United's extraordinary ascent in the 1950s and 1960s would always end his pre-match team talks with one of two valedictions – 'And now, enjoy yourselves', or 'Have fun!' That day, Cantona played as if it had been Busby, not Ferguson, who had sent him on. At one point, he cushioned Ryan Giggs's dipping cross on his chest and, in one movement, swivelled to send a half-volley crashing on to the post. The opposition's manager, Mike Walker, was mesmerized by United's performance. 'There is an aura about [them],' he said. 'They are streets ahead of the rest and their players know it. There is a swaggering arrogance about them, and this is not a criticism. [. . .] You have no idea where their next move is coming from. You plug one hole and another one opens up. You fill that, another player comes at you.' Walker had no hesitation in singling out Cantona as the choreographer of United's ballet: 'He brought it all together last season. His presence has allowed the others to play better. You can see that.' So could Portsmouth, beaten 1–0 in the replay of their League Cup quarter-final, Éric's glancing header setting up Brian McClair for the winner. So could Norwich, dumped out of the FA Cup on 30 January, Keane and Cantona providing the goals in a 2–0 victory – not that the goals provided the talking point in the evening's highlights programme on television.

The 'enthusiasm bordering on fanaticism' about which *The Times* had enthused had shown signs of becoming uncontrollable that afternoon. Phil Neal's 'beast' had come to the fore. The placid Jeremy Goss, who played with Ryan Giggs in the Wales team, was the target of one of Cantona's worst-ever tackles – a dreadful, cowardly assault that pundit Jimmy Hill had every right to call 'vicious', all the more unforgivable as Goss had done nothing to provoke it. The caution Éric escaped with bore no relation to the nastiness of the foul. Nor did Cantona stop there. With a quarter of an hour of the game to go, it was John Polston's head that felt the sting of Éric's studs, an offence that went unpunished. Alex Ferguson stuck to his policy: he publicly defended the indefensible, calling Hill 'a prat' for good measure, while adopting a rather different tone in the privacy of the dressing-room.* Cantona was on the receiving end of a furious tirade, which was also aimed at a number of other hot-headed individuals in the United squad: Hughes, Ince and Keane to name but three.

Ferguson's explosion of anger had some effect on his players, whose behaviour improved markedly (if only temporarily) over the following weeks; but if he had been able to defuse the time bomb ticking in Cantona's head for a short while, there was nothing he could do to alter the growing perception that his United team was behaving like a bunch of arrogant bullies who would resort to violence when things didn't go their way, as if they had a divine right to grind their opponents into the dust. Éric's disciplinary record throughout his first year in England had been commendable, if not examplary, and a number of observers had started to wonder whether the 'bad boy' image he had brought from France was deserved or not. In short succession, Culverhouse, Fairclough, Goss and Polston had received the painful proof that Cantona knew how to 'look after himself' – and others too. As referees talk to each other just as players, fans and journalists do, it wouldn't be long before Éric's reputation would precede him in this circle too, so that he ceased to enjoy the leeway officials were prone to give newcomers in those days. That honeymoon was over.

United had extended their unbeaten run to thirty-one games by mid-February. Éric had buried a predatory header in the net when QPR were defeated 3–2 at Loftus Road, and Giggs's solitary goal against Sheffield Wednesday had brought them within touching distance of the League Cup final. Bookmakers slashed the odds on an unprecedented domestic treble. Life was sweet with France as well. Aimé Jacquet's first game in charge – Éric christening his captain's armband on this occasion – saw *Les Bleus* beat Italy in Italy for the first time since 1912.

---

* This incident marked the beginning of the long feud between Sir Alex Ferguson and the BBC, which eventually led to his boycotting the public broadcaster.

The 'worst night in [his] life' – Bulgaria's triumph in Paris – was fast receding from Cantona's memory.

Then, on 20 February, at Selhurst Park, in front of 27,511 spectators (most of whom were wearing Manchester United shirts), Éric scored one of his most aesthetically satisfying goals, one which has been replayed often enough on television to become a perfect trailer for the film of his English career. It was only the fifth round of the FA Cup; and it was only Wimbledon; but it was also a moment in which it was possible to feel gratitude for Éric's fantasy of the footballer-artist.

Vinnie Jones, in so many ways the antithesis of the player Cantona dreamed himself to be, had been snapping at his heels, calves and knees for most of the game. David Elleray, who refereed on that night, should have sent off the thug-in-chief of the 'Crazy Gang' as early as the 21st minute, for an absurdly high two-foot lunge on Éric. A yellow card gave the adoptive Welshman relative licence to carry on doing his dirty job. He failed to close on his target on this occasion, however. In one movement, Éric defined a space that he alone could inhabit, where there was no place for the Joneses of this world. A ball was floated in from the left wing, which the Dons' defender Gary Elkins could only loop out of the box. Cantona teed it up on the volley with the instep of his right foot, and smashed it into the left corner of Sullivan's net, combining two perfect arcs of the ball to create a perfect goal, a wonder of geometry, poise and violence that had ripples of delight brushing the collective flesh of the crowd.

In any sport, what differentiates greatness from mere exceptional talent is the capacity to invent time and space where there appears to be none; Brian Lara delaying the roll of his wrists to execute an impossibly late cut; Roger Federer picking an Andy Roddick serve on the up, to send it hurrying down the line; Éric Cantona fashioning this goal, exquisite and brutal in its execution, almost proving to us and to himself that he was right in his assertion that football could belong to the realm of art.

I hope I can be forgiven a short pause at this point in Éric Cantona's story, as what I'm writing now, I felt at the time. This ball took a fraction of a second to lodge itself into the net; it also took for ever. Even United's ugly green-and-yellow away strip acquired some kind of beauty at that moment. Then, of course, the beauty became a memory of beauty, no less affecting, but gone all the same. Even the greatest of sports' artists must accept that any thought of immortality is a delusion. To most of them, in any case, what we perceive as an expression of art is, simply, part of their job; you wouldn't have caught Alfredo Di Stefano comparing himself to Velázquez. Federer's astonishing exploration of his gift is a selfish enterprise, an attempt to find the answer to this question: how far can I go? But because this adventurous impulse takes place in a public arena, it becomes almost a gift to others.

We touch here upon a particular paradox that Cantona experienced with a far greater intensity than most, if not all, of the footballers he played with. At certain moments sport has as profound and life-changing an effect as painting or music can bring about on those who witness the act of creation. But no sportsman is an artist, regardless of how much he or she would want to be considered one. I am convinced that Cantona's outbursts of temper, his reluctance to take root, his chronic instability are, when distilled, expressions of his raging at the limitations of his gift and of his awareness (from a very young age: think of the interview he gave to *France Football* in the autumn of 1987, when he was just twenty-one: see page 69) that, no matter how great his on-field achievements may be, he had never become the tormented, misunderstood creator of genius he wished to be in his naïve dreams. Despite the virtual afterlife provided by television, the lifespan of a footballer is a short one, circumscribed by living memory. As Cantona himself has said on many occasions, retirement is 'a form of death'.

Time and again, he has insisted on the expressive dimension of football; to him, expression and creation are one and the same thing. 'Football is the most beautiful of arts' (he was still playing when he said that); or 'art is finding spontaneity in everything. An actor is trying to find the spontaneity of a child when he says a sentence. A painter tries to be as free and as spontaneous as possible' (a statement of such conventionality it would have warranted inclusion in a modern-day Flaubert's dictionary of received ideas). One of his ways of living with the frustration he, a mere ball-kicker, must have felt, was to invent a model of the artist which he could identify with, at least in terms of character and behaviour. I wonder what opinion he may have had of a Charles Ives or a Henri Matisse, bourgeois poets, for whom sitting at the piano or sketching a nude in the studio fitted in a work routine comparable to that of a computer programmer. Matisse was the most reluctant of theorists and phrase-makers when it came to his art. But on the rare occasions when he did speak, he said that, to him, art was about expression, no doubt, but remained rooted in a need to give shape and colour (he could have been talking of musical notes, or textures, or words) to an individual's response to his experience. Art could not be a mere arrangement of forms, presented to the senses of the contemplator.

Football, however, even at its most enthrallingly beautiful, or, if you prefer, 'artistic', is nothing but pure manifestation; it is not a response to anything other than itself; it is an unfolding. The flow of the ball is self-contained, self-referential – and unrepeatable. A perfectly executed free kick might require just as much time on the training field as a bassoonist, say, will spend rehearsing the first bars of *The Rite of Spring* in the concert hall. But whereas the bassoonist will be able to play the same line time after time, finding new shades of tone and refining new articulations, even the greatest footballer we could dream of would fail to repeat a single one of his masterful creations. A football team is not an orchestra. You do not pit two ensembles against each together, playing two scores which are not just incompatible in terms of meter and key, but also try to nullify each other, despite the wildest experiments of avant-garde composers. The greatest of managers is not a conductor, and the footballer-artist is not a soloist: you do not write footballs on a stave. But Éric was driven by the belief that somehow, some were given the ability to do so – Cruyff, Maradona, himself. On that evening in Wimbledon, he wasn't very far from convincing the rest of the world he was right.

Reality reasserted itself quickly after the media had rhapsodized about the Wimbledon wondergoal. United seemed to be cruising at that point in the season, albeit less comfortably than before, as Blackburn Rovers, carried by Alan Shearer's torrent of goals, had closed the gap to seven points (having played one game more). Ferguson's team could nonetheless leave West Ham with a 2–2 draw the following weekend without feeling the need to look nervously behind them – not yet anyway. A 4–1 defeat of Sheffield Wednesday gave United a place in the League Cup final and appeared to have put them back on course. Éric, feeling the effects of a knock on the shin sustained at Upton Park, missed that game and had not fully recovered when Chelsea ended United's series of thirty-four games without defeat. Just as he had done at Stamford Bridge in September, Gavin Peacock scored the only goal of that encounter, neatly bookending United's superb run. And so it was that against all odds, Blackburn had positioned themselves in the champion's slipstream. The rest had no hope of catching up with either club. Arsenal, in third place, were a full 14 points behind United.

The chance of a major upset in the title race soon receded, however. United saw off Charlton 3–1 in an FA Cup quarter-final, despite playing with ten men for the whole of the second half after Peter Schmeichel had been dismissed for a professional foul outside his box. They confirmed they had woken up for good when Cantona orchestrated a 5–0 rout of Sheffield Wednesday on a pitch white with hailstones in mid-March. Éric's timing was splendid. The publication of his autobiography on the 10th of that month had provoked a furore that was quite out of proportion with the book's contents, as we'll see. But there were a number of pundits and commentators who seized on its more controversial chapters to question, again, Éric's work rate, character and contribution to the English game. What a response he gave them. He started by picking up the ball in his own half and, spotting Giggs some 70 yards away, conjured the ball to land sweetly in the path of the winger, who rounded the 'keeper and scored with less than a quarter of an hour on the clock. Two minutes later, one of Cantona's flicks fell for Hughes, who found the net from fully 30 yards. Éric did the job himself for United's fourth after being put through by Paul Ince. But he had kept the best for last. A fluid move released Ince, who fed Cantona, who dummied, let the ball run, wrong-footed the defender, spun on a sixpence and sent the ball into the goal via the inside of a post.

Curiously, the British media hadn't picked up on the original French title of Cantona's book, *Un Rêve modeste et fou* ('A Humble and Crazy Dream', which became *Cantona: My Story* in English, for some reason).

This slim volume had been in bookshops for quite a few months already, but British tabloids did not yet employ French-based staff to scour the local press for recycled 'exclusives', as is the case today. Factually wrong and inexcusably short (142 pages in its original version, excluding Éric's rambling foreword), *Cantona: My Story* still packed a punch – especially if your name was Howard Wilkinson. The book's innumerable mistakes (most of which have been conscientiously reprinted as gospel truth since then) went unnoticed, which wasn't the case of the page-and-a-half – that's all, a page-and-a-half – devoted to Cantona's exit from Elland Road. It can't have been pleasant for the manager who gave Éric his chance to shine in English football to read that his attitude towards the player had been 'bizarre' and 'rather incoherent'. Even more damagingly for his former coach, Cantona, via his ghostwriter Pierre-Louis Basse, insinuated that the real reason for his departure from Yorkshire was Wilkinson's desire to find a scapegoat for his side's poor start to the season, and that his 'solution' was, first, to 'spread rumours' of the player's refusal to accept the authority of his coach, then to accept a ridiculously low offer from Manchester United in order to show that sacrifices had to be made to get rid of the troublemaker. This was not Cantona's finest hour, it must be said. The inelegance of his attack on Wilkinson left a bitter taste in the mouth, especially as he concluded it with a meaningless pirouette: 'there's only a small step to take to say that he doesn't like strong personalities who have an impact on the fans, but I won't take that step'. Really?

Soon after, Wilkinson expressed a desire to slug it out. 'I've kept my own counsel for fifteen months,' he said, 'effectively shielding many of those involved. But given the way Éric has seen fit to reopen the debate, I have no alternative but to spell out the facts.' But he didn't, not until much later, long after Cantona had retired, long after Leeds United had parted with the manager who gave them their only league title in the last thirty-five years – and counting. Whatever the manager's shortcomings may have been, to turn Wilkinson into some kind of Machiavelli reeked of self-serving expediency.

Alex Ferguson supported Cantona, as he had promised himself he would always do. 'I think Éric is a player apart,' he said. 'When I signed him, I thought I had signed a good player, but I didn't think he would make such an impact. He's capable of providing moments of inspiration that we haven't had in the British game for years. He inspires people around him. He changes his way of playing in different games; he has the intelligence to understand the tactical part. Perhaps this club, this stadium, is what he has always needed.' Many years later, in 2005, Ferguson told me how Éric had exceeded his expectations, becoming one of those players 'who do what can't be taught, who, in fact, teach you something you didn't know about football, and can't be learnt, because you had no idea it existed before they did it'. That's as good a definition of greatness as the one I heard from Ferguson's arch-rival Arsène Wenger: 'A player who receives the ball has to solve a million problems within a fraction of a second; a great one is the one who chooses the right solution.' Éric at his best fitted the description more often than not.

All of the United 'family' adopted him as one of their own, the painting, poetry and psychoanalysis notwithstanding. Cantona didn't mind his teammates making gentle fun of him, as when he attempted to buy a packet of chewing-gum with his gold credit card in an airport (Éric hardly ever carried cash on his person). His English was, of course, far better than the media thought, and the more industrial the language, the better he fared. Alex Ferguson encouraged the burgeoning comradeship between the Frenchman and the rest of the squad, making sure he took part in club-organized outings, with unexpected consequences at times. In late 2008 Sir Alex recounted, at a lunch to celebrate Cristiano Ronaldo's *Ballon d'Or*, how on one of these team-bonding exercises (at a racecourse), a group of Liverpool supporters positioned on the balcony overlooking the box reserved for Manchester United relieved themselves on the players below. 'Cantona got up, furious, and started to punch everyone in sight – he took twenty guys on his own! The whole team followed him afterwards, but he'd started on his own . . .'

Such behaviour demanded respect and got it. He had truly become 'one of the lads', someone Roy Keane described as 'funny, [someone who] loved a drink, champagne rather than Heineken', and 'good company', 'one of the best, no real conceit, no bullshit'. Éric would sometimes join the young Irishman and others like Lee Sharpe on one of their sessions in pubs like the Griffin and the Stanford, far enough away from the city centre (the Griffin is located in Altrincham) to avoid trouble-seekers. Éric occasionally patronized venues closer to the heart of the city too, like the Peveril of the Peak, where Pete Boyle met him for the first time on 1 March 1994. 'I was with my mates upstairs,' Pete told me, 'rehearsing "Éric the King" . . . then someone came up and said, "You'll never guess who's downstairs." It was Éric, playing table football with Claude Boli, who was doing an MA in Manchester at the time. I showed him the lyrics to my song, after which we all went to Boli's house, which Éric used to visit regularly – just behind the Kippax' – the legendary stand of Manchester City's now-demolished Maine Road stadium.

Manchester's seediness appealed to Éric, as the French journalists who visited him around this time could testify. He would sometimes show them round some of the less salubrious places where he would have a drink or – an obsession – play or watch snooker. My *France Football* colleague Patrick Urbini (to whom Éric would later say: 'I piss on your arse' live on French television, but that is a different story) told me how, on one such occasion, having been promised 'the best bar on the planet', he found himself in a nondescript public house in a nondescript housing estate. Judging by how relaxed the habitués were in Cantona's company, it was obvious that this wasn't Éric's first visit. When the time came to leave the pub and head back to his car, it was to find out that vandals had broken one of the windows and run away with the radio. Cantona shrugged his shoulders, as if this were a pretty unremarkable occurrence in the life of a Manchester United footballer. And maybe it was. In any case, it showed that Éric's indifference to material belongings was not just pretence. To him, money was a gauge of the appreciation of others, to be earned in great quantity if at all possible, certainly, but also to share; and many friends and former team-mates were either the witnesses or the beneficiaries of one of his acts of generosity.

Roy Keane has told how, one day, Steve Bruce arrived with a cheque for £15,000 – the players' royalties for a Manchester United video; but no one could quite work out how this sum should be divided between the eighteen players. It was agreed to hold a draw. Whoever's name first came out of the hat would pocket the money – all of it – unless some preferred to receive their eighteenth of the sum and not to take part in the lottery. Most of the younger players, for whom this £800 represented a small fortune, opted for the safer solution. Two of them (Paul Scholes and Nicky Butt) decided to try their luck. Éric won – but came in the next morning with two cheques for the losers: their reward for taking the gamble, he explained. 'This was Éric to a "t",' Keane told his biographer, 'the unexpected, a touch of class, also an appreciation of the plight of two young lads more in need of money than himself.'

A father-like manager who played him every week and stood by him in public, teammates who sought his company but also respected his need for solitude, a city he had learned to love, a winning team, supporters who had crowned him 'King' of Old Trafford, the captaincy of the national side, not forgetting a wife and child whom he could visit when it pleased him, money, fame . . . It's easier to draw up a list of the things that Éric Cantona didn't have than the things he did. Yet his inner turmoil hadn't abated, that fire that sometimes caused him 'to do harm to himself, and to others'.

One of these 'others' was John Moncur, the Swindon midfielder who had the misfortune to become tangled with Éric after an untidy tackle. Cantona reacted by donkey-kicking him in full view of referee Brian Hill. It was his first straight red card in England; it could have been his fifth in any other league on the Continent since the beginning of the year. Once more playing with ten men, United surrendered their 2–1 lead and left the County Ground with a single point. An incandescent Ferguson told Éric to 'fucking sort himself out', for the player's dismissal for violent conduct carried an automatic three-game ban, which would rule Cantona out of the FA Cup semi-final. What's more, Kenny Dalglish's Blackburn showed no sign of tiring as the final straight loomed into view: they won 2–1 at Sheffield Wednesday the following day, on 20 March, to cut their deficit to a mere five points.

And it got worse. Arsenal were next in line for United. The scoreline was identical: 2–2, and Éric was sent off again, this time for two bookable offences. He could consider himself hard done by. The referee, Viv Callow, had first punished him for a fairly innocuous (in the context of an ill-tempered game) challenge on Ian Selley, when a horrendous tackle by Paul Ince on the same player had only resulted in a free kick earlier in the match. Within four minutes of receiving this caution, Cantona was ordered off the pitch: Tony Adams had been his target this time. In hindsight, Alex Ferguson probably wished that Aimé Jacquet had not been so understanding of United's needs that he had left his captain out of the national squad – France played a friendly against Chile in Lyon on the very same day. The Scottish manager had had enough. Schmeichel, Ince, Robson, Keane, Bruce, Hughes and Cantona (all of them 'capable of causing a row in an empty house', according to Ferguson) were summoned to his office to be given the famous 'hairdryer' treatment. Once the expletives had been deleted, the speech he gave could be summed up in two words: 'no more'.

'Our disciplinary record lurched towards the unacceptable,' Ferguson later said, falling short of admitting that it was his players' indefensible behaviour rather than their 'disciplinary record' which was the cause of United's difficulties, not so subtly deflecting the blame towards intransigent referees. That 1993–94 side could produce football of quite breathtaking fluidity; I would argue that, in many respects, it was the strongest of all those assembled around Éric Cantona at Old Trafford, if only for the presence of Ince, a stupendous footballer who, when he joined Inter Milan a season and a half later, showed he was adept and skilful enough to play alongside the very best in what was at the time the most technically demanding league the world. Hampered by their inexperience and tethered by the restrictions on 'foreigners' put in place by UEFA, this group of players was unable to express itself fully in Europe. In England, however, they were irresistible at times. They were also shockingly brutal, confrontational and boorish, each one of them egging the other on to emulate their 'manliness' and, one imagines, deriving some perverse pride from finding their name written in the referee's book. Manchester United fans might not like this, but of the great teams of the past, the one which came to mind when comparisons were drawn was Don Revie's Leeds United, not Bob Paisley's Liverpool. With this proviso: whereas Revie had a cynical hand in his side's misdemeanours – according to some accounts, to the extent that his players were told before kick-off who should 'take out' whom, and how to 'rotate the strike' when intimidating a referee – Ferguson merely tolerated them. He would go so far as to exonerate one of his protégés' misconduct when facing the press but, to his credit, addressed the issue of indiscipline in private. Bans harmed the team's prospects, for one thing.

The red mist didn't dissipate immediately. Come the next game, on 27 March,* it was Andreï Kanchelskis who left the field prematurely. His offence was tame in comparison with what had gone on before: a deliberate handball. Aston Villa, humiliated three months previously in the championship, were deserving victors (3–1) of the 1994 League Cup. Cantona, booed at every touch by the Villa supporters, was anonymous – it was as if he was already suspended, a prisoner waiting for the execution of his sentence. There would be no 'historic treble'. A few days later, when Liverpool were beaten 1–0 at Old Trafford, Éric's despondency had increased to such an extent that Alex Ferguson subbed him with twenty-five minutes to play, replacing him with the creaking Bryan Robson.

The six-point lead that United enjoyed over Blackburn was halved at the beginning of April when Alan Shearer – one of Ferguson's targets before Cantona was bought from Leeds – scored a brace for Rovers against the champions. With seven games to go, the prediction made by most at the turn of the year that United would 'walk it' began to look dubious in the extreme, particularly as Éric still had four games of his five-game ban to serve. As so often when he found himself on the periphery of the game, Cantona headed for Marseilles, where he retreated into the cocoon of his clan. The gloom of his mood was matched by the gloom of the Provençal skies: it rained almost incessantly while he was there. Ironically, it was then that he learned that his peers in the PFA – including the magnanimous John Moncur, whom he had assaulted on the field a few weeks previously – had voted

* Éric's brother Joël – a frequent visitor to Old Trafford – had made his debut for Stockport County a day earlier. According to an eyewitness, he featured for fifteen 'not very good minutes' in a home defeat by Bournemouth. The younger Cantona, who'd also played without much success for Marseille, Rennes, Antwerp, Angers and Ujpest, had already been rejected by Peterborough, and rumours were rife at the time that Éric had offered to pay Joël's wages in order to conclude the deal. In any case, within a few months, Cantona junior was back plying his trade in the Hungarian championship.

him the Players' Player of the Year on 11 April, the first foreigner to be deemed worthy of such an accolade.

United stuttered in his absence, edging out Oldham 3–2 at home in the league, and six days later being rescued by Mark Hughes in the last minute of extra time in their FA Cup semi-final against the same tenacious Lancastrian opponents (1–1). They negotiated the replay with some panache, winning 4–1, but fell 1–0 at Wimbledon, which enabled Blackburn (who had played one game more) to join them at the top of the table. How much Cantona had been missed in these three weeks was shown as soon as he was allowed to resume competitive football. Éric's returns from bans or injuries generally turned out to be spectacular occasions, of which he was invariably the focal point, and, once again, he didn't disappoint. He dismantled Manchester City on his own, scoring both goals in a 2–0 victory.

There had been much fighting talk emanating from the City camp before the encounter, some of it so excessive that their manager, Brian Horton, had felt obliged to exclude Terry 'The Scuttler' Phelan from his squad after the left-back had announced he had some 'special treatment' in store for the Frenchman. This didn't prevent Horton from instructing Éric's designated man-marker Steve McMahon to 'get under [his] skin', a piece of advice that the former Liverpool veteran appeared to have taken literally: he was yellow-carded in the fifth minute after his elbow had – just – failed to connect with Cantona's face. Alex Ferguson had predicted that, should anyone intend to intimidate Éric, 'he'd calm them down', and this is what he did, taking advantage of fine work by Kanchelskis and Hughes to bring his tally to 22 goals in 43 games for the season. 'Éric, no matter the tempo or the maelstrom of premier division football,' Ferguson reflected, 'has that ability to put the foot on the ball and to make his passes. That in itself is almost a miracle.'*

Éric excelled once again four days later in Leeds, when the taunts

* The 'miracle' was witnessed by Éric's father Albert, who had got round his notorious phobia of flying by driving his Citroën for 48 hours to be there. Éric's younger brother Joël was there too to see his 'God' (Albert *dixit*), but had a far shorter distance to cover, as he had been awarded a short-term contract by third division Stockport County a month or so beforehand, as we have seen.

of 41,000 baying Yorkshiremen inspired him to deliver one of his most complete performances on the Elland Road pitch. United's convincing 2–0 victory there helped them re-establish their supremacy in the league, as Blackburn had been held 1–1 at home by QPR three days before. United's advantage was far more than the couple of points that now separated the last two challengers for the title: they still had a game in hand with three to play, and their vastly superior goal difference (+39 compared to +29 for Rovers) ensured that parity in terms of points sufficed to ensure triumph.

On the most sombre day of that sporting year, 1 May, the day Ayrton Senna died on the Imola racetrack, another step was made towards the retention of the Premiership title when an 'unsteady' United prevailed 2–1 at Ipswich. Éric had headed the equalizing goal, his 18th in that league campaign, his 23rd in all competitions. Twenty-four hours later, pressure finally got the better of a nerve-racked Blackburn, who were stopped 2–1 in Coventry. As in 1992–93, Manchester United had been crowned without playing, when many had thought that the race would last just a little while longer: Alex Ferguson, for one, was watching snooker on television when his son Jason called him with the news that Coventry had opened the scoring. Steve Bruce, the side's captain, couldn't bear the tension and left his home in search of some champagne. Éric savoured his fourth consecutive national title with more calm than most: he had long been convinced that nothing could stop 'the best team he'd ever played for'.

The Old Trafford crowd cheered their champions on 4 May when Southampton were beaten 2–0 at Old Trafford. This was a red-letter day in more ways than one, as Arsenal won the European Cup Winners Cup at the expense of Parma that evening. Arsenal's success had sufficiently boosted the UEFA rating of English club football to guarantee that Manchester United would enter the following season's competition directly in the group phase – probably the only time in the history of the Gunners that they did a good turn to their bitterest rival in the north-west of England.

There remained an FA Cup final to play, whose outcome was by no means a foregone conclusion, despite United's remarkable statistics in this

1993–94 season: 64 games played in all competitions, 126 goals scored, and only 6 defeats. But their opponents Chelsea had 'done the double' over them in the league. The whole of Manchester, however, had another double in mind – this one with a capital 'D', which only five clubs had achieved since the creation of the Football League in 1888.* United were favourites to become the sixth team, and Cantona the first non-British footballer, to achieve a feat that many had considered impossible in the context of the modern game. Other foreigners had walked up Wembley's thirty-nine steps to receive a FA Cup winner's medal: the Argentinian duo of Osvaldo Ardiles (1981 and 1982) and 'Ricky' Villa (1981), both with Tottenham; much earlier, the Newcastle inside-forward Jorge 'George' Robledo Oliver (in 1951 and 1952), a Chilean international who didn't speak a word of Spanish, as his parents had emigrated to Yorkshire when he was five years old. But none had yet finished a domestic season with the two greatest honours English football had to offer.

Six days before the final, Éric and his teammates did a last lap of honour in their own stadium. Or should it be a stroll of honour? Their opponents that day, Coventry City, had long secured their Premiership status, and Alex Ferguson could afford to give a rare outing to a few fringe players, Dion Dublin among them. The 0–0 scoreline didn't surprise or upset anyone. Éric did his best to provide some entertainment, his bicycle kick forcing Steve Ogrizovic to produce a flying save, one of only two occasions when the crowd rose to its feet; the other was to give a standing ovation to Bryan Robson, who was wearing United's red shirt for the 340th and last time. The Cantona clan had travelled en masse from Marseille for an extended stay, Albert (whose 54th birthday fell on Cup final day) cramming the boot of his car with memorabilia purchased at the club's store, Léonor listening to her son re-enacting his on-field acrobatics, all of them thinking ahead to 14 May, the date of Éric's fifth visit to Wembley,† but the first on which

* Preston North End (1889), Aston Villa (1897), Tottenham Hotspur (1961), Arsenal (1971) and Liverpool (1986).

† After the Charity Shield wins of 1992 and 1993 and the 1994 League Cup final, as well as England's 2–0 defeat of France in February 1992.

the most venerable trophy in world football would be at stake. Joël, as ever, was in adoring attendance.

Cantona slept badly on the eve of the final. Nerves were not to blame, but a recurrence of the back trouble that had been a bane of his career for so long. He usually played through the pain, but the stiffness was such when he woke up that he asked for painkillers before the teams walked out on the pitch. United's medical staff decided against an injection and provided him with three tabs of aspirin instead, which turned out to be remarkably effective on the evidence of his performance that afternoon. Mindful of his condition, he produced a display that was composed rather than flamboyant, controlling the play from a slightly more withdrawn position, finding space on the right wing at times, sustaining a high tempo through quickness of thought and breadth of vision, happy for Giggs, Hughes, Kanchelskis and the marauding Irwin to harry Chelsea's defence.

The final was wrapped up in less than ten minutes, after an hour of play. Before that, Glenn Hoddle's team had proved dogged and resourceful opponents, frequently threatening to pierce United's defence with their quick interpassing. Then, in the 60th minute, Eddie Newton committed a dreadful foul on Dennis Irwin right in front of referee David Elleray, who immediately pointed to the penalty spot. The Chelsea players had no right to feel aggrieved by the decision, but, as Cantona picked up the ball to place it there, one of them, Dennis Wise (who else?), walked up and started remonstrating with the Frenchman – or so the television viewers and commentators thought. Wise intended to disrupt Éric's concentration, there could be no doubt about that, but the method he had chosen to do that was highly original. He asked Cantona: 'Fancy a bet?' to which Éric replied, 'Yes – £100,' before waving him off with a dismissive gesture of the hand. What with Wise's intervention, and Elleray and Cantona taking turns to replace the ball on the spot, the execution of the referee's sentence took over a minute-and-a-half.

The last two penalties awarded on FA Cup final day at Wembley had been saved, but Dimitri Kharine could do nothing about Éric's kick. He struck the ball almost nonchalantly with the inside of his right boot, as if he had been practising on the training ground. Barely five minutes later, the Double became a near certainty when Elleray blew his whistle again, this time after Andreï Kanchelskis had come off worst in a shoulder-to-shoulder challenge in the box. Wise's teammates remonstrated furiously, and not without justification this time, but there was no bet on that occasion (Wise settled his wager at the exit of the dressing-rooms). Éric waited for the tumult to die down, teed the ball – and sent Kharine the wrong way, placing his shot (more a pass into the goal, in fact) precisely in the same spot, to the left of the Russian 'keeper. 'Do not play poker with that man,' as a columnist wrote the next morning. The eerie similarity between the two penalty kicks had something almost comical about it. 'Whatever you do,' Éric seemed to imply, 'we'll beat you on our terms, and there is nothing you can do about it,' which summed up this match perfectly. Chelsea, who showed tremendous spirit throughout, could have played until dusk without scoring, whereas every United move in the second half looked as if it would be concluded with a goal. Éric was only inches away from equalling Stan Mortensen's record of a hat-trick at this stage of the competition, but placed his angled shot in Kharine's side-netting instead. It didn't matter: Hughes capitalized on a defensive mix-up to make it 3–0 in the dying seconds. Then Éric initiated the best move of the game from a Chelsea corner. His superbly timed pass reached Mark Hughes as he was racing towards the halfway line. The Welshman had spotted Paul Ince driving forward, and prolonged the course of the ball in his unimpeded path. Ince rounded the 'keeper and selflessly laid out the simplest of tap-ins for Brian McClair. The lopsided character of the 4–0 scoreline only hardened the growing conviction that the gap Manchester United had opened on their pursuers was turning into an unbridgeable chasm. Alex Ferguson, wearing a red wig, half-walking, half-dancing on the Wembley pitch, assuredly seemed to think as much at the final whistle.

Whereas all the talk prior to the final had been of Ferguson's team emulating legendary sides like Danny Blanchflower's Spurs of 1961, the post-match coverage of the 113th FA Cup final focused on the contribution of one player rather than on the conquest of the Double. The *Daily Mirror*'s headline said it all: 'General De Goal'. Journalists swarmed around the first man ever to score two penalties in the grand

Wembley showcase. Why had he decided to shoot twice to the left of Kharine? 'Because he twice dived to his right,' Éric said. 'If he had twice dived to his left, I would have twice kicked to his right!' Had he not felt nervous? 'If you are nervous,' came the reply, 'you should stop playing football. This is the moment you prepare for all your life. There is the stadium, there are 80,000 people and the ball and the chance to win a Cup final. If that makes you nervous, you should change your occupation.'

Mark Hughes was one of many voices joining in the chorus of praise. 'He has really opened up everyone's football awareness,' the Welshman said. 'We see Éric doing things, and we think, "I'll try that." We're not as good at it as Éric, but he has freed us a little bit, and that's why we now play with that little bit more flair'), but a few dissenting voices could also be heard. Simon Barnes, for example, wrote this cruel barb in *The Times*: 'Éric Cantona is a man who seems to rise to the small occasion.' Barnes, as he often does, had a point, which many others had made and would make again, though not always with the same flair for an epigram: Éric was a flat-track bully. Alluding to the League Cup final defeat by Aston Villa a few months previously, Barnes borrowed from Oscar Wilde to say: 'To lose one Wembley final may be regarded as a misfortune, to lose two looks like a character defect; in particular a defect in the character of Éric Cantona.'

Éric himself could not be held responsible for the adulation that was lavished on him. That he enjoyed it tremendously (and expected it, up to a point) cannot be doubted; the very extravagance of the compliments heaped upon his 'genius' helped him fend off a long-time companion of his – the demon of insecurity. But he could also be a sterner critic of himself than is commonly thought. 'It's too soon to call me a legend,' he warned. 'Before comparing me with George Best, Bobby Charlton or Denis Law, I prefer to be judged after two more years at Old Trafford.' Never before had he suggested so clearly that his future was linked to the future of a particular club – and this at a time when a number of European giants were rumoured to covet him, Real Madrid and Internazionale among the most frequently mentioned suitors. In all likelihood, the Spaniards' infatuation may have been nothing but a journalist's fantasy, but Inter's interest grew into something of an obsession for Massimo Moratti, whose father Angelo had turned the Milanese club into Europe's most feared side in the mid-1960s, and who was desperate to recapture some of that faded glory. Time and again over the next three years, the young oil tycoon (who officially became the *nerazzuri*'s chairman in February 1995) would try and bring Cantona to Serie A. His courtship would not bear fruit, but, as we'll see, it wouldn't be for want of trying.

Twenty-five thousand fans were waiting for the Double winners back in Manchester. Each of them had probably bought or been given a copy of 'Come On You Reds', the first single recorded by a club side* to top the nation's charts. Each of them knew Éric's prodigious statistics for the season: 25 goals in 48 games. Here's the detail: 3 goals scored with his left foot, 19 with his right, plus 3 headers; 21 from within the box, 4 from outside; plus 15 assists. Cantona himself, ten days away from his twenty-eighth birthday, was at the peak of his powers and relishing football as he never had before. Bernard Morlino heard him say on FA Cup final night: 'If I hadn't been a footballer, I would have had to be Jacques Mesrine or Albert Spaggiari to experience emotions as strong as these' (a telling reference that warrants a longer digression for the benefit of English readers, which you will find at the end of this chapter).

After taking part in Mark Hughes's testimonial on May the 16th, the rebel went home to Boothstown, where he was finally reunited with Isabelle and their son in a modest semi-detached house worth less than £100,000, five doors away from the home of one of Ryan Giggs' best friends. He still kept his room at the Novotel. 'It's boring to be in a big house,' he said.

> When there are four of you, why would you buy a house with seven bedrooms? Why would I do that, if not to show people I am rich? I buy a house that I need, not to show people I am

---

* This single, a reworking of Status Quo's 'Burning Bridges', a Top 5 hit in 1988, was recorded by the Manchester United squad with the band, but without Éric Cantona (who nevertheless featured prominently in the accompanying video).

> rich – they already know that. The man who buys the big house with all the bedrooms he doesn't need shows he's rich, but maybe he's not rich inside. For me the atmosphere inside a house is very important: everywhere I have been with my family, it has been cosy. People who are successful want to show they are different, they live in the big house and try to live in another world. I want to live in the same world.

Cantona's rebellion stopped on the doormat. Come June, immediately after Éric had taken part in an inconsequential friendly tournament in Japan,* Isabelle stopped teaching at Leeds University and the collection of cardboard boxes that had cluttered the family residence in Leeds was brought to the home Éric had occupied, alone, for several months already.

Tony Smith, a Manchester United supporter and Boothstown resident, later said that 'the whole village was buzzing with the news that he had come to live among "ordinary" people', rather than hiding away in the exclusivity of the stockbroker belt. But it was not such a shock; he had lived modestly in Leeds, and had stayed in a Worsley motel before bringing his family across the Pennines. The locals quickly became accustomed to seeing Cantona driving through the neighbourhood. 'I had the opportunity to speak to Éric Cantona outside my house during his most traumatic period,' Smith recalled, referring to the aftermath of the Crystal Palace fracas,

> but on learning that I supported United he showed his usual friendliness. He was known among the supporters for understanding the importance of spending a few moments with them and, despite his superstar status, being the most approachable of all the players in the team. During his troubles, journalists camped outside his house seeking uncomplimentary stories, though I never heard a bad word spoken about him. Éric

* France, captained by Éric, won the two games they played in the so-called 'Keirin Cup' on 25 and 29 May. Australia were beaten 1–0, thanks to Cantona's goal, and Japan 4–1 in the final.

eventually left his rented house, and left us with some good memories. It isn't often that Boothstown becomes home to one so famous, but Éric Cantona was more than a celebrity, he was a genuine folk hero.

The names of Mesrine and Spaggiari carry a deep, sombre resonance for the French. Both were notorious gangsters of the 1970s, who became heroes in some sections of society for their daring assaults on symbols of the bourgeois establishment (France's answer to the Kray twins, if you will, but with more panache and, in Mesrine's case, far more violence). To them, or so they claimed, crime was also an act of rebellion, a moral and political statement which somehow drew the offender beyond the accepted boundaries of good and evil. Spaggiari had some justification to make such claims. He pulled off one of the most astonishing heists ever, the robbery of FF50m from the Société Générale in Nice in 1976, daubing the slogan 'sans armes, ni haine, ni violence' *('with no weapons, hatred or violence') on a safe. Mesrine, who, in the best-selling autobiography he wrote in prison (*L'Instinct de mort *– 'The Death Instinct'), boasted to have committed no less than thirty-nine murders, made for a more dubious modern-day Robin Hood. After an implausible escape from an interrogation chamber, Spaggiari spent the last twelve years of his life on the run before dying of throat cancer in Italy. Mesrine, a thug of considerable charm who, chomping a cigar, offered champagne to the police officer who caught him in his hideout, died in a hail of bullets in 1979, hand grenades and automatic weapons at his feet. It's tempting to think that Cantona's reference to these famous criminals was in keeping with the conventions of French society – I remember Spaggiari's and Mesrine's names being mentioned with some admiration around my family's dinner table at the time of their exploits – but, beyond identifying himself with the adventurer-refusenik, it also revealed a political nihilism that has been a constant temptation for individualists in France for over a century.*

Éric's politics cannot be defined in terms of a traditional left–right opposition. Spaggiari and Mesrine were military men who had been decorated for bravery in colonial conflicts, before drifting to the extremes of the political spectrum, the former to the right, the latter to the left. Both had strong connections with the Marseillais milieu and figures like the pimp, racketeer and drugs trafficker Gaëtan Zampa or the idealistic 'lone wolf' Charlie Bauer, for whom robbing at gunpoint and suffering solitary confinement were stages on the path to self-discovery; Zampa, a psychotic thug, Bauer a generous revolutionary at war with hypocrisy. What united Mesrine and Spaggiari – and must have seduced Cantona – was a refusal to recognize authority, any kind of authority. Éric never aligned himself with any party, but was quite happy to stand up and be counted when he was required (by friends or circumstances) to speak against politicians or ideas he felt aversion to. The 'system'. Racism. Miscarriages of justice (he recently expressed support for a Corsican shepherd, Yvan Colonna, who had been convicted of the murder of a high-ranking civil servant, Claude Érignac). This is him talking live in front of French television cameras twelve years after his remark to Morlino: 'Napoleon, celebrated when he re-established slavery . . . a giant who was small and who, today, has been replaced by a Le Pen wearing a mask: [Nicolas] Sarkozy.' Reading through some passages of Mesrine's memoirs, I came across this sentence: 'If you live in the shadows, you'll never get close to the sun,' and thought: Éric could've said that. The boldness of the statement, all front and no hinterland, reminded me of many one-liners he had fed to interviewers ever since he emerged as a footballer of promise at Auxerre: theatricality posturing for truth, still divulging a sense of hope and a need to be seen as a révolté, *a word for which I can find no equivalent in English. A 'rebel', maybe, but whose rebellion stems from an innate thirst for justice, and who knows it cannot be quenched. Cantona's politics cannot be translated either; it might be because they don't necessarily make sense.*

15

Cantona imperator.

THE ROAD TO SELHURST PARK: JUNE 1994 TO JANUARY 1995

'There's a fine line between freedom and chaos. To some extent I espouse the idea of anarchy. What I am really after is an anarchy of thought, a liberation of the mind from all convention.'

Cantona's role in the 1994 World Cup was restricted to that of a pundit for French television. He sat next to his friend Didier Roustan, a charcoal-eyed, dark-haired presenter whose 'hip' delivery betrayed as great a desire to promote himself as to introduce a new style of sporting commentary. I remember Roustan asking Éric shortly before the the start of the final between Brazil and Italy: 'What's this game? A rock'n'roll final?' Cantona, sporting superb shades, his skin tanned by the American sun, paused for what seemed an eternity, before replying, as if explaining the facts of life to a child: 'A football final,' to the delight of many, myself included.

Éric made a fine pundit, clear and forthright in his analysis of pivotal passages of play, rightly determined not to fake enthusiasm for what was mostly a disappointing tournament. The competition didn't pass without incident for him. According to *The Times*, Cantona was 'arrested' by security guards after a scuffle with an official who had questioned the validity of his accreditation and refused him entrance to the stadium where Brazil and Sweden – one of France's opponents in the qualifiers – were to play their semi-final. As no charges were brought, it can be assumed that it was nothing more than one of those irritating encounters with a jobsworth which are all too familiar to travelling reporters.

Of far greater importance to Éric was the fatal shooting of Colombian defender Andrés Escobar, who had scored an own goal in a group game against the USA on 22 June, and was murdered outside a bar in Medellin ten days later, apparently on the orders of a gambling syndicate. The assassin, a bodyguard named Humberto Muñoz Castro, pumped twelve bullets into the body of 'the gentleman of football', as he was known in his native country, allegedly shouting 'Goooooooooooooal!' when he fled from the scene. For Cantona, this, and nothing else, certainly not the victory of a functional *Seleçao*, was what this World Cup should be remembered for. He often mentioned this tragedy to his wife Isabelle and to his closest friends. Was that all there was to football? Violence?

But violence was to be the leitmotiv of Éric's and Manchester United's season, long before 25 January, when he jumped feet first over the advertising boards at Crystal Palace; so much so that it is tempting to see the months that passed until then as a slow build-up to an unavoidable explosion. Many United fans have told me that their 1994–95 side was perhaps the strongest their club had assembled since the heyday of Law, Best and Charlton. It was certainly the most ill-disciplined. Looking back, it is hard not to suggest that they literally 'ran riot' until the consequences of their constant infringement of the rules endangered the very aim of their manager's project.

Éric set the tone with a three-game ban after elbowing an opponent in the last but one of a string of five pre-season friendlies, on 6 August. He had already been shown a yellow card in the same match (against Rangers) for turning his back on referee Andrew Waddell, when the official had intended to issue him with a final warning after a shocking lunge on Stephen Pressley, which thankfully missed its target. His ban wouldn't come into effect until after the Charity Shield, in which he scored a penalty: a routine 2–0 victory over Blackburn which proved nothing except that United were so far ahead of their domestic rivals that they could stroll to a win against one of their supposedly strongest challengers. After which an Éric-less United negotiated their first three Premiership games with a mixture of confidence, slickness and luck: seven points out of nine was a more than decent return, but as Kevin McCarra put it, 'Cantona may be a work of art, but he is of no use to his manager as a still life.'

Éric then left England again, this time to join the French national team, which he captained to a 2–2 draw against the Czech Republic on 17 August, a game that had looked all but lost until the introduction on the hour of the young Bordeaux playmaker Zinédine Zidane, making his debut, who scored twice in the last five minutes. This was to be one of only two games that the two most iconic French players of their era would play together, the other being a goalless draw against Slovakia on 7 September, when 'Zizou' once more came off the bench. Aimé Jacquet already felt that fielding both *registas* in the same line-up would unbalance his team; for the time being, Cantona held the better hand, as he would until he surrendered it through an act of folly, and refused to be dealt a new one in January 1996, as we'll see.

It was a strange season. At times, United only had to show up to turn their opponents over, as when Wimbledon visited Old Trafford on the last day of August. Éric was back, made a joke of Vinnie Jones's attentions, and scored a stupendous header from a Ryan Giggs cross. At others, the Double winners fell victim to their delusions of innate superiority. Leeds beat them 2–1 on 11 September, the first time they had prevailed in that fixture at Elland Road since 1980. Éric scored his side's only goal, and was very close to adding a second when he flicked the ball over Carlton Palmer's head and, while Palmer stood there, bemused, did the trick again, only to volley the ball wide of the post, inches away from reproducing the masterpiece he had created against Chelsea – for Leeds – two years before.

Stop, start, stop, start again. He missed United's European curtain-raiser (a 4–2 demolition of IFK Gothenburg on 14 September) through another suspension: UEFA had banned him for four games after his surreal sending-off in Istanbul. But three days later, it was he who orchestrated a crucial 2–0 defeat of Liverpool, playing a decisive part in the build-up to his team's second goal. Neil Ruddock had decided to spice things up by putting his own collar up, and trying to pull Éric's down every time he was close enough. He also elbowed him, which the referee didn't spot. Almost inevitably, Éric retaliated late in the game, and was booked for a foul on his aggressor. Cantona's reaction? According to Alex Ferguson, who could barely disguise his amusement when he told the story to Erik Bielderman, 'Éric warned Ruddock that he would be waiting for an explanation, "man-to-man", in the tunnel at the end of the game. Once the game was over, Ruddock must have done at least three laps of honour and spent ten minutes saluting the Liverpool fans . . . but Éric was waiting, Ruddock knew it. And I, down there, I was trying to push Éric towards the dressing-room. Fucking hell! He was one tough guy!'

Somehow the team that had defeated Liverpool so convincingly lost 2–3 at Ipswich, a team that had yet to win at home that season – despite United registering twenty-five shots on goal, and Éric scoring his fourth goal in six games, this time from a cross by Roy Keane. His ongoing ban in European competitions prevented Cantona from settling into a consistent rhythm. However, Alex Ferguson believed his team could hang on until the player he had nicknamed 'The Can-opener' made his return in the Champions League: a 0–0 draw in Galatasaray's Ali Sami Yen Stadium gave United top spot in their group in late September, ahead of Barcelona. The Red Devils had returned to hell and come back with a point.

Stop, start, stop, start again. Everton lost 2–0 at Old Trafford in a passionless encounter, Cantona hardly stirring himself. Kevin Keegan's Newcastle, meanwhile, had scored twenty-five goals in eight games so far, to United's fourteen. Then Éric left once more, to play for France in Romania, while Sheffield Wednesday beat his club by the only goal. Their reliance on his gift for conjuring up space was costing them dearly, to the extent that bookmakers no longer considered them favourites to retain the championship. As one of them said at the time, 'In our view, they're more likely to win nothing rather than something.' Come October, there wasn't a single player of Ferguson's in the list of the top ten goalscorers in the league. 'All we're doing at the moment is hanging in there,' the manager said. That meant scrapping for a 1–0 win against West Ham, in which Cantona scored the decider at the very end of a scruffy, confused and confusing game, very much in the image of his club's season. Perhaps minds were already turning to the impending challenge of Johann Cruyff's Barcelona in the Champions League.

Confronted with the 'dream team' of Koeman, Stoichkov and Romário, United responded with the best performance of their season so far, fully deserving of a 2–2 draw which ensured they held on to first place in Group A, with the same number of points as IFK Gothenburg. In their talisman's absence – Cantona still had one game to go before the end of his ban – Ince, Keane and Sharpe proved determined deputies, and United passed the most arduous test they had been presented with so far, raising hopes that they would really kick on once Éric had been restored to the side. More encouragement came their way when Blackburn were outclassed 4–2 at Ewood Park. Rovers hadn't lost at home for thirteen months, while United hadn't earned a single point from their last three away games; but, helped by Henning Berg's harsh dismissal on the stroke of half-time and Cantona's ensuing penalty, United came back within seven points of leaders Newcastle, who would be their next opponents – both in the League Cup and the Premiership.

This double-header was scheduled to take place over seventy-two hours and provided Alex Ferguson with the chance to gain the psychological ascendancy over Kevin Keegan, provided the gamble he had in mind paid off. Mindful of the physical demands that the Champions League and, later, the FA Cup would exert on his squad, he decided to squander the League Cup (which he had already won in 1992), fielding a team of youngsters such as Paul Scholes, Keith Gillespie, Nicky Butt and David Beckham, who were outclassed 2–0 at St James' Park. Three days later, however, the apprentices were back in the reserves, and Cantona reinstated in United's starting line-up for the league encounter. The score was repeated, but at the expense of Newcastle this time, who had turned up without their most prolific striker, Andy Cole, who was suffering from exhaustion. United had now climbed to third place in the table, only four points away from the Magpies, and two behind a surprisingly chirpy Nottingham Forest. But whatever satisfaction Ferguson could derive from this success was swept away in the Camp Nou on 2 November.

Barça too had played only three days beforehand, having to satisfy themselves with a lacklustre draw at Real Sociedad. In truth, United were destroyed that night, their chief tormentor being Johann Cruyff's son Jordi, whose performance so entranced the beaten manager that he brought him to Manchester two years hence on the strength of that game. Ferguson had gambled again, but failed this time. In that age of quotas, he had sacrificed Peter Schmeichel (whom Bobby Charlton had described as 'the best goalkeeper in the world' shortly before the game) in order to accommodate another 'foreigner' in Ryan Giggs. The Dane's replacement, Gary Walsh, had to pick the ball out of his net four times. With the suspended Cantona still sidelined, United created next to nothing on the rare occasions when they had the ball in their possession. 'We were well and truly slaughtered,' Ferguson admitted. As IFK had won in Turkey, he knew that, barring a miracle, his team was condemned to a sickeningly early exit of the premier tournament in European football, and this after having opened their campaign so promisingly. Éric's own frustration was two-fold: he had missed out on the opportunity to show his worth on one of the grandest stages of them all, Barcelona's home ground; and the doubts that he and many others had about Manchester United's ability to bridge the technical and tactical chasm that separated them from Europe's best clubs had received a merciless vindication. Didn't he deserve better?

Consolations could be found on the domestic front, of course, though Aston Villa were unfortunate to be beaten 2–1 in early November when, in truth, they had dominated throughout the game. This didn't prevent the Villa coach Ron Atkinson from being sacked less than a week after this cruel defeat against his old club. Cantona, playing behind Paul Scholes for the first time, had had more productive afternoons, but luckily for his side, Gary Walsh put the Catalan debacle behind him with a succession of match-saving stops. United – and Éric – remained enigmas. Uncertainty seeped through the team and the player who had made such a telling contribution to the previous season's triumphs. It seemed at times that he and they were victims of their own arrogance, as if they didn't really care about the outcome of a match, as if they were too good to be true to themselves. On better days, they could rediscover their swagger and appear unbeatable. They thrashed their City neighbours 5–0 on 10 November, their biggest win in a century of Manchester derbies. Éric provided three assists and a goal of quite breathtaking quality. He flicked a fine cross-field ball from Kanchelskis with the outside of his right boot and drove it past the

City 'keeper with his left, all in one glorious movement. He was unable to carry that new-found form into France's Euro qualifier in Poland, where *Les Bleus* recorded their third consecutive scoreless draw, but shone again when Crystal Palace capitulated 3–0 at Old Trafford in mid-November, a result that took United to the top of the table for the first time that season. For Cantona, a seventh goal in eleven Premiership matches; for United, an eighth victory in as many home league games, despite a number of injuries (Sharpe, Parker, Schmeichel, Keane and Giggs) which had struck them just before the game that would surely decide whether they had a future in Europe or not.

Cantona's return to the Champions League against IFK provided columnists with an easy 1,000 words to deliver. It was all about Éric, again, in the papers as on television. Commercial networks carried a new advertisement for Eurostar, in which the most famous of cross-Channel imports dreamily delivered a line many think (wrongly) he came up with himself: 'Does a bird who sings in a cage sing as sweetly as a bird who is free?' But the pre-match hype fell flat, as United were destroyed by the pace of Jesper Blomquist, another player who would later be brought to Old Trafford by Alex Ferguson. The Scot's team had spent the previous night in the hotel where he had celebrated his Aberdeen side's remarkable victory over Real Madrid in the 1983 Cup Winners Cup final. It didn't bring his new charges any luck. Even with Barcelona losing 2–1 away to Galatasaray, United were as good as out. Their defending had 'disgusted' Ferguson, who stopped short of making comments on the cards that had been shown to three of his players, one yellow each for Hughes and Cantona (for an ugly challenge on Jonas Bjorklund) and a red for Paul Ince. For all his indiscipline, however, Éric had also been his team's most potent weapon – not that it amounted to much: his assist for Hughes's goal came too late to alter the course of the game.

United flew back to England on flight LEI9586 in silence, and landed at 2.30 a.m. in Manchester. Chairman Martin Edwards, one of the passengers on that plane, would have to address his shareholders at the club's AGM later that day. He had much to ponder: that defeat alone had cost his club an estimated £7m. And there was the question that Rob Hughes – without a doubt the most penetrating contemporary chronicler of Éric's English career – dared ask in *The Times*: 'Is it time to say *au revoir* to Cantona?' 'I submit that the Frenchman is at the root of Manchester United's problems,' he wrote, 'as well as being the catalyst for their recent glories. There is the question of Cantona's effect on United's discipline, or rather their indiscipline. His manager has too often indulged the spiteful side of Cantona's nature.'

As the great Manchester City manager Joe Mercer said in December 1972, on the occasion of one of George Best's regular walk-outs from Old Trafford, 'The foundation of success is the strength of the weakest players. Genius is great when it is on song. It's more than a nuisance when it goes bad because it contaminates what is around it.' And the rot was spreading fast, as was shown in a rancorous 0–0 draw between Arsenal and United on 26 November. Seven players were booked, Mark Hughes sent off. Not that Arsenal were models of good behaviour themselves: their tearful playmaker Paul Merson had revealed his cocaine and alcohol addictions (twelve pints a night) a few days before this game. But there seemed to be a wild undercurrent to United's progress that couldn't be attributed only to the brutality then prevalent in the English game. Still, they could be superb when the red mist didn't descend on them, and deserved the luck that often came to their assistance: when Norwich, a fine footballing side, were beaten 1–0 in early December, United had achieved the remarkable feat of a ninth consecutive league victory at home, and without conceding a single goal. Questionable refereeing decisions had considerably eased their task that day, however: the visitors had a valid goal cancelled for a non-existent offside, and should have been awarded a penalty for a blatant foul by Gary Neville in the box. Cantona played with assurance and wit, scoring the decisive goal after combining with Brian McClair.

At no other time in his footballing life did Éric display more sharply the quasi-schizoid nature of his character on the pitch than during these months that led to the Crystal Palace explosion. He delivered another brilliant performance when Galatasaray were pulverized 4–0 in Manchester on 7 December. I should add that the Turkish champions were already out of the competition, and that the 1–1 draw that

Barcelona and IFK agreed to in the Camp Nou made this game an irrelevance. The pressure was off, and Cantona's critics would argue that this was why it was one of the very few occasions when Europe saw him at his best; at his worst too, when he petulantly hacked at the legs of his man-marker Bulent, who had dispossessed him quite legally. The referee put his name in the book.

This hiccuping season next saw him head for Trabzon in Turkey, where Azerbaijan were hosting France for a Euro qualifier, as the political situation in their country made the staging of the match there far too dangerous in UEFA's eyes. *Les Bleus* won 2–0, a mere parenthesis in the chaos that was engulfing Manchester United, who lost at home for the first time since 3 March 1994. Stan Collymore inspired Nottingham Forest to a 2–1 victory that was, again, marred by a flurry of cautions, eight in all, with Ince and Stuart Pearce lucky to escape dismissal in an ugly confrontation. Cantona also scored his ninth goal of the campaign, to no avail: Blackburn now led the Premiership by two points. Éric, 'his touch as delicate, his presence as forceful as ever', added a tenth on Boxing Day, when Chelsea were beaten 3–2 at Stamford Bridge; but he also added another booking to his collection, for time-wasting this time. A bad-tempered 1–1 draw with Leicester followed, then a shockingly violent 2–2 in Southampton on New Year's Eve, where an incensed Ferguson instructed his players to 'go for their fucking throats' at half-time, a recommendation that Cantona followed to the letter, flailing with his hands at Ken Monkou, then slapping Francis Benali (no angel he) to earn yet another caution, all this on the day Alex Ferguson had been awarded a CBE. It looked as if he had washed his hands of his players' uncontrollable behaviour.

January 1995 followed a similar pattern. There were plenty of flowing moves, spectacular goals (Éric scored another three, bringing his tally to a barely credible fourteen in twenty-two domestic games) and controversial incidents – with Cantona in the role of the victim for once, when he was punched by a Sheffield United player in the third round of the FA Cup. United rolled on with growing authority. Lesser teams (Coventry and Sheffield United) were dispatched without fuss, contenders for the title (Newcastle and Blackburn) were dealt with with vim, verve and (sometimes mindless) aggression. Newcastle were fortunate to escape with a 1–1 draw at a torrid St James' Park when Éric uncharacteristically missed two chances to wrap the game up in the final minutes. He was less generous with Rovers, the Premiership leaders, who succumbed to one of the most exhilarating goals of that English season. Ryan Giggs danced his way through Blackburn's defence on the left flank, lost the ball, then, through sheer force of will, regained it inches from the corner flag, and sent a cross to the far post which caught 'keeper Tim Flowers and everyone else by surprise. Everyone, that is, except Cantona, who had timed his run from deep to perfection. Without once breaking his stride, he met the ball with a ferocious header that crashed into the roof of the net. This was not just a magnificent goal, but also a statement. The lead Blackburn still had in the Premiership – two points, with a game in hand – seemed insignificant in the face of United's mighty performance. Give the champions a few more weeks, allow Éric to strike the same rapport with newcomer Andy Cole that he enjoyed with Ryan Giggs, and natural order would be restored. Cantona would see to it. He had always been a slow starter, a luxury car running on diesel. The more he played, the better he became. He was now tantalizingly close to his best, be it with Manchester United or with France, which he captained to an impressive 1–0 victory in the Netherlands.

No one could have guessed he would never hear '*La Marseillaise*' again in a football ground – unless English fans sang it in his honour. He would bow out of international football with a record of 20 goals in 45 games that, in terms of efficiency, is proportionally superior to that of Zinédine Zidane (31 in 108). I'll come back to the prevalent notion that Éric failed in his national team ('in' could be removed from that sentence, in the eyes of many). For the time being, it should be enough to recall these remarkable figures, and be reminded that all but one of these goals were scored from open play, and this when his managers often deployed him in a withdrawn position, as the lower base of an attacking triangle. Many injustices befell Éric Cantona throughout his career; few were less deserved.

On 22 January, an hour or so after Blackburn had been beaten thanks to his goal, Éric met Gary King in the players' car park. The faithful gopher passed him the keys to the Audi; Cantona silently took the wheel and drove back to the Novotel. His solicitor Jean-Jacques Bertrand was due to fly from Paris the very next day to discuss the terms of a new three-year contract with Manchester United. Its terms would be finalized immediately after they had played an away game that shouldn't tax them too much, as their opponents had only won one of their last ten Premiership matches. The champions had no reason to fear Crystal Palace.

Cantona songs still ring around Old Trafford in 2009. In this age when fans have shorter memories than those who filled the (much smaller) stands fifteen years ago, very few players warrant celebration of that kind so long after they've gone. You'll occasionally hear 'Rocky, Rocky, Rocky Rocastle' at Arsenal games – but that is a mourning song for a cult hero whose life was claimed by a dreadful disease before he'd reached the age of 40. Who else? I've heard Peter Osgood's name chanted at Stamford Bridge, but on one occasion only, and that was at the game that followed his death. Cantona is different. There is no tragic undertone to his songs. Singing them is another way of saying 'We are Manchester United', because, to the thousands who join in, Éric was and still is the spirit of the club.

Leading these songs – eight of them – is a man whose name is familiar to anyone associated with the club, its unofficial bard: Pete Boyle, keeper of the flame, poet after his own fashion, conductor of the Éric-worshipping choir. As long as Pete is around, no one will be allowed to forget that Cantona truly was the greatest Red Devil ever. I knew of him through a mutual friend, designer Jim Phelan, himself a Mancunian, who released a small number of records related to Manchester United on his Exotica label in the 1990s. Together with my musical mentor Mike Alway, he also played a prominent role in the conception of the Bend It! Series, which attempted a playful reconciliation of popular music and football long before it became fashionable to write dissertations about 'terrace culture'. (I had a part in these too, in one instance contributing one of my very worst songs to a homage to Éric Cantona which only completists would find worth tracking down.) Pete's own efforts – with a vocal ensemble called 'The K-Stand' – didn't strive for subtlety. He assembled a squad of drinking, chanting companions, and bellowed Old Trafford classics such as 'Éric the King' and 'The Twelve Days of Cantona' (lyrics: Pete Boyle) into a microphone. The result was rousing, chaotic or frightening, depending on which end of the supporting spectrum you found yourself.

I didn't feel completely at ease when Pete and I finally met in a Manchester pub. His friends were not the sort of people I normally associated with in London wine bars. Our phone conversations and emails had been businesslike in tone, and I'd certainly made no mention in them that my own club allegiance was not to United, but to the 'Southern ponces' of Arsenal. I thought I knew his face, as he'd made an appearance in one of the videos United sold by the hundreds of thousands to Cantona's fans. The man I bought a non-alcoholic round for (his mates favoured lager) had changed a great deal from the rather podgy character I'd seen in this film. He was much thinner, almost gaunt, and very, very intense. Soon, however, the awkwardness gave way to the camaraderie that football supporters share to a far greater degree than they're given credit for in England. Pete recounted his tales, which, fine story-teller that he is, needed no embellishment.

This was the man who'd schlepped down to Croydon in a van, and slept in it on a car park, to make sure he'd be given the very first admission ticket to Éric's appeal trial in the spring of 1995 (it is still in his possession). When Éric's sentence was commuted from a jail term to 120 hours of community service, it was he who ran out of the courthouse to exclaim: 'The King is free!' He it was again who had organized the first demonstration of support for his hero outside Old Trafford once the verdict had been announced, and had been chased away by mounted police. I saw a film of it, shot by an amateur video cameraman. There were just half a dozen supporters who chanted their slogans outside the ground. Talking to one of them was like being introduced to the very core of the Cantona cult, to the most exclusive lodge of that Temple. Well over ten years after Cantona's retirement, every weekend, Pete stood on a table in a United pub and led the beer guzzlers into another lung-bursting rendition of 'Éric the King' ('a song we used to sing for Denis Law, and which the crowd picked up on when we played in Budapest' – that would be on 15 September 1993, then).

For some, Pete might seem something of an oddball, an eccentric; but his life has a purpose: Manchester United and, more precisely, Éric Cantona, subjects he talks about with unaffected eloquence. And when he did, our table listened respectfully. This guy knew his stuff. He'd been in the same Budapest hotel as the team when they played Honved in the European Cup. He'd shot pool with Éric and Claude Boli ('in February 1994') in a Castlefield pub called the Peveril of the Peak, which most footballers would make considerable efforts to avoid. He'd then shared a drink with the two of them in Boli's home, 'just behind the Kippax'. Alex Ferguson mentioned his name in interviews.

Pete's fervour brought into sharp relief a shortcoming which is to be found in every single football biography I have come across. It is that fans have no place in them.

Players' lives and careers are told as if they were acted out in an empty theatre. How absurd! An Éric Cantona can only exist when one of his touches of genius is cheered by a roar, or when jeers greet a mistimed pass or a clumsy foul. Pete Boyle haunts Éric Cantona as much as Éric Cantona haunts Pete Boyle. It is true that Éric literally crossed the divide as no other footballer had done before him when he jumped over an advertising board to assault a Crystal Palace fan. Strikingly enough, it is that blurring of the distinction between actor and spectator which was picked on by many of his harshest critics to underline the 'unforgivable' nature of his act.

Why then are supporters erased from the game they own?

It makes no more sense than historians (I'm thinking of another Éric, Eric Hobsbawm) who tell the story of the twentieth century without once mentioning the only socio-cultural activity which linked – physically, emotionally and (arguably) spiritually – billions of human beings who passed through this epoch: football. These are the same academics who'll tear each other apart over the interpretation of some obscure data of wheat production, or will devote chapter after chapter to Socialist Realism without once wondering what could be the significance, in a totalitarian regime, of supporting Dynamo Kyiv rather than Spartak Moscow, or CSKA rather than Spartak. I'll take but one example to illustrate the foolishness, if not the folly, of deleting football from history. How can we hope to comprehend fully the 1956 Budapest Uprising if we fail to keep in mind that Puskas' team had been Olympic champions in 1952, the first team to beat England at Wembley, and were robbed of victory in the 1954 World Cup by – it has been alleged – doped-up West Germans? The pride ordinary Hungarians felt at seeing their nation beating the world's best fed their belief that an escape from the Soviet sphere of influence was possible. Their team played brave, imaginative – dare I say revolutionary – football. It fed a nation's refusal of the grim order that had been imposed on them. For Marxist and post-structuralist historians, this other 'opium of the people', football, belongs to the realm of 'superstructure', an expression of economically driven social changes, and can, therefore, be pushed aside to the touchline while the real game unfolds. This is a belittlement of football's power, a negation of its universality and its centrality to human life. Hobsbawm himself has said: 'The imagined community of millions seems more real as a team of eleven named people.' That 'seems', of course, gives his own game away.

But football writers are just as short-sighted when we espouse the profound-sounding, but ultimately silly pronouncement of French aspiring professional footballer turned philosopher Jacques Derrida: 'Beyond the touchline is nothing.' Compare with Jock Stein's 'Football is nothing without fans'. Derrida's and Stein's 'nothing' aren't the same, of course. Derrida points to the absolute nothingness that lies (or doesn't, if you wish to take this epigram seriously) beyond the pitch on which the laws of football determine human action. I play, therefore I am. By contrast, the manager's 'nothing' is an assertion of the game's essential materiality – football is primarily experienced by the senses, and a perfect strike at goal only acquires its full beauty (and signification) when it is met by the clamour of the crowd.

Some players – Nicolas Anelka is one – have confessed that, should they be given the choice, they wouldn't mind taking part in matches played in front of empty stands. Arsène Wenger once told me that the fervour of English fans 'added to' his joy of managing Arsenal. His choice of words had struck me. It was clear that what mattered most to him was the enactment of the principles he'd instilled on the training ground, which led to the full expression of collective as well as individual talent within parameters he'd defined himself. Stein shared this desire, no doubt. But, to him, 'collective' also meant 'communal'. Éric Cantona was a Steinian. This is how he described his first goal for Leeds United: 'At the exact moment when the ball entered the net, the thousands of supporters who were behind the goal seemed to dive towards the pitch.' Only in England, he said, could such 'ecstasy' be found. Only in England could he communicate (the religious connotations of that word should not be taken as a mere linguistic coincidence) with a mass of strangers whose passion he shared. Some will point time and again to the honours he failed to win on the international stage and argue that their absence invalidates his claim to greatness. They are misguided. Stanley Matthews won just the one FA Cup medal. George Best never played in the World Cup or the European Championships. Yachine had a poor tournament in 1966. Yet all three were undoubted 'greats', and not just because of their unique gifts. They were able to establish an emotional link with the fans that more decorated players found elusive or even saw as a distraction. Go to Old Trafford, and ask anyone: who of David Beckham (ten years at the club, European champion in 1999, six times a Premier League winner) and Éric Cantona (who spent less than half as long in Manchester, and consistently underperformed in Europe) they consider to be a 'great' or a 'legend' of United? Éric, of course. The fans know a 'great' when they see one – they should know: without them, greatness is unattainable. Beyond the touchline is everything.

16

About to face the FA's disciplinary committee.

SELHURST PARK

Sports photographers didn't travel light in 1995. Before digital technology and the internet, they relied on cumbersome mobile equipment, which could only be brought to the stadium in a customized van. Steve Lindsell had arrived at Selhurst Park in one of those, expecting this Premier League evening to pan out as other such evenings normally did, arriving early at the ground, putting on the customary bib, setting his cameras in position, snapping, retiring to the lab, sending his photographs on the wire, going home. But on that night of 25 January, at precisely 9 p.m., his routine was shaken by one of the most extraordinary scenes ever witnessed in an English sporting arena: the infamous 'kung-fu kick' (*ossoto-gari* or *mashawa-gari*? The question still divides Cantona fanatics on internet forums) which ensured Cantona's place in the pantheon of footballing villains. The next day, every newspaper in the country featured the same picture on their front page in their first edition. Lindsell, who took it, had no idea that it would become such a powerful emblem – maybe *the* emblem – of Cantona's troubled career.

It had been a fairly uneventful game up to that point. Palace had set out to disturb United's usual rhythm, and largely succeeded. Defender Richard Shaw (who was voted Palace's 'player of the year' at the end of the season) had been given the task of shadowing Cantona, and was acquitting himself well, much to Éric's annoyance, as the game's referee, Alan Wilkie, seemed to turn a blind eye to the crafty knocks Shaw was landing on his shins on and off the ball. 'No yellow cards, then?' he enquired of the official as they walked back to the dressing-room at half-time. In the tunnel, just as the game was about to restart, Wilkie was asked the question again by a seemingly calm Cantona, and then, in typically more robust language, by an irate Alex Ferguson: 'Why don't you do your fucking job?' The referee ignored them. In the 61st minute of the game, Shaw took advantage of Wilkie turning his back to kick Éric again. The foul had gone unnoticed by the official, but Cantona's retaliation – a kick of his own – hadn't escaped his assistant Eddie Walsh's attention. Another red card was the unavoidable consequence of his flash of temper, of which there had been so many already in the previous months: it was the fifth time Éric had been dismissed in his three years in England, an astonishingly high figure for an attacking player, especially if one bears in mind that none of these dismissals occurred while he played for Leeds United, and that he also collected sixteen cautions during the same period.

The long walk back to the dressing-room was a familiar one to him. He hardly remonstrated. He walked away, turned round after a few steps, looked Wilkie straight in the eye and pulled his collar down, the surest means to indicate he knew his game was over, and that he did not question the validity of the decision. Lindsell trained his camera on the player, who was departing from the pitch at an even pace, and was now going past the dugout where Alex Ferguson stood, looking the other way.

'I was positioned on the opposite side of the ground,' Lindsell told me, 'just following Cantona after his dismissal. Then, all of a sudden, he jumped over the fence and kicked that guy! I snapped, and snapped again. I thought I had a good picture, but couldn't imagine the impact it would have. I went to my van outside Selhurst Park, printed the roll, which must have taken me 15 to 20 minutes, then sent the pictures. The first paper to receive them was the *Daily Mirror*. But it was only the day afterwards that all hell broke loose.'

Images of the incident itself have been played and replayed so often that it seems almost pointless to describe it again in detail. A snarling young man rushed down eleven rows of the stand to shout abuse at Cantona. He later, and quite ludicrously, claimed (in the *Sun*, who paid him for his account of the confrontation) to have said something along the lines of: 'Off you go, Cantona – it's an early bath for you!' According to the numerous eyewitnesses who enjoyed tabloid fame after the explosion, the words that came out of his distorted face were closer to: 'Fuck off, you motherfucking French bastard!' according to Luke Beckley, who was eight at the time.

With his cropped hair, pasty skin and tight-fitting black jacket, Matthew Simmons could have come straight from central casting, the archetypal white thug. But Cantona's victim was no actor. The *Mirror* soon revealed that 'Simmons, twenty, of Kynaston Avenue, Thornton Heath, South London, has a conviction for assault with intent to rob. In 1992, he'd been fined £100 and placed on two years' probation after striking a petrol station cashier.' The cashier in question was a young Sri Lankan who had escaped serious head injuries when the three-foot spanner wielded by Simmons slipped and struck him on the shoulder instead. Quite amusingly, his aggressor was also a qualified referee and, less amusingly, a BNP and National Front sympathizer. Éric had at least been lucky enough to pick on someone who could expect little sympathy from public opinion, or the courts.

'Always be the first to hit! It'll surprise the other,' Albert Cantona had instructed his son. At Auxerre Éric had put this teaching into practice when confronted by a whole team intent on making him pay for an assault on one of their players. He had done the same thing at Martigues when provoked by a foul-mouthed section of the crowd, and Michel Der Zakarian had learnt to his cost that Cantona could do it on the pitch too.

But Selhurst Park was different. From the initial foul to the moment when, escorted by Peter Schmeichel, a terrified Crystal Palace steward named Jim Page, and United's kitman Norman Davies,* Cantona finally entered the tunnel, 88 seconds had elapsed, seconds that felt like an eternity. Cantona had had time to compose himself. He looked as inscrutable as ever as he left the field of play, his chest puffed up, his head held high, apparently deaf to the taunts of the crowd. Why he suddenly lunged over the advertising boards he has never been able to

---

* Known as 'Vaseline' to Manchester United players after his first attempt at getting hold of Cantona failed. Davies made sure to keep the No. 7 shirt Éric was wearing on that night, and passed it on to the curator of the Old Trafford museum.

explain. In 2004, in one of the best interviews he has ever given to the British press, he told Darren Tullett of the *Observer* how, if there hadn't been a barrier, he would have just 'steamed in with [his] fists'. 'You know,' he went on, 'you meet thousands of people like him. And how things turn out can hinge on the precise moment you run into them. If I'd met that guy on another day, things may have happened very differently even if he had said exactly the same things. Life is weird like that. You're on a tightrope every day.' Éric then unconvincingly attempted to justify himself, with the words of a unrepentant egotist. 'The most important thing to me is that I was who I was. I was myself. Even if you understood why you did something, it doesn't mean you won't go and do the same thing tomorrow. The best thing you can do is to take a step back and laugh at yourself. A bit of self-derision.'

Cantona took a while to see things in that light-hearted way. According to Page and Davies, he was 'bloody angry'. So much so that the latter had to position himself at the door of the dressing-room to avoid another, even more dramatic fracas. 'He was furious. He wanted to go out again . . . I locked the door and told him: "If you want to go back on the pitch, you'll have to go over my body, and break the door down."' Once Cantona had recovered some of his composure, Davies brewed some tea for him. The English panacea worked on this occasion. Cantona sipped his cup and headed for the showers without another word being exchanged between the two men. By the time the game had ended in a 1–1 draw, according to Ryan Giggs's recollection, 'Éric wasn't agitated', either in the dressing-room or on the plane that took the team back to Manchester late that night. 'Nothing was said because none of us, the gaffer included, realized the seriousness of what had gone on. Word hadn't got through, and Éric was giving nothing away.'

As he confided to Erik Bielderman many years later, Alex Ferguson failed to realize the 'seriousness' of the situation because he had no clear idea of what had happened after the actual sending-off. 'I wasn't looking at him when he left the pitch. I was focusing on how to reorganize the team tactically, ten versus eleven. I was told [what happened] and, once back at home, my son Jason asked me: "Do you want to see the pictures? I've recorded the game." I refused and went to bed. Sleep wouldn't come. I got up around 3–4 in the morning, and I saw. The shock was huge . . .'

As he wrote in his diary, 'My initial feeling was for letting Éric go. I felt that this time the good name of Manchester United demanded strong action. The club is bigger than any individual.' But Ferguson realized how much Cantona had contributed to making it 'big' again.

'I then thought about a call a friend had given me on our way back from London [*as Ferguson was driving home from Manchester airport*]. We were thinking about what we could do about the media hullabaloo and the punishment that would follow. He told me: "You remember our chat about John McEnroe? I explained to you that Éric and him are the same. John exploded on court, insulted referees, swore against himself. But, off the court, he can be charming. Éric is the same. This guy is fantastic. Don't give up, Alex!"' This friend was a lifelong supporter of Manchester United, Sir Richard Greenbury, who held the positions of chief executive and chairman of Marks & Spencer plc from 1988 till 1999. Ferguson reassured the businessman. He wouldn't let Cantona down.

'The next day,', he went on to tell *L'Équipe Magazine*, 'at breakfast, I told everybody: "We're backing Éric. He's our player. The FA mustn't have his skin. He made a mistake. We all make mistakes." Éric knew I was on his side. He knew he could count on me. He needed someone to help him, someone whom he could trust, who'd support him. I fulfilled this mission.'

And how. As Roy Keane later told Eamon Dunphy: 'I don't think any other football man would have demonstrated the skill, resolve and strength that Alex Ferguson did *managing* the Cantona affair.'

What Ferguson didn't say is that, shortly after the final whistle, referee Wilkie saw an apoplectic Manchester United manager storm into his dressing-room. 'It's all your fucking fault! If you'd done your fucking job this wouldn't have happened!' According to Ferguson's biographer Michael Crick, a policeman had to intervene to stop the stream of abuse and drag the incensed Scot out of the referee's quarters. In many instances, Ferguson's tirades directed at anything that represents the FA's authority, and particularly referees, have been little more than what the tabloids are fond of calling 'mind games', attempts to intimidate officials to gain the upper hand in matches to come. But not in this case. Over the preceding season-and-a-half, his players had stepped over the line with alarming regularity – and viciousness. Manchester United, arrogant Manchester United, ran the risk of earning a reputation for gamesmanship and brutality that would alienate the rest of the footballing world. Other sides (Don Revie's Leeds United springs to mind) had paid a heavy price for such a reputation; Ferguson was aware of that and, despite a well-documented dressing-down of the worst culprits a year before, had failed to throw enough water on the fire raging in his dressing-room. Wilkie bore the brunt of his anger, in the absence of a better target. Ferguson had yet to see Lindsell's photograph that would be on every front page a few hours hence. But, instinctively, he knew. This would be a crisis of enormous, preposterous proportions.

Were there any mitigating circumstances to Éric's moment of madness? Maybe. Ferguson was puzzled enough to have his player tested for hypoglycemia, after a doctor had suggested to him that a low level of glucose in the bloodstream might have triggered the explosion. The test failed to show any proof that this had been the case. More to the point, no one knew at the time that Éric's father Albert had been laid low by a very serious viral infection, which, according to Guy Roux, could have had serious consequences, and had obviously caused tremendous anxiety within the family. As a result, the head of the clan had to be hospitalized in Marseilles for several weeks at the time of the incident. Éric, however, never sought to make an excuse of this. 'I didn't really analyse the situation until the day afterwards,' he said in 2007. 'I didn't know what had happened, and what was going to happen. I wasn't aware of much. One thing was for sure: I wasn't proud of myself. The hooligan who told me: "French son of a whore", I'd heard him 50 billion times. On that day, I didn't react like I'd reacted on other occasions. Why? I've never found an answer to this myself.'

Shocking as Cantona's actions had been, no one could have predicted the near hysteria that swept over the whole country within a few hours of the BBC opening its news bulletin with images of a crazed Éric ploughing into the crowd. Every publication in England seemingly tried to outdo the others in their zeal to condemn Cantona. What he had done was 'scandalous', 'unforgivable', 'unprecedented'. Had not Chief Superintendent Terry Collins, who was in charge of security at the match, said: 'I've never seen anything like it!', adding that 'There could have been a riot' for good measure?

In truth, Cantona was not the first sportsman to administer rough justice to a foul-mouthed heckler. In the early 1930s 'Dixie' Dean had walloped a fan who had insulted him – probably about the swarthy complexion to which he owed his nickname – at the end of an Everton–Spurs Cup game. A policeman stood nearby. Instead of escorting the great centre-forward to the station, he shook his hand, saying: 'That was a beauty, but I never saw it.' Playing before the age of television had its advantages. But there must have been cameras there when, in 1978, Birmingham City's Alberto Tarantini tore into some of his own supporters at the end of a game against Manchester United. Nobody thought much of it, however, and no punishment ensued. Similarly, no action was taken against a rugby player named Gerald Cordle who, playing for Cardiff in 1987, brawled with a supporter of Aberavon Quins. But Dean, Tarantini and Cordle did not have the track record of Éric Cantona, and none of these offenders satisfied the criteria required to become a stereotype, which is what the Marseillais had been ever since he arrived in England; one of them played the gentlemen's game, rugby, where physical violence is viewed with benignity, and is, even now, at least in the minds of some, perversely ennobled as proof of the competitors' manliness.

Ten years after the Heysel disaster, English football had developed an acute sensitivity to anything that could taint its efforts to purge the game of hooliganism. The outside world held even starker views on the periodic outbursts of brutality that still punctuated the football season. Cantona had not just kicked a thug; he had stirred demons that had not yet been put to sleep, he had twisted a blade in a seeping wound.

By squaring up to a foreigner, English football could at least pretend it was 'doing the right thing' without tarnishing the new image it was creating for itself. It would have been far more difficult, and painful, to address two other incidents which took place on the very same night, and which went virtually unnoticed in the furore created by Cantona.

Wimbledon manager Joe Kinnear escaped with a mere caution after verbally and physically abusing referee Mike Reed during a 2–1 defeat to Newcastle. Even more seriously, the Aston Villa goalkeeper, Mark Bosnich, committed, in my opinion, one of the worst premeditated assaults on an opposition player seen on a football field since Harald Schumacher nearly decapitated Patrick Battiston in a famed France–Germany World Cup semi-final, thirteen years previously. Bosnich, who had carelessly left his line, took out Tottenham's Jürgen Klinsmann with a dreadful knees-first lunge that hit the German striker full on the head. Klinsmann, unconscious, had to be carried off on a stretcher and taken to hospital where, fortunately, no lasting damage was detected. Bosnich should have been red-carded and struck with a long ban. Instead of which he was allowed to continue playing, and was not even cautioned. The English press ran a couple of mildly outraged stories in the immediate aftermath of the assault, then promptly forgot it all. It had a far better target to aim at, and wasn't short of volunteers to join in the very public execution of Éric Cantona.

The squeaky-clean Gary Lineker opened the shooting season on the BBC's *Sportsnight* with a toe-curling attempt at a 'joke': 'He's completely lost it, he lost *les* marbles.' Microphones were put under the nose of past Manchester United legends, such as Alex Stepney ('I'm absolutely disgusted that a man of his stature should lower himself to that. He shouldn't play for United any more'), Bill Foulkes ('Going into the crowd is behaving like a hooligan – that's nothing to do with sport. He lost control of himself, and that's very sad to see . . . but Éric is French – they are different to us and he reacts differently') and Shay Brennan ('Sir Matt Busby would have hated anything like this'). The same sanctimonious tune was sung in near unison. In fairness, there were a few more measured comments too, such as Pat Crerand's observation that it was 'very difficult to make excuses for Éric, but the fan got off his seat and had a go at him. I wonder what all these guys in yellow coats [were] doing at Crystal Palace. Are they just along for a night out?', a point of view echoed by Jimmy Greaves, who quite rightly wondered how it was that a couple of banknotes did not just buy a ticket, but also a licence to use the filthiest language imaginable with complete impunity.

Discordant notes of this kind were not heard often, however, and were even more rarely amplified by the media; the fire under the story had to be stoked, even if it took dubious stunts to achieve it. Channel 4's trashy *The Word* sent a dozen teenagers to sing 'peace songs' in Cantona's drive. A young girl, encouraged by presenter Terry Christian, marched up to his house with a bunch of flowers. The door stayed shut, but Channel 4 had its story. The redtops tracked down the spectators who had been next to Simmons when he unleashed his verbal volley, turning one of them, hotel manageress Cathy Churchman (who had come to the game with her two children) into some sort of a celebrity (she turned down an invitation to be a guest on the prime-time TV show *Kilroy* as a result, and later became a sponsor of Crystal Palace FC). In the supposedly more reserved broadsheets, page upon page was devoted to new 'insights' into the troubled character of Cantona, to lengthy and error-ridden accounts of his past misdemeanours, cut-and-pasted from unchecked sources. For weeks, indeed for months, a torrent of words flooded the opinion columns as well as the front and back pages of every single paper in the country, without exception.

Even the *Daily Telegraph* succumbed to Cantona fever, and in an astonishing way. It published two editorials on 28 January. The first was devoted to the fiftieth anniversary of the liberation of Auschwitz; the second, in all seriousness, to Cantona's troubles. It actually was a fine piece of writing, from which the conclusion is worth quoting: 'It has been said that if he [Cantona] had kicked a Leeds or a Newcastle United fan during an away match, he would not have left the stadium alive. That, and not the loutish behaviour of one brilliant but errant player, indicates the deep-seated problem with football.' But if the editorial deserved praise for its thoughtfulness, what could be said of the very idea of juxtaposing the Holocaust with 'the loutish behaviour of one brilliant but errant player'? The notoriously prickly readers of the *Telegraph* didn't complain, though. A number of them immediately removed Cantona from their Fantasy Football League teams (a story that made the front page of the daily), and that was that. The moral high ground is a comfortable place to occupy, and football correspondents slumped in their armchairs with ease.

The 'I-told-you-sos' reminded their readers of how they had predicted that it would all end in tears. Stern headmaster types tut-tutted with a hint of melancholy that the prodigiously gifted Frenchman had betrayed the trust his manager had placed in him. Nonetheless, Alex Ferguson had to shoulder some responsibility for his favourite player's appalling disciplinary record. He had let Cantona get away with numerous breaches of the club's code of behaviour, not out of weakness – most definitely *not* out of weakness – but because he was rightly convinced that there was no better way to guarantee his genius's loyalty. The 'Can-opener' had to retain its sharpness. But it could cut both ways, and Ferguson must have known it. Among the many motives that lie behind his decision to support Éric through thick and thin over the coming months, a place should be found for an admission of partial guilt, and the desire to expiate it. Another, of course, and a far more potent one at that, was plain self-interest. The club's former manager Tommy Docherty asserted that 'Cantona should have been sacked by the club. United's action is all about the perpetrator, not the crime.' He bitterly recalled how he himself 'had been sacked by Martin Edwards for falling in love with a beautiful lady' whom he was still married to, two decades later, while 'they closed ranks around [Cantona]'. Why? 'Because the club sees money. You go to Manchester now, the shirts with his name on the back are flying out of the shops. They've made a martyr out of him.'

More immediately, a Manchester United side deprived of its main attacking threat was far less likely to catch up with Blackburn Rovers, who still led the league. The stock exchange delivered its verdict (£3m was wiped off the club's value the day after the incident, when the shares dropped 5p to £1.26), and the bookmakers agreed with it. They lengthened the odds for Ferguson's team to retain its title from 7/2 to 9/2, joint favourites. Thirty-six hours after Cantona had been sent off, Graham Sharpe, a spokesman for William Hill, announced that not a single bet of £10 or more had been placed on United to win the FA Cup or the Premiership since the incident. In the light of the FA's first statement ('charges of improper conduct and of bringing the game into disrepute will inevitably and swiftly follow'), it was obvious that a lengthy ban was to be expected. But how long would it be?

Manchester United hoped that, by acting quickly, they would be able to defuse the situation enough for the FA to resist the temptation of making an example of Cantona. The man in charge at Lancaster Gate, chief executive Graham Kelly, had led them to believe this could be the case when he faced the media on 26 January. 'What happened was a stain on the game,' he said. 'If any offence is proved [*sic*], the player concerned is bound to face a severe punishment. The FA does not have the power to impose immediate suspension, but we have been in contact with Manchester United throughout the day and are confident that they will be responding in a proper manner.' He carried on in that vein for a while, until his words felt less important than his willingness to repeat them ad nauseam. There was real menace behind the conciliatory tone of his message to the club. 'I gave a clear indication at the start of the day that we expected Manchester United to come out strongly and unequivocally. We understand they are going to do that. We are confident that Manchester United will meet their responsibilities, not just to their own club, but to the widest interests of the game.' Éric had by now been charged by the Football Association, and was given fourteen days to respond. What's more, after two fans had made formal allegations of assault, he was also the subject of an investigation by Scotland Yard. The situation was already out of United's control. A crash-landing couldn't be avoided. All that could be hoped was that Éric would be a survivor when he could be pulled out of the wreck.

The day passed with innumerable telephone conversations between Alex Ferguson, Martin Edwards and other members of United's board. It was agreed to hold an emergency meeting in a luxury Cheshire hotel that night, at which Alex Ferguson was joined by all of the club's top brass. Éric's offence was serious enough to warrant an annulment of his contract, and some of the men present at Alderley Edge had initially felt that no other response could be envisaged, Alex Ferguson among them. One should keep in mind that football was a less forgiving environment then than it is now, when convicted thugs like Joey Barton are offered an unlimited number of 'last chances', despite breaking the game's rules and the law of the land in far more disgraceful a fashion than Éric did. Soon, however, a consensus was reached in Cantona's case. Financial considerations of the kind Docherty referred to may have played their part, although it was far too early in the scandal to guess that the club would, indeed, make millions out of its player's plight and subsequent 'redemption'. Manchester United would not please its rivals by sacking Éric in order to claim moral supremacy.

The in-house trial of Éric Cantona became an exercise in damage limitation. United had to second-guess the FA's intentions, and come up with a punishment that would be severe enough to earn the governing body's respect in order to emerge from this unholy mess with the club's reputation enhanced. Private encouragement was received from Lancaster Gate: should the club act in suitably decisive fashion, the FA would sanction its decision, and the matter would be laid to rest with as little fuss as possible. That, at least, is what United understood. Éric himself was completely unaware of what was happening 150 miles away, and behaved as if nothing had happened. While Isabelle and Raphaël were locked in their semi-detached Boothstown home, besieged by newspapermen and photographers, only opening the door to accept a bunch of flowers sent by an anonymous fan, he walked out through a explosion of flashbulbs, wearing an improbable jumper adorned with, among other things, skulls and bones, got into his Audi without a word, and made his way to United's training ground. A few hours later, disbelieving shop assistants at the club's megastore saw him buying a replica of his own shirt – complete with his name on the back – for his son. 'He walked around as if he didn't have a care in the world,' one bewildered bystander said. This was, of course, a Cantona-esque way of showing the world that he, the son of Albert *et* Éléonore, was above all this nonsense. This display of calculated coolness under fire nearly landed him in serious trouble in the evening when, taking a stroll in Manchester city centre, upon leaving the bar of the Cornerhouse arts centre in the company of an unidentified friend, he came across six young men in suits, who started abusing him verbally in the street, quite violently, for several minutes. Cantona didn't flinch, shrugged his shoulders, and walked back to the same bar, where he had a few more drinks, signing autographs for other customers with his usual good grace. 'Whatever you may think, I can keep my nerve when I want to', was the not-too-subtle message he had set out to communicate to others. Privately, though, he was fully aware of the gravity of his situation, and his nonchalant behaviour may well have been a means of reassuring himself that life, somehow, would carry on as before. It couldn't, of course.

His fate was made public the next morning, when the media assembled to listen to Martin Edwards (Cantona himself received official confirmation of his punishment from a bailiff). The disgraced footballer would play no further part in United's season. He would miss a minimum of sixteen games, and a maximum of twenty, should his team reach the FA Cup final, and the club had fined him two weeks' wages (£10,800, not £20,000 as reported at the time). Edwards justified the club's decisions in the high-minded language that is to be expected in such circumstances: 'The game is bigger than Manchester United, and Manchester United is bigger than Éric Cantona. [. . .] We have proved here that the reputation of Manchester United is above trophies.' There was, however, a thinly disguised promise to Éric in his chairman's message: 'At some stage, we might wish to include him in [practice] matches to maintain his fitness and sanity, [but] that should not happen for a few weeks.'

United were playing a risky game. On one hand, they had fulfilled their promise to the FA, and hit their biggest star as hard as they had said they would: there was no precedent to a punishment of such magnitude in the recent history of the game. It was also hoped that the speed and harshness with which Cantona had been dealt by his club could persuade the criminal justice system to show leniency in its dealings with the player, and maybe even avoid an appearance in court. On the other, by suggesting that Cantona would be allowed to carry on training with his teammates, and even take part in games of an unspecified nature, the United board, wilfully or not, was forcing the FA's hand, opening the door for its disciplinary commission to extend the ban to *all* matches. Should they do so, Cantona's resentment might switch from his employers to the governing body, a neat reversal of responsibility in United's view.

One can see the logic behind this carefully worked-out strategy. Once a decision had been reached to keep Cantona on United's books (a decision that 82 per cent of the club's fans agreed with, according to a poll commissioned by the *Manchester Evening News*), placating the notoriously volatile individual was no less a priority than satisfying the public's opinion and the FA's thirst for 'justice'. By his own account, Éric was a particularly difficult man to live with when deprived of football, be it through suspension or injury. This is how he described his state of mind when forced to sit out two months of a season after the ball-throwing incident that ended his career at Nîmes:

> My body and my head were so completely accustomed to that physical exercise which comes from training and football effort. I was deprived of that motivation and that thirst which make you surpass yourself. I was deprived of the need to work and of that energy you take with you to the stadium. I missed everything, the smells and the atmosphere of the dressing-room, the feeling of belonging to a group, of winning together. I had need for air, for space . . . and I needed the ball.

Whether he played or not, Éric still needed to be managed. Should United fail to care for him and, more importantly, to convince him that they *did* care, for the man as well as for the footballer, others would step in. Rumours already circulated of a departure from England to Barcelona, where Romário had just left to return to Brazil. More seriously, everyone in football knew that Internazionale were circling in the water, waiting for the player to be thrown overboard in time for them to pounce when the Italian transfer market reopened in a few weeks' time. Barring separate action from an international body, an FA ban would only be enforceable in England, and Cantona would be free to play for the *interisti* as soon as a deal was reached. Martin Edwards later confirmed that, hours before the game at Selhurst Park, two emissaries of the *nerazzuri* (a young Massimo Moratti, shortly to become the Milanese club's chairman, a position he still holds today, and his advisor Paolo Taveggia) had met him to discuss Cantona's transfer to San Siro. They later watched the game from the relative comfort of the Selhurst Park directors' box, sitting next Edwards and Éric's solicitor Jean-Jacques Bertrand. 'We had a cup of coffee and a nice little chat,' the United chairman said, 'but it was only out of pure courtesy. I told them that none of the players they were interested in were for sale.' The players in question were Paul Ince – who would indeed join Inter six months later – and Cantona, then valued at £5m. Éric knew of Moratti's interest, and was keener to listen to his proposals than he cared to admit once his future at Old Trafford had been secured. As several members of his close entourage assured me, United's repeated failures in Europe had led Cantona to wonder what could have been if, six-and-a-half years earlier, he had instructed his agents to open negotiations with AC Milan instead of signing for Marseille. Inter could not pretend to be a force on a par with Silvio Berlusconi's team, but it had huge resources at its disposal, and clearly thought of Cantona as a potential catalyst for the club's transformation. To United, Éric's violent outburst was a near catastrophe; to Inter, it was more of an opportunity, and Alex Ferguson knew it. But the United manager also knew that, should he support Éric unconditionally, the surrogate son could never find in himself the strength (or, in his eyes, the weakness) to betray the surrogate father. Cantona had by then transferred so much love on to his elder that ignoring the hand offered to him and running away, to Italy or elsewhere, would have turned Éric into a defenceless child again, alone in a terrifying wilderness.

Hour after hour, it seemed, fresh blows rained in. Éric had unquestionably been a magnificent servant of the French national team for the past two-and-a-half seasons. He had swallowed the huge disappointment of a pitiful Euro 92 better than most, and, after an initial period of rejection, following Michel Platini's resignation from his managerial post, had developed a close relationship with France's new coach Gérard Houllier. The supposed 'big player of small games, and small player of big ones' had put his head on the block when others played the frightened tortoise and withdrew into their shells. In his quiet, unfussy way, he had proved to be a fine captain of the national side. It is often forgotten how important a role he played in the renaissance of *Les Bleus* after the door to the 1994 World Cup had been slammed shut in their faces by Bulgaria. It's true that Cantona may not have been the spark that jump-started Aimé Jacquet's world champions-to-be of 1998. But when others jumped ship, he stood firm. He provided the all-important link between two generations of players, and if he could not be held responsible for the failure of the first, neither should he be airbrushed out of the success of the next. His selfless attitude, the quality of his performances and his *esprit de corps* had earned him many friends within the 'family' of French football, but almost exclusively among fellow players and the technical staff.

It was a different matter in the upper echelons of the administration – the '*idiots*' for whom he had nothing but scorn. The suits he had been lambasting for years in his interviews were given a perfect excuse to exact revenge upon him after the Selhurst Park explosion, which got almost as much coverage in France as it did on the other side of the Channel. FIFA, though cheered on by Cantona's bloodthirstiest critics, showed no immediate inclination to issue their own ban, indicating they would only consider one at the express request of the English FA. The panjandrums of the French Federation could have taken a firm stance without dumping the national team's skipper in the dustbin the way they did. It appears they wavered at first, but not for long. Their chairman, Claude Simonnet, said: 'Éric Cantona was captain yesterday, but I can't say if he will be tomorrow.' Almost in the same breath, he added: 'I am stunned at such behaviour, which is against all sporting ethics. The seriousness of the situation forces me to consider this attitude as incompatible with what is expected of a captain of the national team's colours.' There was no talk of a disciplinary hearing. Éric was tried, convicted and sentenced *in absentia.* He was stripped of the captaincy. Cantona's partisans could almost hear the sound of Capitaine Dreyfus's sword being broken in the courtyard of a barracks. And if the decision itself wouldn't come as a surprise to the culprit, the manner in which it had been reached and made public caused him a great deal of pain. That same day – 27 January – he had called the chairman of the French League, Noel Le Graët,* one of the few administrators he held in some regard, to convey the bitterness he felt at being 'hounded and lynched by the

* Le Graët, currently Guingamps' chairman, had shown great personal courage in instigating the inquiry that had led to Tapie's indictment, following the already mentioned 'OM-VA' scandal in 1993.

press'. The rest of the world should forgive him, he said. Le Graët might have been sympathetic to Cantona, but what could he do? Éric's future had been decided by men whose legitimacy he had torn to shreds in language of the most unequivocal kind. This was pay-back time.

Back in England, where Éric was keeping the lowest of profiles, the media frenzy showed no sign of abating. Psychologists were brought in to enlighten the reading public, in much the same way old generals are pulled out of retirement by the BBC when a conflict erupts in some far-flung country. No one expects them to do much beyond fulfilling a quasi-decorative function. The *Telegraph* ushered in John Syer, who had worked with Spurs for five years in the 1980s, and one Dr Dave Collins, lecturer at Manchester Metropolitan University, who argued that 'Cantona may have found from previous experience that by acting aggressively he gained some advantage, which would make him more likely to do it again. If I'm Vinnie Jones, for example, and I keep seeing my name in the paper all the time, then I'm getting rewarded by fame, or maybe infamy, but at least some sort of respect which I personally find rewarding. Cantona appears more complex than Jones: we hear he is a musician, philosopher, artist and poet. So the reward he seeks is likely to be more complicated.' What this reward could be Dr Collins did not specify. The *Mail on Sunday* dispatched a reporter to Marseilles, whose brief was to dig out clues to Éric's wildness in his childhood. It's fair to say that the locals enjoyed the attention of the *Mail*'s envoy. They spoke a lot, but said little. Jean Olive, the father of one Brigitte Quere, a girl who had known Éric when he was a schoolboy, contributed the revelation that 'Éric's father pushed him with his football and everything else. He was very strict. Even when Éric came to eat with us, he had to be back *at a certain time*.' It is no wonder that, when piffle of that kind was devoured by millions, the father himself felt puzzled. A local television crew parked its van in front of Albert's home in the Hautes-Alpes. After having defended Éric with splendid one-eyedness ('Everyone knows it is unfair'), he sent the journalists away with: 'When my son plays well, you never come here. And now, you're running! Put away that microphone, because, with the fur around it, it looks like a rabbit's tail, and rabbits – I – shoot them!' The crew withdrew.

In retrospect, it is tempting to see in this extravagant pursuit of pseudo-information a defining moment in the history of the English Premier League, as it mutated from a souped-up version of the old championship into a bloated media machine depending on the production of news as well as the scoring of goals to feed its hunger for growth and money. It is now customary for broadsheet newspapers to devote pages by the dozen (and supplements) to transfer rumours, micro-incidents in the lives of Premiership stars and the like. Back in January 1995, most so-called 'quality' papers still distanced themselves from such trivia. Games of secondary importance sometimes went unreported; Monday editions, for example, featured perfunctory accounts of the matches that took place on the Saturday and were sometimes only mentioned *en passant* in a lead article or a review of the weekend's action. Nobody seemed to care about the cost of a Newcastle striker's wedding, and *Hello!* magazine (launched in 1988 in the UK, while its competitor *OK!* waited until 1996 to become a weekly) showed little inclination to pay six-figure sums to footballers willing to invite its photographers to the nuptials.

With Cantona – who never allowed publications of that kind into his own home – all this changed, one is tempted to add, overnight, on 25 January 1995. With one eye on the circulation figures and the other on many of their staff who resented the cheapening of their profession, editors driven by the fear of losing out to competitors oversaw the transition from investigative journalism to mere gossip, while Sky television engineers screwed yet more satellite dishes on the fronts of yet more English homes. Cantona himself was in no way an architect of this transformation, and part of him hated it. But he was also a significant agent for change, and if his conscience was stirred by qualms about pocketing advertisers' fees, he knew how to silence these. His charisma, his exoticism, his excesses gave a veneer of relevance to the pursuit of the inconsequential, if not the meaningless. Offered a chance to explore the gutter press's hunting grounds, the more respectable British papers went in with all guns blazing. If Cantona was not a ringmaster in the Premiership circus, he must at least be considered its first true star attraction.

Cantona's main sponsor, Nike, immediately understood how the disgrace of its figurehead could be put to good use. Its famous posters ('66 was a great year for English football. Éric was born') were not taken down from Matt Busby Way. Its reps had noticed a surge in the sales of Cantona replica shirts, thousands of which found buyers in the week following the Selhurst Park incident. 'Éric's deal will not be affected,' they announced on the 27th. You bet – on the morning after the assault, the *Daily Record* had printed on its front page a picture of a Nike (rugby!) boot, accompanied by the headline 'LETHAL WEAPON'. How much is publicity of that kind worth? The multinational corporation had almost immediately sensed how a sizeable part of public opinion had mellowed towards Éric once the initial shock of his assault on Matthew Simmons had receded, and would later exploit the fracas in characteristically unapologetic style, with a TV advertisement in which Cantona could be heard saying, 'I apologize for my mistakes . . . at Selhurst Park . . .' (in case you are wondering, the punchline was: 'I failed to score a hat-trick. I promise I'll never do it again'). Provocatively, they went on with another advertisement, which was only shown in cinemas because of the coarseness of Éric's language: 'I have been punished for striking a goalkeeper, for spitting at supporters, for throwing my shirt at a referee, for calling my manager a bag of shit. I called those who judged me a bunch of idiots. I thought I might have trouble finding a sponsor.' No, not in an age when Richard Kurt, a regular contributor to the Manchester United fanzine *The Red Issue*, could write: 'Football needs the Cantonas as much as the Linekers – the Establishment might not admit it, but this is an entertainment industry that thrives as much on controversy and bad deeds as it does on good play and clean living. Brawls, bugs, drugs, and karate – we love 'em all. You can save your family values for the tennis club and the PC Nineties.' The mainstream media were trailing behind their consumers, and their ferociousness contributed heavily to a shift in the public perception of Éric's outburst, and of how it should be dealt with by the authorities.

The lunatic was turning into two of the British public's favourite pets: the underdog, and the scapegoat. Within twenty-four hours of 'the incident, hawkers were displaying what can only be described as 'commemorative' Cantona T-shirts, which had been manufactured by so-called 'swag workers' – small companies which specialize in the speedy production of instant memorabilia. It was they – not Manchester United fans – who were responsible for slogans such as 'Rebel with a cause' and 'I'll be back', which they emblazoned on their rags. Others would soon follow. One of them featured Simmons' face, (correct) address and (correct) telephone number, together with the caption 'Wanted for treason'; and whatever one may think of the character or former exploits of Éric's victim, his further vilification left a distinctly bitter taste in the mouth. Simmons paid a very heavy price for what he did and, especially, to whom he did it. He sold his story to the *Sun*, yes, a foolish act he soon regretted. But with no money, no home to hide in other than his mother's flat, no pub he could have a pint in without being recognized and provoked by men very much like him, and with no girlfriend, he was by far the most severe casualty of the fracas, and was still paying for his part in it when my friend Marc Beaugé tracked him down for the French magazine *So Foot* twelve years later. 'I was young and a bit of a cretin,' he admitted, 'but I had a really shitty time afterwards. I lost my job [. . .] and ended up doing shitty jobs for five years. Cantona played again. I was as low as I could be: rotten jobs, no cash, people who looked me up and down, who knew what I'd done. Some of my mates and some members of my family never talked to me afterwards . . .' If only Matthew Simmons had had a sponsor.

Éric, however, did. Nike cleverly adapted the mindset and methods of the swag workers to a mass market. It might not have been edifying, but it worked. In a different, but still revealing vein, the *Manchester Evening News* published a photograph of Éric showering in the nude to accompany a piece entitled 'Why girls love to get their kicks from Cantona', and followed it up with a brief interview with a French florist who had enjoyed Isabelle's custom in her Deansgate shop, and could testify that Éric, whom she had met 'many times', was 'a very nice guy, calm and polite'. Richard Williams lightened the tone of the media coverage in the *Independent on Sunday*: 'You didn't have to look very long and hard at Mr Matthew Simmons of Thornton Heath to conclude that Éric Cantona's only mistake was to stop hitting him. The more we discovered about Mr Simmons, the more Cantona's assault looked like the instinctive expression of a flawless moral judgement.' Talking of the same Simmons, Brian Clough was of the view that an appropriate course of action would have been for Cantona 'to chop his balls off'. The tide was definitely turning.

Non-partisan observers of this quite extraordinary *hallali* now felt bound to express their unease at the sight of a mere footballer being spoken of as if he were a murderer. The most consistently eloquent of these, Rob Hughes, feared for the very values that had led him to confide his doubts on Cantona long before that fateful night in south London. He wrote:

> English football has to decide if it wants to destroy Éric Cantona completely – or rather to complete the destruction he had begun of himself many moons ago. [. . .] Before he is removed from English football for life, it must be asked if he alone was culpable, whether he is beyond redemption, or whether the game is capable of an interim punishment that would allow a man whose touch can be majestic some room to earn a pardon. Cantona is neither a god nor a devil, merely an errant, if sublimely talented, man.

As *The Times*'s football correspondent implied, the idea of a life ban appealed to some diehards within the FA. It was in the disciplinary committee's statutory powers to impose such a sanction and, as we've seen, previous instances of behaviour comparable to Cantona's had never been investigated or incurred punishment. The lack of jurisprudence therefore gave the FA judges a free hand in choosing whichever sentence they thought appropriate. Manchester United could lose their player whether they wanted to or not. Martin Edwards weighed into the game of cat-and-mouse that was developing between club and governing body: 'If Éric was to repeat his actions of the other night, we would have no option but to dispense with his services. Éric has accepted the suspension. If he hadn't, we would have put him on the transfer list.' He was not being firm, merely cautious. In the absence of any statement from the player's side, Éric's 'acceptance' was as close as United could get to an act of contrition.

Given the tornado into which he had been sucked, it is not surprising that Cantona decided to bury himself in silence. The French journalists who had enjoyed remarkable access to Éric since his arrival in England suddenly found it impossible to establish any line of communication with him or his entourage, which had obviously been instructed to shoo away anyone who carried a press card. A brief incident witnessed by Erik Bielderman a week or so after the Crystal Palace game suggests that Alex Ferguson himself was having trouble gauging Éric's state of mind at the time. The Manchester United manager was approached by a BBC television crew, and flew into a frightful rage that couldn't be explained only by his well-known reluctance to talk to the media. Erik enjoyed (and still enjoys) a very close relationship with Ferguson, who felt he had to tell the French reporter why he had reacted so aggressively. It was all about Cantona. 'I don't think we can keep him,' he said, 'I think he's going to go.' This contrasted markedly with the assurances Ferguson had given in the good-humoured press conference that followed a comfortable 5–2 FA Cup win over second division Wrexham on Saturday the 28th (a game which saw the first mass demonstration of support for Éric, in the shape of a few placards appearing here and there in the Old Trafford crowd; a petition would soon follow), and which he reiterated in more detail in a *Mail on Sunday* column a day later. In it, he described Éric's kung-fu kick as 'diabolical' (in *Managing My Life*, the expression he used was 'a lamentable act of folly'), but also confirmed that he would not go back on his decision to keep Cantona within the Manchester United family. 'I intend to keep working on him and with him,' he said. 'He is a joy to watch in training, but when things go wrong on the pitch and he doesn't feel referees are protecting him, he feels a sense of injustice. I have to impress upon him that there will be players and teams who will set out to wind him up. He simply has to be prepared for it and accept it. I still believe he could have an important role at Manchester United.' He also added: 'I sometimes think that he is too quiet and unemotional, that maybe he bottles up things to the point where they are able to burst out disastrously in matches.'

Éric's silence did not mean he was keeping his own counsel. His thoughts, and the thoughts of his closest advisers, such as his solicitor Jean-Jacques Bertrand, were already focused on the fights that lay ahead. He turned to the Professional Footballers' Association chairman, Gordon Taylor, for advice, and asked his union's boss to represent him at the forthcoming hearing, almost a month after the event. It wasn't just an automatic choice dictated by the structure of the game in England, and the necessity to play 'by the book', respecting the arcane hierarchies that had been established by decades of mistrust and often vicious antagonism between the pros and their masters. Taylor felt genuine sympathy for Cantona. Thirteen years later, he told me: 'It was a lynch mob atmosphere at the time. He'd already been heavily punished. United had done what they had to do.' Like most footballers past or present, Taylor was scandalized that one of his peers could be thrown to the dogs *pour encourager les autres.* He could have used the words chosen by the football correspondent of the *Manchester Evening News*, David Meek, who pointed out that 'there are mitigating factors. [. . .] I am also a little bit surprised at the eagerness of the FA to throw the book at the player. I hope they don't make him pay the price for all the other ills in the game. It would be wrong to make an example of Éric Cantona, just because he is an obvious, easy and soft target.' The vindictive nature of the attacks this target had been subjected to could yet turn out to be Cantona's strongest line of defence.

The hearing was still several weeks away, and remaining in England for the time being made no sense to Éric. He had made his vow of silence, but that couldn't suffice. The scene outside his home was reminiscent of Downing Street on days of crisis: tripods on the pavement, hangers-on stopping for a moment, satellite dishes at the ready to beam pictures of precisely nothing happening. Isabelle, by then heavily pregnant with their second child, was living like a prisoner. As Cantona later explained, 'It was impossible to escape the press or the pressure' so long as his family stayed in England. The couple decided to pack their bags and head for the Caribbean, where they hoped they would be granted a modicum of privacy. They were wrong. As they were sunning themselves on a beach at Sainte-Anne, on the island of Guadeloupe, up came, unannounced, ITN reporter Terry Lloyd, who instructed his cameraman to film a bikini-clad Isabelle. Éric erupted and gave Lloyd a good hiding. The reporter apparently suffered a broken rib and, this time, everyone sided with his aggressor. Even the 80-year-old Sir Bert Millichip, the fastidiously conservative chairman of the Football Association, let drop a few words of sympathy.

Alex Ferguson expressed his disgust, saying: 'To film, without permission, a man's six-months-pregnant wife in her swimsuit sitting on a beach is deplorable, and any husband worth his salt would react. This

ITN interviewer has got off lightly in my view' – words that were greeted with appreciative nods of approval, including in the House of Commons, where Éric had found a staunch supporter in Terry Lewis, the Honourable Member for the Worsley constituency. Lewis had already written a footnote in parliamentary history by tabling an unusual motion to the House at the end of January, in which he called for the Manchester United striker to be allowed to return to first-team football before the end of the season. He contented himself with a question this time: 'What is ITN doing half the way round the world tormenting a guy who has gone away for a week or ten days of peace and quiet and then, without permission, taking pictures of his pregnant wife on the beach?' ITN issued a two-line statement, deploring the United manager's stance on Éric's reaction ('We are surprised that Mr Ferguson, as one of Britain's top football managers, believes that a non-violent action warrants a violent response'), then safely withdrew under a rock. Any justification the television network could have come up with was so flimsy that Éric turned the tables on them by instructing his lawyer Jean-Jacques Bertrand to take legal action for 'defamation and invasion of [his] privacy', of which I could find no further trace. Either ITN settled the matter out of court or, which is more likely, the Cantona camp satisfied itself with a gesture designed to highlight the absurdity of the situation.

While columnists went on and on about the deeper significance of an individual player's moment of madness, every week there were reminders of darker evils lurking in the English game. I have mentioned Joe Kinnear and Mark Bosnich, whose offences I for one would argue were of a more serious nature than Éric's. But what of the case of referee Roger Gifford, who was assaulted by a fan after he awarded a penalty in a 1–1 draw between Blackburn and Leeds, on 1 February? Or, even more disturbingly, what of the severe crowd trouble which marred a FA Cup fourth round replay between Chelsea and Milwall seven days later? The pitch was invaded and a vicious free-for-all ensued, in which hundreds of supporters of the two most severely poisoned clubs in the country proved beyond doubt that hooliganism of the most repellent kind was alive and well in England. But when a few merchants of doom asked for metal fencing to be re-erected at Premiership grounds, less than nine years after the Hillsborough disaster, guess which reason they gave for their request? Cantona's kung-fu kick. English football was behaving like a neurotic patient suddenly gushing out incoherently to an absent analyst.

Manchester United still had to defend a league title and, to start with, showed the resilience that is the stuff of champions. 'We'll win it for Éric' was the message passed on by teammate after teammate, most notably by Andy Cole, who, to coin a phrase, had succeeded in creating a misunderstanding with the Frenchman in the two weeks they had spent together. Cantona seemed reluctant to pass the ball to the striker who had left Newcastle in the January transfer window, and had difficulties hiding his dismay at the hotshot's profligacy in front of goal. But Cole toed the party line. 'I know we are going to miss Éric,' he said after finally scoring his first United goal, in the league game that followed Cantona's club-imposed ban (a 1–0 victory over Villa), 'but if the boys win the championship, we'll do it for Éric and that's why we are all pulling together.' By mid-February, with Cole again on the scoresheet against Manchester City (3–0), United's results had given weight to this statement of intent. They had edged closer to Blackburn, who could only draw 1–1 at home to Leeds and were soundly beaten 3–1 at White Hart Lane in their next game. But as the weeks went by, and Dalglish's team regained some form, Ferguson's stuttered, alternating majestic displays – such as a record-breaking 9–0 victory over Ipswich, in which Cole struck five times, another record – and tepid performances, particularly at home, when Cantona's gift to find life in dead matches would have served them well.

In the end, United missed out on a second consecutive Double by the smallest of margins. A single point separated them from Rovers, after Czech goalkeeper Luděk Miklоško played the game of his life to earn West Ham a miraculous 1–1 draw on the last day of the season, while Everton scraped a 1–0 victory in one of the most mediocre Cup finals ever staged at Wembley. To the United manager, the most infuriating aspect of this trophy-less campaign must have been that Blackburn repeatedly threw lifelines that his team did not take advantage of: between 15 and 30 April, Rovers dropped no fewer than eight points out of twelve, but the champions failed to capitalize on those slip-ups. A series of 0–0 draws, all of them at home, against Spurs, Leeds and Chelsea, especially grated with the Scotsman. As he maintains to this day, 'No one's going to tell me, or even try to convince me that he [Cantona] would not have made one goal or scored a goal in one of these three games.' Even when he was banned from playing, Éric still determined United's fate, while his own was taking the most unexpected shape.

He was due to appear in front of the FA disciplinary committee on 24 February, together with Paul Ince, who had allegedly shouted: 'Come on then, we'll take you all!' to the Selhurst Park crowd, and punched a spectator or two when scalding tea had been thrown over his head in the ensuing fracas. His Caribbean holiday had prevented Cantona from accompanying the self-styled 'Guv'nor' to South Norwood police station on the 7 February. Both men were supposed to help the police with their inquiries about the allegations of assault made by a couple of spectators, and his absence was, perhaps inevitably, interpreted as a snub. The Yard did little to help dispel the misapprehension by having a spokesman regret Éric's 'blatant disregard' for authority, when Cantona himself had no idea he had been summoned from his Caribbean retreat. Manchester United's chief legal adviser Maurice Watkins, one of the directors of the club, countered that the police were in fact fully aware that the player was some 5,000 miles away, and that no date or time had been finalized for an appointment. Despite this, most papers printed yet more stories about Cantona showing the law of the land the finger and digging an ever deeper hole for himself.

Éric must have hoped that the hysteria had abated somewhat while he was away. But disappointment was in wait when he landed at Manchester airport in the evening of 19 February. If anything, the furore had reached a crescendo as the date of his appearance in front of the FA's 'wise men' drew nearer. He also discovered that the Audi he had parked in a multi-storey car park had been broken into and vandalized. Welcome back, Éric. He could at least derive some consolation from the soothing words of the Brazilian Sports Minister, then on an official fact-finding mission in Britain. Pelé, for it was he, appealed for moderation. 'He's a human being like everybody else,' the greatest of all footballers said. 'I think he's made a mistake, [but] people try this case [*sic*] like it was the worst case in the world. Of course sport is not to fight, it's to make friends. He has to be punished but not, as I understand a lot of newspapers say, banished from football.'

Maurice Watkins, whom Éric met on the morning of the 20th, felt reasonably confident on the eve of the player's visit to the police. Flanked by the toughest of United's security staff, ex-SAS soldier Ned Kelly, Cantona had barely exchanged a glance with the swarm of pressmen who had reconvened in front of his Boothstown home, and not much more came out of his interview with Scotland Yard detectives, except that Éric and Paul Ince had been charged with common assault, just as everyone had predicted. The hacks would have to wait another four days to get juicier material. The scene of the tragi-comedy shifted from Greater Manchester to St Albans.

At long last, on Friday the 24th, a black limousine glided into the courtyard of Sopwell House, a smart country hotel which had long been a popular haunt of Tottenham and Arsenal footballers. Alex Ferguson was first to climb out of the car, playing the valet for Éric, who was also accompanied by Gordon Taylor and Maurice Watkins, with Ned Kelly keeping the pack of journalists at bay. Inside the building, three men were waiting in a committee room: Geoffrey Thompson, a Justice of the Peace from the amateur county game in Sheffield, who would later become the manager of Doncaster Rovers and rise to the position of chairman of the Football Association; Ian Stott, chairman of Oldham Athletic; and Gordon McKeag, former chairman of Newcastle United and president of the Football League. The trio of establishment mandarins listened to the player's representation and expressions of regret,* then

* According to former FA executive David Davies, who published his memoirs, *FA Confidential*, in 2008, Éric's statement to the commission could have landed him in even deeper trouble. 'I would like to apologise to the chairman of the commission,' Éric began in 'perfect English', according to Davies. 'I would like to apologise to Manchester United, Maurice Watkins and Alex Ferguson. I would like to apologise to my teammates. I want to apologise to the FA. And I would like to apologise to the prostitute who shared my bed last night.' Fortunately for Cantona, if one is to believe this version of events, at least two of his judges didn't understand what he'd said.

retired for three hours of deliberation. A life ban was considered and, according to Graham Kelly, set aside as 'we have to bear in mind that the footballer's life is shorter than in other careers', an odd statement if looked at more carefully. For if a footballer's career is shorter than others, a life ban would surely affect him less severely than it would, say, a doctor or a fireman. Regardless of Kelly's muddled logic, note had been taken that, within the past four weeks, Cantona had been suspended by his club, fined a considerable sum of money, and lost the captaincy of his national team. But the clemency of the FA stopped at these considerations.

To Watkins' surprise, Cantona's bemusement and Ferguson's barely concealed fury, the disciplinary commission doubled the length of the ban imposed by United to six months, extended it worldwide, and added a £10,000 fine of its own.* A measure of satisfaction was given to those who, like Pat Crerand and Jimmy Greaves, believed that the scandal was as much about the trivialization of verbal violence in football grounds as about the frenzied reaction of a footballer who had been subjected to it. The FA had got in touch with various MPs as well as with the Commission for Racial Equality 'in an effort to limit the level of abuse directed at players by supporters'. Visitors to twenty-first-century Premiership grounds will be able to judge for themselves whether these efforts were successful or not. As for Éric, if his misconduct had not been unprecedented, its punishment surely was. Manchester United, however, immediately waived their right to appeal. The club had approached the whole affair in as conciliatory a mood

* This is the full text of the FA's judgement: 'The members of the FA Commission are satisfied that the actions of Éric Cantona following his sending-off at Crystal Palace in the Manchester United match on January 25 brought the game into disrepute. Éric Cantona has therefore been in breach of FA rules. After taking into consideration the previous misconduct of Éric Cantona, the provocation he suffered, the prompt action taken by Manchester United, Éric Cantona's expression of regret to the Commission, the apologies he conveyed to those affected and the assurances he gave to his future conduct, the members of the Commission decided that Éric Cantona should be suspended forthwith from all football activities up to and including 30th September 1995 and in addition fined pounds 10,000.'

as it could muster, up to the smart suit and tie Cantona was wearing for his hearing and at the press conference that followed, in which he said not a single word, in French, English or any other language. Watkins described the FA's sanctions as 'a bit harsh' and himself as 'disappointed'. Ferguson fumed in silence, and waited a few weeks to say what he really felt: 'I don't think any player in the history of football will get the sentence he got unless they had killed Bert Millichip's dog. When someone is doing well we have to knock him down. We don't do it with horses. Red Rum is more loved than anyone I know but he must have lost one race.'

Cantona's arms had remained folded throughout the press conference. As Henri Émile told me, 'I felt that Éric had put a carapace around him. He hardly ever read the papers. He couldn't care less about what was written about him in the press. He didn't suffer, [so long as he] felt at ease with the people he loved.' Reminiscing about another famous football incident, Émile continued: 'Some time after Zizou [Zinédine Zidane] headbutted [Marco] Materazzi in the final of the 2006 World Cup, Éric and I were in Tignes, and a journalist asked him: "Don't you think Zizou will have lost many fans?" "That doesn't matter," he replied. "He'll win others, and these will be sincere."' But what he had done and its consequences, which staggered him, as well as the profound gratitude he felt for the protection Manchester United provided him with, triggered soul-searching of a kind he had never felt the need for previously. 'Before that night [in Selhurst Park], I was behaving like a child,' he confided later. 'I was prepared to repeat the same mistake again and again. After it, I realized that it was an irresponsible habit.'

Éric set out to change with a doggedness he hadn't always shown in the past when things didn't quite go his way. He acted out of personal necessity, but also because he had been shamed into remembering his duty by the kindness and understanding of others, and especially of his manager. This would be his gift to Alex Ferguson, just as, six-and-a-half years earlier, he had literally defied the elements to present Auxerre with an unhoped-for victory at Le Havre, almost bringing tears to the eyes of his mentor Guy Roux. This eagerness to please those who trusted him most points up an essential sincerity at the heart of Éric's character, which should be properly weighed against its perceived flaws. There is true poignancy in his admission: 'I was behaving like a child'. When deciding to mend his ways, wasn't he behaving like one again? And by succeeding in doing so, wasn't he proving himself worthy of the love he craved?

Back in the world of grown-ups, there was still a court action to deal with, as everyone was reminded of when, on the 27th, a newly unemployed double-glazing fitter named Matthew Simmons was bailed and told to appear at Croydon Magistrates Court on 24 March, the day after Cantona's own appearance at the same court. Football was keeping British justice busy at the time. On 14 March the Liverpool goalkeeper Bruce Grobbelaar, together with his Wimbledon counterpart Hans Segers and another member of the so-called 'Crazy Gang', the razor-elbowed striker John Fashanu, were among five suspects questioned by police about their role in alleged bribery and match-fixing for the benefit of Far Eastern gambling syndicates (all of them were eventually cleared in court, but ordered to pay their costs; Grobbelaar and Segers were later banned by the FA for breaching betting regulations). One month earlier, George Graham had been sacked from his managerial post by Arsenal after acknowledging he had received a 'Christmas gift' worth £425,000 from Norwegian agent Rune Hauge, in exchange for the facilitation of a transfer. According to the game's folklore, Graham had just been unlucky: it was rumoured that numerous high-profile managers had received 'brown-paper bags in service stations' to thank them for their part in closing a deal, a practice which everyone within football agrees predated professionalism.

But what a year 1995 was! In late February, 170 English fans rioted in Ostend and were deported from Belgium on the eve of the aptly described European Cup Winners Cup 'clash' between FC Bruges and Chelsea, while one of their heroes, the 'pocket-sized Rottweiler' Dennis Wise, found himself in the dock for assaulting a taxi driver (he was cleared on appeal). Hooligans had caused the abandonment of an Ireland–England international in Dublin. The papers spoke of 'a game in chaos', and dubbed the present campaign 'the season of sleaze'. They had every reason to do so. In fact, had it not been for the identity and the previous record of its perpetrator, Cantona's offence would not have warranted more than a footnote in a litany of far more serious misdemeanours. But its very public nature crystallized the attention of opinion-formers. Cantona had built a formidable career by swimming against the current; when the river finally burst its banks, it was quite natural that he had to be the first to be cast away. He became a symbol of the game's moral decrepitude, a symbol who, after having been crucified by the media, would stand trial on 23 March, the day after a 3–0 victory over Arsenal had brought Manchester United back within three points of Blackburn in the Premiership.

It shouldn't be forgotten that, a year hence, England too would stand trial. UEFA had awarded the privilege of hosting the 1996 European Championships to the country where football was born. This highly controversial decision – which turned out to be an inspired one – was meant to be a gesture of goodwill towards the football authorities in England for their courage in addressing the problem of hooliganism, and a spur to pursue the government-endorsed drive towards eliminating the 'cancer of the game'. Extreme conditions sometimes require extreme treatment.

The throng that assembled for Éric's walk to the scaffold was worthy of a royal engagement – Charles I's execution springs to mind. Reporters and photographers turned up in their hundreds, and came to blows to claim a vantage point. No fewer than twenty television crews vied for space. One cameraman hired a hydraulic lift to give himself the best possible chance of catching every single step of Cantona's progress from the Croydon Park hotel to the entrance of the Magistrates Court, 200 yards away. The police had offered Éric a car to take him to the tribunal, but Éric refused. This was his show, after all. The King would walk, and, as noted by a contemporary columnist, 'dozens of snappers' retreated before him, walking backwards, 'in a bizarre parody of a royal protocol'. The way Éric had dressed for this coronation of a kind bewildered his co-defendant Paul Ince (who was cleared of common assault). 'So we got up in the morning,' he recalled, 'and I've got me suit on – the nuts, know what I mean? I knocked on Éric's door and he's standing in jacket [*on the lapel of which he had pinned a small replica of the Statue of Liberty*], white shirt, long collars like that, unbuttoned so you can see his chest. "Éric, you can't go to court like that!" I told him and he says,

"I'm Cantona, I can go as I want." So he got in the dock and he got fourteen days in prison. I thought, "Oh my God! It must be the shirt. It has to be the shirt, Éric!"'

Fourteen days in jail. A few miles away, on the very same day, Alex Ferguson was collecting a CBE from Her Majesty the Queen at Buckingham Palace. Indie-rock band Ash was making its first appearance in the British Top 60 with 'Kung Fu' (with, yes, Steve Lindsell's photograph reproduced on the sleeve). How surreal could it get? Cantona, in truth, could have been punished even more severely: the maximum sentence for the offence he had committed was six months' imprisonment and a £5,000 fine. A few words fell from Éric's lips: 'If they lock me up, that'll be a new experience.' The chairperson of the bench that sent him to prison was one Mrs Jean Pearch, 53, a retired music teacher and mother of four who told him: 'You are a high-profile public figure with undoubted gifts, and as such you are looked up to by so many young people. For this reason, the only sentence that is appropriate for this offence is two weeks' imprisonment forthwith.' Cantona's admission of guilt and expression of remorse, which were conveyed in a contrite statement read out to the court by his barrister, David Poole QC, had not been enough to save him from jail. Éric gave a half-smile when a French interpreter confirmed the sentence. He had understood everything, of course. An appeal was immediately lodged against the verdict, but a request for bail was rejected. Éric was locked in a cell for three hours until Judge Ian Davies of Croydon Crown Court finally set him free, on condition he paid a £500 guarantee. He had spent this time signing autographs for well-wishers.

A few minutes later, Éric, flanked by the now ever-present Ned Kelly, finally made his way out of the court, but not without some difficulty. The crowd of newspapermen and television crews had been swelled by a group of youths who taunted the freshly convicted footballer, screaming, 'Scum!' and, 'You're going down!' Or should they have shouted: 'You're going out of the country'? For, outside Britain, the pariah's future elicited more than curiosity or outrage. Strange ideas took root in strange places. Casal de Rey, chairman of Sao Paulo FC, had already told the Brazilian press that he was about to make an offer for Cantona to Manchester United (he never did). In Italy, Massimo

Moratti stuck to his 'one declared passion, and that is Éric Cantona'. Internazionale would soon make a move for 'a great player and a man of culture, not at all stupid', and this despite the fact that, at the beginning of the month, FIFA had extended Éric's ban worldwide, as its statutes demanded it did. Two days after sentence was passed on Cantona, the irrepressible Moratti faxed Manchester United, 'to sound out whether they [were] prepared to sell the player'.

Should the sentence be upheld on appeal, which would be heard eight days later, there was little doubt that Cantona would quit English football in even more dramatic fashion than he had run away from his own country. On the night of the verdict, another of Éric's advisers, who doubled up as vice-chairman of UNFP, the French footballers' union, Jean-Jacques Amorfini, was interviewed on French radio. 'They are all out to get him,' he said, 'and I can tell you, he won't stay in that country a lot longer. I think people are trying to make Cantona disgusted with England and, obviously, I believe he is going to have to leave the country.' Amorfini went further, and suggested that Manchester United were partly to blame for his client's plight: 'We are dumbfounded and absolutely shocked because Manchester United's English lawyers advised a guilty plea so English justice would show clemency.' What Amorfini didn't take into account was that the club genuinely expected that this would be the case, even if there was a measure of disingenuity in Martin Edwards' statement that 'the whole thing has got out of hand. He [Cantona] has been punished three times for the same offence.' For how could the Manchester United chairman argue that a football club, the FA and the Crown Prosecution Service somehow shared the same jurisdiction? But his shock was not feigned. Everyone was 'stunned' by the harshness of the punishment. Gordon Taylor said that the court had made an example of Cantona because of his fame: 'It looks as though footballers are being made the whipping boys for many of the [*sic*] society's ills. We are in danger of getting [in]to a lynch-mob mentality.'

In France, too, the reaction was one of disbelief, and was voiced in language which suggested another hundred year war was about to erupt between the two countries. The national coach Aimé Jacquet, who had just given the captain's armband to the future Lyon and

Rangers manager Paul Le Guen, denounced the Croydon magistrates' verdict as 'absurd, incomprehensible, out of proportion'. Michel Platini, by now president of the 1998 World Cup organizing committee, added one adjective: 'disgraceful'. Philippe Piat, the chairman of the French PFA, chimed in: 'It is really shocking to send someone to jail because he reacted to [the provocation of] a convicted criminal. It is another proof of the English ostracism of the French who live there.' Piat added, somewhat gnomically, 'We all remember the campaigns against Merle, the rugby player, and Gachot, the motor racing driver.' Jean-Pierre Papin urged that Matthew Simmons 'should be banned for ever from every stadium', which he was, but for one year only, the longest ban that he could be served with under the terms of the 1989 Football Supporters Act. There were few dissenters in the family that had risen to defend its beleaguered son. When Noel Le Graët stated, quite reasonably, that 'the demands and extreme media coverage of high level sport impose some duties on the players and managers' and that they 'must have exemplary behaviour and cannot consider themselves above rules and laws', few were prepared to listen.

Thankfully, oil was poured on these choppy waters when, on 31 March, judge Ian Davies commuted the original sentence to 120 hours of community service, a popular kind of punishment with disgraced sportsmen: the snooker player Jimmy White, for example, had been requested to clean an old people's home to atone for a drink-driving offence. A handful of diehard Manchester United supporters, Pete Boyle among them, who had secured the first ticket available for the tribunal's public gallery, ran out of the court, shouting, 'The King is free! The King is free!' One of these fans, thirteen-year-old Sebastian Pennels, had risked the wrath of the court by presenting Éric with a good luck card during the hearing. An interpreter was on hand to pass on the verdict to Cantona, who again greeted it with the hint of a smile. Judge Davies, summing up, said: 'We express the hope that he [Éric] will be able to be used in carrying out his public duty by helping young people who aspire to be professional footballers [. . .] and others who merely aspire to play and enjoy it. Cantona reacted in a way that was out of character and would not have done so but for the provocative conduct aimed at him.' He concluded with words that must have tasted like honey to Éric: 'Whatever the defendant's status, he is entitled to be dealt with for the gravity of his offence and not to make an example of a public figure.' Short of an acquittal, Judge Ian Davies could not have done more to satisfy the player's thirst for justice. With his common sense and fairness, he had also made sure that, should Éric play football again, it would be in England, and for Manchester United.

It's time to bring Guy Roux back into Éric's story again.

'Canto's mother called me on the day of his appeal. Nobody had ever interrupted one of my training sessions in thirty years. But she was beside herself with worry. Éric had told her that, should the judge uphold the sentence, he'd beat him up! Oh dear . . . I told her: I am not God. But . . . I knew Béatrice Main, who'd been under-prefect of Château-Chinon, and was now President Mitterrand's chef de cabinet *[private secretary]. Fourteen years before, I'd agreed to do a picture of our team with Mitterrand, who was then campaigning for the presidency. He had retained a soft spot for Auxerre, and had even told me once, "If you ever have a problem, call Béatrice, and we'll see what we can do." I told her that I had never bothered the President before – I wasn't going to ask his help for a parking ticket, was I? – but that we were now facing a serious situation: Cantona was facing the judges. Her reaction was predictable: "We are not going to give lessons to the English, who invented the independence of the judiciary!" Yes, I said, of course, but I've found a way round it. If the President sends a cable to the Queen, saying, 'If Cantona goes to jail, it will have a serious adverse effect on the relationship between the youth of England and the youth of France,' maybe it will be of some use . . . She replied, "You're absolutely mad. I knew it." "Well, could you just tell him?" It was on a Wednesday, the day the* Conseil des Ministres *[Cabinet] met at the Élysée Palace. She told me she'd call me back in the afternoon. And she called me back at 3 p.m.: "Only mad people succeed on this earth of ours. The President has asked a high-ranking civil servant to send a cable to the Home Office." At 3 p.m., Cantona had his sentence commuted, and went back home.'*

'Months passed by. We didn't talk about it. Then [French television network] TF1 sends me to Manchester United–Dortmund, and asked me

to organize an interview with Cantona, who hadn't talked to French television for a year. Éric said: "Guy Roux – yes. With a cameraman and no one else." We locked ourselves in and did the interview. Then I told him the story . . . and he says: "Of course, that's it! I hadn't understood at the time! My lawyers were rubbish!"

'Was it so? No one will ever know, until the archives are open to the public.'

17

THE AFTERMATH AND THE RETURN OF THE KING: APRIL–DECEMBER 1995

'My lawyer and the officials wanted me to speak. So I just said that. It was nothing, it did not mean anything. I could have said, "The curtains are pink but I love them."'

Soberly dressed in white shirt, black V-necked jumper, grey flannel jacket and matching two-tone silk tie, Éric Cantona sat down to confront the throng of journalists who had assembled at the court-house. The incessant clicking of the cameras and the fizz of the flashing lights made a noise like thousands of raindrops clattering on a tin roof. Éric delivered a single sentence of twenty words in precisely fourteen seconds, fated to become one of the most celebrated quotes in the history of football.

> When the seagulls [*a sip of water*] follow a trawler [*the 'a' almost inaudible, leaning back, smiling, pausing again*], it's because they think [*another pause*] sardines [*and another*] will be thrown into the [*slight hesitation*] sea [*a smile and a quick nod*]. Thank you, very much.

Incredulous guffaws accompanied Cantona as he made his way out of the heaving room. The bemusement of the journalists was under-standable: they had been expecting a press conference, possibly more words of repentance, instead of which 'Le nutter' had just cocked a snook at his tormentors, pirouetted on his heels and left them with gaping mouths. Much was made of the 'sybilline' nature of the pronouncement, when, in truth, everyone understood Cantona's meaning; but no one could bring themselves to accept that he had had the cheek to steal the show in such a light-hearted – and memorable – manner. The 'seagulls' (the press, of course) could have been other animals – vultures, for example. Incredibly, the carcass had spoken. It hadn't been thrown overboard after all, and wouldn't give the scavengers as much as a bone to chew on. The disingenuousness of some commentators, who claimed these words were those of a certifiable lunatic, did not fool the general public. All of England – then, within hours, most of the watching world – fell about laughing. Éric's team-mates joined in the merriment. Steve Bruce and Gary Pallister would rib Cantona for months to come in the dressing-room – sardines-this and sardines-that – to Éric's undisguised delight. He had never told a better joke. He had diverted the media's attention from the consequences of his faux pas, and given them another basis on which to build the legend ever higher. He would never speak to a journalist again while at United, unless he had been dispatched by his club to provide material for an official book or video, one of several steps he took to wipe the slate clean and draw a new picture of himself.* It took time to take shape, naturally, and it wasn't until much later in the season to come that it became clear that Cantona, against all odds and all predictions, had succeeded in doing so.

---

* Cantona had granted a number of interviews to French journalists until that point, but had been deeply hurt by the headline of *L'Équipe* on the day they reported the Crystal Palace kung-fu kick: 'INDÉFENDABLE' (Indefensible). How hurt he had been was revealed in March 2001, when he launched a furious verbal attack on two of the paper's leading writers, Christian Ollivier and Patrick Urbini (now my colleague at *France Football*), live on a popular TV programme, *Côté Tribune*. 'I piss on your arses,' he said, and repeated, with such fury in his voice that Patrick, fearing that blows might be exchanged, chose to leave the set fifteen minutes before the end of the transmission. To Éric – who said he had been bottling up his anger 'for ten [*sic*] years' – '*indéfendable*' meant that all he deserved was to be cast out in the wilderness and never allowed to return. He also hinted at the pain his close family had had to endure because of this, but stopped short of recognizing his own culpability in the incident, referring to his attack on Matthew Simmons as 'a small assault on a small supporter' which could be forgiven.

Films of Cantona shot during his ban show him on his own, running around a training pitch or lifting weights in United's gymnasium. In fact, he trained with his teammates throughout his enforced absence, apparently taking 'it all in his stride', according to Ryan Giggs. Most observers were convinced that it would only be a matter of weeks before a foreign club, probably Italian, and more precisely Inter Milan, would rescue Cantona from his English predicament, but Alex Ferguson thought otherwise. 'We know it will be difficult for [him] to return to normal football in this country,' he said as early as 4 April, 'but we think it is possible. I've said all along we want him to stay, and together we can work it out.'

The *Daily Mirror* disagreed. On 12 April, on the day a Crystal Palace fan called Paul Nixon was killed in a scuffle before their FA Cup semi-final replay against United (in which Roy Keane was sent off and 'appalling' Cantona songs rang around Selhurst Park), the tabloid announced that Éric's transfer to Internazionale was now a certainty. Cantona had instructed his adviser Jean-Jacques Bertrand to open negotiations. The Italians would increase the player's salary five-fold, to £25,000 a week, while offering his present club £4.5m. Bertrand immediately denied that a deal had been struck, but admitted that there had been some contact, which was the truth; as we know, Moratti had approached the United board long before Éric's troubles, and was unlikely to let go now that his target seemed to have forsaken a future in English football. In Manchester, meanwhile, supporters could hardly be reassured by club statements such as: 'We've always said that we wanted Éric to stay, but we want players who want to stay with us' – which was as good as saying that the door leading Cantona out of Old Trafford had been left ajar, if not quite opened for him. Martin Edwards professed more optimism himself – United were conducting their own negotiations with Bertrand – but only up to a point. 'A lot depends on what Éric wants to do,' he said. 'If he wants to play for United he is certainly going to receive a very good offer from us, but if he feels he has had enough of England or that he is in an impossible position because of the problems he has had, then that is a different matter.'

Doubts would linger for months to come. One close confidant of Cantona's told me that the player had indeed been 'that close' to moving to Italy at the time. The urge to leave England and the lure of phenomenal wages were not the only factors preying on Éric's mind. He felt that Manchester United should have made far more effort to bring in the top-class players required to achieve the club's oft-stated ambition to rejoin Europe's footballing elite. The names of Gabriel Batistuta, Marcelo Salas and even Zinédine Zidane had been mentioned. None of them came to Old Trafford, of course, and a number of Cantona's friends believed they had been bandied only to pacify the one genuine star the club possessed: Éric himself. In an interview Marc Beaugé and I conducted in March 2009, Alex Ferguson admitted that – with the benefit of hindsight – he regretted not having been more forceful in his efforts to strengthen his squad at that time. And when I asked him if he thought it could have been a factor in Éric's decision to call it quits a year hence, his answer was a plain 'yes'. Cantona wished to prove himself on the European stage, which he wasn't sure that United could help him do any more. Looking back, however, had he not been in a similar situation when he had found himself frozen out of the Marseille team four years previously? He could have chosen to walk out, but bided his time. Leaving would have been quitting, admitting defeat. He would not give his enemies the satisfaction of knowing that they had succeeded in hounding him out of England after they had made it impossible for him to live and play in France. And the children of Manchester played their part too.

The first of Éric's 120 hours of community service was spent signing autographs at The Cliff, surrounded by the now familiar gaggle of cameramen, security personnel and hardcore fans, who were augmented that day – 18 April – by Liz Calderbank, a supervisor of the Manchester Probation Service, whose presence was the only reminder that Cantona was expiating a crime. It was he who had suggested that his time would be best employed coaching children from the Manchester area, and this he did over a period of three months, to the delight of some 700 boys and girls, the first of whom were a dozen players from Ellsmere Park Junior FC, aged 9–12. That club had no strip and no pitch to train and play on; in fact, it had barely come into existence, having been involved in a mere three games before Cantona took them under his wing for a two-hour session.

Few of the boys had managed to get a minute's sleep the night before and couldn't contain their excitement when the moment finally came to meet their idol in the club's gymnasium. Paul Thompson, aged twelve, enthused: 'We just ran up to him cheering. He was totally brilliant. I thought he would be a bit harsh, but he was great. I talked to him in French, and he told me not to get rough because I would be sent off.' Journalists then moved on to Aiden Sharp, 11, and wrote in their notebooks: 'He worked really hard and made us work the whole time. Éric was a very nice man, very patient and gentle. I've learnt tons from him today.' *The Times* had sent Rob Hughes to Salford, who heard another of the beaming children tell him: 'He were [*sic*] terrific, showed me I could score. He told me to concentrate on one corner of the net, to aim for that, and now I score every time.'

Éric adored children, in whom he saw a reflection of his former and truer self, before he had been emotionally maimed by the corrupting power of professional football. He had said so himself on many occasions – he couldn't be granted the privilege of being a child again, but playing brought him as close as could be to this unattainable aim. There, at The Cliff, the uncontrollable pupil, Guy Roux's '*caractériel*', turned into a patient guide for starstruck youngsters who could barely speak through the tears when the time came to leave their 'King' for good. 'It was the best day of my life,' one of them said, shaking with a mixture of grief and elation, wishing that tomorrow, and the day after that, and every other day, he could jump from his team's minibus to meet his hero, distraught by the realization that this would never happen again. The haunting image of that boy's face has never left me, and I don't think it has left Cantona's mind either. He truly loved every single one of these kids, and wasn't playing to the audience when he said, later in the year: 'It wasn't a punishment. It was like a gift,' adding after a half-thoughtful, half-mischievous pause a 'thank you' that, I believe, was partly but not entirely ironic, as it was certainly meant for the children he spent the end of the spring with as much as for the court that had 'punished' him. To one of them, ten-year-old Michael Sargent, he had confided that he 'would really like to stay [at United]'. He owed them a debt, one that was light to carry, and that he was happy to honour. These children had 'helped [him] a lot', he said. Judging by the transformation of his character over the coming year, they clearly had. He had told a boy called Simon Croft: 'If you're going to get a yellow card, walk away and don't argue with the referee,' words that others like Célestin Oliver and Sébastien Mercier had drummed into him when he was a *minot* himself. At long last, he was about to take on board the advice he had been given, and I'm not so sure it would have been the case if he hadn't had to pass it on to others.

Éric wouldn't return to competitive football until 30 September 1995 at the earliest. Ahead of him lay five months of inactivity, boredom, rumours, and the odd trumpet lesson with John MacMurray, the Canadian principal of the Hallé Orchestra. He found he had limited gifts for this instrument, and soon moved on. Support came from unlikely sources, like the bass player of The Stranglers, his compatriot Jean-Jacques Burnel, who toyed with the idea of including a tribute to Éric in the band's forthcoming twentieth anniversary tour. '[Cantona] has done more for Anglo-French relations than anyone since Brigitte Bardot,' the punk musician said. 'You English should be grateful for him.' It's true that Burnel had his own reasons for empathizing with Cantona: he had once attacked a spectator at a Stranglers gig: 'He insulted my mother, so I put down my guitar, leapt off the stage and landed him in hospital.' Incidentally, Burnel taught karate when he wasn't playing with The Stranglers. Meanwhile, in France, the editor of *Paris-Match* magazine, Patrick Mahé, was putting the finishing touches to his book *Cantona au Bûcher* ('Cantona at the Stake'), oddly described in its blurb as 'an impassioned plea for the celebrated footballer against the anti-French hysteria of the Anglo-Londoners'. Make of that what you will.

As for football, by the end of April, a verbal agreement had been reached to extend Éric's contract at Old Trafford – or so it seemed, as his agent Jean-Jacques Amorfini was still waiting for a written proposal. Éric, whose present deal was due to expire a year hence, would commit himself to Manchester United until the end of the 1997–98 season. Despite Amorfini's warning that things 'could take longer', the papers which had predicted Cantona's exit swiftly announced that a resolution could be achieved 'within a few days', and they were right. Éric put his signature to a new, improved three-year agreement (which would bring him £750,000 a year, and not £1m, as most contemporary sources had it) on the very day English football's only other true foreign star of the time, Jürgen Klinsmann, headed back to his native Germany: 27 April. It was Éric's first appearance in front of the media since his 'sardines' quip. He looked heavier, which wasn't much of a surprise, as his weight tended to fluctuate wildly when he wasn't playing regularly. There was even the hint of a double chin on the face that emerged from a candy-striped pink jacket Jeeves would have instantly removed from Bertie Wooster's wardrobe. 'I can forget everything,' he told the press, 'and we can win everything. We are bigger than the people who have sometimes been so hard and so wrong' – among whom he obviously didn't include himself.

The news was greeted with relish by those who had stood by him back in January, the former Manchester United midfielder Pat Crerand among them. 'I'm delighted that Éric has the courage to turn around and show two fingers to a lot of people in England,' he said. 'So many clowns have jumped on the bandwagon.' Brendon Batson, speaking on behalf of the Professional Footballers' Association, who had voted Cantona their player of the year in 1994, gushed: 'we didn't want to lose a talent like Éric's. Now we just hope that when he does reappear on a football pitch that he receives a decent reception.' Many shared his apprehension, like the fan who called a local radio station to say he wondered whether 'he [Cantona] could cope with what he's going to get next season'.

But while others celebrated, and fretted, Éric slipped away to France. He had more urgent matters to attend to. Isabelle gave birth to their second child, Joséphine – named after Cantona's beloved grandfather Joseph, who had died in 1991 – on 7 July. Then, one week later, the new father had another birth to attend – his own, in the guise of a theatrical character. He drove to the Avignon festival to attend the premiere of *Ode à Canto*, a play written and directed by the alarmingly prolific Gérard Gelas, which claimed to be based on Antonin Artaud's *Trip to the Land of the Tarahumaras*. 'Play' might be the wrong word, as it was little more than a comic dialogue between a regal

Cantona – the actor Damien Rémy, clad in the red of Manchester United, collar up, of course – and an aspiring footballer called Lorenzo. Éric took his seat among the few hundred spectators of the Théâtre du Chêne noir, where Gelas had been based since 1967. French television cameras were there too, all of them trained on the footballer's face in the small crowd. Thankfully, the King was amused. 'I felt close to the main character, all through the play,' he said. 'That shows how an actor can do anything. We're just footballers, and I don't know if we can do anything but play football. It's a good thing that the main character says things I might not have said myself, but which I could have said, yes.' Cantona was referring – obliquely – to the political subtext of the farce, in which unsubtle references were made to Jean-Marie Le Pen's National Front, renamed '*Affront National*' by Gelas. I must say that my blood froze when I watched a video recording of *Ode à Canto*. The odd declamatory tone and self-conscious poetry of the lines reminded me of an amateur staging of one of Dario Fo's anarchic plays I had once attended in the Auvergne, a ghastly memory that will never leave me. But I could understand how Cantona was taken with passages such as '. . . Marseilles, bitten by the wind of corsairs, children of Greek sailors, Italian stonemasons, Armenians, Algerians or Africans . . . Marseilles, which affords herself the luxury of being an island in the midst of a continent . . .' If every man's an island, that one suited him, the son of Les Caillols, born and raised on a rocky spur, sharp and unyielding as stone itself. A Marseillais, always.

The hero of Gelas' imagination left the Provençal sun soon after his consecration on the stage. *Ode à Canto* would be one of the playwright's most resounding successes; his troupe toured with the play for three years at home and abroad, carried by the notoriety of its subject. Cantona himself travelled back to Manchester, where Alex Ferguson had organized a pre-season friendly between his team and Rochdale. Unaware that he might be breaking the terms of his ban by taking part in this match played behind closed doors at The Cliff, Éric found himself in the eye of yet another storm. On 30 July, five days after the game had taken place, FA spokesman Mike Parry read the following statement to the usual shoal of 'sardines': 'We became aware of the fact that Éric Cantona had played through newspaper reports and have written to Manchester United asking for their observations, and to ask them under what sort of conditions the match was played. The ban imposed on Cantona said that he should be suspended from all football activities until the beginning of October, so we assume Manchester United have a plausible explanation. We'd just like to know what it is – to clear the matter up.'

The price tag – £7.5m, second only to Alan Shearer's, and £3m more than Newcastle recruit David Ginola's – that *The Times*'s new 'interactive team football' game had put on Cantona suddenly looked far less attractive, even if the affair didn't make much noise at first. The sporting public was looking elsewhere. Linford Christie had failed at the World Athletics Championships, and Jonathan Edwards was about to produce a staggering triple jump of 18.29m to win the gold in Gothenburg, setting two world records in the process. England's cricket team had woken up at last against the West Indies. Manchester United fans were getting used (with a great deal of difficulty) to the idea of living without Paul Ince and Mark Hughes, who had been sold to Inter and Chelsea respectively, while Andreï Kanchelskis was – rightly – said to be on his way to Everton. They didn't know that a furious Cantona had headed straight back to France when he had heard that the FA was considering bringing another charge against him.

They wouldn't have to wait for long. Jean-Jacques Bertrand delivered Éric's ultimatum in Paris, on 7 August. 'Éric Cantona will not return to England unless the FA goes back on its decision, which forbids him from taking part in training games behind closed doors for his club,' he said. The authorities were given a strict deadline: 'Friday the 11th of August, 1995, at midnight.' The ploy worked. The FA, who had faced almost unanimous criticism in the media for their rigid stance, crawled back under a rock: '[We] received a response from Manchester United in regard to our inquiry about Éric Cantona. We are entirely satisfied with their explanation and we have conveyed that to the club'. But the camel's back appeared to have been broken for good before Éric's persecutors had beaten a sheepish retreat.

Cantona had faxed a transfer request to his club, as was acknowledged by United's press officer Ken Ramsden. '[Éric] was very upset at the recent inquiry by the FA concerning his involvement in the training session of 25 July,' he said. 'He told Martin Edwards that he felt he had little future in the English game and that his career would be best served by a move abroad,' which everyone guessed meant Inter Milan in Italy. However, 'The board has considered the request very carefully but is not prepared to agree to it, believing that it is in the best interests of both the club and player that he remains with them.' Alex Ferguson's task was to convince Cantona that his 'best interests' would indeed be protected if he chose not to carry on his threat of leaving. In public, he just expressed the hope that 'things [would] settle down over the next few days'. Away from the cameras, while still trying to bring the protracted transfer of Andreï Kanchelskis to Everton to a satisfactory conclusion (it had now been referred to the Premier League), Ferguson embarked on a quite extraordinary rescue mission to Paris. Perhaps he felt a degree of responsibility in the affair, even though he had genuinely believed that the confidential friendlies he had scheduled against teams such as Oldham, Bury, Rochdale and apparently a few others as well, did not fall within the scope of 'organized matches' which Cantona was not permitted to play in. All he had wanted to do was to involve Éric in the day-to-day life of his team, keep him fit, and sate his hunger for the ball. It hadn't helped that United had flown out to Malaysia for one of their money-spinning summer tours almost immediately after the friendly which was at the heart of the dispute: Éric had literally been left behind.

As soon as he had been informed that Cantona was packing his bags, Ferguson had driven to Worsley, where he had found a distinctly unresponsive Frenchman who had chosen to rely on room service to avoid mingling with the seagulls waiting for him in the restaurant. Ferguson could and did empathize with the plight of his player, to the point that, had it not been for a late-night conversation with his wife on his return, he might well have concluded that losing Cantona was unavoidable. But Cathy Ferguson felt that her husband shouldn't yield so easily, and slowly brought him round to share her point of view. The next morning, Ferguson, who had barely slept, informed Bertrand that he wished to speak to Éric, who had now left for

France, and that he was willing to head for the airport straight away. Cantona's adviser agreed to a meeting, which would take place on 9 August, the day after the manager was due to attend a book launch in London. Wine tends to flow freely on such occasions, and that night was no exception. A relaxed Ferguson made some unguarded remarks to his dinner companions, a number of whom were journalists who immediately informed their news desks that they had better dispatch their special forces to Heathrow and Roissy. How could Ferguson beat his pursuers?

The phone rang in the room he'd booked at the George V hotel. It was Jean-Jacques Amorfini, one of Cantona's closest confidants as well as the vice-chairman of the French PFA. He would come and collect Ferguson in the evening. All he would have to do would be to follow the porter when he turned up at his door, which he did shortly before 7.30 p.m. as arranged. The two men made their way through a maze of corridors, through the kitchen, down to a side exit where Amorfini was waiting, holding two motorcycle helmets. Ferguson donned his, and sat on the pillion of a Harley-Davidson. The bike roared and quickly slipped out of sight in the Parisian streets. Its destination was a quiet, almost deserted restaurant – its owner had taken the precaution to place a '*fermé*' sign on the door. Éric was there, as were Jean-Jacques Bertrand and a secretary.

Cantona, delighted as he was by his manager's presence, at first showed no signs of going back on his decision. Soon, however, Ferguson turned on the charm and used his remarkable powers of persuasion to change Éric's mind. He told him how Maurice Watkins and United had taken the fight to the FA, how public opinion and the press had shifted in his favour in the past week or so and how he, Ferguson, was sure that 'everything would be all right' in the longer term. These were the words Éric wanted to hear, spoken by the very man who could give them meaning.

A couple of weeks later, on the occasion of a short trip he made to Amsterdam, where he presented the Dutch Young Player of the Year award to Michael Mols of Twente Enschede (whose hero he was), Cantona explained how 'morally, it would be impossible for me to leave Manchester United after what the people there have done for me'. Ferguson and his assistant Brian Kidd had shown 'more respect' towards him in these troubled months than he had ever experienced in his entire life, he said, and never more poignantly than on that evening in Paris. Talk soon drifted to other subjects, as happens when old friends get over a misunderstanding and choose to go back to shared convictions and memories to feed the conversation. Player and manager now reminisced about great games of the past, as they hardly needed to articulate what they both knew would happen: Cantona would come back to Manchester. Ferguson had handled him magnificently, and could justifiably write four years later: 'Those hours spent in Éric's company [. . .] added up to one of the more worthwhile acts I have performed in this stupid job of mine.' Stupid? Really?

On Monday 14 August Cantona reported for training at The Cliff, four days after Manchester United had called a press conference to pass on the good news. The Italian transfer window had shut shortly before, as Amorfini angrily reminded a reporter who had contacted him on the phone, and there was no question of Éric joining Inter as a 'joker', that is, signing a pre-contract agreement and waiting until the reopening of the transfer market in November to become a *nerazzuro*. 'His future is secure with us,' Ferguson announced. 'I haven't had much sleep, but I'm happy the job has now been done.' That much was settled. But there were still another seven weeks to go before Cantona could resume playing for United, when Liverpool, supposedly their main rival for the title (according to the bookmakers), would travel to Old Trafford on 1 October.

The abrupt departure of Ince, Hughes and Kanchelskis, who had been at the heart of United's surge over the past three years, had left many observers unimpressed with the team's chances for the new season. Cantona's success had convinced several of the main league contenders to look beyond Britain's borders for reinforcements. The brutally tedious 1–0 victory of Everton over Blackburn in the Charity Shield was perhaps the last occasion when traditional 'British' values decided the outcome of a domestic trophy game. Few guessed so at the time, but both clubs were throwbacks and would soon slump into mid-table mediocrity – in Blackburn's case, relegation, a mere four years after securing the

1994–95 Premiership title. It could be argued that football, one of the most insular, not to say most reactionary of businesses, entered a new century earlier than many other manifestations of working-class culture in England. This was football's 'Big Bang', a decade after the London Stock Exchange had mutated into a hitherto unknown beast thanks to deregulation. Football swooned into cosmopolitanism, at a time when it had become habitual for summer holidaymakers to ride donkeys in Corfu rather than Blackpool. Suddenly, each club had to have their foreign 'star' (a bit like most indie-pop bands had to have a female bassist or guitarist towards the end of the 1980s). David Ginola joined Newcastle; Dennis Bergkamp, incredibly, swapped Inter for Arsenal; Ruud Gullit now wore the blue of Chelsea – and let's not forget the dazzling Georgian Georgi Kinkladze, who would enchant Manchester City fans for three memorable seasons.

Not everyone thought that 1995–96 could be a high watermark in Cantona's career. Some still maintained that the reopening of the Italian transfer market on 1 November – for a week only – would see Moratti pounce again, this time decisively. Rob Hughes was one of the very few observers who believed that with his namesake Mark Hughes and Paul Ince gone, Bryan Robson retired and Steve Bruce nearing 30, the time was right for Cantona to become the lynchpin of the side, and not just in a playing sense. Far-sighted as he was, the journalist was actually describing what had already happened rather than what could be hoped for. Éric was already a captain in all but name. No other senior player on United's staff exerted the same positive influence on his younger teammates, all of whom were hungry for guidance. In December 1994, immediately after United's 4–0 trouncing of Galatasaray in the Champions League, Alex Ferguson had made his way to the dressing-room, where he had found Cantona standing by the tactics board, explaining passages of play to an awe-struck David Beckham and Gary Neville, two of the players who now stayed behind to train with Éric long after they were supposed to leave The Cliff. Cantona had always been a believer in Chateaubriand's maxim: 'Talent is a long apprenticeship.' To the delight of his manager, he was now passing on this conviction, first to a small group of youngsters, then to the whole of the United squad, one of many ways in which his legacy can still be felt at Old Trafford, where the pupils of old, like Neville, Paul Scholes and Ryan Giggs, have now turned into mentors themselves. 'Now they all stay [behind after training] except for Steve Bruce, who needs his rest,' Ferguson said. 'On Fridays I have to tell them to come in.'

But this transformation was taking place behind the scenes, and on the evening of 19 August, after United had melted away 3–1 at Villa Park on the opening day of the season, it certainly looked as if Alex Ferguson's gamble to build a new side around products of the club's academy (all of whom had been part of the 1992 FA Youth Cup-winning team) had been ill-judged, and catastrophically so. No less than four of them – six if one includes substitutes John O'Kane and David Beckham, who replaced Phil Neville at half-time, and scored a late consolation goal – took part in a match that could have been billed 'men against boys'. What no one foresaw – except Ferguson – was that the 'boys', placed under the tutelage of Éric Cantona, would soon eclipse the 'men'. The former Liverpool captain-turned-pundit Alan Hansen (who won his first English league title at the age of twenty-two) later became the target of much ridicule, having famously asserted that 'you can't win anything with kids' in the season's first *Match of the Day* programme. His mistake was to speak as if he was enunciating a self-evident truth, with more than a hint of scorn towards Ferguson's project. He had also chosen to ignore that, despite the absence of the injured Steve Bruce, a back four of Parker, Irwin, Pallister and Gary Neville, supposedly shielded by the 'anchor' Roy Keane, should have done more to protect Peter Schmeichel. Hansen's opinion was shared by most observers, however, who were stunned when this defeat proved to be an aberration. There were another six Premiership games to play before the end of Cantona's ban, and of these, United won five and drew the other, defeating English champions Blackburn 2–1 at Ewood Park on 28 August, the twenty-year-old Beckham scoring the decisive goal.

This is not to say that United had found a way to live without Éric. As September drew to a close, and Old Trafford was readied for the outcast's return to centre stage, Ferguson's inexperienced team exited two competitions in less than a week. On the 20th – the day the

Advocate-General of the European Court of Justice Carl Otto Lenz found in favour of Belgian footballer Jean-Marc Bosman and changed the face of football for ever – a deliberately weakened United side was blown away 3–0 by second division York City in the League Cup. At home. In truth, Ferguson cared little for this competition, far less than for the UEFA Cup, which his club had never won, and which still retained much of its prestige. But six days later, Rotor Volgograd, a strong side if not exactly Europe's most glamorous club, held on for a 2–2 draw in Manchester – despite 'keeper Peter Schmeichel scoring the only goal of his English career from a header. United, who had brought back an encouraging 0–0 from the first leg, exited the competition on the away-goals rule.

In other circumstances, this early exit from Europe would have triggered a thorough examination of United's dismal recent record in international competitions, but the debate was short-lived, as everything was piffle compared to the return of the 'King'. On the morning of 28 September the media were given the very rare privilege of attending a short training session on the Old Trafford pitch, which was little more than a chance to snap Cantona wearing his no. 7 red shirt again. The fans – who had been singing Cantona songs throughout his ban – had been kept out, and it was only the presence of a few workmen busying themselves on the stadium's new stand that gave a semblance of reality to the scene. Éric predictably refrained from making any public comment, and Alex Ferguson sounded guarded when he met the press at the conclusion of this photo opportunity. Did he feel confident? Reasonably so, he said, before adding, 'I wouldn't think that anyone would want to go down that road again. I don't think he'll want to suffer all that, himself or his family. The stigma is always going to be there in the history books.'

Judging by the press coverage, the only topic of interest for the English public was Éric Cantona. Even London's Stock Exchange was not immune to this collective fever. On the 29th Manchester United shares rose 3p to an all-time high. It was expected that the club would announce record profits within the week (they did, to the tune of £18.8m, £8m more than in the previous tax year), which accounted in part for the optimism of the traders, but in part only: Cantona's return would undoubtedly boost his team's performance on and off the pitch. Merchandise bearing his likeness or his name represented a disproportionate slice of the club's sales of memorabilia: £4m, over 20 per cent of their turnover in that sector alone, three times what Paris Saint-Germain, one of France's leading clubs, could hope to earn from sales of replica shirts and the like over a whole season.

Keeping Éric – I daren't say at all costs – made sense economically as well as in sporting terms, for Manchester United and for the player's sponsor, Nike, who did everything in their power to increase the visibility of one of their most precious assets (whom they paid £200,000 a year for the use of his image). Posters appeared on advertising boards throughout the country. They showed Cantona, collar up, back to the camera, a ball in his left hand, about to step onto the pitch. The open gate couldn't have looked more like prison bars. The tag? 'He's been punished for his mistakes. Now it's someone else's turn.' Pierre Canton (no relation), who managed the Cantona account for Nike in France, explained: 'His personality corresponds with that of our company, irreverent and a touch rebellious.' Very clever too. A stark, strikingly simple TV ad featuring Éric and Newcastle centre-forward Les Ferdinand was put on heavy rotation on commercial networks. Its objectives were manifold: to promote a message of tolerance, obviously, making anti-racism 'cool' for the younger, hipper football supporters who were also customers of Nike; but also to re-establish Cantona as *the* towering figure in the game, the Premier League's premier personality, and assimilating any abuse that might be directed at the disgraced footballer to an attack, not just on an individual, but on values that no one in their right mind could fail to share. It was a means of protecting Éric from the provocation it was thought he would constantly encounter in months to come. The subtext of this short film was clear: hecklers must be xenophobic, if not outright racist, and had to be shamed into silence.

There was a real fear that something would go wrong. The hostility of the crowds towards a player they loved to hate would redouble, and it could be expected that no quarter would be given to Cantona on the field of play. His opponents would rile and taunt him, the referees would be on the lookout to punish his slightest misdemeanour. Hadn't David Elleray, the Harrow schoolmaster who would officiate in his first game back, already dismissed Roy Keane earlier in the season? It couldn't be long before 'another Crystal Palace'; only this time, there could be no way back. 'It'll be ten times worse than before,' predicted George Best. 'He'll have to show to everyone, and especially himself, that he is able to face it, [. . .] that he has grown and has become a man.'

All observers peppered their columns with grave words of warning – and all of them were proved wrong. This would be the season of redemption, for player and fans alike. The revolting chants that had been heard while Éric was serving his ban died down in the stands, and the presence of United's chief security enforcer Ned Kelly by his side was soon felt to be an unnecessary reminder of a darker past. Defenders didn't go out of their way to make Cantona's life easier on the pitch; but nor did they try to exploit the supposed fragility of his character, and the next eight months passed almost without a blemish from one side or the other. This showed the respect his fellow professionals had for Cantona, a respect his exemplary conduct certainly demanded. Éric himself was deeply touched by the fairness of his opponents, and developed an even stronger bond with England and its football as a result, not that anyone could have predicted how smooth the path to reacceptance would be – except, maybe, Alex Ferguson himself. 'He was ready to confront the crowds, the media and all the rest,' the manager confided to Erik Bielderman many years later. 'I had to show as much courage as he had shown himself, by supporting him. Publicly, but also within the team. Éric came back a stronger man. He came back more mature, too. He was also more wary. I'm flabbergasted by the strength with which he went through this ordeal. I discovered myself to be even closer to the man than before.'

Necessary as they were, physical fitness and mental readiness did not guarantee that Cantona could waltz in and perform as if he had never been away. Éric's successful rehabilitation also depended on his acquiring an understanding of the tactical changes that had affected English football in his long absence, namely the adoption of three-man central defences by a number of teams in the Premiership. Today, the 3-5-2 system may seem an antiquated formation only deployed by backward-looking Eastern European and Asian teams, as the flat back four it replaced for a while is now the common denominator of all modern formations. But 3-5-2 was the height of sophistication then: it had been imported from the Continent, after all. It was believed to pose near insurmountable problems to attacking players who hadn't come across it. When Alex Ferguson was asked whether Cantona could deal with it, he brushed the doubters aside with another affirmation of his striker's unique talent. 'He just takes centre-backs into an area where they don't know whether to go or stay. He has an awareness of where he is pulling people. He drifts into midfield, drifts behind a striker, sometimes he drifts out on to the line. But when a cross comes in or something is going to happen in the box, he is not far away.' Few shared the Scot's confidence: the time had finally come for Éric to demonstrate that it hadn't been misplaced.

The first of October 1995. Hawkers had set up their stalls well in advance on Matt Busby Way, loading their tables with commemorative T-shirts ('Back with a vengeance', among many others). A group of hardcore United fans had placed cheeky advertisements in national newspapers, which read: 'We'll never forget that night at Crystal Palace (when you buried that amazing volley against Wimbledon).' Due to the work carried out on a new stand, Old Trafford could only accommodate 34,101 spectators that afternoon, but thousands more milled around the stadium, many of them clutching copies of the matchday programme, whose cover was half-filled by a portrait of a smiling Éric. Reporters had been dispatched from all over Europe to cover the event, which was not a top-of-the-table clash (United trailed Newcastle by a single point, Liverpool by two), but the homecoming of Éric Cantona. In the absence of any new material to broadcast, BBC Radio Five Live aired an hour-long interview with '*Dieu*' which had been taped a year previously. 'God was back among his disciples', as David Lacey wrote in the *Guardian* (adding presciently that the real test would be at Chelsea, three weeks later, where he would be 'the Devil incarnate'), and cameras were there in extraordinary numbers to record the resurrection: *one hundred and eight* television crews (I feel compelled to write out this scarcely believable figure in full) were positioned around the pitch. The public address system drowned Old Trafford with the main theme of *The Magnificent Seven.* And at 15:58 the last of the Manchester United players to exit the dressing-room made his triumphant entrance on the field: Éric Cantona, 248 days, 18 hours and 22 minutes after he had last performed for his club in a competitive game. Old Trafford was a sea of tricolours, each flag-brandishing fan a wave in an ocean. It was as if the crowd was intent on staging their own version of Bastille Day, with FA chairman Bert Millichip, one presumes, in the role of Louis XVI climbing the steps to the guillotine.

One of these spectators was the French character actress Sabine Azema, whom Éric had met on the set of *Le Bonheur est dans le pré,** and who had never attended a football game before. 'As you approached the ground,' she recalled, 'it was as if you were in Lourdes, except that instead of pictures of Bernadette Soubirous [*the young shepherdess who claimed to have had visions of the Virgin*], it was pictures of Éric Cantona. The closer you got, the louder people were screaming, their fists raised. For me, the queen of the cowards, it was hell – I started to panic, to weep, and I can't remember who won that day'. No one did: the game finished 2–2.

One of the linesmen was called Messiah, a fact that didn't escape the wits in the press box. Cantona received a '9/10' from the *Manchester Evening News,* one of many rave notices which should have been enough to make him footballer of the season, let alone of the day. 'Éric de Triomphe' (*Daily Mirror*), 'Super-Can' (*Sun*), had touched the ball 49 times, completing 31 of 43 passes. The Monday papers were full of such statistical titbits, dissecting every one of Éric's moves to the point of absurdity. His first touch occurred on sixty-seven seconds. Andy Cole passed him the ball on the left wing. Cantona took a couple of strides, crossed, Nicky Butt surged and scored his first goal of the

* This film, directed by Étienne Chatillez and shot in the late spring of 1995, marked Cantona's acting debut. His brother Joël was also given a small speaking part. Both attracted decent if slightly condescending reviews for their performances.

season. Easy. The most dynamic player in a strangely lethargic side, Cantona supplied Lee Sharpe with another sumptuous pass, but the winger missed from eight yards out. Liverpool then scored twice through Robbie Fowler (who, as his manager Roy Evans later argued with some justification, had been the 'real man of the match' in terms of performance), before Jamie Redknapp tugged Ryan Giggs' jersey in the box, earning the hosts a penalty. Cantona immediately took the ball under his arm, waited for the recriminations to die down, walked to the spot, and sent David James the wrong way. He was not one to strike carefully choreographed poses after he had scored a goal. To him, it was both an individual release and a chance to share in collective joy: a choreographed celebration would have debased the act of scoring and dulled the raw emotion. But that successful penalty kick was unlike any he had taken before. He ran on towards the crowd, and pole-danced on the left stanchion of Liverpool's goal.

Strangely, what should have been a stern examination of Éric's temperament turned out to be a tepid affair, as if all the players – except Cantona himself – had really soaked up the hype to such an extent that they believed this game was about one man only. Even Neil Ruddock kept his own counsel – no collar jokes this time and, as David Lacey rightly pointed out, hardly any tackles either. Alone among the twenty-two players, only Cantona seemed to want more. With the score at 2–2, he could be heard shouting at the bench, 'How long? How long?'

Éric's hunger was in evidence again two days later, when United travelled to York's Bootham Crescent ground, forty coachloads of fans in tow, to try and make up for the 3–0 defeat they had conceded in Manchester in late September. They failed – just, Paul Scholes scoring a brace in a 3–1 win. The result was a setback, but was balanced by the fact that Cantona had played the full ninety minutes, and wanted more. So, on 7 October, 21,502 spectators turned up to watch their god in action against Leeds United – in a reserve game that attracted a bigger crowd than any other match played that Saturday in England. Éric unfortunately had to limp off the pitch after eighteen minutes, having hurt his right knee in a collision with Jason Blunt. The injury appeared to be slight at first, but caution had to be exercised in view of the forthcoming Manchester derby, an occasion which Cantona had always relished in the past. Mindful of the disappointment felt by the spectators, Éric had a message of apology read out on the ground's PA by physio Robert Swaires, a gesture that was much appreciated. He also pulled out of a friendly played in Swansea in honour and for the benefit of former Bury manager Bobby Smith, against a Welsh XI that featured Ryan Giggs. This rest was to no avail: the knock he had suffered was more serious than thought – a medial ligament strain – and he could play no part in United's 1–0 victory over City in the 123rd Mancunian derby. Frustratingly, he would have to wait until 21 October to play again. The Liverpool game had been a quasi-religious celebration of his relationship with the faithful; what awaited him at Stamford Bridge promised to be an ordeal instead of a *grand-messe.*

Éric hadn't been back to London since the Crystal Palace fracas. One of the Premiership's most hostile crowds was waiting for him. What's more, the referee of that game was none other than Alan Wilkie – the man who had dismissed him at Selhurst Park nine months earlier. Chelsea did all they could, and probably more than they should, to protect him. Every time he emerged on the field or left it, he was accompanied by a guard of eight stewards clad in DayGlo overalls – plus an impressively built security guard for good measure. The press were denied access to him. In fact, it was as if a magnetic field had been created around the player, which extended on to the pitch where the Blues gave such a feeble account of themselves that, ten minutes after the game had started, their supporters had changed the target of their jeers from Cantona to their own players. Éric couldn't have hoped for a more comfortable afternoon, and contributed to three of his side's four goals without really doing much more than walking the ball down the left wing. United, 4–1 winners, now stood second in the table, four points behind Newcastle.

The next match (a visit by Middlesbrough), a homecoming of sorts for Bryan Robson, now Boro's manager, was littered with ugly fouls and bookings, plus a sending-off, when Roy Keane reminded Jan-Aage Fjortoft of his days sparring in Cork's boxing clubs by sending him to the ground with a powerful right hook. Three minutes before the final whistle, Éric cushioned the ball beautifully, turned it between Boro's two central defenders, and served it up to Andy Cole on a silver platter. United won 2–0. The goals were not flowing as freely as before his ban (only one in four games since his return, and that from a penalty), but this was partly due to a slightly more withdrawn position on the pitch, behind Cole and the twenty-year-old Paul Scholes. But, slowly, Éric was finding his feet – and showing he could keep the lid on his temper. He still looked tentative at times, unsure of his rhythm, struggling to link up with Cole as he had done so naturally with Mark Hughes. He was also suffering from the uncertainty that could be detected in United's play as a whole.

In early November, Alex Ferguson's work in progress was checked at Arsenal (0–1), as Newcastle dug deep to overcome Liverpool 2–1 at St James' Park to establish a six-point cushion at the top of the league. United's engine briefly clicked into gear after this reverse, admittedly helped by the mediocrity of the opposition. First Southampton, then Coventry assented to the former champions' supremacy, shipping four goals each, Éric content with adding two assists to his account along the way. Then Nottingham Forest (who Cantona had described as 'the most defensive side in the league', somewhat harshly) produced a magnificent performance to earn a 1–1 draw on 27 November. Éric was back at his best, conjuring a penalty in the final third of the game when Chettle fouled him in the box. He converted it himself. Less than a week later, it was the Frenchman again who inspired a workmanlike Manchester United to another 1–1 draw, against Chelsea, teasing the Blues' six-man midfield with his subtle runs and unerring vision: only Andy Cole's profligacy cost Éric's side two points, not for the last time that season.

His team was undoubtedly struggling: Sheffield Wednesday left Old Trafford with a 2–2 draw, Liverpool prevailed 2–0 at Anfield, and United had now collected only 4 out of 12 possible points. In both games, however, Cantona had been the catalyst of almost all of United's more dangerous moves: two goals (the second a beautiful volley which brought the scores level five minutes from time) rewarded him in the first game, while he showed admirable restraint in front of constant crowd abuse in Liverpool. But that wasn't quite enough. By the time

Leeds beat them 3–1 on Christmas Eve, United trailed Newcastle by 10 points, a gap that hardly a soul believed could be bridged. Keegan's 'Cavaliers' cut quite a dash, while the tireless but awkward Andy Cole – a former Magpie himself – had become an infuriating symbol of and a scapegoat for all that was wrong with United, which was rather a lot. Nearly two months had passed since their last victory. Had it not been for Cantona's superb form, their position would've been even more desperate, but they were given a chance to regain some pride and a modicum of hope when the leaders travelled to Manchester on 27 December. They seized it. Goals by Cole (at long last) and Roy Keane decided the game, Cantona winning hands down his duel with David Ginola, whom Dennis Irwin snuffed out of the proceedings.

It had been a convincing victory, inasmuch as it confirmed that United could hold their own against any opposition on their day. But a single result couldn't decide the outcome of the race for the championship. United could stir themselves out of a slump, but still lacked the substance to use an outstanding success as a foundation for consistency. Every team must learn how to hang on when its turn inevitably comes to cope with injuries, but Alex Ferguson's assortment of youths and older hands had yet to coalesce into a real unit. With Steve Bruce, David May and Gary Pallister sidelined with a variety of complaints (Dennis Irwin and Peter Schmeichel would soon join them on the sick list), the manager turned to one of Éric's former Auxerre teammates, William Prunier, to shore up his defence. Signed on Cantona's recommendation, Prunier became a cult hero when he set up the first goal in United's 2–1 grim win over QPR on 30 December, smacking the bar later in the game for good measure. But this would be the shortest-lived cult in the history of Manchester United. On New Year's Day, Spurs beat them 4–1 at White Hart Lane, their biggest defeat in three years, for which the disconsolate 'other Frenchman', at fault on two of the goals, would pay dearly. Alex Ferguson would never select him again. The manager's only consolation was that Andy Cole had scored his fourth goal in four matches.

His friend's humiliation may still have affected Éric when Sunderland came close to ending his club's progress in the FA Cup third round later in the week. 'When [Cantona] is subdued, United are only half the team,' as a journalist wrote in his account of the 2–2 draw. Subdued or not, he still rescued his team with a header from a Lee Sharpe free kick shortly before the final whistle. He had also looked within himself, and decided to demonstrate his attachment to United's cause with a very public gesture: he shaved his head.

He had done so once already when at Auxerre. But this had been the prank of a twenty-year-old who wanted to needle his then manager, Guy Roux. It was now a means of identification with the youth of his adoptive city, and a statement of intent as well: this was the look that many of the foremost musicians on the 'Madchester' scene had adopted, Shaun Ryder of The Happy Mondays and Black Grape, for example, and which had been copied by many of the young working-class fans who moved between the Hacienda nightclub and Old Trafford in their spare time. It also evoked pictures of commandos readying themselves for action on the front line – hard, uncompromising, fearless. At the end of the first match he played in this new guise – a goalless draw against Aston Villa, on 13 January – he walked off the pitch without shaking a single hand. This remoteness was understood at the time as an expression of his frustration with Andy Cole, which he had made obvious by huffs and puffs throughout the match. Nothing seemed to work any more. Even the two telepathists, Giggs and Cantona, played as if they were reading an absent friend's mind. But I would argue that Éric was also building up his reserves of anger, coiling a spring that only he knew existed. Only he – and Alex Ferguson, who still believed, or claimed to believe in his side's chances of regaining the title. 'The Premiership is like the Grand National,' he said. 'People are falling at hurdles every week and Newcastle are going to come up against a testing time. Of that I am certain.' So was Éric. But Éric had his own hurdle to jump over: what he intended to do for Manchester United, could he do for France as well?

Éric Cantona was never afraid to contradict himself. 'I talk a lot of bullshit,' he once reminded a journalist. But it is one thing to change one's mind, and quite another to hold two mutually exclusive opinions simultaneously, which is precisely what Cantona appeared to do when it came to money. The man who 'wanted to be poor' in 1987 was also by 1995 *one of the best-paid non-American sportsmen on the planet. Éric the King was also the king of endorsements,* Nike's number-one weapon in their war against other sportswear corporations in Europe. He could hardly be blamed for making the most of his commercial opportunities, especially when they were exploited with some style and inventiveness. But Cantona's relationship with the American manufacturer (which, revealingly, his retirement from football hardly affected) went far beyond what George Best did for a sausage-maker or David Ginola for a popular brand of shampoo. In truth, it belongs to another dimension altogether; and, for a long time, I struggled to make sense of it – until I shared a plate of pasta in the North London footballers' belt with Alex Fynn, a man who played a key role in the establishment of the Premier League but has always remained 'an outsider looking in', as he puts it himself, when it comes to football. It was Alex who stood up in the middle of a recent Arsenal AGM to remind the club's board they had made no mention of their recently departed vice-chairman David Dein in their annual report – the equivalent of the best man mentioning the groom's ex-girlfriend in his wedding speech. Alex, to quote another friend, has cojones.*

So, when I mentioned to him that I was writing this book and he told me that he had a couple of things that could be of value to me, I was naturally interested – very interested. I knew Alex had helped put together a largely pictorial account of Éric's career. The book itself – Cantona on Cantona *– nice enough to leaf through, was a money-spinning exercise about which Alex had no illusions. He had been brought in at the eleventh hour by the company that dealt with United's commercial interests, as they despaired of ever convincing Éric to sit down and honour some of his contractual obligations – such as contributing to books and videos about himself, which could be sold to United fans for Christmas. Cantona showed very little inclination to talk to anyone at the time; he was in the middle of the ban inflicted on him after the Crystal Palace*

* A non-exhaustive list would include: Bic razors, Sharp camcorders, Partouche casinos and online betting facilities, the Irish Lottery, Eurostar, Lipton's iced tea, as well as Nike. In 1996 the Canadian brewing company Molson also recreated the Crystal Palace 'kung-fu kick' for an advertisement – with a Cantona lookalike. Éric was not amused. The ad was subsequently withdrawn.

fracas. Alex – who spoke and could write decent French, and was not intimidated by his subject's reputation – accepted the assignment, all the more eagerly since he had formed his own ideas about how best to exploit the Cantona 'brand', to the player's as well as to the club's advantage. His ambitions were not purely mercenary. He had been struck by the effectiveness of the Nike anti-racism campaign mentioned earlier in this chapter. Its success showed how the intelligent use of sporting 'icons' could have a far greater impact on public opinion than far costlier official 'initiatives'. With this in mind, Alex believed that it was possible for the French football star to create a trust or foundation that would control and exploit his image rights for the benefit of many – without prejudice to his own earnings. Such a set-up had met with remarkable success for the Brazilian Formula 1 world champion Ayrton Senna, for example.

Over the course of the two days Alex spent in a hotel with Cantona to 'write' the book (two days!), he mentioned his plans more than once, but always drew the same response from the player: Éric was not remotely interested. Such talk bored him. The interviews bored him too. Alex – who had been a top executive at Saatchi & Saatchi for a very long time – could not comprehend such apathy. What he was proposing – with the assent of the club and of the company representing the club's interests in marketing and merchandising – could add a great deal of value to the Cantona brand, fill everyone's pockets, and achieve a great deal of good for causes close to the player's heart, should there be any, of course (something Alex had no means to ascertain). Only when photographs of Éric in action were laid out on the table did the player show any animation, indeed excitement. As long it was about him and him only, Cantona was no shrinking violet. He was happy to go along with what Nike and others offered him. Some of it was funny, some pompous, some distasteful, such as the use of the shaven-headed Cantona's resemblance to Benito Mussolini to recycle fascist imagery and design in a later advertisement for La République du Football, *a Nike-sponsored 'football village' set in the outskirts of Paris.*

Some of the comments Cantona made to justify his willingness to go along with almost anything strike me as utter – well, utter bullshit, to be frank. I have tried to find words more suited to the gravitas of a biographer, but failed. Here's one of those comments. 'Yeah, I acted that moment [at Crystal Palace],' he said (the bullshit detector is already quavering). 'It was a drama and I was an actor. I do things seriously, without taking myself seriously' (it's now vibrating dangerously). 'I think Nike found that side of my character and used it very well. Even when I kicked the fan it is because I don't take myself seriously' (evacuation orders are issued). 'I didn't think because of who I was I had a responsibility not to do it. No, I was just a footballer and a man. I don't care about being some sort of superior person. I just wanted to do whatever I wanted to do. If I want to kick a fan, I do it' (the place is now empty). 'I am not a role model. I am not a superior teacher telling you how to behave. I think the more you see, the more life is a circus.' Who is the clown?

He also hammed it up as a ringmaster in a Terry Gilliam superproduction that featured 'jailed' footballers aboard a prison ship, and not without showing a certain talent for comedy. But he wasn't merely playing a game. Three years ago, a charity game was organized with the help of Guy Roux between French and German sides, for which Éric was drafted at the last minute. He kindly consented to play, and all went well until he realized he had been given boots from the 'wrong' manufacturer – at which point he panicked. Rebellion has its limits.

Nike's exploitation of Éric's status as an institutional rebel flattered his ego, fed his perception of himself as a messenger (I daren't say an angel) of freedom. The 'message' might have been a universal one (joga bonito, play the beautiful game as it should be played, if one forgets about the sickly sentimentalization of Brazilian football that underpins the marketing exercise), but there was no doubt as to who would deliver it: Éric Cantona. When, in 1996, a celebrated 'Nike stars v The Devil' 'super-ad' was shot at the Coliseum in Rome, it was Éric who dispatched the demon goalkeeper with a perfectly timed 'Au revoir'. To me, if there is a shadow hanging over Éric's personality, which must lead to uneasy questions about the sincerity of his sincerity, it has to be his self-serving compliance with the agenda set for him by his commercial partners, and his reactions when he felt his interests were threatened by outsiders in this regard, as the independent publisher Ringpull Press found to its cost in 1995.

This minuscule company had come up with the idea of collecting Cantona's best sallies in a volume titled La Philosophie de Cantona, gathering the material from a number of public sources, including the

English-language version of Éric's autobiography. The publishers of that book, Headline, had not given their consent, however. Nor had Manchester United, and the owners of Ringpull Press had no choice but to stop the distribution of La Philosophie, *remove the passages which amounted to a breach of copyright, and add the club's logo to the book's cover. The revised edition went into production, with a print run of 30,000 copies. It is at that moment that Éric's lawyers were instructed to act. His agents objected to the picture of their client used on the dust jacket: a beret and a goatee beard had been added to Cantona's face. Ringpull had to take its book off the shelves, and the company collapsed.*

18

The relief of scoring.

THE MAN WHO WASN'T THERE: JANUARY–MAY 1996

'I should have been born English. When I hear "God Save the Queen" it can make me cry, much more than when I hear "La Marseillaise". *I feel close to the rebelliousness and vigour of the youth here. Perhaps time will separate us, but nobody can deny that here, behind the windows of Manchester, there is an insane love of football, of celebration and of music.'*

Éric Cantona committed suicide in January 1996 in a Manchester hotel room. But none of the three people present – Éric, Aimé Jacquet and Henri Émile – remembers precisely when the trigger was pulled. Émile's only recollection is that some time towards the end of that month, a few days before France beat Portugal 3–2 in a friendly, he and the manager of *Les Bleus* made a rare joint visit to England. As Manchester United played (and won 1–0, Éric scoring the winner) at West Ham on the 22nd, and the French were in action forty-eight hours later in Paris, the meeting must have taken place just before the game at Upton Park. But it is impossible to be more precise than that. Jacquet had a proposal for Éric, who hadn't played for France since he captained the side to a 1–0 defeat of the Netherlands on 18 January 1995, one week before the events at Crystal Palace. The fortunes of the national team had improved significantly in Cantona's absence. Three of the four Euro qualifiers that had been played before his suspension had ended in goalless draws.* Since

* France drew 0–0 with Slovakia, Romania and Poland, and beat Azerbaijan 2–0, between September and December 1994.

then, France had taken wing with four wins in six games, including a crucial 3–1 away victory in Romania, scoring twenty goals and conceding only two along the way. Jacquet, however, was distraught at the idea of not taking Éric along to the 1996 European Championships in which his team had now earned a place. In Émile's words, leaving Cantona out 'would be to inflict hurt on the man who'd been the first to join the adventure'. But others had stepped into the breach since then. Jacquet couldn't ignore the idea that France was close to finding a new, intriguing balance, thanks to the emerging genius of Zinédine Zidane and to the understanding the Bordeaux playmaker had developed with PSG's Youri Djorkaeff.

Both were consistent goalscorers, but neither operated within the conventional parameters of centre-forward play. They drifted, looked for space and angles of attack which were strikingly modern (in that they did away with the idea of a focal point, a *point de fixation* in the forward line, years before teams like Spalletti's AS Roma and Ferguson's post-Van Nistelrooy's United showed that penetration and success didn't depend on the presence of an old-style predator). The lack of a 'natural-born killer' in French football at that time forced Jacquet's hand to an extent. Jean-Pierre Papin (then 31 years old, and playing the last of his two seasons at Bayern Munich) would have been a shoo-in had it not been for recurrent knee injuries that rendered him largely ineffectual. No obvious replacement was available, although quite a few were tried – and found wanting. The names of Patrice Loko, Nicolas Ouédec and Mikaël Madar (one of France least successful exports to England, where he spent a forgettable season with Everton in 1997–98) were unlikely to strike fear in France's opponents. Stéphane Guivarc'h's colossal work-rate will always come second to the strange fact that as the designated lone striker of the French team, he didn't score a single goal in their victorious 1998 World Cup campaign.

Jacquet, quite reasonably, worried that making space for Cantona would slow down his team's impetus; he couldn't upset his system to accommodate a particular player. Éric, until his moment of folly, had been deployed as an attacking midfielder in a fluid version of the manager's favoured 4-4-2, in which the two centre-forwards frequently sought out space on the flanks, creating a 'free zone' in the middle of the pitch. Cantona could glide there naturally, as if sucked in by their lateral movement. But France lacked strikers of proven international class, and had evolved towards a 4-3-2-1 formation which revolved around the combined skills of Djorkaeff and Zidane and their talent for improvisation. The front player they moved behind would hustle the opposition's central defenders, a kind of advanced 'water-carrier' who was expected to disrupt the back line and create holes for others to exploit. This tactical formation could look frustratingly negative when the two *fantasistas* were not on song; when they were (which was most of the time) the music they made together was ravishing, and extremely effective. Jacquet had no desire and no reason to disrupt that harmony. He had never closed the door on Cantona (or Ginola, for that matter, who was captivating crowds in England with Newcastle). Earlier that month, he'd told journalists that 'they [were] players of international calibre' whom he couldn't 'cut out'. 'All will depend on their output between now and the tournament,' he explained. Some thought Jacquet was paying lip-service to public opinion and nothing more, as Cantona's estrangement from the national squad had developed into a matter of national debate in France. Éric's exploits (and rehabilitation) with Manchester United hadn't gone unnoticed, to say the least, up to the point that they fed yet more rumour-mongering when news of his exclusion from the national squad was broken in May 1996. What Cantona's supporters didn't know was that it was Éric himself who refused the hand Jacquet held out to him.

'Neither Aimé nor myself thought that what happened at Crystal Palace would signify the end for Éric as a French national team player,' Émile told me. 'The events meant that he took himself out of the team because of his ban. And the team was winning without him. Still, Aimé had an idea. When Éric came back after his eight-month suspension, we had qualified for Euro 96. As a manager, should Aimé question what had been positive and ensured qualification? Should he yield to the pressure of the media which lobbied for Éric to return in the role he'd played before, as skipper, playmaker and orchestrator from midfield? Or should he do something which meant evolving from the set-up we'd put in place?' After a great deal of soul-searching, Jacquet decided to gamble: he would ask Cantona to return to the fold. And on that evening in Manchester, he did.

The coach's decision was not solely motivated by Éric's superb performances in the Premier League. Euro 96 would take place in England; what's more, should they qualify for the latter stages of the tournament, France were likely to play at Old Trafford.* With Cantona on the field, the French could count on the support of the largely Mancunian crowd, as foreign fans were not expected to travel in large numbers to a country still seen as a hotbed of hooliganism. Jacquet explained to Cantona that France would carry on playing as they had done in the previous months, adding that they needed a centre-forward. He then put the question to Éric.

'Do you want to be that player?'

'Éric said no, straight away,' Émile recalls. But Cantona, who seemed 'strangely distant', didn't offer any explanation for his refusal. Shaken but undeterred, Jacquet told him that he would 'draw the consequences he [needed] from this', but that under no circumstances could he envisage having Éric Cantona as a mere substitute. However, should Zidane or Djorkaeff be unavailable for one reason or another, could he count on him? Éric made no reply. Jacquet put the question to him again and, at the third time of asking, an answer finally fell from Cantona's lips. 'You can count on me,' he said, 'but you'll have to call me beforehand, so that we can talk it over.'

Now in his 75th year, Émile still spends a great deal of time with Cantona through his involvement with the French beach-soccer team, which Éric took to the world title as a manager in May 2005. He has tried to get to the heart of Cantona's incomprehensible *froideur* that night on a number of occasions, but his repeated enquiries get short shrift every time. 'Éric says he can't remember much of what happened then,' he told me disbelievingly. 'If he'd agreed to be in the team, he'd have been in the starting eleven, and we could have been European champions – as we lost on penalties in the semi-finals.' He could also have carried on to the 1998 World Cup, been part of the unit that

* They did, going out 6–5 in a penalty shoot-out against the Czechs in the semi-final after the game had finished scoreless after extra time.

beat Brazil 3–0 in an unforgettable final, and silenced all the detractors who single out the absence of any international honour at senior level in his collection of trophies to deny him footballing greatness. But he said no. He turned his back on the greatest chance he'd been given in his whole career, as if it were meant to be that way. But it wasn't. He chose not to have a last opportunity to fail. Why? It couldn't be because the position didn't appeal to him any more: he had occupied it for Manchester United regularly, as he had done at Auxerre and Marseille, and would do so again in his last season in England. Had the 'fear of losing' that he claimed was his greatest motivation to play finally overwhelmed him? Was he scared to be found wanting as he had been in 1992?

Not once has he mentioned the reasons behind his decision to walk away from France in the numerous interviews he's given since then. Only a very small number of people have been aware – until now – that it could and probably should have been Éric Cantona and not Patrice Loko or Stéphane Guivarc'h who led France's attack not just at Euro 1996, but at the 1998 *Mondiale* too. Cantona himself did little to silence those who muttered that Jacquet had been obeying 'orders from above' to leave him by the wayside. Later that year, he took advantage of a guest appearance on a popular French TV programme to criticize the omission of his and Jean-Pierre Papin's names from the Euro 96 squad. 'I'm still available,' he insisted. '[The French football authorities] would be very happy if I said I wasn't.' The 'Cantonians' (Bernard Morlino among them) went further: many of them still argue that their hero was shunned because he was under contract with Nike, not Adidas, the French team's official sponsor. This is utter nonsense. In fairness, Cantona himself toned down his criticism over time. In 2007 he said that he 'understood Jacquet's decision [to leave him out]', adding this telling caveat, '*in a wider context*'. 'My eight-month ban had allowed a new generation to claim their place,' he told *L'Équipe Magazine*, 'and they were winning. It was normal that they should stay.' But Cantona didn't stop at this magnanimous comment. He added: 'I think I could've played. Sincerely, I could have played just as much as Stéphane Guivarc'h did, couldn't I? I feel like I'm belittling myself when I say that. To quote Charles Bukowski, "Truth is evidence that no one tells."'

Hadn't Guivarc'h played as a centre-forward? The real truth is that Éric froze at the precise moment when he was called back in. His reluctance to admit it, his lapses of memory, speak of a fragile man who will forever carry 'the greatest regret of his career' (that much he has confessed, speaking of his missing out on two extraordinary years in the history of the French national team) as if it had happened to someone else. If retiring, for a footballer, is 'a kind of death', the cause of it in Éric's case was not murder. 'You cannot go against the choice of such a player,' Émile told me, 'and only Éric could tell you why he made that choice.' But Éric left no suicide note.

No Euro 96 meant no World Cup. It also meant that Cantona could never exorcize the demons of November 1993, never know what could have been; he would remain, for ever, the nearly man of a nearly team. He would play on through the remaining year-and-a-half of his career with no hope of doing for France what his hero Diego Maradona had done for Argentina in 1986, and been so close to doing in 1990 and 1994. '[If I had been selected by France for Euro 96], with the World Cup in 1998, I would certainly not have stopped in 1997,' he confessed much later, in April 2007. 'And if we'd won the European Cup with Manchester that year, maybe I'd have carried on too.' But isn't it significant that he himself has never spoken publicly about his conversation with Jacquet, that, even in private, he claimed not to remember a word of it? It's tempting to see in this denial of one of the most pivotal decisions in his life a desire to stamp out the vertigo that must have engulfed him when Jacquet and Émile left his hotel room. And then, as if freed from an unbearable weight, he devoted himself to the cause of Manchester United, and did for them what he had made sure he couldn't do for France: be the architect of victory.

There seemed to be no hope of catching up with the runaway leaders, Newcastle, who were twelve points ahead of their nearest pursuers Liverpool at that stage, and were now rumoured to have captured one of Serie A's most potent attackers, Parma's Colombian Faustino Asprilla. United themselves trailed in third after their 1–0 victory at West Ham, sending a mixed message to their supporters. Once again, they had finished with ten men after Nicky Butt received two yellow cards, and had Éric to thank not just for a stupendous winning goal, scored from a very acute angle, but also for defusing an ugly confrontation between Julian Dicks and Roy Keane which could have led to further dismissals. His convict's hairstyle may have made him look more threatening than ever, but his peacemaking role earned a few admiring comments in the Tuesday papers. There was also the confirmation that Manchester United's reliance on their French talisman was growing by the game. He was again a central figure in a brutal dismantling of first division Reading (3–0) in the fourth round of the FA Cup, in which the only surprise was to see the psychic Uri Geller practise one of his spoon-bending tricks on Bobby Charlton and Cantona's father Albert, who had come on one of his increasingly numerous Éric-watching trips to England.

Albert was in the stands again on 3 February, the guest of honour of Wimbledon's chairman Sam Hammam, to see his son return to Selhurst Park a year and a week after the infamous game against Crystal Palace. United won at a stroll (4–2), with Éric at the heart of every single one of their attacks – Éric wearing the captain's armband after Steve Bruce, his forehead badly gashed, had been forced to leave the field. The first of his two goals was as exquisite in its conception – a bewildering exchange of passes with David Beckham – as it was brave in its execution, as defender Chris Perry had raised his boot to reach the ball when Cantona headed it. He then rounded off the scoring with a penalty, and the Dons' manager Joe Kinnear joined the long list of English coaches who had praised their chief tormentor. 'He's got everything that's great about a player,' he gushed. 'He drifts in, ghosts in and out, making it almost impossible to do anything about him. Some say he's a lesser player since he came back, but I can't see that.'

Manchester United had played their last four games away from home, and won them all, Éric scoring four times. The pattern for the rest of the season had been established. Cantona had, it seemed, made a vow to himself. I do not choose the word 'vow' at random. His tonsure and his silence in public had a quasi-monastic quality. There was a sense of a man inhabited by a kind of ferocious but controlled anger, of a zealot bent on redressing an injustice and imposing a greater truth. Nothing would stand in his way, certainly not Blackburn, who were next on his list of victims. Of the seven chances United created in 90 minutes, he was involved in five, including that which led to Lee Sharpe's winning goal. Then Manchester City were disposed of 2–1 in the fifth round of the FA Cup. Once again, he had made the difference in one of the tightest Mancunian derbies in recent years, which United might well have lost had it not been for a controversial equalizing penalty, awarded by that man Alan Wilkie for a foul by Michael Frontzeck on, who else, Éric Cantona. City's left-back wrapped both his arms around Cantona's shoulders, the whistle blew to the bafflement of both culprit and victim, which didn't prevent the victim from turning executioner with his customary efficiency.

United's ferocious rhythm did not slacken: Everton – fielding the 'traitor' Andreï Kanchelskis, who was booed relentlessly on his return to Old Trafford – lost 2–0, Cantona having a hand in both goals. On 25 February it was Bolton's turn to face Éric's wrath. United eviscerated their hosts 6–0, Cantona walking off the pitch to be replaced by Paul Scholes (who scored a brace) with 15 minutes to go: the job had already been done, and Ferguson could give his star player a rest. This was United's eighth victory on the trot in all competitions, their fifth in the Premier League, and the tremendous pressure applied by their challengers started to have a telling impact on Newcastle. A couple of disappointing results in late February (a 2–0 defeat at West Ham, and a 3–3 draw at Manchester City) had seen their lead dwindle to four points. They had a game in hand, however, and would have an opportunity to blunt United's chances in the very next game. Alex Ferguson and Kevin Keegan were to come head to head on 4 March at St James' Park, in one of the most anticipated top-of-the-table clashes one could remember. The two French outcasts, David Ginola and Éric Cantona, would also resume their game of one-upmanship in English football. Should Newcastle win, the title, their first since 1927, would become a near certainty.

Keegan stuck to his principles of blitzing the opposition from the outset, fielding an ultra-attacking side which included just the one all-out defensive midfielder (Éric's former Leeds teammate David Batty, who was making his debut for the Magpies) to United's two, Roy Keane and Nicky Butt. Ginola, Asprilla and Peter Beardsley could be relied on to provide the ammunition for their powerful centre-forward Les Ferdinand, who tested Peter Schmeichel twice in the first half. Little was seen of Cantona in that first 45 minutes: his own midfield had been too busy trying to soak up Newcastle's offensives to supply him with decent service. How much this was part of Alex Ferguson's pre-match strategy is impossible to say. It may have been that he had instructed his team to work the ball like an opening batsman on a tricky pitch: block, and block again, wait for the bowlers to tire, then open your shoulders. This they did five minutes after the resumption and, inevitably, it was Cantona who applied the decisive stroke. Phil Neville found himself on the left of Newcastle's penalty area and lobbed a cross towards the far post, where Éric was lurking on the six-yard line, free of any marking. He met the ball with a solid right-foot volley which hit the turf before beating Pavel Srníček's dive. Silence engulfed St James' Park. There would be no way back for Newcastle, not in that game anyway. They were still one point ahead with a game in hand, but fear had chosen its camp.

For Cantona, this game marked the beginning of one of the most astonishing purple patches enjoyed by a player in the history of English football, to which, in all honesty, I have been unable to find any equivalent. It's not only that the 1–0 win on Tyneside was the first in a series of six games in which he never failed to score. In terms of statistics, others have done better, Thierry Henry and Cristiano Ronaldo among them recently. It is also that, every single time, his goals proved decisive – in the context not just of the matches themselves, but also of the progress his club made towards the second Double of its existence, and at a time when many of his teammates were experiencing a dip in their own form. On 11 March United ensured their qualification for the semi-finals of the FA Cup by beating Southampton 2–0. Éric had opened the scoring against the run of play with a goal of breathtaking beauty, in front of the biggest crowd of the English season so far (45,446 spectators): he had combined with Cole and Giggs before surging at the far post, again with deadly effect. Southampton stirred and threatened for a while, but Cantona applied the killer touch, drawing their 'keeper Dave Beasant from his line and squaring the ball for Lee Sharpe to poke in. Incredibly, Éric had yet to lose a single FA Cup tie since his arrival from France three-and-a-half years earlier, and maintained his record of scoring at least once in every round of that year's competition. United were now 5/1 on for the Double with most bookmakers.

On the 16th, a day the British had woken up to the dreadful news of the 'massacre of the innocents' in Dunblane, QPR were close to halting United's juggernaut. It looked as if most around Éric had lost the plot, some commenting that Andy Cole, who spurned chance after chance, had never grasped it to start with. The Reds looked set to suffer their first defeat since 1 January when Cantona decided to take the matter into his own hands – but not before unleashing a verbal volley at Cole which showed that his command of the vernacular was far better than some might have thought. In the third minute of added time, Cantona looped the ball into the QPR goal and United left London with a deserved but unlikely point which ensured they stayed within touching distance of Newcastle (3–0 victors at West Ham), and kept a resurgent Liverpool (who won 2–0 at Chelsea) at arm's length in third place.

Four days later, when Arsenal, who had gone six games undefeated, visited Old Trafford, it was up to Cantona to compensate for his teammates' wastefulness once more, Andy Cole doing nothing that would elevate him in his striking partner's estimation. Éric exploited a misunderstanding between Andy Linighan and David Seaman, chested the ball, took two steps forwards and struck a dipping volley under the bar. 'It had to be a special goal, and we got one,' Ferguson said. 'The most thrilling part was the way he advanced, it was sheer class – like a ballet dancer.' Newcastle, meanwhile, were shedding points like a team destined for relegation. When Arsenal beat them 2–0 at Highbury on the 23rd, they had only earned four out of fifteen in their last five outings, and United took full advantage of this slip-up a day later. Another 'Cantona special' was enough for them to prevail 1–0 over Tottenham, the last team to have beaten them, fifteen games previously. Michael Henderson hit the nail on the head in his match report for *The Times*. 'Day by day,' he wrote, 'piece by piece, the picture is becoming clearer. When the championship jigsaw is complete, it will surely reveal a central image. Éric Cantona, of course, for the brilliant

Frenchman seems determined to bring the trophy back to Old Trafford on his own.' Andy Cole had failed again, and been substituted. Éric stepped up to the crease. With 50 minutes gone, he picked up the ball well within the Spurs half, brushed off two challenges, drifted into an inside-left position, and drilled a shot to the opposite side of the goal from 20 yards. He had found the net for the fifteenth time that season – a season, it should be remembered, that had only started for him on 1 October. His failure to find the target in his club's next game – a 2–1 victory over Chelsea that gave them their third straight appearance in an FA Cup final at Wembley – was jokingly seen as an aberration, and so it proved to be. He opened the scoring against Manchester City with a penalty (3–2), three days after Newcastle had famously surrendered a 3–1 lead at Anfield to lose 4–3, and guaranteed all three points against Coventry with a forty-seventh-minute strike two days later, on 8 April. He had now scored in six consecutive league games.

I am aware of the repetitive, almost rebarbative nature of this account of Éric's most prodigious spring, a litany of goals, victories and mind-boggling statistics. My defence would be that it seemed exactly that way at the time: repetitive and strangely unexciting for unaffiliated observers, magical for Manchester United fans, galling for the rest. The unwavering sense of purpose of Cantona's crusade forced admiration and demanded a re-evaluation of his character. But it didn't prevent a form of regret from taking hold in a substantial part of the public: Newcastle, for all their brittleness, had produced thrilling football for most of the campaign, playing with an abandon and a sense of joy that only Arsène Wenger's best sides emulated afterwards; Peter Beardsley, in particular, had been in superb form, and put paid to the idea that England could not produce footballers as skilful and imaginative as their Continental counterparts. The relentlessness of United's pursuit of the title was remarkable – the degree to which it was owed to a single man even more so – but it was difficult not to feel for Keegan's Cavaliers and, for some, to think of Ferguson's troops as Roundheads.

I remember one of these afternoons when, detained at the BBC World Service, I had lost track of a game in which United were locked in a 0–0 draw at half-time. My phone rang.

'Guess what happened?' my caller asked.

'Cantona scored?' I replied, somewhat wearily. We're easily contemptuous of the familiar, and unfair towards what we believe to be predictable: Éric's achievement was of colossal proportions. The magnitude of his success, perhaps inevitably but perversely all the same, lent it an air of unreality and dulled some of its sheen. But what he did in those few weeks, when his club's hopes only gained substance through his singlemindedness and unceasing excellence, deserves to be ranked among the greatest contributions any individual footballer has made to the fortunes of an English club.

United now topped the table, but only just, and a surprising 3–1 defeat at Southampton on 13 April (with three games to go) reminded everyone how, when a trophy is in sight, its horizon can appear to recede with every step. Alex Ferguson's team had been caught cold and conceded two goals within twenty minutes. This scenario was highly unusual: not since Tottenham had humbled United on the first day of the calendar year had their rearguard been at fault so early in a game, and not even Cantona's endeavour could regain the lost ground. Newcastle played their part in rekindling suspense, narrowly beating Aston Villa at St James' Park to bridge the gap to three points. What's more, United could expect no favours from their next visitors, Leeds. In fact, while Keegan's team showed considerable grit to edge out Southampton 1–0 at home, Ferguson's side narrowly avoided a potentially catastrophic 0–0 draw when Roy Keane scored deep in the second half. Cantona's obvious frustration found its usual target in Andy Cole (who was subbed again), whereas his manager's took a subtler form when he expressed the hope that Leeds would show as much spirit against Newcastle, whom they would host a couple of weeks later, after an international break which only served to increase the tension on the domestic scene.

Kevin Keegan's extraordinary response to his rival's innuendo, his voice quivering with emotion, his index finger wagging at SkySports' camera ('I would love it if we beat them, love it!') later became a symbol of Newcastle's capitulation. If we give in to lazy preconceptions, the hypersensitive Keegan had let the canny Scot get under his skin, and lost it – 'it' being the Premier League title as well as his composure. What is often forgotten is that Keegan exploded after his team had *won* 1–0 at Elland Road, where Leeds had done everything in their power to dispel the notion that they were quite happy to roll over when their opponents were not Manchester United. When Keegan exclaimed: 'We're still fighting, and he [Ferguson] has got to go to Middlesbrough and get something,' as if each word was punctuated with an exclamation mark, it was not a defeated man who was speaking. With two games to go, the race could still go either way, even if United held the upper hand with their three-point lead and marginally superior goal difference: +20 against +18, which had been boosted by a 5–0 hammering of Nottingham Forest at Old Trafford on 28 April.

Éric was majestic that afternoon; his best moment, perhaps, a magnificent reverse pass which switched play from one wing to the other, and brought on United's third goal via the boot of David Beckham. In the 89th minute, as a young boy wearing a no. 7 shirt on which had been printed '*Dieu*' was about to leave the ground, 'God' scored the fifth and last of United's goals with a crisp strike from 12 yards. He had already shaken a post from three times that distance with the outside of his right boot.

No one could be in any doubt that the Football Writers Association had chosen the right man to be its footballer of the year a week earlier.* Alex Ferguson hailed the pressmen's choice as 'a triumph for British justice', Cantona himself as 'an honour for me and my country [and a] wonderful tribute to the rest of my colleagues at United'. *Paroles de circonstance*, maybe. But there was no denying the poignancy of this award. Many of the journalists who cast their vote in favour of the Frenchman had censured him pitilessly fifteen months previously, in some instances to the point of mindlessness. The violence of their comments had prepared the ground for the FA and the law of the realm

---

* Cantona was the third foreign footballer to be distinguished by the FWA, after Dutchman Frans Thijssen (Ipswich, 1981) and German striker Jürgen Klinsmann (Tottenham, 1995). The trophy was presented to him – as tradition demands – on the Thursday evening preceding the FA Cup final, in this case on 9 May, in London.

to hit the renegade footballer with all their might. It was more than a symbolic pardon, it was also a crucial step in Cantona's journey of redemption, a theme he had become obsessed with, and not without reason. A French journalist had once asked him to name the three novels that carried the deepest resonance for him. Éric chose *A Picture of Dorian Gray, The Monk* (as revised by French 'mad genius' Antonin Artaud) and Herman Hesse's *Narcisse and Golmund*, the selection of a well-read man who could also read well. All three, he explained, explored the fateful transitions from temptation to culpability and, ultimately, redemption. To him, a book was also a mirror.

The rehabilitation of Éric Cantona took a farcical turn when an editorial in *The Times* suggested that President of the French Republic Jacques Chirac could do worse than making him his ambassador during his forthcoming state visit. This apparently caused quite a lot of head-scratching in staff meetings of France's Foreign Office. How was Chirac supposed to add a footballer to his retinue at such an occasion? No provisions of that kind could be found in the official protocol. Fortunately, Cantona eased the civil servants' headache by letting it be known that he had no wish to be seen in his president's company. Chirac had not quite finished with Cantona, however. The Speaker of the House of Commons, the Rt. Hon. Betty Boothroyd, greeted him with these words: 'I'm so glad to meet the second most famous Frenchman in Britain.' No prize for guessing how Boothroyd responded when the statesman asked her who could be the first.

The hopes Kevin Keegan had placed in Middlesbrough stopping his rival evaporated as early as the fifteenth minute of United's last game of the league season, when David May scored for the visitors. That in itself suggests a measure of their superiority: May found the net nine times in as many seasons at Old Trafford. In any case, it would have taken a small miracle for Newcastle to leapfrog United at the last: Boro had to win, and so had the Magpies – by two goals – against Tottenham at St James' Park. The groan that went round the stadium when news of United's first goal reached the fans effectively drained Keegan's players of what little energy they had left. Forty-five miles away, a quiet Cantona let Ryan Giggs run the show in his stead, then steal it with a virtuoso finish to seal a 3–0 win, United's 16th in their last 17 games in all competitions. The game was truly up: 36,000 disconsolate Geordies applauded their heartbroken team at the conclusion of an anticlimactic 1–1 draw, and for the fourth time in five years, Éric finished the season as a national champion; for the second in three, the Double* was six days – or 90 minutes – away. Only Liverpool now stood in his way.

It is hard to say which was the poorer of the two: Manchester United's FA Cup final song or the game itself. Thankfully for his club, Cantona wasn't as discreet on the Wembley pitch as he had been in the recording studio, miming 'Move, Move, Move' with the smile of someone who's just realized he's gatecrashed the wrong birthday party. United shaded a first half of misplaced passes and spurned chances, the best of which fell to Andy Cole, who let them pass him by. The game hardly improved afterwards. Éric forced David James to save smartly when his volley looked set to sneak in at the foot of a post. The biggest cheer of the afternoon greeted the substitution of the hapless Cole after 63 minutes; more celebration ensued 11 minutes later when it was Stan Collymore's turn to make way for Ian Rush, who was playing his last competitive game for Liverpool before leaving on a free transfer. The match seemed destined for two periods of extra time that nobody was looking forward to when Cantona produced a goal worthy of his contribution to United's season, if not of what was supposed to be the most prestigious event on the footballing calendar. James, hitherto imperious in the air, had a rush of blood and raced from his line to clear a David Beckham corner, colliding with two players on the way. As he lay on the ground, the ball came to Éric, who had positioned himself on the edge of the penalty area, took three quick steps back and volleyed the rebound from the centre of the 'D', his movement and execution a study in poise and elegance. Sixteen players were encamped in the box at this point, most of them directly in his line of vision – but the ball travelled through a forest of chests and legs to lodge itself in the net. The

* Each Manchester United player stood to earn a £100,000 bonus if they won the FA Cup, a fifth of which had been earmarked for the Dunblane appeal.

whole phase of play had lasted less than four seconds, but so pure was Cantona's strike that time appeared to slow down to a halt. His father Albert turned towards his neighbour and said: 'The locksmith has found the key, yet again! And heaven knows the hole was small!' Isabelle fell sobbing into her brother's arms. Aimé Jacquet left the ground without a word.

Liverpool, who had had a shocking afternoon anyway, spent the few remaining minutes in a stupor. The clamour saluting Cantona's wondergoal had scarcely died down when referee Dermot Gallagher signalled the game was at an end. The BBC commentator got it right when he said: 'The FA Cup goes to Cantona and to Manchester United,' in that order, as the trophy was presented to the stand-in captain by the Duchess of Kent. Back on the pitch, United's skipper Steve Bruce, who had been deprived of this final by a hamstring injury, clapped with his customary generosity. When Éric had suggested it should be he who walked up the thirty-nine steps, Bruce had waved the Frenchman away with a gentle smile, as if to say: 'This is your day, enjoy it to the full.' But it was also Alex Ferguson's day. Back in August, his decision to part with Mark Hughes, Paul Ince and Andreï Kanchelskis and replace them with untried youngsters from the club's academy had been deemed an act of folly, and not just by Alan Hansen on the BBC. Cantona was still serving his suspension, and when Aston Villa beat his 'kids' 3–1, no one gave a chance to a side in which the Neville brothers, Nicky Butt, Paul Scholes and David Beckham were to be found. No one predicted they would go on to collect a total of 355 England caps (and counting, in Beckham's case) between them. No one had any inkling that a second Double was in the offing. But in truth, none of this would have ever happened without Éric Cantona's astonishing resurgence, which started with a goal against Liverpool in the league on 1 October and ended with another at Wembley on 11 May. During that period, he scored nineteen times in thirty-seven appearances. He was also a mentor to a new generation, a prolific provider and, most importantly, a credit to himself, demonstrating powers of renewal that astonished his harshest critics. But he wouldn't take part in the European Championships.

*

On 19 May, three days after Alex Ferguson had signed a new, vastly improved four-year deal with Manchester United,* Aimé Jacquet addressed journalists at a packed press conference organized at the French FA's headquarters. Just as everyone expected, Cantona's name didn't appear in the list of twenty-two players he had selected for Euro 96. As early as 21 February, on the occasion of a friendly against Greece, the manager, not mentioning the private meeting he had had with Éric in Manchester, had made clear that he 'didn't think that [Cantona] could bring something to the team at the moment. [. . .] His presence would force me to re-evaluate everything, and this time has passed, I believe.' Three months on, he explained that Éric had been left aside 'for purely sporting reasons'. 'Something happened which everybody is aware of,' he added, 'which it is not for me to comment upon. And I took the decision not to select him because, since then [the Crystal Palace incident and Cantona's subsequent suspension], the French team has made progress.' It was clear from Jacquet's presentation that Euro 96 represented a springboard towards the World Cup that was to take place in France two years afterwards, in which he was proved right. 'The problem is that Euro 96 taught us we were on to something on the way to the World Cup,' Henri Émile told me.

> It was a necessary step to have a successful France 98. Because we lived together for a month-and-a-half, because we saw the qualities of this and that player, because a style of play was emerging, because we could tell that the players who had been on the bench had the right attitude to carry on training and working seriously. Euro 96 enabled us to think we could master these elements. Éric? It was finished. He would not play centre-forward. New midfielders had emerged, like 'Manu' Petit. Zizou's influence on the game kept growing. So there couldn't be a way back, unless there was an avalanche of injuries.

---

* Said to be worth £1m a year. The Bank of Scotland advertised a new mortgage product with a picture of the beaming manager accompanied with the tagline: 'Even he couldn't set up a better transfer deal than this', referring, of course, to Cantona's capture from Leeds United.

Jacquet's preparation had gone without the slightest hiccup so far: his team, transformed by the elevation of Youri Djorkaeff and Zinédine Zidane to the role of dual playmakers, had now gone twenty games unbeaten and qualified for the final tournament at a canter. 'A *sélectionneur*,' he said, 'is there to make choices. This group of players shares the same ideas about the game, based on rhythm, movement, "explosion". They live well together. Why break up this rhythm, this desire to win? I didn't have to take the English public into account. I'm only accountable to the French.' What he didn't add was that, according to a poll commissioned by *L'Équipe*, 83 per cent of his compatriots wished Cantona to be recalled. But it was also clear that, within the French camp, a number of players were unwilling to welcome him back, Djorkaeff and Zidane being two of them. 'Why should our places be taken?' the first asked, 'Zizou' nodding in the background. Marcel Desailly showed he had been raised in a family of diplomats by saying: 'Before, we were a collection of richly talented individuals. Now we have a collective unit, each player knowing his responsibilities. The coach had to make difficult sacrifices to achieve that.' The coach – not Éric's former teammates.

Other players had been left behind, David Ginola and Jean-Pierre Papin among them. But their exclusion, or that of Metz's Cyrille Pouget, to whom Mikaël Madar had been preferred, hardly got a mention: it was all about the man who wasn't there, Éric Cantona. Harried by the media – who had been clamouring for his return, and in whose spotlight he had never felt entirely at ease – Jacquet looked on the back foot throughout, and gave the impression that there were reasons behind his decision that he didn't want to get into. This much was true, but the tone he adopted misled his audience into thinking that these reasons were indefensible if sporting criteria alone had formed his judgement. Not for the last time, Jacquet's decency – and the very respect he had for the jettisoned Cantona – played against him. Later, in a more reflective mood, he admitted that the day he finally lanced the abcess 'had been the hardest in [his] life as a national coach'. 'I understood I couldn't shy away [from the decision to leave Cantona out],' he said, 'as I was running the risk of leading everyone up a blind alley. You always believe that you'll succeed in changing the player. You never do.'

Cantona had not been under any illusion that he might get a reprieve at the last minute, but felt the shock no less keenly. So much had happened since that night in January. He had led a group of largely untested players to an unhoped-for Double, and established himself as the most influential footballer in the English Premier League. His on-field behaviour had been a model of sportsmanship. He now had to watch France play in the country that had adopted him, captained by a man, Didier Deschamps, who teased him during the French squad's get-togethers by mimicking his 'Picasso' puppet. He had to watch France go through their semi-final against the Czech Republic without registering a single shot on target, and exit the competition on penalties at – of all places – Old Trafford. Some French players went shopping in the stadium's megastore after their elimination, but no one knows whether they slipped one of the hundreds of replica no. 7 shirts bearing Éric's name into their bags.

Just as they had done in 1994, the Cantona clan gathered in Manchester for the climax of the season. Albert formed the vanguard, to be rejoined by the rest of the family at the beginning of May. Éric's parents had now moved to a mountain hideaway in the Alpes de Haute-Provence, where radio reception was so poor that they had to rely on Bernard Morlino's match summaries to keep abreast of their son's progress. Morlino travelled to Manchester himself, as did Isabelle's brother Nino. In the days preceding the FA Cup final, Éric whiled away the time in the city's bookstores in the company of his writer friend. I was deeply moved when I learnt that one of the volumes he had picked was Yves Bonnefoy's collection of poems Rue Traversière, *whose hieratic yet sensual beauty was burnt indelibly in my own memory. Bonnefoy's readers are few; but all of these few consider themselves blessed, and, to me, the idea that Cantona was one of them is oddly thrilling: it provides another sign that, willing as he was to hear the advice of others, as when Didier Fèvre led him to discover the films of Max Ophüls, he trusted his own instinct, and that the unsteady hand that was guiding him had a sure aim. Sprawled on the bookshop's floor, he also read through Ezra Pound's* Drafts and Fragments, *attracted, perhaps, by the punning aptness of 'Cantos 111–117'. 'Cantos for Cantona' would make a sweet title in its own right, would it not?*

19

The last game; the last shirt.

THIS IS THE END, BEAUTIFUL FRIEND, THIS IS THE END: MANCHESTER 1996–97

'I do not want any inscription on my tombstone. A blank stone, because what I would like to leave behind me is the sentiment of a great mystery.'

'My dream was to live in the world of creation. In football I did that; now I have other opportunities to do that. The only thing I fear is death. Sometimes, when I take a flight I am a little afraid, because we can die in a plane crash very quickly. In cars too, but in cars you have some control. I have things in my memory stick and I never take that with me when I am flying. I say to my partner, the person I am living with, "If something happened to me, I want you to read what is on that memory stick and do what is there." I tell her, "I want you to do these things if you can, to say to people – 'It was Éric's wish that this should happen.'" If I die with the memory stick, I die with everything. I want to go with the possibility that what I haven't achieved will be achieved by somebody else. I've always thought, now more than ever, that it is not how you live your life that counts, but how people will remember you.'

Éric loved and still loves The Doors. Whether 'The End' rates among his favourite songs of theirs I don't know, but it seems a good one to play as the background track to that funereal season that was 1996–97, all the more so since Francis Ford Coppola added it to the soundtrack of *Apocalypse Now*, and since Cantona's physique now bore more than a passing resemblance to that of Joseph Conrad's Captain Kurtz as portrayed by Marlon Brando.

The 1996–97 season is not one I've been looking forward to writing about. It was a dull affair, grey as a November sky, a blanket of clouds heavy with unshed rain, lifeless. Manchester United won the league again, to which I'm tempted to add: so what? There wasn't anybody to win it from. Éric had his moments of brilliance, as ever. But he also ambled from game to game like a farmer from field to field in late autumn, his boots heavy with mud. This was the year a light dimmed and was switched off, a procession of days leading to retirement – footballing death.

I reread my notes for the month of August:

> United take part in the 'Umbro Tournament', which also features Ajax, Chelsea and Nottingham Forest. United has recruited Jordi Cruyff, Ronnie Johnsen and one of the stars of Euro 96, the Czech winger Karel Poborsky. Newcastle has paid £15m for Alan Shearer, a new British and world record, and are close to bringing Patrick Kluivert from Ajax. Gianluca Vialli makes his debut for Chelsea.

Patrick Vieira, Roberto Di Matteo and Fabrizio Ravanelli also made their bow in the Premiership that season. The pioneer's task was all but completed. The exotic colours with which Cantona had enlivened English football were fast disappearing under a flurry of brushstrokes. The time of surprise had passed.

Selected moments of brilliance: 11 August was one. 'Cantona steals Shearer's show' is how one paper put it in its report of the Charity Shield. Éric scored a goal full of poise in the 24th minute, teasing Srníček before beating him, offering another to Nicky Butt, then playing a part in the build-up to the third by producing a superb backheel which Beckham controlled expertly before firing past the Czech 'keeper. Cantona then ran 15 yards to confront Belgian defender Philippe Albert (who had just been fouled by Gary Neville) and shake him by the neck, which should have earned him a red card, but didn't. Newcastle were eviscerated 4–0. Éric was named man of the match, as he had been in 1993 with Leeds. But Charity Shields didn't matter much to Cantona any more: this one was his third in four years. 'This season,' he said, 'everybody at United wants to win the European Cup. We want to be famous all around the world, not just in our country.' Just as 1994–95 could be seen as a slow, inexorable march towards Crystal Palace, the true nature of 1996–97 would only be revealed when Borussia Dortmund denied United a place in the Champions League final.

Éric had changed, physically; there was the hint of a double chin on the face of the United captain, and a certain regal (not Falstaffian) portliness about him. It was as if Cantona had been poured into a new, bigger shell. Inspirational against Newcastle in the Charity Shield, he conducted another masterclass in the season's first properly competitive game, a 3–0 victory at Selhurst Park against Wimbledon, a game that is remembered for David Beckham spotting that the Dons' goalkeeper Neil Sullivan had strayed off his line and beating him from inside his own half. Éric scored himself, controlling an awkward ball with his left foot and propelling it into the net with his right, making it look the easiest thing imaginable. He was also booked – his second caution in two games. I hope I'll be forgiven, though, for not sticking to the day-to-day account of Cantona's progress in the Premiership as I've done up to this point. As it soon became apparent, something was broken: his club's progress and his own had become disjointed. Until then, recounting one was akin to describing the other. The supreme effort he had produced all through the previous spring for United had brought them another Double. It had been his gift, his offering to the club and the manager who had rescued him. But what else was there to prove, now that international success was no longer an option? What life could be found after committing suicide? Europe, and only Europe could provide him with a life worth living.

I turn to my notes again.

> 21 August: United and Cantona struggled against the ruggedness and physical power of Everton. A 2–2 draw was a just reflection of what deserved to be called a 'battle'. 25 August: Man U–B'burn, 2–2. Blackburn had been cheeky enough to send a fax requesting the purchase of Éric Cantona during the summer (ha-ha). Alex Ferguson recognized that Rovers had

> been superb; for the second game in a row, both at home, the visitors' doggedness had been rewarded with a point, and Éric had failed to shine, a sign, maybe, that his idle summer had left him somewhat short of fitness. Ole-Gunnar Solskjær, then 23 years of age, provided the most inspiring performance of a compelling afternoon, despite featuring for fewer than 30 minutes in the game. 4 September: Derby–Man U, 1–1. Man United are 7th in the league after this result, 6 points behind Sheffield Wednesday. Their third draw in a row, and a lucky one at that, rescued by a David Beckham thunderbolt under the eyes of the spies sent by Juventus, who were hosting United in the Champions League a week later. Cantona, physically well short of peak condition, only glimmered intermittently – a flick here, a pass on the turn there, a beautifully executed overhead kick, but to little effect.

A litany, sometimes broken by an unexpected reminder that every weekend, Éric Cantona had to do his job, and that, regardless of his increasing disaffection with football, he couldn't just clock on and clock off. On 7 September he missed a penalty. Éric Cantona missed a penalty! United had crushed Leeds 4–0 at Elland Road, but space was found to mention his failure in the headlines, and Simon Barnes would remember it months later, when Éric's decision to retire was made public. 'When Cantona missed that penalty,' he wrote, 'he was forced to come face to face with the fact that he was, after all, like everybody else. His doctrine of personal infallibility had been shattered, his notion of his own perfection was forever flawed, his myth was spoiled. Nothing could ever be quite the same again.' But he had also scored his side's fourth goal, and produced a majestic performance in a position he was not accustomed to – as a lone centre-forward, in a dress rehearsal of the game plan that Alex Ferguson had prepared to counter Juventus. In January 1996 Aimé Jacquet had failed to convince Cantona that he could have a future with France if he took on that role; but Éric had refused, as you will recall. Only a handful of people were aware of the poignancy of the situation – all eyes were already trained on the Stadio delle Alpi. In the words of a contemporary reporter, when Cantona scored in Leeds, 'he turned, raised his arm to the taunting crowd like a gladiator, and turned again, his face turned towards Turin'. This celebration consummated a revenge as well: by leading United's demolition of his former club, he had hammered the final nail into Howard Wilkinson's coffin: the manager who had given him his first taste of competitive football in England was dismissed after the weekend.

Marcello Lippi looked after a formidably well-organized Juventus team which was renowned for its miserliness in defence, but also possessed almost unrivalled riches in attack, as could be expected of any side counting Zidane, Bokšić, Del Piero and Vieri in its ranks. Ferguson feared Juve's creativity with good reason; the last time United had met a European team of similar pedigree in Europe, they had been swept away: Barcelona had murdered them 4–0 in the Nou Camp, a memory seared into the Scot's brain. To avoid a repetition of that catastrophe, he deployed a thick midfield curtain, with Cantona his single target man. The absence of the injured Roy Keane partly accounted for this cautiousness but in truth, as he later admitted, Ferguson didn't know what his best team was.

For Éric, these considerations came a distant second to the excitement he felt at playing 'what is already a final'. Milan and Inter had both been close to taking him away from first French, then English football, but he had never played on Italian soil before. There was the added spice of coming across a fellow *Bleu*, a footballer he didn't rate and a man he despised, midfielder Didier Deschamps. Cantona, who had refused to talk to journalists for close to two years, broke his silence for an interview with *La Gazzetta dello Sport*, in which he took the gloves off and slipped on a knuckleduster. 'Deschamps,' he said 'is there because he always gives 100 per cent of himself, but he'll always be a water-carrier [*a phrase that stuck, as you know*]. You find players like him on every street corner.' Anger simmered behind the scorn. 'Today, Didier speaks as if he were a monk. He gives moral lessons, but he'll end up succumbing to all the vices of the world.' What he was hinting at can only be guessed; but I remember feeling at the time that he could only be alluding to the rumours that had been sullying Marseille's reputation when Deschamps was in Bernard Tapie's employment –

which, in Eric's estimation, automatically made him one of the OM chairman's 'creatures'.

But his appetite for revenge, sharp as it was, went unsated. A change in the UEFA rulebook allowed the United manager to field as many 'foreigners' as he liked, for the very first time, and it was hoped that his players could now give a truer account of themselves. Judging by what they did on that night of 11 September, they weren't very good. United were outplayed, out-thought, outpaced, and ultimately fortunate to escape with the narrowest of defeats, by a single goal scored by Zinédine Zidane. Cantona, with the fearsome Uruguayan Paolo Montero on his coat-tails, could not find an inch of space, whereas the Leeds defenders had left him with acres four days beforehand. He was barely seen. The lone-striker experiment had failed. Ferguson singled out Éric for praise, though, blaming the severity of his team's defeat (in manner if not according to the scoreline) on their inexperience. 'We have the players to improve,' he said, 'but they must take the lesson from Éric Cantona. He never gave the ball away once.' In truth, he had seen very little of it.

How far United still had to go (and how long Éric would have to wait) before they were able to compete with, let alone beat the best of Continental opposition was demonstrated *a contrario* when they destroyed Nottingham Forest 4–1 three days after their humbling in Turin. Forest hadn't yet lost all of the football Brian Clough and Peter Taylor had taught them, but couldn't contain a side that had regained its exuberance when it returned to its default setting, a 4-4-1-1 formation in which Cantona had the freedom to roam behind Ole-Gunnar Solskjær. Were United's shortcomings Éric's as well? With no Deschamps to cut the supply from midfield and no Montero to spoil it, Cantona created two goals and scored a brace himself, the eighth double of his United career. In the next game, though, a scoreless draw at Villa Park, he drifted into anonymity, nor did he shine in the 2–0 victory over Rapid Vienna that followed – Roy Keane, in his second game since coming back from a knee operation, was United's catalyst in this unremarkable success against feeble opposition.

Blowing hot and cold on the field, Éric remained a prize asset off it. Nike presented him with an improved contract, rumoured to be worth £500,000 a year, which tied him to the American company for a further four years.

Éric had turned thirty in May, an age at which, today, most players opt for a lucrative last contract if they don't opt out altogether. But football hadn't yet become a young man's game in 1996. A number of the Premiership's most popular players were Cantona's elders: Ruud Gullit (thirty-four), Chris Waddle (then with Bradford, thirty-five), Ian Wright (thirty-two), Gianluca Vialli (thirty-two), Stuart Pearce (thirty-four), not to mention most of the Arsenal back four, of course, or Teddy Sheringham, Éric's almost exact contemporary, for whom life began at thirty. Still, Cantona paced himself as if he were five years older, choosing his games with great care when, six months earlier, he had thrown himself whole into every minute of every match and willed his team to two trophies. To quote a journalist who reported on a crucial 1–0 win over league leaders Liverpool in mid-October, Éric strove to 'make himself invisible'. Alex Ferguson had his own theory to explain this disappearing act: now that he was no longer selected to play for his country, Cantona had to train on his own during the international breaks. This argument didn't hold water. Éric had never been more influential, and inspired, than in the five months that preceded the Euro 96 tournament in which he had refused to take part. There is no doubt that the realization that he would never put the blue jersey on again – and that a new team was gelling into a tremendously dangerous unit before his very eyes, without him, their former captain – led him to withdraw into regrets he was too proud to confess. Like Maupassant's character who, one evening, discovering white strands in his hair, mutters, 'Finished,' Cantona had to face his own mortality. But the lure of Europe still glowed in the near distance, fresh oxygen to feed a weakening fire.

United were back in Istanbul on 16 October, the city where Bryan Robson and Éric had been roughed up by policemen and where United hadn't scored in their two previous visits. Their opponents were not Galatasaray this time, but Fenerbahçe, whose fanatical support couldn't prevent them from slumping to a 2–0 defeat. A beaming Ferguson told the press he now believed that 'this team can go all the way in this competition'. Cantona's display, one of his very best in the Champions League, gave substance to this profession of faith. Frequently dropping back to midfield to beat a steady tempo, United's conductor helped create David Beckham's goal and provided the finish for his side's second. He had now scored five in fifteen European games.

Then he sank, as did all around him. Four days after the elation felt in the Şükrü Saracoğlu Stadium, Newcastle blew United to smithereens at St James' Park. Final score: 5–0 (and five bookings for the visitors, one of them for Éric, who reprised his private war with Philippe Albert that afternoon). This was Alex Ferguson's worst-ever managerial defeat. United then folded abjectly at Southampton, shipping six goals and having Roy Keane sent off, as Cantona should have been for a nasty, cowardly kick at Ulrich van Gobbel, whose only crime was to have won the ball cleanly from him. Another, later foul earned Éric the yellow card he fully deserved. Fenerbahçe were next to exploit United's frailty, winning 1–0 in Manchester. Never before had the Old Trafford crowd seen their team lose at home on a European night, and there had been 56 of these since United became the first English team to enter the European Cup, in the 1956–57 season. Strangely, Ferguson chose to play a 4-5-1 formation again. Cantona didn't play in the hole: he vanished into one, and by the end of a woeful week, his team had dropped out of the Premiership's top five. Chelsea took advantage of two bad mistakes by Peter Schmeichel to bring three points back from Old Trafford. Thankfully, another international break followed, giving Alex Ferguson a fortnight to reflect on his team's current failings and prepare for their second game against Juventus.

Éric looked refreshed by this period of rest, far sharper than he had been for a good while, awoken, perhaps, by the prospect of avenging the 1–0 defeat conceded at the Stadio delle Alpi in September. Arsenal, now managed by Arsène Wenger, lost in Lancashire – a fast, bruising affair in which Peter Schmeichel rediscovered his old authority. Juve, however, resisted United's vibrant challenge and came out victors once more, again by a single goal. Éric himself had exerted close to no influence on the game. His timing had gone astray, and his temper too – he was booked for a typical 'striker's tackle' on Bokšić. Across the halfway line, he could see the man he had called a 'water-carrier' control space with unerring intelligence, winding Juve's spring with simple, measured passes. But while Deschamps was magnificent, Cantona remained a spectator, gauche and ineffectual.

By the time Leicester had been beaten 3–1, on 30 November, Cantona hadn't scored in eight games. He looked heavy – he *was* heavy, close to 90 kilos. I'm examining a photograph taken at United's next game, a 2–0 victory in Rapid Vienna's Gerhard Hanappi Stadium. On the left, Ryan Giggs, perfectly balanced, hair flowing, is gliding past an Austrian defender while, two yards away from him, on the right, Cantona looks on. A huge Cantona, with the thighs of a weightlifter, a huge neck, a huge chin. He still exudes strength, but there is something awkward about him. No wonder people had started to talk about the 'old Cantona'.

This was, however, Éric's best game for some considerable time. He played his part – as a lone striker, again – in setting up Giggs's opening goal, when he went past Zingler with a delightful shimmy, and put the result beyond doubt when he was found by an impeccable David Beckham pass in the penalty box. But he couldn't sustain that night's excellence, sometimes a passenger, sometimes the pilot, often within the same match. He didn't do much when United drew 2–2 at West Ham, but what he did, he did superbly, threading a peach of ball to send Solskjær in on goal when he noticed a fleeting moment of hesitancy in the Hammers back four, who were unsure whether they should use the offside trap as a weapon against the Norwegian striker. That was almost his only contribution to the game – but it had been decisive. Rarely, too rarely, he conjured a display of athleticism and elegance no other player – bar Dennis Bergkamp – could match in England, as when Sunderland, a gritty side which had drawn at Anfield and beaten Chelsea, were annihilated 5–0 three days before Christmas. He had already scored a penalty when, twelve minutes from time, he created one of his masterpieces. I've watched footage of this miraculous goal dozens of times, but the beauty of its execution still astonishes me. Just inside Sunderland's half, harnessed by Ord and Ball, he set himself free with a stupendous double feint, somehow found McClair, who instantly returned the ball to him, which, still running, he chipped from 18 yards over the head of his former Nîmes teammate Lionel Perez. What is extraordinary is that Éric found a way to stop without stopping, slowing down imperceptibly to compose himself and brush the underside of the ball with his bootlaces, sending it to the only spot where the rushing 'keeper couldn't reach it. The celebration was almost as memorable as the goal. Éric, affecting a haughty inscrutability, did nothing but straighten his back and puff out his chest, a Roman imperator savouring his triumph: all that was missing was David Beckham holding the laurels above his shaven head. Then Cantona broke into a beautiful smile, as if to say: 'Did you see that one? Did you see?' How could you not love such a player?

True to that season's pattern, Éric, having hit his stride, soon enough lost it. There was a superb volley in the 4–0 deconstruction of Nottingham Forest on Boxing Day, which shook the bar and offered Solskjær a chance he didn't miss, and a successful penalty kick against Leeds, following a double one-two with United's other telepathist, Ryan Giggs. But whereas Keane, still recovering from injury, was in and out of the side, Cantona was in and out of form, looking a spent force one day, a match-winner the next. Part of the problem was his obvious lack of complicity with Andy Cole, to whom he could hardly bring himself to pass the ball. The flicks and backheels did not find the intended player as often as before. United 'stumbled to second top' in the league, to quote Alex Ferguson, and, going for an unprecedented fourth straight appearance in the FA Cup final, struggled to get past a Tottenham side missing six first-team players in the third round of that competition. The emergence of David Beckham counterbalanced Éric's inconsistency to a degree, but United's satisfactory position in the Premiership – only two points behind leaders Liverpool, after registering those three consecutive league defeats in the autumn – owed more to the feebleness of their challengers than to the quality of their own football. Newcastle, seductive but so fragile, hadn't got over the trauma of the previous season's sickening endgame, Blackburn were fading after the briefest of blossomings, and Arsenal were still in the process of being reinvented by Arsène Wenger. The rest? Mere fodder: Coventry (2–0), Wimbledon (2–1), Southampton (2–1, a double-chinned and unshaven Éric scoring the scrappy winner to end a scrappy game), three victories, nine points that made one feel like adding a verse to Peggy Lee's 'Is That All There Is?'.

Cantona's influence on the team was dwindling. The yellow cards he had accrued meant he missed two of that season's pivotal games through suspension, a 2–1 win at Highbury and a 1–1 draw at Stamford Bridge. In both cases, what was noticed was that his absence was hardly noticeable; as was his presence when Wimbledon took United out of the FA Cup in a fourth round replay, on 1 February. This was the only defeat Éric ever suffered in this competition (an extraordinary statistic, as he had played his first FA Cup tie three years and a month previously), but, judging by his expression at the final whistle, he might as well have lost a friendly. He must have cared – he couldn't help but care – but it didn't show.

In truth, Éric was already thinking of another future, of an existence beyond football. The international breaks had given him a chance to travel to Paris regularly over the past few months. He had become a familiar figure in the capital's theatres, not just as a mere spectator, but also as a producer, in partnership with one of France's finest stage and screen actors, Niels Arestrup, who had collaborated with arthouse directors such as Alain Resnais, Chantal Ackerman and István Szabó. Cantona was no neophyte in that regard. As early as 1989, he had helped launch the career of comedian Patrick Bosso, a fellow Marseillais who had actually played four years as a sweeper in OM's under-18 team. Assisted by his brother Joël, whose role and influence were growing as Éric's disenchantment with football deepened, he increased his involvement in Arestrup's company, Caargo, both financially and emotionally. Their first common project had been a revival of Edward Albee's *Who's Afraid of Virginia Woolf?* at the Théâtre de la Gaîté Montparnasse in November 1996, which received excellent notices and did decent business at the box office. Éric then threw himself into the production of *Derrière les collines,* a play written by Jean-Louis Bourdon which had been passed on to the fledgling producer by the owner of a brasserie in the Opéra quarter, where Cantona happily mingled with a bohemian clientele of actors, writers and critics. 'We never talked about football,' Bourdon told me. 'We talked about art. He was *formidable,* passionate, eager to listen to others, and so kind.' The two men first met over dinner, where the playwright was delighted to welcome an unexpected guest at their table: the boxing legend Jake La Motta, Martin Scorsese's 'Raging Bull' in person. Compare such charmed evenings with the privileged but humdrum life of a professional footballer: no wonder Éric often gave the impression he would rather be elsewhere when the time had come to don a jersey.

Cantona's *ennui* was nothing new: it had been his companion ever since he had signed his first contract with Auxerre. 'It is better to live with your passions on the margins [of the football milieu] than to let yourself be eaten alive by this system,' he said, long after he left it for good. French photographer Isabelle Waternaux – whose Géricault-like study of Cantona appears on this book's dustjacket – told me how her subject had confessed he'd 'had enough of this circus' more than two years before his retirement. Sitting at the bar of the Novotel, a baseball cap screwed on his head in a vain and almost touching attempt to hide his identity, Éric told her how much he had come to despise the British press, how everything that was happening off the pitch encouraged him, if that's the word, to think of another life for himself, away from what had made him a celebrity. 'I have nothing to prove, and I have no duty to show who I am to the people whom I find interesting,' he said, enigmatically, in the first interview he gave – to *Libération* – after his decision to leave England and football. 'To the others – I have nothing to say.'

Nothing to prove? Now that the 1998 World Cup would be played without him, there remained one aim to reach: victory in Europe, and that prospect alone was enough to make him find resources within himself that many believed were now exhausted. Éric Cantona had not given up – not yet.

Manchester United's opponents in their Champions League quarter-final were FC Porto, the first leg to be played at Old Trafford on 5 March. For Ferguson, this was the opportunity to exact revenge for the controversial defeat his Aberdeen side had suffered at their hands in the 1984 Cup Winners Cup, when allegations (which remain unsubstantiated) that the officials had been bribed surfaced shortly before the game. The 'Dragons' would be no pushovers, as their recent record in Europe's top competition showed. Bobby Robson had led them to the semi-finals in 1993–94, further than United themselves had gone for twenty-nine years, and they had also reached the quarters of the Cup Winners Cup a season later. But Alex Ferguson's team swept past the Portuguese champions that night: the 4–0 scoreline gave a fair reflection of the hosts' dominance. This was one of the very few matches Éric played in Europe which could rank with his best performances in the league or the FA Cup. The consensus in the press box was that Porto had been torn to shreds by prospective European champions. The pounding rain hardly affected the fluidity of United's passing. Cantona's goal, United's second, was not a classic – a long punt upfield by Schmeichel, flicked on by Solskjær, bundled by Aloisio, thumped by Éric past a flailing Hilario – the same Hilario who made a few cameo appearances for Chelsea a decade later. On the hour, it was Cantona again who kindled United's fire, addressing a slide-rule pass along the touchline to Andy Cole, who found Giggs, who scored. United's last goal was also Éric's creation. He cushioned a hopeful ball by Ronnie Johnsen, and found the exact millisecond at which he could release the ball into the path of Andy Cole, who finished off the move deftly with his left foot. 'One of the best performances of my time,' enthused Ferguson afterwards, 'a hell of a performance.' The following day the value of United's stock rose £10m to £430m.

As could be expected, the glorious winners fell back to earth when they had to resume their quest for the championship title. Sunderland picked up the pieces of a team suffering from a collective hangover and won 2–1. Éric barely looked interested.

United's play was the reflection of his own, and vice versa, exhilarating in fits and bursts (as when Éric found Cole in a packed penalty box with an exquisite pass for the first goal of a 2–0 victory over Sheffield Wednesday), otherwise ponderous, flat, uninspired. It's true that they could afford to relax in the comfort of the Premiership, as no other team showed the talent or the drive required from would-be champions. Energy could be saved for the all-important European semi-final to come, after a demoralized Porto could only achieve a goalless draw in the second leg of a tie that had already been won in Manchester.

Éric's form in the games preceding the clash with Borussia Dortmund (who had seen off his old club Auxerre in the previous round) showed some improvement: even when Derby surprisingly won 3–2 at Old Trafford, he scored his second goal in two matches, following a nonchalant volley in a 2–0 win over a desperately poor Everton. Confidence was high in Manchester, so high that Peter Schmeichel made the quite ridiculous assertion that the current United team would beat the European champions of 1968 by 10 goals to nil. It didn't bring him luck: he suffered an injury just before kick-off in Dortmund on 9 April, and had to leave his place in goal to Raymond van der Gouw. Alex Ferguson hadn't been as reckless in his pre-match predictions, but had nonetheless brushed away suggestions that Cantona could struggle if the German champions man-marked him, as was expected, an apprehension that was shared by Gary Pallister. In the defender's view, it was primarily the tighter man-marking practised by Continental teams that explained why Éric never really expressed himself fully in European competitions, rather than some flaw in his character. But Ferguson disagreed. 'I don't think Éric will be too worried about it,' he said. The manager's remarkable confidence was shared by most observers, with some justification. Dortmund, a fine side which had won two Bundelsiga titles on the trot, would be deprived of no fewer than seven of their regular first-teamers in the first leg, including the internationals Stéphane Chapuisat, Karl-Heinz Riedle and Jürgen Kohler, all of them injured, as well as their inspirational skipper Matthias Sammer, the future 1997 *Ballon d'Or*, who was suspended.

Luck certainly didn't smile on United in the awe-inspiring Westfalenstadion, packed with 48,500 vociferous supporters. René Tretschok's late winner (scored a quarter of an hour from time) was deflected by Gary Pallister's foot – after Nicky Butt, David Beckham and Cantona had all spurned good chances to score a crucial away goal. Éric had been sent clear by Butt, but from 15 yards, and with only Stefan Klos to beat, put his attempt high and wide. Then Butt (served by Cantona) hit a powerful shot which cannoned off the post. Finally, the Frenchman provided Beckham with an excellent ball on the hour, but the midfielder's strike was too weak: Martin Kree had time to rush behind the beaten Klos and clear the ball off the line. United's already wretched night took a turn for the worse when Roy Keane picked up yet another yellow card, which triggered an automatic ban for the return match, much to Cantona's annoyance.

The role Éric played in his team's best three chances might suggest that he had been one of their best performers on the night, but this was not Keane's judgement. The Irishman later told Eamon Dunphy that he felt Éric had been one of 'the one or two of our players' who had been 'backing off' on this occasion. He went further: 'Éric will never rank alongside the truly great European players. This is the stage that really counts. Maybe Éric's not capable of it. Never will be.' Alex Ferguson was kinder to his protégé, but only marginally so. Cantona had been 'so low-key and marginal in Dortmund', he recollected later, 'that I was left searching for a reason. I questioned myself about whether there had been an alteration in my method of dealing with him.' Reflecting on their defeat, Ferguson wondered if he 'had been talking to him less than [he] should'. He had sensed that Cantona needed more space, more freedom to find out how he could best lead the team. The captaincy he had inherited after Steve Bruce had retired at the end of the previous season was not a natural role for him. While admitting that there might have been 'a mental block' in Éric's persona when it came to so-called 'big European nights', a puzzled Ferguson argued that 'there were such occasions when Éric played marvellously for us'. But which ones could he be thinking of?

I read the reports and watched the videos, trying to find these elusive moments of personal triumph, and could only come up with two: a late equalizer against Galatasaray and the trouncing of Porto in Manchester, when a couple of early goals had rocked the Portuguese side and precipitated a state of euphoria in the whole United side. Compare this with the record of another French superstar in whom many see a 'choker' on the European stage, Thierry Henry. Cantona never scored a winning goal at the Bernabéu, a double at San Siro or a hat-trick at the Stadio Olimpico. Henry did, and when it mattered. Éric himself has never won an international trophy with club or country, unless the 1988 European under-21 title is taken into account – and you may remember a ban had prevented him from playing in the second leg of the final. That a player blessed with such strength of character and such talent could prove an almost complete failure in European competitions is a mystery for which I can only offer a few clues – but no definite explanation. One such clue is that Éric had felt – and for quite a long time – that his club wasn't prepared to spend the money needed to purchase the proven matchwinners who could help him lift United to success in Europe. These promises failed to materialize, adding to Éric's disillusionment with a club that he believed was now prioritizing its image as a marketing commodity.

Retirement wasn't uppermost in his mind just yet, however. Three meetings had been held with United chairman Martin Edwards since the beginning of March, and both parties appeared to favour a new extension to Cantona's present contract, which had over a year to run. There was no reason to believe that the tap-in he scored against Blackburn (3–2) on 12 April, three days after the Dortmund heartbreaker, would be his last goal for Manchester United – or for anyone else, which it was. He was at the apex of his fame, I'd almost say his popularity, as he'd overcome the consequences of his moment of madness at Crystal Palace with great dignity. The adulation he received in his adopted city showed no sign of abating. Thirteen thousand people visited the City of Manchester Art Gallery in the last two weeks of April, to gaze on *The Art of the Game*, a 10ft by 8ft painting by local artist Michael Browne.* The composition was based on Piero Della Francesca's *Resurrection of Christ* and Andrea Mantegna's *Julius Caesar on his Triumphal Chariot*, in which Cantona's likeness had been substituted for the Lamb's, to the outrage of a few and the amusement of many. 'To the person on the street it will be tongue in cheek,' the artist said. 'I don't believe people will take it seriously as an insult. It reflects street humour – the kind of humour the fans have.'

---

* Éric had been aware of Browne's project ever since the two men had met by chance in a Castlefield bar named BarCa in the summer of 1996. To help the artist, he agreed to pose for a series of photographic studies, and was so taken by this work that he purchased it before it was completed. 'I felt that Eric was a very private man,' Browne told me. 'But he is also incredibly warm and generous once you get to know him.' The two men met regularly in Manchester and, ten months later, once in Paris, where Éric was signing reproductions of *The Art of the Game.* Browne hasn't forgotten how the superstar helped him carry the crate of prints along the street and up a staircase, a far cry from the diva he was supposed to be. Contrary to legend, Cantona never asked for visitors to leave the gallery when the work was first exhibited, in order to be alone with his painted self: another of those factual distortions which show him, wrongly, in an unfavourable light.

Naked but for a cloth wrapped around his hips, Éric the Saviour emerged from the tomb, surrounded by Phil Neville, David Beckham, Nicky Butt and Gary Neville. Alex Ferguson lurked in the background. Browne's work was meant to be taken with a pinch of salt, but also provided a poignant allegory of Cantona's redemption.

Prolonging his stay at Old Trafford guaranteed Éric another shot at European glory, even if Dortmund were to prevail later in the month: United, helped by one of 'keeper David James's more eccentric displays, snuffed out Liverpool's last hopes of taking the title by winning 3–1 at Anfield on 19 April. Cantona, with one eye on the European semi-final taking place four days later, didn't exert himself unduly that afternoon, not that he had to. His team now needed just five points from their last four games, three of them at home, to make sure they claimed the Premiership for the fourth time in five years. This was a stupendous achievement, no doubt about it, especially as Alex Ferguson had had to rebuild his squad after the sale or retirement of a number of key players, and found the courage to replace them with products of the club's academy. Stupendous as it was, though, it was overshadowed by the expectancy surrounding the coming of Borussia to Old Trafford on the 23rd. At the end of these 90 minutes was a place in the grandest of all club finals, which carried extra significance for Manchester United that year, as it would be played in Munich, where, on 6 February 1958, BEA flight 609 crashed on a snow-shrouded runway, claiming twenty-three victims, eight of whom were members of Matt Busby's famed 'Babes' team.

'Old Trafford's biggest night for thirty years' – since United had beaten Real Madrid 1–0 in their 1968 semi-final – was meant to be Éric's own coronation as the King of Europe, not just England. But what 53,606 spectators witnessed was an abdication. Their team squandered chance after chance against a side still missing their captain, and Cantona was the worst culprit. When the young midfielder Lars Ricken shot Borussia into the lead with seven minutes on the clock, United now needed to score three to go through. Incredibly, they could – they should – have done it. In the sixteenth minute, Cole's cross-shot was pushed out by Klos, fell to Cantona, just a few yards from goal – with just Kohler, already off balance, to beat. He could have skipped past the defender and pushed the ball into the net. But no, he blasted it against Kohler's legs. Minutes later, the ball trickled to him just outside the area, in what should have been a perfect position to shoot, but he dithered, as did Cole. On fifty-three minutes, finally, the ball broke to Éric's feet, on the edge of the six-yard box. He dinked the ball over Klos – but too weakly, and Dortmund cleared it off the line.

Cantona's ghost had been playing, the ghost of a player who had died at the end of the previous season, as his adviser Jean-Jacques Bertrand all but confirmed when he said, towards the end of May, that 'Éric's decision to stop playing football was due to the fact that [Aimé] Jacquet decided not to pick him for the French team from 1995. His decision to end his career was because he knew he will never play in the World Cup.' In other words, when he had committed suicide in January 1996.

Immediately after the game, Ferguson exploded in the dressing-room, where Éric, the captain, visibly sickened, remained absolutely silent. The morning after, Cantona asked for a face-to-face meeting with his manager, who talked about it – to Erik Bielderman – for the first time ten years after the event. 'I had a bad premonition. I could guess what he was about to tell me. I had noticed several changes in his mood and his physical appearance.'

Cantona had had enough. Football was over for him. He had decided to retire, to quit at the top. The fact that he broke the news to a man he not only respected, but loved, so soon after this catastrophic defeat leads me to suspect that he had thought about leaving the sport that had been his life since he was a *minot* in Marseilles long before Dortmund killed off the last dream he had as a player. He had often acted on impulse, a leaf carried by the wind of his enthusiasm, his grudges and his disappointments, but not this time. United's supporters were probably too much in shock to digest what their manager dictated to his *Manchester Evening News* amanuensis: 'It looks as if the chances he missed – not to mention his relatively quiet performance – have prompted him to question his future.'

Ferguson's first reaction was one of disbelief. To him, the league winner of 1996–97 had 'another two good years in his legs' (an opinion shared by Henri Émile, who saw Cantona play a superb game in a testimonial two days before the annoucement of his retirement). 'But in his mind, the standards he set himself were so high that he felt he had almost betrayed himself with his disappointing performances towards the end of the 1996–97 season.' Ferguson did everything he could to try and convince Cantona to think it over again. When he realized that nothing he could say would make Éric change his mind, he reverted to an old trick. 'Go and see your father, talk to him, and come back to see me,' he said. Éric agreed to discuss his decision with Albert; but when he came back, a week later, his resolution had hardened. A wish, a choice which could have been inspired by the bitterness of yet another adieu to consecration in Europe, had now become an irrevocable decision. 'When [Éric] has got something in his head,' Ferguson told Bielderman, 'it is almost impossible to make him drop it.'

Still, for a while, in fact for most of the following summer, he believed it might be possible to bring Éric back. All his entreaties failed, even though, unbeknown to his ex-manager, Cantona toyed with the idea of a comeback. In a neat twist, one of the clubs that tried to attract him was Nagoya Grampus Eight, in Japan, the country where he had wanted to escape to after his first retirement in 1991. But it was more of a defence mechanism, one way to deal with the huge void of his footballing death – a means for Éric to mourn Cantona. There were still four games to play. The teamsheets tell us that Éric took part in all of them, but it was as a transient presence, a corruption of the great player he had been. Had Manchester United's rivals possessed the belief and the physical resources needed to chase the champions in the last furlong of the title race, had they identified and exploited the gaping hole that had appeared in the team after the Dortmund disasters, maybe – just maybe – another name would have been engraved on the Premier League trophy that year. United finished the season in neutral, with Éric withdrawn in the role of a playmaker behind Andy Cole and Ole-Gunnar Solskjær. They drew 2–2 at Leicester, 3–3 at home against Middlesbrough: four points dropped. Meanwhile, their supposed rivals were doing their best to go into reverse themselves. Arsenal lost at home, and then on 6 May Liverpool capitulated at

Wimbledon and Newcastle conceded a pitiful 0–0 draw at West Ham. Another title had fallen into Alex Ferguson's lap, irrespective of what would happen in the last two games of this strangely unsatisfying campaign. And Éric, quintuple champion of England, would never win the title in front of his home crowd.

In Prestbury, Isabelle was already packing the family's belongings into the cardboard boxes that had been part of her life for ten years. Among the photographs she put away was one of her son Raphaël, Claude Boli and Gary King posing alongside the trophies Éric had won in 1996. It had been displayed on the fireplace until then, but it no longer belonged to the present. 'In football, yesterday happened a long time ago,' as Billy Bremner said. 'When I was younger,' Éric confided to *Libération* in the summer, 'I loved the idea of theatrical tours, like they did in Molière's time. Sometimes, they'd be on the road for a year. Leaving – that's what I've always done in football.' This time, it was for good, and for Barcelona, soon after the season was over. Raphaël would be enrolled in the local English school – English, not French – in a city 'close to the idea I have of life. [It is] open, capable of unearthing talents. People haven't stopped at Gaudi or Miró here, even if they haven't forgotten what they owe them. To stop [. . .] is to accept death. And I'll never be ready for that. I've got so many things to see, so many things to live before I die.'

In the photographs of the champions posing with the trophy (which Cantona didn't kiss) on the Old Trafford pitch, which was presented to them after they had beaten West Ham 2–0 on 11 May, Éric is at the back, permitting himself a gentle smile. His is the face of a 40-year-old man, though. It's raining softly. He had already received his 'Manchester United Player of the Year' award in the centre circle. His last meaningful gesture as a player had been to deliver a pass of delightful accuracy to Jordi Cruyff (who had come on as a substitute, possibly because his father Johann was at the ground that day), who smashed it past Luděk Mikloško.

'I swapped my shirt with some guy,' he remembered later. 'I've heard that he sold it at an auction later on, probably for charity.' The 'guy' was John Moncur, whom he had almost beheaded with a donkey kick in March 1994 – Éric's first red card in England. 'I didn't feel anything. Because I wanted to stop. I'd had enough. And I was telling myself I could come back whenever I wanted. I was thinking: "You're young, you train for two months, you're back." I thought that way for a long time. I couldn't find the fire [in me]. Football had been my life, the passion of my childhood. The day when the fire goes out, why go on? To go to the Emirates and pocket 300 billion euros? I wasn't interested in that.'

Contemporary reports suggested that Cantona '[had] received no firm commitment about his future since his below-par performance in [United's] European Champions League exit against Borussia Dortmund, and there have been suggestions that for financial reasons, he will not get any such commitment'. They were well wide of the mark, as United were desperate to hold on to their prize asset – and it was precisely this 'assetization' that rankled with the player, as he explained.

> The environment contributed a lot to the extinction of that fire. Manchester, it's a lot of merchandising. You're sometimes needed for a video, a book, photographs, interviews . . . to avoid chaos, I signed very clear contracts with the club. I gave them exclusivity on my photographs. But they didn't respect [the contract]. I went to see Ferguson, then the chairman. I told them – careful, some things are happening. To give you an example, one morning, before a game, on my way to having breakfast, I came across a magazine on which I was on the front page. There are people who couldn't care less about being on the cover of a celebrity magazine. They're even proud of it. Me, it destroys me, even if I play a game, it becomes more important than the game. I live this as a kind of betrayal. So, on the day I told the club I was retiring, I warned them: 'OK, I'm stopping, but you should know I'll sue the merchandising.' The problem is that England is very beautiful in many respects, but very ugly when it comes down to the image and to the press. It's unhealthy.

Éric won his suit against World Foot Center and Manchester United Merchandising Limited in 2000. The companies paid compensation thought to have been worth £50,000.

Éric's decision to retire was conveyed to the general public by Martin Edwards on Sunday 18 May, at 15:38 precisely. Within minutes of the agency reporters filing their copy, half of Manchester was in mourning. Hundreds of supporters, many of them in tears, converged on Matt Busby Way, not knowing what to do, not knowing what to say, as nothing could have prepared them for the abruptness of their hero's departure. Manchester United's shares dropped 22.5p when the markets reopened. The next morning, paper after paper referred to the 'funereal atmosphere around Old Trafford', and, for once, the cliché rang true: the King was dead, and no *dauphin* was in sight. Of Éric himself, of his whereabouts, all that was known was that his family was holidaying abroad: in fact, he had sought refuge at his parents' hideaway in the Provençal village of Villar, where a French paparazzo snapped him sitting his son Raphaël on a Harley-Davidson motorbike.

The shock that engulfed Manchester United supporters was also felt keenly among the players, even though Gary Pallister, for one, had felt that Cantona's mood throughout the season, and especially in the last few months, had been suspiciously morose. Ryan Giggs asked himself the rhetorical question 'Were we surprised?' in 2005, and came up with this answer: 'Life with Éric was one long surprise.' 'You never knew what he would do next,' he told Joe Lovejoy. 'There were no farewells or anything like that, and I didn't really believe he meant it until he failed to turn up the following season. He was a fit lad, and he could definitely have gone on longer.'

I'm not so sure. What had snapped could not be mended, what is dead cannot be revived; and when Cantona reflected on the last trick he played on his audience, as he did surprisingly often in years to come, it was always in unequivocal terms, with a stark awareness of what it means for a performer to leave the stage for good: it is death. And quite appropriately, the dozens of columns printed in the British press on that Monday morning read like obituaries. Simon Barnes even gave his the title 'Intimations of Mortality'.

That word, 'death', kept coming back in a fascinating interview Éric gave to David Walsh of the *Sunday Times* in 2006. 'When you are a footballer,' he told the journalist, 'you do something very public, you do it because it is a passion and you feel alive when you're doing it. You feel alive also because people recognize you for the job you do. Then you quit and it's like a death. A lot of footballers are afraid and that is why they go on TV to speak about the game. They do it for themselves. It is important because it helps them to feel alive again, to deal with their fears about this death.'

A bemused Amelia Gentleman had recorded similar thoughts for the *Guardian* in 2003.

> If you only have one passion in life – and pursue it to the exclusion of everything else – it becomes very dangerous. When you stop doing this activity, it is as though you are dying. The death of that activity is a death in itself. Often there are players who have only football as a way of expressing themselves and never develop other interests. And when they no longer play football, they no longer do anything; they no longer exist, or rather they have the sensation of no longer existing. Too many players think they are eternal.

Éric Cantona's life was brief. He was born as a professional footballer on 5 November 1983, in Auxerre, and died on 11 May 1997 at Old Trafford. Less than fourteen years, a blink within a blink within eternity. The man lived on, became an actor, took France to a world title in beach soccer, divorced Isabelle, remarried, might even come back to football as a manager for all we know. It is not a sad story; at least I hope that the story I've told is not a sad one. He achieved a great deal, he failed sometimes. He erred. But he was true to his half-truths when most are content to lie, and that – lying – he never did. He was naïve, flawed, arrogant, self-serving, violent, egotistical. But he was also the most generous of men, for what he gave he gave for the sake of giving. He enriched the lives of millions, he fed their dreams and – sometimes – realized them. As I'm about to say goodbye to him, that is the one picture of Éric I want to keep: Cantona the provider of beauty, the eternal child doomed to age, who knows it and chooses to give two fingers to fate. I'll be my own man, he says, and fuck the whole lot of you who think I can't do it. It is pathetic, it is admirable, it is Éric Cantona.

Michael Browne puts the finishing touches to The Art of the Game.

Acknowledgements

My task as a biographer was two-fold. I first had to assemble and sift through thousands and thousands of pages of documentation on my own, which I did by reading through every single piece written about Cantona in the French and English publications I believed to be the most trustworthy,* starting from his professional debut at Auxerre, when he was just seventeen. collating all the interviews he'd given from 1987 to the present day; and watching every video of Éric in action that I could get access to. The staff of the British Library in Colindale must be thanked for their willingness to carry hundreds of rolls of microfilm throughout the best part of two years for my sake, and so should my colleagues at *France Football*, who bore my constant questioning with fortitude for an even longer period.

I owe a huge debt of gratitude in that regard to my French fellow journalists, three of them in particular: Erik Bielderman, Jérôme Cazadieu of *L'Équipe Magazine* (whose superb 2007 'Cantona Special' provided me with vital first-hand material) and Jean-Marie Lanoé of *France Football*. Their generosity in passing on and allowing me to use the information they had at their disposal I'm not sure I can ever repay. This was a rewarding exercise: a great deal that appeared mysterious at first found a ready explanation in contemporary accounts, provided one

* In France, *L'Équipe*, *L'Équipe Magazine* and my own paper, *France Football*; in England, *The Times*, the *Guardian*, the *Observer*, the *Telegraph* and, for obvious reasons, the *Yorkshire Evening Post* and the *Manchester Evening News*. I also dipped into the British tabloid press, the *Sun* and the *Mirror* in particular, though not with the same ferocity.

was prepared to search long and hard for a credible source – and spend the time and effort to check it. Most of this material has never been made available to the British public before. Cantona, despite his reputation of being a silent, brooding type, was remarkably approachable and forthright with French reporters until the long ban that was imposed on him in the spring of 1995, but the British tabloid press had yet to acquire its present habit of cherry-picking 'exclusives' in foreign publications. The translations are mine; the awkwardness of some of Éric's statements is more often than not a fair reflection of his idiosyncratic speech patterns rather than that of my own limitations, however.

Once I had established a factual foundation for my work, I approached many of the most most significant protagonists in Cantona's story, who were not always the most famous ones. As they number into the hundreds, I hope to be forgiven if I single out Gérard Houllier, Guy Roux, Didier Fèvre, Henri Émile, Célestin Oliver, Gary McAllister and Sir Alex Ferguson, as their testimonies (Sir Alex's in person on two occasions, but mostly through the conduit of Erik Bielderman, with whom he enjoys a truly unique relationship) provided the spine of much of this work. I should also add that several of my interviewees asked for their anonymity to be preserved, and that I respected their wish: their discretion had purely personal motivations, and, crucially, none of them used it as a licence to blacken Éric's character – in fact, the contrary was true.

Thus armed, I threw myself into the actual writing of this biography. Though French, it is in English that I composed it, and as I'm neither Joseph Conrad nor Vladimir Nabokov, it was fortunate that I had, in Richard Milner and Jon Butler, two editors of tremendous skill and sensitivity, as unstinting in their encouragements as they were in their hunt for gallicisms. Foreigners tend to ripen their adopted language to the extent that a mouthful of it can tease the palate, and another one make you feel like retching (as this sentence illustrates). Thanks to them, and – in the last furlong – to Natasha Martin and John English, the worst was averted. Jonathan Harris and David Luxton, without whom this book wouldn't have existed in the first place, showed me that 'agent' needn't be a dirty word, and can sometimes be synonymous with 'friend'. Photographer Isabelle Waternaux didn't just provide me with a magnificent portrait for the cover of this book, but also with precious reminiscences. Dermot Rice, who describes himself as a 'cantonista', showed me he amply deserved this epithet by suggesting a number of corrections before this paperback edition. Last, a *merci* to Jonathan Wilson, the sharpest of readers, who spared me a few blushes by pointing out some factual errors which would have greatly endangered what standing I enjoy in the press box had they gone unnoticed.